1987
FamilyCircle®
COOKBOOK

Other Books by Family Circle:

The Best of Family Circle Cookbook
1986 Family Circle Cookbook
The Family Circle Christmas Treasury

To order **FamilyCircle** books, write to Family Circle Special Projects Dept.,
488 Madison Avenue, New York, NY 10022.

To subscribe to **FamilyCircle** magazine, write to Family Circle Subscriptions,
488 Madison Avenue, New York, NY 10022.

Special Project Staff

Project Editor—JoAnn Brett-Billowitz
Book Design—Bessen & Tully, Inc.
Typesetting—Vickie Almquist, Helen Russell
Special Assistants—Kim Gayton, Joanne Hajdu, Marty Heebner, Susan McQuillan
Illustrations—Lauren Jarrett

Family Circle Staff

Project Manager—Margie Chan-Yip
Associate Project Manager—Carol Guasti
Project Coordinator—Karen Wang

Food Editor—Jean Hewitt
Senior Associate Food Editor—David Ricketts
Copy Editor—Wallace A. Kunukau, Jr.
Photocomposition Manager—Wendy Allen

Photographers—Debold, Ron G. Harris, Laszlo, Allen Lieberman, Bill McGinn,
Rudy Muller, Ron Schwerin, Gordon E. Smith, Theo, John Uher, René Velez

Published by The Family Circle, Inc.
488 Madison Avenue, New York, NY 10022

Copyright ©1987 by The Family Circle, Inc.

Manufactured in the United States of America

10 9 8 7 6 5 4 3 2 1

Library of Congress Cataloging in Publication Data
Main entry under title:

1987 Family circle cookbook.
Includes index.
1. Cookery.   I. Family circle (Mount Morris, Ill.)
TX715.B485555   1985   641.5   86-4465
ISBN 0-933585-03-9
ISSN 0890-1481

1987
FamilyCircle®
COOKBOOK

The Editors of Family Circle

Contents

Cover Recipe, page 132.

Reuben Brunch Casserole (page 98)

Introduction

O nce again, Family Circle presents the year's finest recipes in one handy volume! From appetizer openings through dessert finales, here are the makings for some of the best meals you'll ever serve. Like all of our Family Circle creations, these recipes are triple-tested so each one is guaranteed to be fail-proof. What's more, our many helpful hints will guide you every step of the way.

There's something here to satisfy every set of tastebuds—recipes range from the savory and exotic to the sweet and familiar, and every flavor in between. You'll find over 75 menus for all types of occasions as well, so you'll never again have to agonize over what to fix for breakfast, lunch or dinner. Each of our recipes and menus has been coded, so you'll know whether it's quick and easy, make-ahead, for entertaining, low cost or low calorie. And, of course, we've included the nutritional value per serving of each recipe—handy information if you're concerned with health and fitness.

But that's not all! You'll also find microwave directions for many recipes, as well as lower-calorie versions to help you watch your weight (these recipes are boxed). Look for them when you have little time or few calories to spare. If your schedule is a hectic one, you'll love our final chapter with its complete meals that can be prepared in half an hour—or less! Plus, we've provided shopping lists and work plans to save you even more time.

Sit back and spend some time flipping through the pages of your new treasure. We're sure you'll be enticed to start cooking—right away!

Cooking Helps

Every recipe and menu is coded by type, identifiable with the following symbols:

N Quick

KKK Make-Ahead

Y Entertaining

$$ Low-Cost

≣ Low-Calorie

Keep in mind that:
1. *Baking powder* is double action.
2. *Brown sugar* is firmly packed.
3. *Corn syrup*, unless specified, can be either light or dark.
4. Doubling recipes is not wise. It is best to make the recipe a second time.
5. *Eggs* are large.
6. *"Eggs, slightly beaten"* means just break the yolks.
7. *"Eggs, lightly beaten"* means to create a smooth mixture.
8. Most commercial brands of cake or all-purpose flour come presifted from the manufacturer. Some of our recipes indicate additional sifting to produce a lighter product.
9. *Heavy cream* for whipping is 40 percent butterfat.
10. *Herbs and spices* are dried unless noted otherwise.
11. Measurements are level.
12. *Milk* is whole homogenized.
13. *Vegetable shortening* is used for greasing pans.
14. *Vinegar* is cider, unless otherwise noted.

Good Meals— Good Health

Good nutrition is the secret for being physically and mentally fit. A well-nourished person possesses a well-developed body of ideal weight, clear, smooth skin, shiny hair and clear eyes.

Consume a variety of foods in moderate amounts to supply a complete range of vitamins and minerals. Eat foods that provide plenty of complex carbohydrates, such as whole grains, fruits and vegetables, for energy and high-fiber content. Avoid eating foods containing a lot of fat, cholesterol, sodium and sugar.

The Nutrient Value Per Serving is included with each recipe in this book to help you plan daily menus that are well balanced and healthful. Refer to the Daily Nutrition Countdown Chart below for the daily requirements of average adult men and women.

Daily Nutrition Countdown Chart

	AVERAGE HEALTHY ADULT	
	Women	Men
Calories[1]	2,000	2,700
Protein[2]	44 g (176 cal.)	56 g (224 cal.)
Fat[3]	66 g (594 cal.)	90 g (810 cal.)
Sodium[4]	1,100 - 3,300 mg	1,100 - 3,300 mg
Cholesterol[5]	300 mg	300 mg

Calories (cal.) that do not come from protein or fat should be derived from complex carbohydrates found in whole grains, fresh fruits, vegetables, pasta, etc.

[1]RDA [2](8-12% of calories) RDA [3](30% of calories) Amer. Heart Assoc. and Nat'l Acad. of Science [4](USDA) [5]Amer. Heart Assoc.

Due to rapid growth rate and body changes during the developmental years, nutritional needs for children vary more than for adults. Therefore, we suggest you supervise your children's daily dietary intake to make sure they're eating well-rounded meals and developing healthy eating habits. If you're not certain about specific dietary needs for your child, consult a registered dietitian or qualified doctor. *Note:* For calorie-cutting guidelines, see page 16.

Important Measures

Dash	under ⅛ teaspoon
½ tablespoon	1½ teaspoons
1 tablespoon	3 teaspoons
1 ounce liquid	2 tablespoons
1 jigger	1½ ounces
¼ cup	4 tablespoons
⅓ cup	5 tablespoons plus 1 teaspoon
½ cup	8 tablespoons
⅔ cup	10 tablespoons plus 2 teaspoons
¾ cup	12 tablespoons
1 cup	16 tablespoons
1 pint	2 cups
1 quart	2 pints
1 gallon	4 quarts
1 pound	16 ounces

Measuring Equipment

MEASURING FLOUR

Measure the all-purpose flour called for in most of the recipes in this book by spooning flour from the bag or canister into a standard dry measuring cup, heaping slightly. (Note: The top of the cup is flat; there is no spout in a dry measure, as there is in a liquid measuring cup.)

Place the heaping cup of flour over the bag of flour or canister and run the flat side of a long knife across the top to level off the cup. (Note: Use this technique for granulated sugar too.) Do not tap or shake the cup to level.

PACKING BROWN SUGAR

Measure light or dark brown sugar by packing it into a standard dry measuring cup, using the back of a tablespoon.

MEASURING SHORTENING

Measure vegetable shortening by scooping it with a rubber scraper into a standard dry measuring cup; run the flat blade of a long knife over the top, then scoop it out of the cup with a rubber scraper into the mixing bowl.
● Shortening can be measured before or after it is melted.
● One stick of butter or margarine equals 4 ounces; 4 sticks equal 1 pound or 2 cups.

MEASURING LIQUID

Place a standard liquid measuring cup on a flat surface and stoop to be at eye level with the measuring cup; pour the liquid to the desired measure printed on the side of the cup. (Note: When measuring a syrup, such as molasses or honey, grease the cup with butter or margarine. Then the syrup will pour out easily.)

Oven Temperatures

Ovens need not be preheated for meats, vegetables and most casserole dishes. Recipes that *need* preheated ovens have the direction inserted in the recipe to allow the 15-minute margin for preheating either gas or electric ovens.

Very Slow	**250°-275°**
Slow	**300°-325°**
Moderate	**350°-375°**
Hot	**400°-425°**
Very Hot	**450°-475°**
Extremely Hot	**500°+**

Casserole Measurement Chart
Casseroles are international dishes created all over the world. Each country has its own system for measuring volume or quantity. The chart below will help you to convert your casserole's measurements from one system to another so that you can be assured your recipe will bake to perfection.

Cups	=	Pints	=	Quarts	=	Liters
1		½		¼		0.237
2		1*		½*		0.473
4		2*		1*		0.946
6		3		1½		1.419
8		4		2		1.892
10		5		2½		2.365
12		6		3		2.838

In Canada, 1 pint = 2½ cups; 1 quart = 5 cups.

Emergency Ingredient Substitutes

WHEN THE RECIPE CALLS FOR:	YOU MAY SUBSTITUTE:
1 square unsweetened chocolate	3 tablespoons unsweetened cocoa powder plus 1 tablespoon butter, margarine or vegetable shortening
1 cup sifted cake flour	⅞ cup sifted all-purpose flour (1 cup less 2 tablespoons)
2 tablespoons flour (for thickening)	1 tablespoon cornstarch
1 teaspoon baking powder	¼ teaspoon baking powder plus ⅝ teaspoon cream of tartar
1 cup corn syrup	1 cup sugar and ¼ cup liquid used in recipe
1 cup honey	1¼ cups sugar and ¼ cup liquid used in recipe
1 cup whole milk	½ cup evaporated milk plus ½ cup water
1 cup buttermilk	1 tablespoon vinegar plus enough sweet milk to make 1 cup; let stand 5 minutes
1 cup sour cream (in baking)	⅞ cup buttermilk or sour milk plus 3 tablespoons butter
1 egg (for custards)	2 egg yolks
1 cup brown sugar (packed)	1 cup sugar or 1 cup sugar plus 2 tablespoons molasses
1 teaspoon lemon juice	½ teaspoon vinegar
¼ cup chopped onion	1 tablespoon instant minced onion
1 clove garlic	⅛ teaspoon garlic powder
1 cup zucchini	1 cup summer squash
1 cup tomato juice	½ cup tomato sauce plus ½ cup water
2 cups tomato sauce	¾ cup tomato paste plus 1 cup water
1 tablespoon fresh snipped herbs	1 teaspoon dried herbs
1 tablespoon prepared mustard	1 teaspoon dry mustard
1 cup bread crumbs	¾ cup cracker crumbs

Emergency Baking Dish and Pan Substitutes

If you do not have the specific-size baking pan or mold called for in a recipe, substitute a pan of equal volume from the list below.
● If the pan you are substituting is made of glass, reduce the baking temperature by 25°.
● If you are substituting a pan that is shallower than the pan in the recipe, reduce the baking time by about one-quarter.
● If you are substituting a pan that is deeper than the pan in the recipe, increase baking time by one-quarter.

HANDY CHART OF KITCHEN MATH
You'll never have a cooking crisis when you use our handy charts. Need a 4- or 6-cup baking dish? Will your fancy mold be the right size for the recipe? See below for the answers, plus much more!

COMMON KITCHEN PANS TO USE AS CASSEROLES WHEN THE RECIPE CALLS FOR:

4-cup baking dish:
9-inch pie plate
8 x 1¼-inch round layer-cake pan—C
7⅜ x 3⅝ x 2⅝-inch loaf pan—A
6-cup baking dish:
10-inch pie plate
8 or 9 x 1½-inch round layer-cake pan—C
8½ x 3⅝ x 2⅝-inch loaf pan—A
8-cup baking dish:
8 x 8 x 2-inch square pan—D
11 x 7 x 1½-inch baking pan
9 x 5 x 3-inch loaf pan—A
10-cup baking dish:
9 x 9 x 2-inch square pan—D
11¾ x 7½ x 1¾-inch baking pan
15½ x 10½ x 1-inch jelly-roll pan
12-cup baking dish and over:
13½ x 8½ x 2-inch glass baking dish (12 cups)
13 x 9 x 2-inch metal baking pan (15 cups)
14 x 10½ x 2½-inch roasting pan (19 cups)
Three 8-inch-round pans:
two 9 x 9 x 2-inch square cake pans
Two 9-inch-round layer-cake pans:
two 8 x 8 x 2-inch square cake pans, or 13 x 9 x 2-inch pan
9 x 5 x 3-inch loaf pan:
9 x 9 x 2-inch square cake pan
9-inch angel-cake tube pan:
10 x 3¾-inch Bundt® pan, or 9 x 3½-inch fancy tube pan

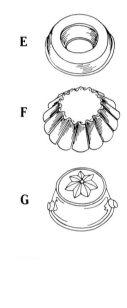

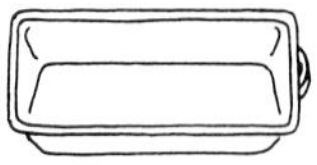

TOTAL VOLUME OF VARIOUS SPECIAL BAKING PANS

Tube pans:

7½ x 3-inch Bundt® tube pan—K	6 cups
9 x 3½-inch fancy tube or Bundt® pan—J or K	9 cups
9 x 3½-inch angel-cake or tube pan—I	12 cups
10 x 3¾-inch Bundt® or Crownburst pan—K	12 cups
9 x 3½-inch fancy tube mold—J	12 cups
10 x 4-inch fancy tube mold (Kugelhopf)—J	16 cups
10 x 4-inch angel-cake or tube pan—I	18 cups

Melon Mold:

7 x 5½ x 4-inch mold—H	6 cups

Springform Pans:

8 x 3-inch pan—B	12 cups
9 x 3-inch pan—B	16 cups

Ring Molds:

8½ x 2¼-inch mold—E	4½ cups
9¼ x 2¾-inch mold—E	8 cups

Charlotte Mold:

6 x 4¼-inch mold—G	7½ cups

Brioche Pan:

9½ x 3¼-inch pan—F	8 cups

Food Equivalents

Berries, 1 pint — 1¾ cups

Bread
1 pound, sliced — 22 slices
Crumbs, soft, 1 cup — 2 slices
Cubes, 1 cup — 2 slices

Broth
Beef or Chicken, 1 cup — 1 teaspoon instant bouillon or 1 envelope bouillon or 1 cube bouillon, dissolved in 1 cup boiling water

Butter or Margarine
½ stick — ¼ cup or 4 tablespoons
1 pound — 4 sticks or 2 cups

Cream and Milk
Cream, heavy, 1 cup — 2 cups, whipped
Milk, evaporated, small can — ⅔ cup
Milk, instant, nonfat dry, 1 pound — 5 quarts liquid skim milk
Milk, sweetened condensed, 14-ounce can — 1⅔ cups

Cheese
Blue, crumbled, 4 ounces — 1 cup
Cheddar or Swiss, 1 pound, shredded — 4 cups
Cottage, 8 ounces — 1 cup
Cream, 8-ounce package — 1 cup
Parmesan or Romano, ¼ pound, grated — 1¼ cups

Chocolate
Unsweetened, 1 ounce — 1 square
Semisweet pieces, 6-ounce package — 1 cup

Coconut
Flaked, 3½-ounce can — 1⅓ cups
Shredded, 4-ounce can — 1⅓ cups

Cookies
Chocolate wafers, 1 cup crumbs — 19 wafers
Graham crackers, 1 cup fine crumbs — 14 square crackers
Vanilla wafers, 1 cup fine crumbs — 22 wafers

Dried Beans and Peas
1 cup — 2¼ cups, cooked

Eggs (large)
Whole, 1 cup — 5 to 6
Whites, 1 cup — 7 to 8
Yolks, 1 cup — 13 to 14

Flour
All-purpose, sifted, 1 pound — 4 cups
Cake, sifted, 1 pound — 4¾ to 5 cups

Gelatin, unflavored, 1 envelope — 1 tablespoon

Nuts
Almonds, 1 pound, shelled — 3½ cups
Peanuts, 1 pound, shelled — 3 cups
Pecans, 1 pound, shelled — 4 cups
Walnuts, 1 pound, shelled — 4 cups

Pasta
Macaroni, elbow, uncooked, 8 ounces — 4 cups, cooked
Noodles, medium width, 8 ounces, uncooked — 3¾ cups, cooked
Spaghetti, 8 ounces, uncooked — 4 cups, cooked

Rice
Enriched precooked rice, uncooked, 1 cup — 2 cups, cooked
Long-grain white rice, uncooked, 1 cup — 3 cups, cooked

Sugar
Brown, firmly packed, 1 pound — 2¼ cups
Granulated, 1 pound — 2 cups
10X (confectioners' powdered), sifted, 1 pound — 3⅓ to 4 cups

Vegetables and Fruits
Apples, 1 pound — 3 medium-size
Bananas, 1 pound — 3 medium-size
Cabbage, 1 pound, shredded — 4 cups
Carrots, 1 pound, sliced — 2½ cups
Herbs, chopped fresh, 1 tablespoon — 1 teaspoon dried
Lemon, 1 medium-size, grated — 2 teaspoons lemon rind
Lemon, 1 medium-size, squeezed — 2 tablespoons lemon juice
Mushrooms, 1 pound, sliced — 3 cups
Onions, small white silverskins, 1 pound — 12 to 14
Onions, yellow cooking, 1 pound — 5 to 6 medium size
Orange, 1 medium-size, grated — 2 tablespoons orange rind
Orange, 1 medium-size, squeezed — ⅓ to ½ cup orange juice
Peaches, 1 pound — 4 medium-size
Potatoes, all-purpose, 1 pound — 3 medium-size
Tomatoes, 1 pound
  Large — 2
  Medium-size — 3
  Small — 4

Maximum Cupboard Storage Times

Use foods within the times recommended in this chart. Foods stored longer than recommended are still good to eat, but may be less flavorful and nutritious.

Baking powder	18 months
Baking soda	18 months
Barbecue sauce*	12 months
Bouillon cubes, instant	12 months
Cake Mixes	12 months
Canned foods* Fruit, gravy, sauce, meat, poultry, milk, seafood, soup, vegetables	12 months
Casserole mixes	18 months
Catsup*	12 months
Cereal	6 months
Chili sauce*	12 months
Chocolate for cooking	12 months
Coconut*	12 months
Coffee* In vacuum-packed cans	12 months
Instant	6 months
Flour* all types	12 months
Frosting mixes or cans	8 months
Fruit, dried*	6 months
Gelatin plain and sweet	18 months
Herbs/spices (refrigerate red spices) Ground	6 months
Whole	12 months
Honey	12 months
Jam/jelly*	12 months
Molasses	24 months

Nonfat dry milk powder	6 months
Oil* Olive	1 month
Vegetable	3 months
Olives/pickles*	12 months
Pancake mixes	6 months
Pasta	12 months
Peanut butter	6 months
Piecrust mixes	6 months
Potato mixes or instant	18 months
Pudding mixes	12 months
Rice Brown, wild	12 months
Regular long-grain	24 months
Salad dressing*	6 months
Shortening	8 months
Soup mixes	6 months
Sugar Brown or 10X	4 months
Granulated	24 months
Syrup* Corn, maple	12 months
Tea Bags or loose	6 months
Instant	12 months
Vegetables Onions and potatoes	1 to 2 weeks
Winter squash	1 to 3 months
Yeast active dry	follow package date

refrigerate after opening

Maximum Freezer Storage Times

Use foods within the times recommended in this chart. Foods stored longer than recommended are still good to eat, but will be less flavorful and nutritious.

What Not To Freeze

You *can* freeze most foods, but some suffer at freezer temperatures: *Canned hams* become watery and soft; *cooked egg white* gets rubbery; *salad dressings or mayonnaise* (unless in very small amounts in a mixture) separate; *milk sauces* curdle; *fresh salad ingredients* wilt; *processed meats* (such as cold cuts) have a high salt content which speeds rancidity; *cooked white potatoes* become mealy; *home-stuffed whole poultry* (still on carcass) can get contaminated due to slow freezing; *gelatin-based dishes* "weep" upon thawing; *cream pie fillings* become watery and lumpy.

Appetizers	(Canapes, hors d'oeuvres)	½ to 1 month
Breads	**Quick**	
	Baked muffins, biscuits and simple quick breads	2 to 3 months
	Rich, fruit, nut or spicy quick breads	1 to 2 months
	Unbaked dough	1 month
	Yeast	
	Baked bread and rolls	3 months
	Danish pastry	3 months
	Doughnuts, cake or yeast	3 months
	Half-baked (brown 'n' serve)	2 to 3 months
	Rich sweet breads	2 months
	Unbaked	1 months
Cakes	Any type butter cake,* frosted or unfrosted	4 to 6 months
	Angel or chiffon	2 months
	Fruit	12 months
Cooked Combination Dishes	Casseroles, pasta or rice base	2 to 4 weeks
	Pizza	2 to 4 weeks
	Sauces and stews	1 to 3 months
Cookies	Baked	6 to 8 months
	Unbaked, refrigerator	6 months
Dairy Products	Butter	6 months
	Margarine	12 months
	Cheese	
	Cottage, uncreamed	2 to 3 months
	Cream cheese, for use as an ingredient	2 months
	Natural Cheddar (all forms) and Swiss	1½ months
	Processed cheese**	4 months
	Cream	
	Heavy cream (thawed cream may not whip)	2 months
	Half-and-half	2 months
	Whipped cream	1 month

Desserts	Cream puffs or eclairs	1 to 2 months
	Fruit	2 to 4 months
	Ice cream, sherbet	6 months
Eggs	Whole, yolks or whites separated	12 months
Meats, raw	**Beef**	
	Ground beef	2 to 4 months
	Steaks, roasts	8 to 12 months
	Stew meats	2 to 4 months
	Lamb	
	Chops	3 to 4 months
	Roasts	6 to 9 months
	Pork	
	Chops	3 to 4 months
	Cured (bacon, ham)	2 months
	Roasts	4 to 8 months
	Sausage	1 to 3 months
	Veal	
	Roasts, cutlets, chops	6 to 9 months
Meats, cooked and processed	Bologna and luncheon meats	Not recommended
	Casseroles, pies, prepared dinners	3 months
	Frankfurters	3 months
	Gravy, broth	2 to 3 months
	Loaves	2 to 3 months
Poultry, raw	**Chicken**	
	Cut up	9 months
	Livers	1 month
	Whole	12 months
	Duckling, whole	6 months
	Turkey	
	Cut up	6 to 9 months
	Whole	12 months
Poultry, cooked	Casseroles, pies, prepared dinners	6 months
	Fried	4 months
	Stuffing†	1 month
	Without gravy or broth	1 month
	Whole, unstuffed†	6 months

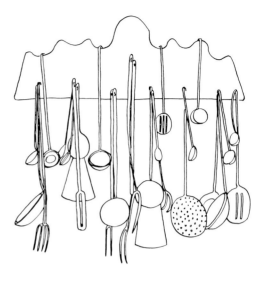

Fish and shellfish, raw	Lean (bass, cod, perch pike, sunfish)	6 to 8 months
	Oily (catfish, herring, mackerel, salmon)	2 to 3 months
	Shrimp (unbreaded)	9 to 12 months
Cooked		3 months
Nuts	Unsalted	9 to 12 months
	Salted	6 to 8 months
Pastries	**Pastry dough**	
	Unbaked	1½ to 2 months
	Baked	6 to 8 months
	Pies††	
	Unbaked	2 to 4 months
	Baked	6 to 8 months
	Chiffon	2 months
Sandwiches	Meat, poultry, cheese, jelly or jam mixtures	1 to 2 months
Soups	Including concentrated and stock	1 to 3 months
Vegetables, blanched	Most	12 months

Do not freeze cakes filled with custard or cream.
**Processed cheese is identified on the label. If not so designated, it is natural.*
†*Do not freeze home-stuffed poultry, because of the danger of bacterial contamination.*
†† *Do not freeze custard or cream pies or those with a meringue topping.*

If Your Freezer Breaks Down...

Or if you have a power failure, follow these tips to avoid food spoilage:
● Keep the freezer door closed tightly. If the freezer is fully stocked, the contents will stay frozen for at least two days; if it is half-full, the food will stay frozen for about one day.
● For periods longer than a day or two, buy dry ice—25 pounds for each cubic foot of freezer space—and place large chunks (with gloved hands) on top of the food. If the freezer is fully stocked, the dry ice will keep the food frozen three to four days; in a half-filled freezer, up to two to three days.
● If foods have partially thawed, but still have ice crystals in their packages, they can be safely refrozen. To make sure food is only partially thawed (when ice crystals are not discernible), slip a thermometer between the food and its wrapping. If the temperature is 40°F. or lower, the food can be safely refrozen.
● If uncooked foods have thawed, cook, then safely refreeze. Any cooked foods should be heated and eaten right away.

How to Get the Most From Your Microwave

These tips will help you use your microwave oven to its full potential.

GENERAL TIPS

1. To test whether a dish is microwave-safe or not, place it in the microwave oven next to a glass measuring cup half full of water. Heat at full (100%) power for 1 minute. If the dish is hot, it should not be used in the microwave oven. If it is warm, use only for reheating. If the dish is at room temperature, it is safe to use for all microwave cooking.

2. Pay attention to standing times in recipes! Internal heat finishes the cooking after the dish is removed from the oven.

3. Make sure the cooking utensil rests on a solid heatproof surface during the standing time or resting time specified in the recipe.

4. Set a timer for the minimum cooking time called for in a recipe. Check the doneness of food, then microwave for the additional time, if necessary.

5. When frequent stirring is necessary for a dish, leave a wooden spoon or microwave-safe utensil in the dish in the microwave oven.

6. To prevent messy boil-overs, use a cooking container two to three times larger than the volume of the sauce, soup, drink or other liquid dish you are preparing.

7. If cooking uniform pieces of food, such as meatballs or chicken wings, arrange in a circle in the cooking utensil for even cooking.

8. Place tougher or thicker parts of food toward the outside edges of cooking pan or tray.

9. Do not use gold- or silver-trimmed dishes in a microwave oven; arcing may occur. Arcing is an electrical current that flows from the oven wall to metal in the oven, causing a light flash and popping sound. This may cause damage to the magnetron tube, the interior oven wall or the cooking utensil.

10. If arcing occurs, turn the power off immediately.

11. If there are small children in your house who might reach the controls and accidently turn the microwave oven on, keep a glass measure or bowl containing about 1 cup of water in the oven to prevent damage to it.

12. A microwave oven works especially well with foods that have a naturally high moisture content, such as fish, poultry, fruits and vegetables.

13. Dense foods, such as potato, will take longer to cook in a microwave oven than lighter-textured foods, such as a cake.

MEATS & FISH

14. Cook clams and mussels right in their shells for an easy-to-prepare appetizer. Arrange on a pie plate, hinged-side toward the outside of the plate, and cover loosely with wax paper. For three 5-ounce clams, microwave at full (100%) power for 3 to 5 minutes or until the shells open.

15. If your roast beef is too rare, microwave the slices right on the dinner plate until the desired doneness.

16. For one-step cooking and draining of excess fat, crumble ground meat into a microwave-safe plastic colander set in a casserole. The fat will drain into the casserole during cooking.

17. No-fuss, fancy hors d'oeuvres: Wrap pineapple chunks or water chestnuts in bacon and fasten with a wooden pick. Place on paper toweling and microwave at full (100%) power until the bacon is thoroughly cooked.

18. For an instant hot dog in a warm bun, lightly score a fully cooked frankfurter and place in the bun. Wrap loosely in paper toweling and microwave at full (100%) power for 30 to 45 seconds.

19. For barbecued spareribs and chicken, microwave until tender, then grill long enough for a charcoal flavor and a crisp exterior.

20. Remember: Boneless meats cook more evenly than meats on the bone, because bones attract more microwave energy than meat.

FRUITS AND VEGETABLES

21. To get the maximum amount of juice from citrus fruits, microwave at full (100%) power for 15 to 30 seconds before squeezing.

22. Peel, core and pierce whole fruit, such as apples, before microwaving to allow steam to escape and avoid spattering.

23. When microwaving cabbage-family vegetables, such as fresh broccoli or cauliflower, cover loosely with wax paper for better flavor and color.

24. For an easy, quick single serving of frozen vegetables: Put ½ cup of frozen vegetables with 1 tablespoon of water in a custard cup. Cover with wax paper. Microwave at full (100%) power for 1½ to 2 minutes.

25. Here's how to cook crisp frozen hash-brown or French-fried potatoes in half the time! Partially thaw first in the microwave oven, following the package directions, then fry or bake conventionally to finish.

26. To plump raisins and other dried fruits, place in a small bowl and sprinkle with a few drops of water. Microwave at full (100%) power for 15 to 30 seconds.

27. Use your microwave to dry fresh herbs. Wash and pat dry on paper toweling. Measure 1½ cups of leaves (without stems). Spread on a double thickness of paper toweling and microwave at full (100%) power for 4 to 5 minutes, stirring several times.

28. Shortcut acorn squash: Pierce the skin of a medium-size (1¼ pounds) squash and microwave at full (100%) power for 4 minutes. Cut in half, remove the seeds and microwave another 4 minutes. Let stand for 5 minutes.

29. Cook broccoli or asparagus with the tender flower ends pointing toward the center and with the tougher stem ends pointing out.

KITCHEN HELPS

30. Separate cold bacon in its package: microwave at full (100%) power for 30 to 45 seconds.

31. To soften solidly frozen ice cream for easier scooping, microwave the container at low (30%) power for 20 to 40 seconds.

32. Soften 1 stick of butter at half (50%) power for 45 to 55 seconds. Remove any foil wrapping before microwaving.

33. To soften cream cheese, remove the metallic wrapper and loosely wrap in wax paper. Microwave at low (30%) power for 1½ to 2 minutes for the 3-ounce size and 3 to 4 minutes for the 8-ounce size.

34. Use doubled paper muffin-pan liners for microwaving muffins; the liners will help absorb any excess moisture.

35. Loosen hard brown sugar by adding an apple slice or a few drops of water to the box; microwave at full (100%) power for a few seconds.

36. To melt chocolate, microwave in a micro-wave-safe cup at full (100%) power for 45 to 60 seconds per ounce of chocolate.

37. To make chocolate curls, place an unwrapped block of chocolate on a microwave-safe plate. Heat at half (50%) power for 8 to 12 seconds. Scrape off the curls with a vegetable peeler.

38. "Toasted" coconut: To brown 1 cup of shredded coconut, spread out on a microwave-safe pie plate. Microwave at full (100%) power for 2 to 3 minutes, stirring several times.

39. Make your own chocolate syrup for milk: Combine 1¼ cups of granulated sugar, 1 cup of unsweetened cocoa powder, ¾ cup of water and ⅛ teaspoon of salt in a 1-quart measuring cup. Microwave at full (100%) power for 2 minutes or until mixture boils. Stir. Continue cooking 2 minutes longer, stirring every 30 seconds; don't let the mixture boil over. Stir in ½ teaspoon of vanilla. To serve, stir 2 tablespoons of the syrup into an 8-ounce glass of milk. The syrup will keep for up to 1 month when tightly covered in the refrigerator.

40. For fried or poached eggs, always pierce the yolks with a wooden pick *before* microwaving to prevent bursting.

41. Quick cup of tea, instant coffee or cocoa: Heat the water directly in the cup instead of boiling a large kettle of water conventionally. A cup with 6 ounces of water microwaved at full (100%) power will be steaming after 1¼ to 2 minutes. Two cups will take 2½ to 3 minutes.

42. Speedy toasted cheese sandwich: Toast 2 slices of bread (white or whole wheat) in a toaster or toaster oven. Place a slice of cheese on one piece of toast. Spread with mustard, if you wish, then top with the remaining piece of toast. Place the sandwich on a paper plate and microwave at medium-high (70%) power for 15 to 20 seconds or until the cheese melts.

WARMING UP FOODS

43. Microwave dinner rolls in a napkin-lined straw serving basket at full (100%) power for 15 to 30 seconds, depending on the number and size of rolls.

44. Wrap a sandwich in paper toweling and microwave—the paper absorbs excess moisture.

45. Heat pancake syrup in its own container, cap removed, or in a serving pitcher at full (100%) power for 15 seconds.

46. Heat gravy in a serving bowl or gravy boat at full (100%) power for 1 minute per cup.

47. To warm a 12-ounce jar of sundae or fruit sauce topping, remove the lid and microwave at full (100%) power for 45 to 60 seconds.

48. Reheat take-out fast food in its own paper wrapping at full (100%) power. If a container has a foil top, remove and cover loosely with wax paper.

49. Reheat fast-food double-decker hamburger in its plastic package at full (100%) power for 20 to 40 seconds.

50. To crisp and renew fresh flavor of day-old cookies, crackers or potato chips, microwave at full (100%) power for 5 to 15 seconds.

51. Warm a slice of apple pie with "melty" cheese on top by microwaving at full (100%) power for 15 to 20 seconds.

52. Popped corn can be reheated at full (100%) power for 15 to 20 seconds per cup.

53. As a general rule, to reheat foods, allow 1½ to 2 minutes for each cup of refrigerated mixture.
54. Hot pancakes: arrange 3 already-cooked pancakes, overlapping on a microwave-safe plate. Cover loosely with wax paper and microwave at full (100%) power for 20 to 30 seconds.

DEFROSTING
55. Defrost and heat foods in boilable plastic bags right in the bag. Place the bag in a microwave-safe pie plate and cut an "X" in the bag above the liquid line for venting.
56. Frozen juice can be defrosted in its container. Remove the lid from one end. Defrost at half (50%) power for 2 to 2½ minutes for a 6-ounce can and 4½ to 5 minutes for a 12-ounce can.
57. Thaw frozen fish fillets right in their own packaging at low (30%) power.

Watching Calories?

We're all interested in learning as much as possible about diet and fitness so that we look and feel as good as possible. For many of us, this involves not only reducing caloric intake but also developing new eating patterns. To start, check out our health and nutrition guidelines, (see Good Meals–Good Health, page 6), then keep an eye out for *boxed recipes*—these are low-calorie versions that will help you create healthful and delicious dishes, using substitute products or less fat. In some cases, we've reduced portion sizes so you can consume all the ingredients you enjoy—but just in smaller amounts.

GENERAL DIETING GUIDELINES
Caloric intake should equal the calories you expend. And 3,500 calories equal 1 pound of fatty tissue. Keep that all-important formula in mind if you're trying to maintain your weight.
Calories do count: Most women will lose weight eating 1,200 to 1,700 calories per day. Eating less may actually impede weight loss by lowering the body's basal metobolic rate. Most men will lose weight by eating 1,600 to 2,000 calories per day. However, any attempt to lose weight should be discussed with a doctor beforehand.
Water: Drink at least 8 glasses of water per day. It cleanses the system, helps to digest food properly, and helps create the feeling of being full.
Carbohydrates: Pasta, whole-wheat breads, rice, beans, potatoes, fresh fruits…complex carbohydrates are not fattening! This food group should make up more than ½ of the total calories con-

sumed in one day (60% to 65%). If you eat the right amount of complex carbohydrates, it will help avoid that starved feeling and food cravings.
Protein: Protein is important, but should not be the main source of calories in your diet. Forget the "high-protein, quick weight-loss" diets. Only 20% of the daily calorie total should come from protein.
Fat: Fattening. Don't consume more than 17% of total calories in fat.
Fiber: Fresh fruit, vegetables, oatmeal, brown rice, lentils, beans…fiber may help reduce cholesterol, decrease the risk of cancer and prevent a variety of diseases. Plus, fiber gives that "full" feeling.
Fad diets have one big drawback: They don't teach you how to change your eating habits permanently. When the diet ends, so does your ability to control your weight.
Junk foods—candy bars, sugary drinks, chips, cookies—are O.K. as an occasional treat. But avoid a steady diet of "empty calories."
Metabolism is one of the key factors in weight control. Active people burn more calories *all of the time,* not just while exercising.
Nutrient-rich foods pay off—in clear skin, shiny hair, strong teeth. Be sure to get your daily quota of vitamins and minerals.
Osteoporosis—"brittle bones"—is eight times more common in women than in men. Recent studies indicate that regular exercise and a calcium-rich diet can help keep bones strong.
Vitamins are vital for optimal health. Get them by eating a well-balanced diet—fresh fruits and vegetables, lean meats, fish, poultry, whole grains and dairy products.

CALORIE-CUTTING AND SUBSTITUTIONS
1. A tablespoon of butter has the same calorie count as a tablespoon of margarine. But substitute an equal amount of diet margarine, and you'll shave off up to 50% of the calories.
2. Look for margarine with "liquid oil" as the first ingredient instead of "hydrogenated oil" or butter.
3. Use corn, soybean, safflower or sunflower oil instead of peanut, palm, coconut or olive oil.
4. Instead of legs or thighs, use *skinless* chicken breasts for chicken salads, pot pies, curries, stews and soups. White meat has fewer calories than dark meat and most of the fat is in the skin.
5. To keep chicken moist, cook it with the skin on, but remove the skin before serving.
6. Part-skim milk products can often be substituted for their whole-milk cousins, without affecting a recipe. You'll find part-skim or low-fat milk,

cheeses and yogurt at supermarkets.

7. Substitute low-fat plain yogurt for sour cream.

8. Create low-fat "cream cheese" by blending 1½ cups of ricotta cheese (partially skimmed) with ¼ cup of plain yogurt. Refrigerate.

9. Substitute 2% or skim milk for whole milk.

10. Replace evaporated skim milk for cream in recipes.

11. Know where calories come from: 1 tablespoon of sour cream on a baked potato adds more calories than 1 tablespoon of sugar sprinkled over a grapefruit half. (Fat provides double the calories compared with carbohydrates and protein.)

12. Switch from whole milk to skim. If you've never been able to get used to the taste of skim milk, mix half whole with half skim; you'll cut 36 calories from each 8-ounce glass.

13. Make a two-egg omelet, using one whole egg with just the white of the other egg. By eliminating the second yolk, you'll save more than 250 mg of cholesterol and 65 calories.

14. Instead of American cheese as your omelet filling, substitute leftover steamed vegetables and herbs. You'll save about 210 calories and 16 grams of fat per 2 ounces of cheese.

15. Try some of the low-fat varieties of these cheeses: Edam, Gouda, mozzarella, Parmesan, ricotta, Monterey Jack, cottage, Cheddar.

16. Make a mock mayonnaise by blending 2 tablespoons of low-calorie mayonnaise with 1 cup of yogurt.

17. Try reducing sugar and salt in recipes by half.

18. Choose fresh fruit and vegetables in season instead of canned or frozen when possible.

19. Sauté foods in chicken broth instead of oil.

20. Trim fat from beef and poultry. Avoid marbled meat.

21. Use only nonstick skillets for sautéing—you'll need less oil. Remember to drain the fat when possible.

22. Roast, bake or broil meats and poultry on a rack to ensure maximum fat runoff. Then, remove skin and all visible fat before eating.

23. Eliminate bacon in stews, casseroles and soups and avoid cooking with bacon fat.

24. Try some of the new lower-fat products now available: sausage-rice breakfast links, chicken and turkey franks, and lower-fat luncheon meats.

25. If you're a tuna fish fan, save 300 calories per 6½-ounce can by using tuna packed in water rather than oil.

26. Substitute whole-wheat or spinach pasta for white pasta.

27. Use brown instead of white rice.

28. Try lentils, bulgur or kasha as alternatives to rice, noodles and mashed potatoes.

29. Make French fries without the oil: Cut a raw potato into 16 wedges. Place on a cookie sheet and bake at 400°…sprinkle with garlic, onion or chili powder.

30. When baking, substitute whole-wheat flour for half of the white flour.

31. Forego crumb toppings, icings and glazes on home-baked goods.

32. Garnish desserts with slices of fresh fruit and fresh mint leaves rather than with a dollop of whipped cream.

33. Try substituting a low-calorie whipped topping mix in a recipe that calls for sweetened whipped cream.

34. Try two shredded wheat biscuits with 4 ounces of skim milk for a filling, low-fat, high-fiber, 225-calorie lunchtime meal.

35. Have a low-calorie California-style salad: Slices of oranges and fresh spinach leaves make a salad with lots of eye appeal that is also high in iron and vitamin C. Sprinkle with lemon, vinegar or a low-calorie dressing.

36. Mix ½ cup of tangy buttermilk with ½ cup of tomato juice. Just 67 calories.

37. Mix ½ cup of buttermilk with ½ cup of low-calorie borscht. Only about 60 calories and a refreshing summer soup, too.

38. Boost your calcium intake by adding a tablespoon of dry skim milk powder to a glass of skim milk. Only 23 extra calories.

39. Create a healthful, low-calorie thirst-quencher by mixing ½ cup of mineral water with ⅓ cup of your favorite juice.

40. Another low-cal, healthful drink: 2 ounces of orange juice mixed with a squeeze of lime and enough cold water to make one cup. Only about 30 calories.

41. Have a spritzer—equal parts of wine and club soda. If you use just 2 ounces of wine, it's about 35 to 45 calories.

42. Rule of thumb for alcoholic beverages: The "proof" determines the calories—80-proof vodka instead of 100-proof, for example, saves you about 25 calories per 1½ ounces.

43. Sip your cocktail from a large glass filled with ice. There will be less room for liquid.

44. Opt for lower-calorie dry wines over sweet ones. (Champagne is a good choice.)

45. If you prefer no alcohol at all, sip a glass of mineral water with a slice of lemon, lime or orange. It will help take the edge off your appetite.

Tomatoes Stuffed with Ham Salad (page 176), Regal Peach Crown (page 270)

Menu Themes and Ideas

Having trouble deciding what to fix for your next meal? This chapter's here to rescue you with over 75 complete menus to make your life easier. You'll find menus for breakfast, lunch and dinner, as well as some for brunches, holidays and other special occasions. Every menu contains recipes from our cookbook, and we've also suggested other foods to serve with our delectable dishes.

To make things even easier for you, we've used our coding system in arranging these menus:

"Quick" meals, with their suggestions for packaged convenience items and simple-to-prepare foods, can be ready to eat within an hour.

"Make-ahead" meals include recipes that can be prepared, all at once or in stages, ahead of time. That leaves only last-minute details for those hectic moments just before meal-time.

Meals "for entertaining" are those reserved for special occasions and special "someones" when you want everything to be just a bit more elegant.

"Low-cost" meals will enable you to scrimp on your grocery bill but not on nutrition or taste. Meatless courses, such as pasta or vegetable dishes, are just one way to reduce your food bill, and they can even make your diet a healthier one.

"Low-calorie" meals are very popular with people who are concerned about their waistlines. Our exciting and delicious low-calorie creations let "foodaholics" satisfy cravings without loading up on those unwanted calories.

As complete and irresistible as our menus are, you should still feel free to juggle our choices and create your own combinations. The possibilities are limitless!

Meals for Two

BREAKFAST

BREAKFAST ON THE GO
FOR 2
Grapefruit Juice
Egg on a Muffin, page 165
(make the recipe two times)

BREAKFAST IN A MINUTE
FOR 2
Fresh Fruit Cup
Assorted Cheese Slices
Buttermilk and Bacon Corn Muffins,
page 60
Butter   Jam
Coffee   Tea

FOR FITNESS FANATICS
FOR 2
Grapefruit Half
Homemade Granola Crunch, page 274
with Skim Milk
Peanut Butter on Whole-Wheat Toast
Caffeine-Free Coffee or Tea

BREAKFAST IN A GLASS
FOR 2
Orange Juice
Banana-Berry Shake, page 284
(make the recipe two times)
Cinnamon-Raisin English Muffins

BRUNCH

HIS FAVORITE
FOR 2
Sliced Cantaloupe
Mushroom Omelet   Broiled Bacon
Flaky Biscuits, page 66
Butter   Marmalade
Coffee   Tea

LUNCH

JUST YOU AND ME
FOR 2
Cream of Asparagus Soup
Tomatoes Stuffed with Ham Salad,
page 176 (halve the recipe)
Corn Sticks   Herb Butter
Fresh Fruit and Tapioca Parfaits
Iced Tea with Lemon

LUNCHEON TRAY
FOR 2

Creamy Cauliflower Soup
Chicken, Orange and Beet Salad,
page 181 (halve the recipe)
Whole-Grain Rolls   Butter
Peanut Brittle and Rice Pudding
with Nectarines, page 270
Coffee

LADIES' NIGHT
FOR 2

Gazpacho
Shrimp with Cilantro Mayonnaise,
page 176 (halve the recipe)
Marinated Cherry Tomatoes
Whole Wheat Bread, page 54   Butter
Lemon Mousse with Whipped Cream
White Wine

CHICKEN & VEGGIES LUNCH
FOR 2

Poached Chicken Cutlets
Vegetable Curry with Fruit, page 195
(halve the recipe)
Hot Cooked Rice
Vanilla Ice Cream
Beer

BACHELOR SPECIAL
FOR 2

Cheese and Crackers
Salad Bar Minestrone, page 163
(halve the recipe)
French Bread   Butter
Chocolate Chocolate-Chip Ice Cream
Red Wine

DINNER

LO-CAL DINNER
FOR 2

Beef Broth with Mushroom Slices
Confetti Primavera with Mozzarella,
page 157 (halve the recipe)
Mixed Green Salad with Yogurt-Tomato
Dressing
Sunshine Sundae, page 271
Light White Wine

ANNIVERSARY DINNER
FOR 2

Chicken with Hazelnuts Sublime,
page 113 (halve the recipe)
Brown Rice with Mushrooms and Herbs
Steamed Broccoli
Leaf Lettuce and Radicchio Salad with
Pineapple-Lemon-Mint Dressing,
page 89 (halve the recipe)
Ice-Cream Parfaits
White Wine

Meals for Four

STIR-FRY SPECIAL
FOR 2

Egg Drop Soup
Stir-Fried Chicken and Vegetables in
Oyster Sauce, page 118 (halve the recipe)
Steamed Rice
Orange Sherbet   Almond Cookies
Green Tea

DINNER IN A FLASH
FOR 2

Beef Consommé with Sliced Mushrooms
Vealballs with Dilled Fettuccine,
page 101 (halve the recipe)
Stir-Fried Green Beans and Red Peppers
Apple-Walnut Squares
Sparkling Water with Lemon

QUICK-FIX DINNER
FOR 2

Vegetable Soup
Grilled Open-Face Club Sandwich,
page 99 (halve the recipe)
Coleslaw   Dilled Pickle Spears
Gingerbread with Lemon Sauce
Apple Cider

BREAKFAST

BREAKFAST SKIPPER'S BREAKFAST
FOR 4

Fruit Smoothie, page 285
Cheese Chunks
Apple-Spice Granola Muffins, page 59
Butter
Coffee   Tea

PERFECT FOR SUMMER
FOR 4

Fresh Fruit Cup
Poached Eggs
Citrus Lime Muffins, page 61
Orange Butter
Coffee   Tea   Milk

BRUNCH

TRADITIONAL AND TASTY
FOR 4
Orange Juice Mimosas
Buttermilk Pancakes, page 67, topped
with Fresh Blueberries and Blueberry
Syrup
Canadian Bacon
Coffee   Tea

FAST-FOOD BRUNCH
FOR 4
Gazpacho, page 81
Egg, Bacon and Cheese Monster Muffins,
page 164
Coffee   Tea   Milk

WELCOME HOME BRUNCH
FOR 4
Cranberry Juice Cocktails
Eggs au Gratin, page 165
Whole Wheat Muffins, page 63
Strawberry Butter
Coffee   Tea   Milk

LUNCH

BRIDAL LUNCHEON
FOR 4
Cold Fruit Soup
Cucumber Surprise, page 177
Asparagus Spears
Wheat Germ Muffins, page 62
Herb Butter
California Oranges Jubilee, page 261
(halve the recipe)
White Wine

SUN AND SURF PICNIC
FOR 4
Bean and Potato with Ham, page 162
Coleslaw Vinaigrette
Whole-Wheat Pita Bread
Watermelon Wedges
Beer   Soda

IN-A-MINUTE MELTS
FOR 4
Cream of Tomato Soup
Zesty Avocado, Bacon and
Swiss Cheese Melts, page 168
Orange Wedges
Chocolate Cupcakes
Apple Juice

ONE-DISH LUNCH
FOR 4

*Chicken with Lemon-Yogurt Dressing,
page 182
Sliced Bananas and Kiwi
Whole Wheat Bread, page 54
Orange Butter
Granola Cookies
Iced Tea with Fresh Mint*

LET'S GO ITALIAN
FOR 4

*Spinach-Prosciutto Roll Lasagne,
page 178
Red, Green and Yellow Pepper
Vinaigrette
Garlic Bread
Tortonis
Rosé Wine Spritzers*

CALORIE CRUNCHER
FOR 4

*Chicken Broth with Green Onion Slices
Ravioli with Red Pepper and
Tomato Sauce, page 156
Fresh Pineapple, Papaya and Raspberry
Compote with Lime
Sparkling Water*

DINNER

PATIO SUPPER
FOR 4

*Mixed Vegetable Salad with
Yogurt-Mushroom Dressing,
(halve the recipe, if you wish), page 89
Mustard-Crusted Flank Steak, page 94
Steamed Broccoli with
Toasted Sesame Seeds
Baked Potato   Butter
Plain Yogurt Mixed with Chopped Chives
Lemon Sorbet   Butter Cookies
Rosé Spritzer, page 282
(make the recipe four times)*

LIGHT UP THE GRILL
FOR 4

*Key West Ribs, page 145
Grilled Summer Squash, page 152
Buttered Noodles   Cucumber Salad
Pineapple-Orange Ice, page 268
Apple Iced Tea, page 284*

SUMMER FAREWELL COOKOUT
FOR 4

*Cold Cantaloupe Soup, page 81
Corn 'n' Chicken, page 148
Baked Potatoes   Mixed Green Salad
Spice Cakes with Banana Cream Filling,
page 228 (halve the recipe)
Lemonade*

ORIENTAL COMBINATION
FOR 4

Chicken Broth with
Chopped Green Onions
Sweet and Sour Chicken, page 119
Hot Cooked Rice
Orange, Pineapple and Banana Chunks
Sprinkled with Coconut
Hot Tea   Beer

THREE-DAY WEEKEND CELEBRATION
FOR 4

Artichoke Vinaigrette Appetizer,
page 77
Curried Swordfish, page 149
Grilled Mushrooms, page 152
Hot Cooked Rice
Vanilla Ice Cream with Port Wine Sauce,
page 275
White Wine

HEARTY AUTUMN DINNER
FOR 4

Pork Chops in Beer, page 105
Red Cabbage   Boiled Potatoes
Pear Waldorf Salad
Warm Gingerbread with Vanilla Ice
Cream
Hot Cider   Milk

SOMETHING ELEGANT
FOR 4

Lemon-Roasted Cornish Hens, page 124
Spinach Bake, page 190
Brown and Wild Rice
Fresh Pineapple and Orange Slices on
Leaf Lettuce
Chocolate and Vanilla
Pudding Parfaits
White Wine
Coffee   Tea

PASTA FAVORITE
FOR 4

Pasta with Sausage and Peppers,
page 160
Sliced Tomatoes on Lettuce
Butter-Toasted Onion Rolls
Wine-Poached Pears
Beer   Iced Tea

TURKEY AND IT'S NOT THANKSGIVING
FOR 4

Turkey Cutlets with Fresh Tomato and Coriander Sauce, page 133
Brown Rice   Steamed Broccoli Spears
Cucumber Vinaigrette
Pineapple Sorbet
Sparkling Water with Lemon

ANYTIME FEAST
FOR 4

Easy Roast Duckling, page 126
Creamed Onions
Candied Baby Carrots
Belgian Endive and Watercress Salad
with Vinaigrette Dressing
Country Home-Baked Bread,
page 56
Butter
White Wine

BREAKFAST

KIDS'LL LOVE IT
FOR 6

Orange Juice
Banana Kabobs, page 259
Honey Raisin Bread, page 64
Milk

BRUNCH

FESTIVE WEEKEND BRUNCH
FOR 6

Assorted Melon Balls Laced with
Champagne
Belgian Waffles with Maple-Blueberry
Topping, page 273
Brown-and-Serve Sausage Links
Assorted Cheeses
Coffee   Tea

MAKE-AHEAD BRUNCH
FOR 6
Iced Buttermilk-Lemon Soup, page 81
Broccoli, Mushroom and
Sweet Pepper Pie, page 172
Sliced Orange and Avocado with
Fruit Dressing
Raspberry Sherbet with Pound Cake
Coffee   Tea

LUNCH

ALL-SEASON SALAD
FOR 6
Curried Turkey-Rice Salad, page 182
Sliced Bananas and Fresh Pineapple
Slices with Toasted Coconut
Whole-Wheat Pita Breads
Individual Birthday Cakes,
page 226 (halve the recipe)
Sparkling Water with Lime Twists

CHILLY OUTSIDE-CHILI INSIDE
FOR 6
Vegetarian Chili, page 164
Grapefruit and Orange Sections
on Romaine Lettuce
Assorted Crackers and Breadsticks
Fresh Coconut Layer Cake, page 213
Beer/Soda   Coffee/Tea

BACK-TO-SCHOOL FAVORITE
FOR 6
Tomato Soup
Croque Monsieur, page 170
Coleslaw
Pineapple-Strawberry Fruit Pops,
page 260
Milk   Soda

AUTUMN VEGETABLE LUNCH
FOR 6
Deep-Dish Vegetable Pie, page 175
Mandarin Oranges and Green Grapes
with Toasted Almonds on Boston Lettuce
Mocha Bar Cookies, page 235
Hot Tea

ONE-DISH LUNCHEON
FOR 6
Cheese Tart with Tomato, page 166
Mixed Green Salad with
Vinaigrette Dressing
Fresh Fruit Compote
White Wine

DINNER

RIB-STICKING SUPPER
FOR 6

Sausage and Garbanzo Beans with
Tomato Sauce, page 106
Lettuce Wedges with Russian Dressing
Dark Rye Bread, page 54   Butter
Apple Crisp, page 257
Beer   Milk   Coffee

HARVEST MOON DINNER
FOR 6

Scandinavian Meatballs, page 128
Fettucine   Mixed Vegetables
Creamy Yogurt Cucumbers
Orange Bread Pudding, page 264
Coffee   Tea   Milk

LIGHT 'N' DELICIOUS
FOR 6

Watercress Cream Soup, page 80
Poached Sole with Oranges,
page 139
Rice Almondine   Brussels Sprouts
Shredded Carrot Salad
Lemon Loaf Cake, page 225,
with Raspberries and Whipped Cream
White Chardonnay Wine
Demitasse

DINNER IN NO TIME
FOR 6

Fresh Raw Vegetable Platter
Chicken in a Bun with
Special Sauces, page 117
Pear and Apple Slaw, page 85
Family Circle's Carrot Cake, page 226
Apple Juice

BEEF IT UP
FOR 6

Beef Turnovers, page 96
Baked Turnips, page 195
Sautéed Mushrooms
Alfalfa Sprouts with
Creamy Italian Dressing
Sliced Nectarines on Pound Cake with
Cream Cheese Topping, page 258
Coffee   Tea   Milk

TEX-MEX NIGHT
FOR 6

New Mexican Pork Chili, page 103
Gazpacho, page 81
Assorted Crackers
Yogurt-Lime Parfaits, page 256
Sangria Spritzer, page 282
(make recipe six times)

Meals for Eight

BRUNCH

GRANDPARENTS' DAY DINNER
FOR 6

Cranberry Juice Cocktails

Lamb Burgundy, page 109

Special Spinach-Mushroom Salad,
page 83

French Bread Baguettes   Whipped Butter

Pink Grapefruit Snow with
Warm Orange Sauce, page 255

Red Wine   Coffee   Tea

FRIDAY NIGHT COOKOUT
FOR 6

Vino Round Steak, page 145

Grilled Potatoes, page 152

Grilled Corn-on-the-Cob, page 152

Sliced Tomatoes on
Boston Lettuce Leaves

Blueberry Lemon Tarts, page 270

Red Wine

MEMORIAL DAY BARBECUE
FOR 6

Scallops en Coquille, page 148

Rice Pilaf

Grilled Asparagus, page 152

Radicchio-Romaine Salad with
Chili-Lime Dressing, page 88

Cornsticks   Butter

Hazelnut Roll, page 217

White Wine Coolers   Coffee

CHAMPAGNE BRUNCH
FOR 8

Champagne Cocktails

Broiled Grapefruit Halves

Creamed Eggs over
Steamed Asparagus

Croissants

Pecan "Stickies" Ring, page 40   Butter

Coffee   Tea

APRIL SHOWER BRUNCH
For 8

Mixed Berry Compote Laced with
Orange Juice

Sour Cream Waffles with
Brown Sugar Syrup, page 67

Whipped Butter

Center-Cut Ham Slices

Coffee   Tea

LUNCH

▨▨▨

VEGETARIAN'S TREAT
FOR 8
Fresh Vegetable Lasagne, page 168
Mixed Green Salad with
Chive-Onion Dressing, page 89
Hard Rolls   Butter
Fresh Fruit
Flavored Sparkling Water

▨

POCKET LUNCH
FOR 8
Falafel, page 163
Sliced Cucumbers in Yogurt Dressing
Mocha Bar Cookies, page 235
Iced Tea with Fresh Mint

▨▨

LADIES' LUNCHEON
FOR 8
Chilled Madriléne
Vegetable and Feta Cheese Pie, page 169
Tomato Wedges on Green Leaf Lettuce
Mint Bavarian with Chocolate Sauce,
page 275
White Wine   Coffee   Tea

▨▨▨

GRADUATION DAY
FOR 8
Turkey Tacos with Desired Toppings
Chick-Pea Salad, page 162
Fresh Fruit Flan
Limeade

DINNER

▨▨

SUNDAY BEST
FOR 8
Rolled Flank Steak, page 93
Parsleyed New Potatoes, page 194
Asparagus with Mustard–Cream Sauce,
page 189
Salad of Watercress, Cherry Tomatoes
and Boston Lettuce, page 83
Strawberry-Rhubarb Cream Pie, page 250
Red Wine   Coffee

▨▨

ON A HOT SUMMER'S DAY
FOR 8
Smoked Salmon and Caviar
Cheese Torte, page 72
Peppery Grilled Chicken, page 147
Breadstick Salad, page 86
Athenian Vegetable Bake, page 153
Baked Alaska, page 265
Fruit-Tea Punch, page 278

SPRING CELEBRATION
FOR 8
*Cornish Game Hens
with Savory Stuffing, page 124
Green Pea and Mushroom Timbales,
page 193
Vegetable Rice Pilaf, page 193
Salad of Radish, Cucumber
and Romaine, page 83
Cream of Coconut Cake, page 212
White Chardonnay
Wine   Cappucino, page 286*

CHASE THE CHILL DINNER
FOR 8
*Platter of Red and Green Pepper Rings
and Cucumber and Zucchini Sticks
Beef Tomato and Rice Soup,
page 97
Country Home-Baked Bread;
Cheddar Variation, page 56
Banana Chiffon Cake, page 214
Milk*

INDEPENDENCE DAY BARBECUE
FOR 8
*Champagne Cocktails
Red and Green Pepper Phyllo Triangles,
page 73
Butterflied Lamb, page 147
Grilled Corn-on-the-Cob, page 152
Minted Green Peas
Country Home-Baked
Bread-Pan Rolls, page 58
Butter
Peach Melba Ripple Ice Cream,
page 267*

THANKSGIVING DINNER
FOR 8
*Brandied Cider, page 287
Shrimp Roulade, page 75
Green Pea and Onion Soup, page 79
(double the recipe)
Crisply Roasted Goose, page 126
Fruited Stuffing, page 200
Perfect Pan Gravy, page 200
Fruit Bowl
Mashed Potatoes
Creamed Green Peas and Onions
Gingered Carrots
Cranberry-Orange Relish
Chewy Pecan Pie, page 252
Coffee   Tea*

ITALIAN FEST
FOR 8
Eggplant Rollatini, page 183
Spinach and Mushroom Salad with
Oil and Vinegar Dressing
Italian Bread, page 57
Garlic Butter
Frozen Semi-Freddo, page 268
Red Wine

DINNER FOR THE GANG
FOR 8
Onion Soup au Gratin
Flounder and Salmon Roulade, page 137
Wild Rice with Mushrooms and Herbs
Steamed Baby Carrots
Belgian Endive on Watercress with
Walnuts and Vinaigrette Dressing
White Wine

A FORMAL AFFAIR
FOR 8
Chilled Zucchini Soup, page 80
Baked Red Snapper, page 138
Potatoes au Gratin
Steamed Asparagus
Sliced Cucumbers on Radicchio with
Yogurt-Chive Dressing
Sacher Torte, page 207
White Wine   Coffee   Tea

CHRISTMAS BUFFET
FOR 10
Gorgonzola Toast, page 77
Stuffed Turkey Breast, page 132
Champagne Choucroute with
Smoked Meats, page 105
Parsleyed New Potatoes, page 194
Zucchini Boats with Bulgur Pilaf,
page 197
Pear-Ginger Pudding with Lemon
and Nesselrode Sauces, page 262
Cranberry Linzer Torte, page 261
Holiday Punch, page 279

ITALIAN HERITAGE GALA
FOR 10
Mozzarella Cheese and
Basil-Marinated Cherry Tomato Kabobs
Veal and Rice Gremolata, page 100
Crusty Italian Bread   Butter
Fresh Fruit Bowl
White Wine Spritzers

VALENTINE DESSERT BUFFET
FOR 10
Raspberry–Nut Pinwheels, page 235
Orange Loaf, page 210
Meringue Rice Pudding, page 272
Chestnut Ice Cream Log, page 267
Valentine Cheesecake, page 221
Coffee   Tea

RED, WHITE AND BLUE BRUNCH
FOR 12
Tomato Juice Cocktails
Red, White and Blue Waffle Shortcake,
page 273
Sliced Canadian Bacon
Coffee   Tea

Meals for Twelve

SOUP AND SALAD LOVER'S BUFFET
FOR 12
Won Ton Soup
Oriental Beef Salad, page 97
(double the recipe)
Chow Mein Noodles   Stir-Fried Broccoli
Pineapple-Yogurt Sherbet, page 266
(make the recipe two times)
Fortune Cookies
Hot Tea

BON VOYAGE BRUNCH
FOR 12
Leek and Potato Soup, page 80
(double the recipe)
Chicken and Vegetable Brochettes,
page 115 (double the recipe)
Hot Cooked Rice
Spiced Coffee Vienna, page 286
(double the recipe)

SUPER BOWL GET-TOGETHER
FOR 12
Nacho Mushrooms, page 72
Mole Chili, page 95
(double the recipe)
Assorted Raw Vegetable Platter
Creamy Dip
Hard Rolls   Butter
Vanilla Ice-Cream and
Strawberry Topping Parfaits
Beer   Soda

Cream Cheese Loaf (page 44), Mincemeat Braid (page 44)

Fresh Baked Breads

Baked bread that's fresh from the oven—who can resist it? The wonderful smell and anticipated taste are enough to make anyone's mouth water. Yeast breads, whether they're made with regular active dry yeast or the faster-rising kind, are particularly aromatic and flavorful. Try Viennese Raisin-Nut Coffee Cake (page 41) as a tasty example.

When time is of the essence, the increasingly popular fast-rising yeast breads (such as Mushroom Bread Magnifique, page 48) can't be beat. Not only do you get the same delicious results, but you get them in half to a third of the time!

Quick breads are exactly that—quick to make—since leavening agents, such as baking powder and baking soda, eliminate the rising time. But these ingredients still produce light and airy biscuits, pancakes and doughnuts, as well as delicious coffee cakes, muffins and tea breads, like Cranberry-Nut Bread (page 62).

Most yeast and quick breads can be made well in advance and frozen. Plan to set aside one day to devote to baking some of your favorites from the following pages, and then freeze them for last-minute needs—or when the craving for homemade bread strikes!

Quick

Make Ahead

Entertaining

Low Cost

Low Calorie

Yeast Breads

Yeast as an Ingredient

Yeast causes dough to rise and gives bread its porous texture. Yeast is actually a small plant or cell that "grows" or multiplies under the proper temperature conditions. Yeast feeds on the sugar and produces carbon dioxide; it is this gas that causes dough to rise. It is yeast that is primarily responsible for the marvelous aromas and flavors of breads. Yeast is available as compressed cakes which must be dissolved before using or as the dry granular form which can, in some recipes, be mixed directly with the dry ingredients.

Compressed yeast is moist, creamy white and firm in texture. It is perishable and must be kept refrigerated. Look for it in the supermarket dairy case packaged in foil. It is best when used within a few days from purchase or it can be wrapped in heavy-duty aluminum foil and frozen. It keeps for up to 6 months stored at 0°F. Defrost it overnight in the refrigerator before using. Compressed yeast must be dissolved in lukewarm liquid (80° to 90°) before using.

Dry yeast is a strain of yeast that has been dried and packaged in envelopes or jars. Two level teaspoons of dry yeast equals a single ¼-ounce envelope or a ⅝-ounce cake. Dry yeast can be stored for over 6 months unrefrigerated. In areas of the country with high temperatures, refrigeration will help keep it fresh. Dry yeast is activated by dissolving it in warm liquid (110° to 115°). To be sure your envelope is alive and well, mix the yeast with a bit of sugar while it is dissolving. A fresh envelope will bubble nicely within 10 minutes. Dry yeast should be used before the expiration date which is stamped on the envelope.

Cardamom Rolls

For a sweet breakfast treat, pour a thin sugar glaze over the tops.

Bake at 375° for 10 to 15 minutes.
Makes about 2½ dozen rolls.

Nutrient Value Per Roll: 108 calories, 3 g protein, 3 g fat, 18 g carbohydrate, 66 mg sodium, 22 mg cholesterol.

1 envelope active dry yeast
½ cup sugar
¼ cup warm water
1 cup evaporated milk
¼ cup (½ stick) butter
1 teaspoon coarsely crushed cardamom seeds
½ teaspoon salt
4 to 4½ cups unsifted all-purpose flour
2 eggs, slightly beaten

1. Sprinkle the yeast and ½ teaspoon of the sugar over the warm water in a small cup; stir to dissolve the yeast. Let stand until bubbly, for 10 minutes.
2. Combine the remaining sugar, milk, butter, cardamom and salt in a small saucepan. Heat just until the butter melts. Pour into a large bowl. Cool to lukewarm. Stir in the yeast mixture.

3. Beat in 3 cups of the flour until smooth. Beat in the eggs, one at a time, until well blended. Gradually stir in enough of the remaining flour to make a soft dough.

4. Turn out onto a lightly floured surface. Knead until smooth and elastic for about 8 minutes. Press into a buttered bowl; bring the buttered-side up. Cover with buttered wax paper and a towel. Let rise in a warm place, away from drafts, until doubled in volume, or for about 1 hour.

5. Punch down dough; knead a few times.

6. Roll the dough into "knots" or "snail-shaped" rolls: Pinch off about 2 tablespoons of the dough for each roll. Roll each into a 9-inch-long rope. For "knots," tie each rope into a knot; tuck ends under and place on greased cookie sheets. For "snails," hold one end of the rope down on the greased cookie sheet; wind the other end around and around in a tight spiral, and tuck the end under. Arrange the rolls about 2½ inches apart on the sheets. Cover with buttered wax paper and a towel. Let rise in a warm place, away from drafts, until doubled in volume, for about 45 minutes. Meanwhile, preheat the oven to moderate (375°).

7. Bake in the preheated moderate oven (375°) for 10 to 15 minutes, or until golden brown. Transfer to wire racks to cool. Serve warm.

Hints for Better Breads

● Use the specified pan size called for in the recipe. A pan that is too large will yield a flat bread. Too small a pan will cause the dough to overflow.

● The material the pan is made of can affect the baking time. Uncoated metal pans need longer baking. Glass and enamel pans need a lower oven temperature; reduce the oven temperature called for in the recipe by 25°.

● For a shiny crust on a loaf of yeast bread, brush it with an egg beaten with a little water. For a soft crust, rub with softened butter or margarine just after the bread is removed from the pan to cool.

Preheated Ovens for Baking Bread

Bake breads in a preheated oven. The final rising of the dough takes place during the first 10 to 15 minutes of baking time.

Flour Range in Bread Recipes

Most bread recipes offer a range in the amount of flour to use since the results of a recipe will be affected by the type and brand of flour to be used, the amount of moisture in the flour, the time of year it is used and such variables as the size of eggs.

Useful Tips For the Best Coffee Cakes You'll Ever Make

Mixing

When making a yeast coffee cake, check that the yeast is active. Add water that is 105° to 115° F. If the yeast mixture does not bubble within 10 minutes, just start over with fresh yeast and check the water temperature carefully. A milk mixture, on the other hand, should always cool to lukewarm, and that temperature is a low, low 85° F. Investing in a candy or water thermometer would be a great help, until you can judge temperature for yourself. Baking-powder coffee cakes are made with a quick-mix method—all in one bowl.

Kneading

A good part of the kneading in several of our coffee cake recipes is done with the electric mixer, so actual kneading time is fairly short.

Rising

Keeping the dough warm is essential. Here is a good method: Put the bowl of dough on top of (not in) a large pot of hot tap water. Cover with buttered wax paper and a towel; put the bowl and pot in an unheated oven. For a gas oven with a pilot, leave the door ajar. With an electric oven, close the door. Buttering the wax paper to cover the dough keeps expanding dough from sticking to the paper. Risen cakes can be safely removed to the countertop while the oven is heating.

Baking

Many ovens are too hot. A hot oven will over-brown the cake before it is baked. An oven thermometer assures accuracy. Baking-powder cakes should go into a preheated oven with no delay, so the leavening will do its job.

Wrapping and Storing

Wrap thoroughly cooled cakes in plastic wrap or foil. They will keep fresh for several days at room temperature. To freeze: Omit icings if you plan to freeze cakes. (Ice after reheating.) Wrap the cakes tightly in foil, then overwrap in freezer-weight plastic wrap or bags. To reheat frozen cakes: Remove from plastic; reheat cakes right in their foil wrapping. Ten to 20 minutes, depending on size, in a preheated moderate oven (350°) will bring them back to their just-baked state.

To Freshen Coffee Cakes

Coffee cakes are so delicious when served warm. Wrap as much as you need for that meal in foil. Preheat the toaster oven to moderate (350°), then heat the cake for 5 minutes. Baking-powder coffee cakes can be frozen and reheated, following the yeast directions.

Christmas Stollen

Bake at 350° for 30 to 35 minutes.
Makes 2 stollens (about 12 slices each).

Nutrient Value Per Slice: 199 calories, 4 g protein, 8 g fat, 29 g carbohydrate, 169 mg sodium, 25 mg cholesterol.

- ¾ **cup milk**
- ½ **cup water**
- ½ **cup (1 stick) unsalted butter, at room temperature**
- 4 **to 4¼ cups unsifted all-purpose flour**
- ½ **cup sugar**
- 1¾ **teaspoons salt**
- 2 **envelopes active dry yeast**
- 1 **egg, at room temperature**
- ½ **cup golden raisins**
- ½ **teaspoon ground mace**
- 2 **tablespoons brandy**
- ¾ **cup chopped mixed candied fruits**
- ⅔ **cup coarsely chopped blanched almonds**
- 2 **tablespoons unsalted butter, melted**
  10X (confectioners') sugar

1. Combine the milk, water and the ½ cup of butter in a small saucepan. Heat over low heat until warm (120° to 130°) and the butter is melted. Remove from the heat.
2. Combine 1¼ cups of the flour, sugar, salt and yeast in a large bowl. Gradually beat in the milk mixture. Beat for 2 minutes at medium speed, scraping down the sides of the bowl occasionally with a rubber spatula. Beat in the egg and ¾ cup of the flour. Beat at high speed for 2 minutes. Stir in 2 cups of the flour or enough to make a stiff batter. Transfer to a lightly oiled bowl; turn to bring the oiled-side up. Cover tightly with plastic wrap. Refrigerate for 2 to 3 hours.
3. When ready to shape, remove the dough from the refrigerator. Combine the raisins, mace and brandy in a small saucepan. Heat gently over very low heat just until the brandy begins to simmer. Cool to lukewarm. Add the candied fruits and almonds. Set aside.
4. Grease 2 cookie sheets. Turn out the dough onto a lightly floured surface. Knead in the fruits and nuts. Divide the dough in half. Roll each half into a 12 x 6-inch oval. Fold each in half lengthwise. Transfer to the prepared cookie sheets. Curve the ends of each slightly to form a crescent shape. Cover with buttered wax paper and a towel. Let rise in a warm place, away from drafts, until doubled in volume, for about 1 hour. Meanwhile,

preheat the oven to moderate (350°). Bake in a preheated moderate oven (350°) for 30 to 35 minutes until golden brown and the undersides sound hollow when tapped with the fingers. Remove to wire racks to cool. Brush with the melted butter while still warm. Sprinkle evenly with the 10X sugar.

Bread Doneness Check

Breads should be checked for doneness near the end of the suggested baking time. Breads are done when they are nicely browned and sound hollow when tapped lightly on top. Remove loaves from the pans so they do not becomes soggy. Cool completely on wire racks.

Rich Coffee Cake Dough

A flavorful dough base for Prune-Nut Pinwheels or Pecan Stickies Ring. Experiment with your own favorite coffee cake variation using this dough as a base. A rich dough you can use as the basis for many different coffee cakes. This recipe makes 2 coffee cakes—one to enjoy immediately and one to freeze, if you wish.

1/3 **cup milk**
1/2 **cup (1 stick) butter or margarine**
1/2 **cup sugar**
1/2 **teaspoon salt**
1 **envelope active dry yeast**
1 **teaspoon sugar**
1/4 **cup very warm water**
2 **eggs**
2 **egg yolks (reserve whites for coffee cake toppings)**
2 **tablespoons grated orange rind (optional)**
4 **to 4½ cups unsifted all-purpose flour**

1. Stir together the milk, butter, the ½ cup sugar and salt in a small saucepan over very low heat just until the butter is melted. Pour into a large bowl; cool to lukewarm.
2. Sprinkle the yeast and the 1 teaspoon sugar over very warm water in a 1-cup glass measure. ("Very warm water" should feel comfortably warm when a few drops are sprinkled on your wrist.) Stir to dissolve the yeast. Let stand until bubbly, about 10 minutes.

3. Stir the eggs, egg yolks, orange rind, if using, the yeast mixture and 2 cups of the flour into the cooled milk mixture. Beat with an electric mixer until batter is smooth; beat for 2 minutes longer. Stir in enough of the remaining flour to form a soft dough.
4. Turn the dough out onto a floured surface. Knead until smooth and elastic, about 5 minutes, using only enough additional flour to prevent sticking.
5. Press the dough into a buttered large bowl; turn to bring buttered-side up. Cover with buttered wax paper and a towel. Let rise in a warm place, away from drafts, until doubled in volume, for about 1 hour.
6. Punch the dough down. Turn out onto a floured surface. Shape and bake following Prune-Nut Pinwheel or Pecan Stickies Ring directions.

Once one has started making a yeast dough, can the process ever be interrupted?

That depends on when you stop. If you've just prepared the dough, cover the bowl very securely with plastic wrap and refrigerate it without punching it down. The dough will stay perfectly fresh for up to 18 hours. If the dough has already risen and you have to leave it before it's formed, punch it down, cover securely and refrigerate.

Prune-Nut Pinwheel

Bake at 350° for 35 minutes.
Makes 1 coffee cake (8 slices).

Nutrient Value Per Pinwheel: 392 calories, 8 g protein, 18 g fat, 53 g carbohydrate, 91 mg sodium, 92 mg cholesterol.

- ½ **recipe Rich Coffee Cake Dough (see recipe, page 39)**
- 1 **cup pitted prunes, cut up**
- 4 **tablespoons sugar**
- 1 **teaspoon grated lemon rind**
- ¾ **cup chopped walnuts**
- 2 **tablespoons unsalted butter or margarine, softened**
- 1 **egg white**
- 1 **teaspoon ground cinnamon**

1. Prepare Rich Coffee Cake Dough through first rising.
2. Combine the prunes, 2 tablespoons of the sugar, lemon rind and ½ cup of the chopped walnuts in a small bowl; reserve.
3. Butter a 9 x 1½-inch-round layer-cake pan.
4. Punch the dough down; turn out onto a floured surface. Press or roll into an 18 x 8-inch rectangle. Spread with the butter; then evenly spread the prune mixture to within ½ inch of the edges. Starting with a long side, roll up jelly-roll fashion; pinch firmly along seam to seal. Pick up the roll and gently stretch to lengthen to 30 inches. Hold down one end of the roll in the center of the prepared pan; coil the roll loosely in a spiral in the pan. Cover with buttered wax paper and a towel. Let rise in a warm place, away from drafts, until doubled in volume, for about 45 minutes.
5. Meanwhile, preheat the oven to moderate (350°).
6. Beat the egg white in a small bowl until soft peaks form; spread over the top of the dough. Combine the remaining ¼ cup walnuts, the remaining 2 tablespoons sugar and cinnamon in a cup; sprinkle over the egg white.
7. Bake in the preheated moderate oven (350°) for 35 minutes or until the coffee cake is golden brown and sounds hollow when tapped with fingers. Remove the cake from the pan to a wire rack; cool.

Softening Butter

The best way to soften butter is to let it stand at room temperature until it is soft enough to beat into a creamy mixture. If you haven't done this, cut the butter into pieces in a bowl and begin stirring with a wooden spoon. Then, for no more than 2 seconds at a time, place the bowl over another bowl of hot water. You want the butter to soften, not melt.

Pecan "Stickies" Ring

A caramel-glazed ring that breaks apart into individual pinwheels.

Bake at 350° for 35 minutes.
Makes 1 coffee cake (8 pinwheels).

Nutrient Value Per Pinwheel: 366 calories, 5 g protein, 16 g fat, 50 g carbohydrate, 90 mg sodium, 100 mg cholesterol.

- ½ **recipe Rich Coffee Cake Dough (see recipe, page 39)**
- ¼ **cup firmly packed brown sugar**
- 4 **tablespoons unsalted butter or margarine, softened**
- 1 **tablespoon light corn syrup**
- ⅓ **cup pecan halves**
- ⅓ **cup firmly packed brown sugar**

1. Prepare Rich Coffee Cake Dough through first rising.
2. Combine the ¼ cup of brown sugar, 2 tablespoons of the butter and the corn syrup in a small saucepan. Cook over medium heat, stirring constantly, until the butter melts.
3. Grease a 6½-cup ring mold. Arrange the pecan halves evenly over the bottom of the ring mold. Pour the sugar and butter mixture evenly into the mold.
4. Punch the dough down; turn out onto a floured surface. Roll or press the dough into a 16 x 8-inch rectangle. Spread with the remaining 2 tablespoons of butter; sprinkle with the remaining ⅓ cup of brown sugar to within ½ inch of the edges. Starting with a long side, roll up jelly-roll fashion; pinch firmly along the seam to seal. Cut into 8 equal portions. Arrange the pinwheels evenly in the prepared pan, seam-side down and cut-sides next to each other. Cover with buttered wax paper and a towel. Let rise in a warm place, away from drafts, until doubled in volume, for about 45 minutes.

5. Meanwhile, preheat the oven to moderate (350°).

6. Bake in the preheated moderate oven (350°) for 35 minutes or until the coffee cake is golden brown and sounds hollow when tapped with the fingers. Invert onto a large cookie sheet. Let stand for 1 minute. Lift off the pan. Serve warm. Break into individual pinwheels or buns.

Sifted Vs. Unsifted

Most commercial brands of flour come pre-sifted from the manufacturer, making additional sifting unnecessary in most cases. Some of our recipes indicate additional sifting in order to produce a lighter product. Do *not* sift unless the recipe specifically calls for it.

Viennese Raisin-Nut Coffee Cake

A simplified version of the famous Austrian Kugelhopf, this exceptionally light coffee cake requires no kneading.

Bake at 350° for 30 minutes.
Makes 1 large coffee cake (12 slices).

Nutrient Value Per Slice: 316 calories, 7 g protein, 13 g fat, 44 g carbohydrate, 150 mg sodium, 91 mg cholesterol.

⅔ **cup milk**
½ **cup (1 stick) butter or margarine**
¼ **teaspoon salt**
½ **cup granulated sugar**
1 **envelope active dry yeast**
1 **teaspoon sugar**
¼ **cup very warm water**
3 **eggs**
4 **teaspoons grated lemon rind**
3¼ **cups sifted *all-purpose flour***
1 **cup golden raisins**
½ **cup sliced blanched almonds**
   10X (confectioners') sugar (optional)

1. Stir the milk, butter, salt and the ½ cup of sugar in a small saucepan over very low heat just until the butter is melted. Pour the mixture into a large bowl; cool to lukewarm.

2. Sprinkle the yeast and the 1 teaspoon of sugar over very warm water in a 1-cup glass measure. ("Very warm water" should feel comfortably warm when a few drops are sprinkled on your wrist.) Stir to dissolve the yeast. Let stand until bubbly, for about 10 minutes.

3. Stir the eggs, yeast mixture, lemon rind and 2 cups of the flour into the cooled milk mixture. Beat with an electric mixer at low speed until blended. Increase the speed to medium; beat for 3 minutes longer.

4. By hand, beat in the remaining flour until the batter is smooth; beat for 1 minute longer. Stir in the raisins. Cover with buttered wax paper and a towel. Let rise in warm place, away from drafts, until doubled in volume, for about 50 minutes.

5. While the batter is rising, butter a 10-inch (12 cup) Bundt® or Kugelhopf pan. Sprinkle the bottom and side evenly with the almonds.

6. Stir the batter vigorously for about 30 seconds. Turn into the prepared pan. Cover with buttered wax paper and a towel. Let rise in a warm place, away from drafts, until almost doubled in volume, for about 45 minutes.

7. Meanwhile, preheat the oven to moderate (350°).

8. Bake in the preheated moderate oven (350°) for 30 minutes, or until golden brown and cake sounds hollow when tapped with the fingers. Remove from the pan to a wire rack; cool. Sprinkle lightly with the 10X (confectioners') sugar, if you wish.

Flaky Croissants

Bake at 400° for 20 minutes.
Makes 1½ dozen.

Nutrient Value Per Croissant: 311 calories, 7 g protein, 12 g fat, 114 g carbohydrate, 245 mg sodium, 47 mg cholesterol.

7 **cups unsifted all-purpose flour**
1 **envelope active dry yeast**
¼ **cup very warm water**
2 **cups lukewarm milk**
1 **teaspoon salt**
½ **cup sugar**
1 **cup (2 sticks) butter, softened**
1 **egg**
1 **tablespoon milk**

1. Measure 2 cups of the flour into a large bowl; make a well in the center.

2. Sprinkle the yeast over the very warm water in a cup; stir to dissolve. ("Very warm water" should feel comfortably warm when a few drops are sprinkled on your wrist.) Pour into well in the flour; let stand until the yeast mixture is bubbly, for about 5 minutes. ▶

3. Add the milk, salt and sugar. Beat at low speed until blended; then beat at medium speed until smooth. Mix in enough of the remaining flour, ½ cup at a time, scraping down the sides of the bowl with a rubber spatula, to form a soft dough.

4. Turn the dough out onto a lightly floured surface. Knead for about 3 minutes, using only enough additional flour to prevent the dough from sticking.

5. Transfer dough into a large, lightly greased bowl; cover with buttered wax paper and a towel. Let rise in a warm place away from drafts, until doubled in volume, for about 1½ hours.

6. While the dough is rising, knead the 2 sticks of butter with a dough scraper or stiff-bladed putty knife until soft but not melted. Shape into an 8 x 6-inch rectangle, ½ inch thick.

7. Roll out the dough to a 12 x 10-inch rectangle on a lightly floured surface; let it rest for 10 minutes.

8. Place the butter on top of the dough so that the 8-inch edge is parallel to the 10-inch edge, leaving a 1-inch margin on 3 sides and 5 inches on the remaining side. Fold the 5 inches of dough over to cover half the butter. Lift the uncovered butter-and-dough layer up and fold over the covered butter as for a letter. (The layers will be dough, butter, dough, butter, dough.) Press the dough firmly to seal. Turn the dough so the folds are at right angles to the lower edge of work surface.

9. Lightly flour the work surface. Roll out the dough to a 14 x 8-inch rectangle about 1 inch thick. Fold in thirds as for a letter. Let rest for 10 minutes.

10. Give the dough a quarter turn so that the folds will be at right angles to the front edge of the work surface. Roll to a 14 x 8-inch rectangle. Fold in thirds again. Repeat rolling and folding once again.

11. Wrap the dough in the moist cloth; refrigerate for about 1½ hours. If refrigerating overnight, overwrap with wax paper.

12. For shaping, roll the dough on a lightly floured surface to a 25 x 10-inch rectangle, about ¼-inch thick. Divide the dough into 2 long strips, each 5 inches wide. Let the dough "relax" for about 5 minutes. Mark each strip lightly into 5 even divisions. Mark and cut each of these fifths diagonally to make 2 triangles each. Shape each croissant: Roll each from the base to a point with a rolling pin, pressing a little to make a larger and thinner elongated triangle. Roll up from the base of the triangle to the point.

13. Place the croissants on baking sheets, 1½ inches apart. Curve the ends slightly to form a crescent shape. Beat the egg and milk in a cup; brush over the croissants.

14. Let the croissants rise, at room temperature, for 30 minutes. Brush again; let rise for 30 minutes longer or until doubled in volume.

15. Meanwhile, preheat the oven to hot (400°). When the oven is ready, brush the croissants for the third time.

16. Bake in the preheated hot oven (400°) for 20 minutes, or until golden brown. Cool on a wire rack. If the croissants are to be frozen, take from the oven when just a light brown. To bake, allow to thaw, then bake in a preheated hot oven (400°) for 8 minutes, or until golden brown.

Croissant

Although the word is French for crescent, croissants originated in Budapest in 1686 to celebrate Hungary's defeat of the Turks. The Turks were invading the city by tunneling through the walls. The bakers, virtually the only people awake during the late-night hours, heard the invaders, sounded the alarm and saved the city. In honor of the event, the bakers invented a pastry shaped like a crescent, the Turkish emblem.

Croissants are made of a yeast dough with butter layered into the dough using the puff-pastry method. Their rich, buttery flavor makes them well worth the effort to make.

Yeast-Raised Doughnuts

Makes about 2 dozen doughnuts.

Nutrient Value Per Doughnut: 170 calories, 4 g protein, 6 g fat, 25 g carbohydrate, 130 mg sodium, 31 mg cholesterol.

1¼ **cups milk**
⅓ **cup butter or margarine, cut up**
5 **cups unsifted all-purpose flour**
2 **envelopes active dry yeast**
½ **cup sugar**
1 **teaspoon salt**
1 **teaspoon ground nutmeg**
2 **eggs**
Vegetable oil

1. Combine the milk and butter in a small saucepan. Heat over low heat until very warm. ("Very warm" should feel comfortably warm when a few drops are sprinkled on your wrist.)

2. Combine 2 cups of the flour, yeast, sugar, salt and nutmeg in a large bowl. Gradually beat in the milk mixture.

3. Beat for 2 minutes at medium speed, scraping down the sides of the bowl occasionally with a rubber spatula. Beat in the eggs and ½ cup of the flour.

4. Stir in about 1½ cups more of the flour to form a soft dough. Turn the dough out onto a lightly floured surface. Knead until smooth and elastic, for about 8 minutes, using only enough of the additional flour to prevent the dough from sticking.

5. Transfer the dough to a lightly oiled bowl; turn to bring the oiled side up. Cover with buttered wax paper and a towel. Let rise in a warm place, away from drafts, until doubled in volume, for about 1 to 1½ hours.

6. Punch the dough down; knead 8 to 10 times to remove any large bubbles; cover with the bowl; let rest for 15 minutes. Meanwhile, grease 2 large cookie sheets.

7. Roll out the dough on a lightly floured surface to a ¼-inch thickness; cut with a floured 3-to-3½-inch doughnut cutter. Lift off the trimmings and the doughnut centers. Press the trimmings together; reroll and cut. Transfer the doughnuts to the cookie sheets; brush the tops with oil to prevent a skin from forming. Cover with buttered wax paper and a towel. Let rise in a warm place, away from drafts, until doubled in volume, for about 45 minutes.

8. Fill a large saucepan or Dutch oven half full with vegetable oil. Heat to 370° on a deep-fat thermometer.

9. Transfer the doughnuts to the hot oil with a flexible spatula or pancake turner, frying 2 or 3 at a time. Fry, turning once, for 3 minutes, or until golden. Drain on paper toweling. Cool.

Storing Flour

All flour should be stored in airtight containers in the refrigerator or freezer, if possible.

Fast-Rising Yeast Breads

For the old-fashioned flavor of homemade yeast breads in a lot less time, use fast-rising dry yeast.

Tips for Using Fast-Rising Dry Yeast

Follow these pointers for using the new yeast in our delicious breads, as well as in your own favorite recipes.

● Always include water in the ingredients. If your recipe calls for all milk or liquid other than water, decrease the amount of liquid by ¼ cup per envelope of fast-rising yeast used and substitute an equal amount of water.

● Combine the yeast with about two-thirds of the flour and the other dry ingredients in a large bowl. No need to dissolve the yeast in a liquid first. See note, below.

● Heat the liquids and solid or liquid fats, but not the eggs, in a saucepan until *hot* to the touch, 130°. This is hotter than the 110° to 115° usually required if the yeast is being dissolved directly in a liquid.

● Stir the hot liquids into the dry ingredients; add the eggs, if using. Blend at low speed with an electric mixer; then beat at medium speed for 3 minutes. Stir in enough remaining flour to make a soft dough.

● Follow the recipe directions for kneading and rising (the rising time is reduced by one-half to one-third). Start checking the dough halfway through the suggested rising time in a recipe calling for regular yeast.

Substituting Regular Active Dry Yeast for Fast-Rising.

Note: When combining the yeast with a portion of the flour and other dry ingredients, combine with about one-third of the flour (instead of two-thirds as with the fast-rising) and other dry ingredients. Also increase the rising times by one-third to one-half.

Cream Cheese Loaf*

- 6 cups unsifted all-purpose flour
- 2 tablespoons white sugar
- 1 teaspoon salt
- 1 envelope fast-rising dry yeast
- 1 cup water
- 1 cup milk
- 2 tablespoons margarine
- 4 ounces (half of 8-ounce package) cream cheese, at room temperature
- 1 egg yolk mixed with 1 tablespoon water
- 4 teaspoons instant onion flakes

Mincemeat Braid*

- 4 cups unsifted all-purpose flour
- ¼ cup firmly packed brown sugar
- 1 teaspoon salt
- 1 envelope fast-rising dry yeast
- 1 cup milk
- ¼ cup water
- 2 tablespoons butter or margarine
- 1 egg
- 1½ cups bottled mincemeat Sugar Glaze (see Step 7D)

1. MIX
Stir together the flour (3½ cups for *Loaf;* 2 cups for *Braid),* white or brown sugar, salt and yeast. Heat the water, milk and margarine to 130° (mixture should feel comfortably hot to the touch). Add to the flour mixture.
For Loaf: Add the cream cheese.
For Braid: Add the egg.

2. BEAT
Loaf: Beat at low speed until blended; then beat at medium speed for 3 minutes. Mix in 1½ cups more of flour, ½ cup at a time, scraping down the sides with a spatula.
Braid: Beat at low speed until blended; then beat at medium speed for 3 minutes. Mix in 1 cup more flour, ½ cup at a time.

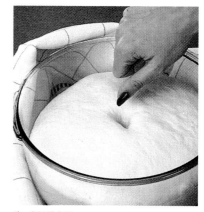

3. KNEAD
Turn the dough out onto a floured surface. Knead for 5 minutes: Fold the dough over; push away with the palm of hand; rotate one-quarter turn. Repeat until smooth and elastic, adding up to 1 cup more of flour.

4. SHAPE
Shape the dough into a ball; place in a large oiled bowl, turning to bring the oiled side up. Cover with a dish towel and let rise in a warm place, away from drafts, until doubled in volume, for about 30 minutes.

5. CHECK
Press a finger into the dough. (You'll know the dough has doubled when a finger indentation remains in the dough.) Punch the dough down.
For Loaf, knead briefly, then proceed to step 6.
For Braid, proceed to step 7.

* These recipes also appear on page 46 to 47.

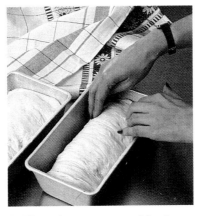

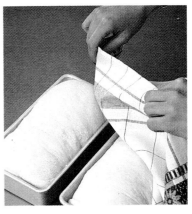

6. FOR CREAM CHEESE LOAF
A. Divide the dough in half. Roll out each half into a rectangle, about 12 x 8½ inches. Roll up from a short end; pinch edges together.

B. Place in two greased loaf pans (8½ x 4½ x 2½ inches), seam-side down.

C. Cover and let rise in a warm place, away from drafts, until doubled in volume, for about 30 minutes. Meanwhile, preheat the oven to slow (325°). Bake in the preheated slow oven (325°) for 30 minutes.

D. Brush with the egg yolk mixed with water; sprinkle with onion flakes. Bake for 10 minutes more or until golden brown and the loaves sound hollow when tapped. Remove from the pans; cool on wire racks.

7. FOR MINCEMEAT BRAID
A. Divide the dough into 6 equal pieces; roll each between the palms into a "sausage" about 10 inches long. Flatten each piece with a rolling pin until 3 inches wide. Spoon ¼ cup of mincemeat lengthwise down the center of each piece.

B. Bring the long sides up together over the filling and pinch to seal. Braid three mincemeat "sausages" together to make 1 loaf. Pinch the ends together to seal. Repeat to make second braid. ▶

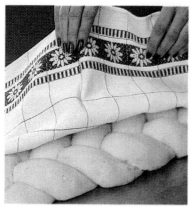

C. Transfer each braid to a greased cookie sheet. Cover and let rise in a warm place, away from drafts, until doubled in volume, for about 30 minutes. Meanwhile, preheat the oven to moderate (350°). Bake in the preheated moderate oven (350°) for 45 minutes, or until browned.

D. Cool on wire racks. To glaze: Place 1 cup of *sifted* 10X (confectioners') sugar in a small bowl. Gradually stir in 1 to 2 tablespoons of milk until thin enough to drizzle over the braid.

Cream Cheese Loaf

Bake at 325° for 40 minutes.
Makes 2 loaves (15 slices each).

Nutrient Value Per Slice: 122 calories, 3 g protein, 3 g fat, 21 g carbohydrate, 98 mg sodium, 14 mg cholesterol.

- **6 cups unsifted all-purpose flour**
- **2 tablespoons sugar**
- **1 teaspoon salt**
- **1 envelope fast-rising dry yeast**
- **1 cup water**
- **1 cup milk**
- **2 tablespoons margarine**
- **4 ounces (half an 8-ounce package) cream cheese, at room temperature**
- **1 egg yolk mixed with 1 tablespoon water**
- **4 teaspoons instant onion flakes**

1. Combine 3½ cups of the flour, the sugar, salt and yeast in a large bowl; stir to mix.
2. Combine the water, milk and margarine in a small saucepan. Heat to 130° (mixture should feel comfortably hot to the touch). Add to the flour mixture; add the cheese. Beat at low speed until blended; then beat at medium speed for 3 minutes. Mix in 1½ cups of the remaining flour, ½ cup at a time, scraping down the sides with a spatula.
3. Turn the dough out onto a lightly floured surface. Knead until smooth and elastic, about 5 minutes, using up to 1 cup of the remaining flour.
4. Shape the dough into a ball. Place in a large oiled bowl, turning to bring the oiled side up. Cover with buttered wax paper and a towel. Let rise in a warm place, away from drafts, until doubled in volume, about 30 minutes. Press finger into the dough; you'll know dough has doubled when the finger indentation remains in the dough.
5. Grease 2 loaf pans (8½ x 4½ x 2½-inches).
6. After the dough has risen, punch down. Knead briefly. Divide in half. Roll out each half into a rectangle, about 12 x 8½ inches. Roll up from the short end; pinch the edges together. Place in the prepared pans, seam-side down. Cover with buttered wax paper and a towel. Let rise in a warm place, away from drafts, until doubled in bulk, about 30 minutes.
7. Meanwhile, preheat the oven to slow (325°).
8. Bake in the preheated slow oven (325°) for 30 minutes. Brush with the egg yolk mixture;

sprinkle with the onion flakes. Bake for 10 minutes more or until the loaves are golden brown and sound hollow when tapped with fingers. Remove the bread from pans to racks to cool.

Mincemeat Braid

Bake at 350° for 45 minutes.
Makes 2 braids (16 slices each).

Nutrient Value Per Slice: 121 calories, 2 g protein, 2 g fat, 24 g carbohydrate, 121 mg sodium, 12 mg cholesterol.

4 cups unsifted all-purpose flour
¼ cup firmly packed brown sugar
1 teaspoon salt
1 envelope fast-rising dry yeast
1 cup milk
¼ cup water
2 tablespoons butter or margarine
1 egg
1½ cups bottled mincemeat
Sugar Glaze (recipe follows)

1. Combine 2 cups of the flour, the sugar, salt and yeast in a large bowl; stir to mix.
2. Combine the milk, water and butter in a small saucepan. Heat to 130° (mixture should feel comfortably hot to the touch). Add to the flour mixture; add the egg. Beat at low speed until blended; then beat at medium speed for 3 minutes. Mix in 1 cup of the remaining flour, ½ cup at a time, scraping down the sides with a spatula.
3. Turn the dough out onto a lightly floured surface. Knead until smooth and elastic, about 5 minutes, using up to 1 cup of the remaining flour.
4. Shape the dough into a ball. Place in a large oiled bowl, turning to bring the oiled side up. Cover with buttered wax paper and a towel. Let rise in a warm place, away from drafts, until doubled in volume, about 30 minutes. Press finger into dough; you'll know the dough has doubled when the finger indentation remains in the dough.
5. After the dough has risen, punch down. Divide into 6 equal pieces. Roll each piece between palms into a "sausage," about 10 inches long. Flatten each piece with a rolling pin until 3 inches wide. Spoon ¼ cup of mincemeat lengthwise down the center of each piece.

6. Bring the long sides up over the filling and pinch the edges closed to seal. Braid the 3 mincemeat "sausages" together to make 1 loaf. Pinch the ends together to seal. Transfer the braid to a greased cookie sheet. Repeat to make a second braid.
7. Cover the braids with buttered wax paper and a towel. Let rise in a warm place, away from drafts, until doubled in volume, about 30 minutes.
8. Meanwhile, preheat the oven to moderate (350°).
9. Bake in the preheated moderate oven (350°) for 45 minutes or until the braids are browned and sound hollow when tapped with fingers. Cool on wire racks.
10. Drizzle the Sugar Glaze over the bread.

Sugar Glaze: Place 1 cup *sifted* 10X (confectioners') sugar in a small bowl. Gradually stir in 1 to 2 tablespoons milk until thin enough to drizzle over the braids.

Keep Your Flour Fresh

Regular all-purpose flour can be stored in an airtight container at room temperature. Whole-wheat flour and rye flour should be stored in the freezer in an airtight freezer bag or container if you will not be using them right away.

Crunch-Topped Hamburger Rolls

Bake at 350° for 20 to 25 minutes.
Makes 12 buns.

Nutrient Value Per Bun: 345 calories, 9 g protein, 8 g fat, 59.8 g carbohydrate, 831 mg sodium, 16 mg cholesterol.

4 cups unsifted unbleached flour
2½ cups whole-wheat flour
⅓ cup instant nonfat dry milk powder
2 teaspoons salt
2 envelopes fast-rising dry yeast
1¼ cups water
⅔ cup Dijon-style or whole-grain mustard
⅓ cup butter or margarine
¼ cup honey
1 tablespoon butter or margarine, melted
Instant chopped onion, sesame seeds and poppy seeds for topping ▶

1. Set aside 1 cup of the unbleached flour. Mix together the remaining 3 cups of unbleached flour, whole-wheat flour, milk powder, salt and yeast in a large bowl.
2. Combine the water, mustard, the ⅓ cup of butter and honey in a medium-size saucepan. Heat to 130° (the mixture should feel comfortably hot to to the touch). Mix into the dry ingredients. Stir in enough of the reserved 1 cup flour to make a fairly stiff dough.
3. Turn the dough out onto a lightly floured surface. Knead until smooth and elastic, 8 to 10 minutes. Cover; let rest for 10 minutes.
4. Divide the dough into 12 equal pieces. Form each into a smooth ball. Place about 2 inches apart on greased cookie sheets; press to flatten slightly. Cover with buttered wax paper and a towel. Let rise in warm place, away from drafts, until doubled in volume, for 35 to 45 minutes.
5. Meanwhile, preheat the oven to moderate (350°).
6. Brush the tops of the rolls with the melted butter. Sprinkle with the instant chopped onions. Sprinkle half the rolls with sesame seeds and half with poppy seeds.
7. Bake in the preheated moderate oven (350°) for 20 to 25 minutes, or until the rolls are browned and they sound hollow when tapped with the fingers. Remove to wire racks to cool.

Mushroom Bread Magnifique

Bake at 350° for 45 minutes.
Makes 2 loaves (12 slices each).

Nutrient Value Per Slice: 321 calories, 9 g protein, 10 g fat, 46.79 g carbohydrate, 357 mg sodium, 37 mg cholesterol.

Mushroom Filling:
- *2 pounds mushrooms, sliced*
- *1 small onion, chopped (¼ cup)*
- *3 tablespoons vegetable oil*
- *1 package (8 ounces) cream cheese*
- *1 cup dry fine bread crumbs*
- *½ cup plain yogurt*
- *½ cup dairy sour cream*
- *⅓ cup chopped parsley*
- *2 cloves garlic, finely chopped*
- *2 teaspoons lemon juice*
- *½ teaspoon caraway seeds*
- *½ teaspoon pepper*

Dough:
- *10 cups unsifted all-purpose flour*
- *⅓ cup instant nonfat dry milk powder*
- *1 tablespoon sugar*
- *1 tablespoon salt*
- *2 envelopes fast-rising dry yeast*
- *2½ cups water*
- *¼ cup vegetable oil*
- *2 eggs, slightly beaten*
- *1 tablespoon butter or margarine, melted*

1. To prepare the Mushroom Filling: Sauté the mushrooms and onion in oil in a large skillet until the mushrooms give off their liquid. Continue cooking, stirring occasionally, until liquid evaporates. Add the cream cheese; stir until melted. Stir in the bread crumbs, yogurt, sour cream, parsley, garlic, lemon juice, caraway seeds and pepper. Set aside.
2. To prepare the Dough: Set aside 1 cup of the flour. Mix together the remaining 9 cups flour, dry milk powder, sugar, salt and yeast in a large bowl.
3. Combine the water and oil in a saucepan. Heat to 130° (mixture should feel comfortably hot to the touch). Mix into the dry ingredients. Mix in the eggs. Mix in enough reserved 1 cup flour to make a soft dough.
4. Turn out onto a floured surface. Knead until smooth and elastic, for 8 to 10 minutes. Cover; let rest for 10 minutes.
5. Divide the dough in half. Roll out each half on a lightly floured surface into a 15 x 12-inch rectangle. Spread each with half the Mushroom Filling to within ½ inch of edges. Starting at a long side, roll each up jelly-roll fashion; pinch along the seams to seal. Place seam-sides down on greased cookie sheets. Make cuts in the top of each loaf, three-quarters of the way through and at 1½-inch intervals. Twist every other slice to opposite side. Cover with buttered wax paper and a towel. Let rise in a warm place, away from drafts, until doubled in volume, about 45 minutes.
6. Meanwhile, preheat the oven to moderate (350°).
7. Bake in the preheated moderate oven (350°) for 45 minutes or until the loaves are browned and sound hollow when tapped with fingers. Remove the breads from the cookie sheets to wire racks to cool; brush with the butter. Serve warm or at room temperature. Store in the refrigerator.

Apricot-Yogurt Chestnut Bread

Bake at 375° for 35 minutes.
Makes 2 loaves (6 slices each).

Nutrient Value Per Slice: 200 calories, 5 g protein, 4 g fat, 32.9 g carbohydrate, 194 mg sodium, 32 mg cholesterol.

3 cups unsifted unbleached flour
1 cup cooked shelled chestnuts, chopped
      OR: 1 cup walnuts, chopped
⅓ cup dried apricots, chopped
¾ teaspoon salt
½ teaspoon baking soda
1 envelope fast-rising dry yeast
1 cup apricot yogurt
⅓ cup apricot nectar
¼ cup water
¼ cup milk
3 tablespoons butter or margarine
1 egg
Garnish (optional):
      Apricot preserves, strained
      Cooked shelled chestnuts
      Dried apricot halves

1. Set aside 1 cup flour. Mix together the remaining flour, chestnuts, apricots, salt, baking soda and yeast in a large bowl.
2. Combine the apricot yogurt, apricot nectar, water, milk and butter in a medium-size saucepan. Heat to 130° (mixture should feel comfortably hot to the touch). Stir into the dry ingredients. Mix in the egg. Mix in just enough of the reserved 1 cup flour to make a very thick batter. Cover the bowl; let rest for 10 minutes.
3. Divide the batter evenly into two greased 8½ x 4½ x 2½-inch baking pans or other 6-cup baking pans. Cover with buttered wax paper and a towel. Let rise in warm place, away from drafts, until doubled in volume, about 45 minutes.
4. Meanwhile, preheat the oven to moderate (375°).
5. Bake in the preheated moderate oven (375°) for 35 minutes or until the centers spring back when lightly pressed with fingertip and the bottom sounds hollow when tapped with fingers. Remove the breads to a wire rack to cool.
6. Prepare the optional Garnish: Brush the loaves with the strained apricot preserves. Garnish the top of the loaves with a chestnut placed on each dried apricot half. Arrange the apricots down the center of the loaves.

Whole-Wheat "Yamadamia" Bread

Bake at 350° for 60 minutes.
Makes 2 loaves (8 slices each).

Nutrient Value Per Slice: 345 calories, 12 g protein, 9 g fat, 65.2 g carbohydrate, 458 mg sodium, 12 mg cholesterol.

9½ cups whole-wheat flour
1 cup mashed cooked yams
⅔ cup macadamia nuts, chopped
1 tablespoon salt
1 envelope fast-rising dry yeast
3 cups milk
⅓ cup water
1 tablespoon honey
1 tablespoon molasses
3 tablespoons butter or margarine
      Confectioners' Glaze (recipe follows; optional)

1. Set aside 1 cup of the flour. Mix together the remaining 8½ cups flour, yams, macadamia nuts, salt and yeast in a large bowl.
2. Combine the milk, water, honey, molasses and 1 tablespoon of the butter in a medium-size saucepan. Heat to 130° (mixture should feel comfortably hot the the touch). Stir into the dry ingredients. Stir in just enough of the reserved 1 cup flour to make a stiff dough.
3. Turn the dough out onto a lightly floured surface. Knead until smooth and elastic, for 6 to 8 minutes. Cover; let rest for 10 minutes. ▶

4. Divide the dough in half. Shape into 2 loaves. Place in 2 greased 8½ x 4½ x 2½ -inch baking pans or other 6-cup baking pans or molds. Cover with buttered wax paper and a towel. Let rise in a warm place, away from drafts, until doubled in volume, for 45 to 55 minutes.

5. Meanwhile, preheat the oven to moderate (350°).

6. Bake in the preheated moderate oven (350°) for 60 minutes or until the loaves are browned and sound hollow when tapped with fingers. Remove the breads from the pans to wire racks to cool.

7. Spread the Confectioners' Glaze over the top of the bread, if you wish, allowing the glaze to run down the sides. Sprinkle tops with chopped macadamia nuts, if you wish.

Confectioners' Glaze: Combine 1 cup 10X (confectioners') sugar and 1 to 1½ tablespoons milk and ¼ teaspoon vanilla in a small bowl, stirring until smooth and good spreading consistency.

Healthy Hi-Rise White Bread

If desired, substitute 1 cup of wheat germ for 1 cup of the flour.

Bake at 400° for 30 minutes.
Makes 2 round loaves (10 slices each).

Nutrient Value Per Slice: 284 calories, 7 g protein, 5 g fat, 53 g carbohydrate, 227 mg sodium, 14 mg cholesterol.

3 envelopes fast-rising dry yeast
½ cup honey
3 cups very warm water
9 to 10 cups unsifted unbleached white flour
4 teaspoons salt
5 tablespoons vegetable oil
1 egg, lightly beaten with 1 teaspoon water
   Sesame seeds

1. Dissolve the yeast and honey in very warm water in a very large bowl. ("Very warm water" should feel comfortably warm when a few drops are sprinkled on your wrist.) Stir until the yeast is completely dissolved.

2. Add half of the flour and the salt; beat well with a large wooden spoon, to form a smooth batter. Add the remaining flour and blend well.

3. Pour oil over; punch and knead into the dough for 2 minutes. Cover with buttered wax

paper and a towel.

4. Let rise in a warm place, away from drafts, until doubled in volume for about 45 minutes. Punch down the dough; turn out onto a lightly floured board or pastry cloth. Knead lightly; divide the dough in half. Shape each half into a round loaf; place in a greased 8-inch springform pan. Cover with buttered wax paper and a towel.

5. Let rise in a warm place, away from drafts, until doubled in volume, for about 30 minutes. Brush with the egg beaten with 1 teaspoon of water. Sprinkle with the sesame seeds.

6. Meanwhile, preheat the oven to hot (400°).

7. Bake in the hot oven (400°) for 30 minutes, or until the tops of the loaves are golden brown and the loaves sound hollow when lightly tapped. Cool completely on wire racks before wrapping. Cut with a serrated knife on a wooden board.

Flour Substitution

Unbleached white flour may be used in place of all-purpose flour.

Healthy Hi-Rise White Bread (page 50), Braided Egg Bread (page 53),
Dark Rye Bread (page 54), Whole Wheat Bread (page 54)

HOW TO KNEAD AND SHAPE BREAD

1. Turn soft dough out on a floured board. Flour hands lightly, then pat dough to flatten slightly. Begin to knead this way. Pick up the edge of the dough with your fingers and fold over toward you.

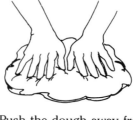

2. Push the dough away from you with the heels of both hands. If the dough sticks to the board, have a metal spatula handy to scrape the board clean; then re-flour and continue.

3. Give the dough a quarter turn, then repeat folding, pushing, turning. As you knead, you will develop your own speed. You'll find that well-kneaded bread dough is satiny, elastic and smooth.

4. An easy way to determine when dough has doubled in volume: Press the dough flat in a bowl, mark its level, then remove the dough. Fill the bowl with water to double the first mark; mark the level.

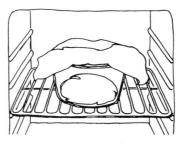

5. For a warm, draft-free place to let dough rise, use the oven with the door closed. If the oven is electric, warm to 200°, then turn off and let cool for 5 minutes. If gas, the pilot light will keep the dough warm with oven door ajar.

6. To shape a handsome loaf of bread: Roll or pat the dough out to a rectangle with the short side equal to the length of a bread pan. Roll up the dough, in jelly-roll style, pressing the turns firmly.

7. When the loaf has been shaped, make sure the dough is even on both ends. Then, with your fingers, pinch long seam firmly—to seal and keep from unrolling. Put in the pans, with the seam on the bottom.

8. How to smooth the ends of the loaves: Press the dough down on each end of the loaf with the sides of your hands. Tuck the thin strips formed under the loaf. Lift the loaf to the pan without stretching.

9. To shape long loaves of bread: Roll up, in jelly-roll style, pinching the seam, as in Fig. 7. Then, with the palms of your hands, taper the ends by rolling the loaf back and forth on a board.

Braided Egg Bread

A spectacular 4½ pound braid, perfect for a large buffet.

Bake at 375° for 55 minutes.
Makes one very large loaf (20 slices).

Nutrient Value Per Slice: 217 calories, 6 g protein, 4 g fat, 39 g carbohydrate, 368 mg sodium, 61 mg cholesterol.

2 envelopes fast-rising dry yeast
1¾ cups very warm water
½ cup sugar
¼ cup (½ stick) butter or margarine, melted
1 tablespoon salt
4 large eggs, beaten
7 cups unsifted unbleached white flour
Melted butter or margarine
Poppy or sesame seeds

1. Dissolve the yeast in very warm water in a large bowl. ("Very warm water" should feel comfortably warm when a few drops are sprinkled on your wrist.) Stir in the sugar, melted butter or margarine and salt until well blended.
2. Blend in the beaten eggs and 3 cups of the flour. Beat well with a large wooden spoon. Add the remaining flour, a little at a time, beating with a spoon until the dough is too stiff to use a spoon. Then mix with hands.
3. Turn out the dough onto a floured bread board or work surface. Knead for 10 minutes, or until smooth and elastic. Place in a very large greased bowl; turn to coat dough all over. Cover with buttered wax paper and a towel.
4. Let rise in a warm place, away from drafts, until doubled in volume, about 1 hour. Punch down the dough; turn out onto a board. Cut the dough in half; cover one half.
5. Cut the remaining half into 3 equal pieces; roll each piece into a strip, about 18 inches long. Braid the strips together. Place on the diagonal onto a greased cookie sheet. Take ⅔ of the remaining dough; cut into 3 equal pieces; roll into strips, braid and place on the first braid. Repeat the process with the remaining dough, gently placing the braid on top of the other braids.
6. Gently brush the loaf with melted butter or margarine. Cover with buttered wax paper and a towel. Let rise in a warm place until doubled in volume, about 30 minutes.
7. Meanwhile, preheat the oven to moderate (375°).
8. Bake in the preheated moderate oven (375°) for 45 minutes, or until the top is golden brown.

Home-Style Bread

Vary the proportion of unbleached white and whole-wheat flours to suit your taste.

Bake at 375° for 40 minutes.
Makes 4 loaves (12 slices each).

Nutrient Value Per Slice: 132 calories, 4 g protein, 2 g fat, 25 g carbohydrate, 97 mg sodium, 1 mg cholesterol.

3 envelopes fast-rising dry yeast
2 cups very warm water
½ cup sugar
¼ cup vegetable shortening, melted
1 tablespoon salt
2 cups milk, scalded
2 cups cold water
6 cups unsifted unbleached white flour
6 cups whole-wheat blend flour

1. Dissolve the yeast in very warm water in a very large bowl. ("Very warm water" should feel comfortably warm when a few drops are sprinkled on your wrist.) Let stand for 5 minutes.
2. Combine the sugar, melted shortening and salt in another bowl; blend in the milk, then the cold water. Cool slightly.
3. Add the milk mixture to the yeast mixture, stirring until well blended. Add the white and wheat flours, a little at a time, beating with a large wooden spoon. When the dough gets too stiff, use your hands to mix in the flour, if you wish.
4. Turn out the dough onto a floured bread board or work surface. Knead for 15 minutes, or until smooth and elastic. Place in a greased very large bowl; turn to coat dough all over. Cover with buttered wax paper and a towel.
5. Let rise in warm place, away from drafts until doubled in volume, about 45 minutes. Punch down the dough. Turn out onto a floured board; cover with bowl; let rest for 15 minutes.
6. Divide the dough into 4 even pieces; shape each piece into a 9-inch loaf and place in the greased 9 x 5 x 3-inch loaf pans. Cover with ▶

buttered wax paper and a towel. Let rise until doubled in volume, about 30 minutes.
7. Meanwhile, preheat the oven to moderate (375°).
8. Bake in the preheated moderate oven for 40 minutes, or until the tops are golden brown and the loaves sound hollow when lightly tapped. Cool completely.

Baker's Tip: Or form dough into 2 large round loaves on greased cookie sheets; brush with 1 beaten egg mixed with 1 teaspoon water, and sprinkle with poppy or sesame seeds.

Oven Rack Positioning

When baking two loaves, place them on the center rack in the oven; for four loaves, use two racks, placed in the bottom and next to the highest positions.

Whole Wheat Bread

Perfect for sandwiches, if it's not all eaten while still warm!

Bake at 400° for 10 minutes,
then at 350° for 40 minutes.
Makes 2 loaves (12 slices each).

Nutrient Value Per Serving: 175 calories, 6 g protein, 4 g fat, 30 g carbohydrate, 206 mg sodium, 5 mg cholesterol.

   2   *envelopes fast-rising dry yeast*
   1   *cup very warm water*
   2   *cups milk*
   ½   *cup firmly packed brown sugar*
   2   *teaspoons salt*
   7   *cups whole-wheat blend flour*
   ¼   *cup butter-flavor vegetable shortening*
       Butter or margarine, melted
       Coarse salt (optional)

1. Dissolve the yeast in the very warm water in a large bowl. ("Very warm water" should feel comfortably warm when a few drops are sprinkled on your wrist.) Let stand for 5 minutes.
2. Scald, but do not boil, the milk in a medium-size saucepan. Remove from the heat; stir in the brown sugar and salt until dissolved. Cool slightly.
3. Add the milk mixture to the yeast mixture in the bowl, stirring constantly with a large

wooden spoon. Add 3 cups of the flour and the melted shortening, still stirring constantly. Gradually beat in the remaining flour, adding more flour if necessary, to form a dough that doesn't stick to the bowl.
4. Turn out the dough onto a lightly floured bread board. Knead for 10 minutes, or until smooth and elastic. Shape into a ball; place in a greased bowl; turn to coat the dough all over. Cover with buttered wax paper and a towel.
5. Let rise in a warm place, away from drafts until doubled in volume, about 45 minutes. Punch down the dough; turn out onto a floured board. Let rest for 5 minutes.
6. Cut the dough in half; roll each half into a 12 x 9-inch rectangle; roll up tightly from a short end; place seam-side down in a greased 9 x 5 x 3-inch loaf pan. Brush with the melted butter or margarine; sprinkle with coarse salt, if desired. Cover with buttered wax paper and a towel. Let rise until doubled in volume, about 30 minutes.
7. Meanwhile, preheat the oven to hot (400°).
8. Bake in the preheated hot oven (400°) for 10 minutes. Lower the oven temperature to moderate (350°). Bake for 40 minutes longer, or until the tops are golden brown. Cool on wire racks.

Dark Rye Bread

Use this bread as a base for hors d'oeuvres, especially smoked ham.

Bake at 375° for 35 minutes.
Makes one large round (12 slices).

Nutrient Value Per Slice: 271 calories, 7 g protein, 4 g fat, 57 g carbohydrate, 251 mg sodium, 28 mg cholesterol.

   2   *cups rye flour*
   ½   *cup cocoa powder (not a mix)*
   1   *tablespoon instant coffee powder*
   2   *envelopes fast-rising dry yeast*
   1½   *cups very warm water*
   1½   *cups molasses*
   2   *tablespoons brown sugar*
   2   *tablespoons caraway seeds*
   2   *teaspoons salt*
   2   *tablespoons butter or margarine, melted*
   2½   *cups whole-wheat blend flour*
   1   *egg, lightly beaten with*
        1 teaspoon water
        Caraway seeds

1. Combine the rye flour, cocoa and instant coffee in a small bowl. Dissolve the yeast in ½ cup of the very warm water in a cup. ("Very warm water" should feel comfortably warm when a few drops are sprinkled on your wrist.)
2. Combine the molasses, sugar, caraway seeds and salt with the remaining 1 cup very warm water in a large bowl; stir with a wooden spoon to blend.
3. Stir in the rye flour mixture, yeast mixture, melted butter or margarine and 1 cup of the whole-wheat flour. Beat until the batter is smooth.
4. Sprinkle the remaining 1½ cups whole-wheat flour on a bread board or work surface. Scrape the dough out of the bowl onto the flour. Work in the flour, adding more flour, if necessary, to form a dough that doesn't stick to the surface. Knead the dough until smooth and elastic, about 10 minutes. Place in a greased large bowl; turn to coat dough all over. Cover with buttered wax paper and a towel.
5. Let rise until doubled in volume, about 30 minutes. Shape into a large round on a cookie sheet. Brush the top with the egg beaten with 1 teaspoon water; sprinkle with additional caraway seeds.
6. Meanwhile, preheat the oven to moderate (375°).
7. Bake in the preheated moderate oven (375°) for 35 to 40 minutes, or until the loaf sounds hollow when lightly tapped.

Rye Flour

Rye flour is milled from the entire rye kernel. It is available in three grades: white, medium and dark. Rye flour produces gluten of low elasticity; therefore it should be combined with white flour in bread recipes in order to produce a better loaf.

Pumpernickel Raisin Bread

Bake at 375° for 40 minutes.
Makes 1 loaf (12 slices).

Nutrient Value Per Slice: 178 calories, 5 g protein, 2 g fat, 33 g carbohydrate, 390 mg sodium, 1 mg cholesterol.

> 2   **packages active dry yeast**
> 1   **cup whole-wheat flour**
> 1   **cup rye flour**
> 1½ cups sifted **all-purpose flour**
> ½   **cup instant dry milk powder**
> 2   **teaspoons salt**
> 1½ cups **very warm water**
> ¼   **cup molasses**
> 2   **tablespoons vegetable oil**
> ½   **cup raisins**

1. Combine the yeast, whole-wheat flour, rye flour, ½ cup of the all-purpose flour, dry milk and salt in a large bowl.
2. Add the water, molasses and oil. ("Very warm water" should feel comfortably warm when a few drops are sprinkled on your wrist.) Beat for 3 minutes at medium speed, scraping down the sides of the bowl occasionally with a rubber spatula. Stir in the remaining flour to make a stiff dough. Stir in the raisins.
3. Cover the bowl with buttered wax paper and a towel. Let the dough rise in a warm place, away from drafts, until doubled in volume, for about 45 minutes.
4. Stir the dough down. Spoon into a greased 9 x 5 x 3-inch loaf pan, pushing the dough well into the corners.
5. Cover with buttered wax paper on a towel. Let rise again in a warm place away from drafts, until doubled in volume, about 35 minutes.
6. Meanwhile, preheat oven to moderate (375°).
7. Bake in the preheated moderate oven (375°) for 40 minutes, or until the bread sounds hollow when tapped. Cool on a wire rack.

Whole-Wheat Flour

Whole-wheat flour is a coarse-textured flour ground from the entire kernel. This flour has a small amount of gluten, so baked products tend to be heavier and denser than those made with all-purpose flour. For better baking results, combine whole-wheat with white flour. Whole-wheat flour is rich in B-complex vitamins, vitamin E, fat, protein and some minerals. It is more susceptible to spoilage than other flours because of the fat in the wheat germ.

Start with one basic recipe and choose your favorite flours, sweeteners, herbs or spices, cheese or fruit and nuts from the choices on the following page. Shape into a variety of rolls or breads and have enough baked goodies to serve today with some for the freezer, too. It's much easier than you think.

Country Home-Baked Bread

There is no better way to fill the house with the aromas of baking than to make yeast bread or rolls.

Bake at 375° for 40 minutes for bread, for 30 minutes for rolls.
Makes 2 loaves (12 slices each) or 2 dozen rolls.

Nutrient Value Per Serving: 121 calories, 3 g protein, 2 g fat, 23 g carbohydrate, 153 mg sodium, 4 mg cholesterol.

2 envelopes fast-rising dry yeast
1½ cups very warm water
5 to 6 cups unsifted all-purpose flour
½ cup dry milk powder (optional)
1 to 2 teaspoons salt
1 to 6 tablespoons sweetener (see chart)
3 tablespoons butter or margarine, melted
2 eggs (optional)

1. Sprinkle the yeast over very warm water in a large glass or ceramic bowl; add 1 teaspoon sugar and stir until well blended. ("Very warm" water should feel comfortably warm when a few drops are sprinkled on your wrist.) Allow to stand for 5 minutes, or until bubbly.
2. Stir in 3 cups of the flour, dry milk powder, if used, salt and sweetener with a wooden spoon. (Use 1 or 2 tablespoons sugar for a plain, wheat, cheese or herb dough; increase the sweetener when making a spicy, fruit or nut dough.) Beat the eggs in a small bowl and add, if used. (Dry milk powder and eggs add richness to the dough; the bread

or rolls will be smoother textured and with a soft crust. Do not use either for a crisp crust.)
3. Beat with a wooden spoon until very smooth, add the desired ingredients from the next page and enough of the remaining 3 cups flour to make a soft dough. Turn out the dough onto a lightly floured pastry cloth or board.
4. Knead the dough, adding just enough flour to keep the dough from sticking, for 5 minutes, or until smooth and elastic.
5. Wash the mixing bowl in hot sudsy water, rinse with hot water and dry; grease generously with butter or margarine. Shape the dough into a ball and place in bowl; turn to coat the top; cover the bowl with buttered wax paper and a towel.
6. Let rise in a warm place, away from draft, until doubled in volume, about 45 minutes; punch the dough down.
7. Turn the dough onto a pastry cloth or board and knead for 10 times; divide the dough and shape, choosing from the selection that follows. (Note: You can make half the dough into a loaf and half into rolls, if you wish.)
8. Cover dough with buttered wax paper and a towel. Let rise in a warm place away from draft, for about 20 minutes or until doubled in volume.
9. Meanwhile, preheat the oven to moderate (375°).
10. Bake in the preheated moderate oven (375°) for 20 minutes for rolls, or 40 minutes for bread, or until the tops are golden brown and the bread gives a hollow sound when tapped with fingertips.
11. Invert the bread onto a wire rack, then turn right-side up, or remove the rolls from the pan with a spatula; cool the bread before slicing; serve the rolls warm. Or cool completely; wrap in heavy duty aluminum foil, or place in freezer plastic bags and seal; label, date and freeze.

Basic Loaf—Roll out half of dough to an 12 x 8-inch rectangle; roll up, starting at the short end, into a tight roll; press the ends to seal; place, seam-side down, in a greased 9 x 5 x 3-inch loaf pan; brush with butter, just before baking.

Round Loaf—Shape half of the dough into a ball and place, rounded side up, in a greased 8-inch springform pan; brush with melted butter just before baking, if you wish.

Italian Bread—Roll out half of dough to a 15 x 10-inch rectangle; roll up, starting at a long end, into a tight roll; place, seam-side down, on a large cookie sheet greased and coated with cornmeal; taper the ends; cover with plastic wrap; let rise for 20 minutes; make diagonal slashes on the top with a sharp knife and brush with ice water, just before baking; brush with water while baking several times.

Braided Loaf—Makes 1 loaf from the recipe. Divide the dough in half; divide one half into one-third and two-thirds. Divide the half portion of the dough into 3 parts; roll each part to an 18-inch-long rope. Braid the rolls on a large greased cookie sheet. Divide the two-thirds portion into three parts and roll out each to a 15-inch rope; braid these ropes on a lightly floured pastry cloth or board and place on top of the first braid. Divide the third portion of dough into 3 parts and roll each part into a 12-inch rope; braid the ropes and place on top of the second braid; cover with plastic wrap and let rise for 30 minutes; brush with 1 egg beaten with 1 tablespoon of water, just before baking for 45 minutes, or until golden.

Crescent Rolls—Roll out dough to an 18 x 15-inch rectangle on a lightly floured pastry board. Cut into 3-inch squares; cut each square diagonally into a triangle. Roll up the triangle, starting at the long ends; place, pointed end to the top, on a greased cookie sheet; turn the ends to shape into crescent; brush with a beaten egg, just before baking.

Breadsticks—Divide the dough into 24 parts and roll each part into an 8-inch rope on a lightly floured pastry board; place on a cookie sheet; brush with water and sprinkle with sesame seeds, just before baking.

Herbs—Add:
- 2 tsp. leaf basil
- 2 tsp. dill weed
- 2 tsp. Italian herbs
- 1 tsp. leaf oregano
- 1 Tbsp. dried parsley
- 1 Tbsp. chopped chives

Cheese—Add:
- ½ cup grated Cheddar
- ⅓ cup Parmesan
- ½ cup grated Swiss
- ¾ cup cubed Edam

Nuts—Add:
- 1 cup chopped peanuts
- ¾ cup chopped walnuts
- ¾ cup sliced almonds
- 1 cup chopped pecans

Sweeteners—Add:
- 1 to 6 Tbsp. sugar
- ¼ cup brown sugar
- ⅓ cup honey (reduce water by ¼ cup)
- ¼ cup molasses (reduce water by ¼ cup)

Grains—Substitute for 2 cups all-purpose flour:
- 1½ cups whole wheat flour
- 1½ cups rye flour
- 3 cups oatmeal
- 1½ cups bran
- 3 cups wheat germ

Vegetables—Add:
- 1 cup grated zucchini
- ¾ cup grated carrot
- 1 cup grated potato
- ¾ cup chopped onion
- 1 cup chopped leeks
- 1 cup chopped mushrooms

Fruits—Add:
- 1 cup flaked coconut
- 1 cup raisins
- 1 cup grated apple
- ¾ cup chopped dried apricots
- 1 cup chopped raw cranberries
- ¾ cup chopped dates
- 1 Tbsp. orange rind
- 2 tsp. lemon rind

Spices—Add:
- 1 tsp. pumpkin pie spice
- 1 tsp. ground cinnamon
- 1 tsp. ground nutmeg
- ½ tsp. ground cloves

Glazes—Brush on:
- Butter or margarine
- 1 egg white beaten with 1 Tbsp. water
- Melted apple jelly
- Honey

Toppings— Sprinkle before baking:
- Sesame seeds
- Poppy seeds
- Sunflower seeds
- Parmesan cheese
- Chopped chives
- Partially cooked diced bacon.

HOW TO SHAPE YEAST ROLLS

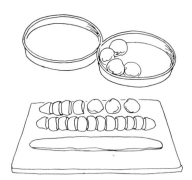

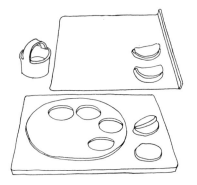

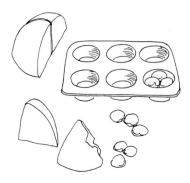

Pan Rolls: Divide the dough into three equal parts and shape each into a fat roll, 12 inches long. Slice each roll crosswise every inch; roll the slices into balls; place ¼ inch apart in greased 9-inch layer-cake pans.

Parker House Rolls: Divide the dough in three equal parts; roll, one part at a time, on a floured board into a circle 9 inches across. Cut into rounds with a lightly floured, 2½-inch biscuit cutter; brush each round with softened butter or margarine, make a crease across each slightly to one side of center, then fold the smaller "half" over the larger, forming half-moons, and place on greased baking sheets 1 inch apart. Pinch the edges lightly to seal.

Cloverleaf Rolls: Divide the dough into four equal parts, then working with one part at a time, pinch off small pieces of dough; shape into balls about the size of marbles. Place three balls of dough in each cup of greased muffin pans, forming "three-leaf clovers."

Pinwheels: Divide the dough into three equal parts and roll, one part at a time, on a floured board into a 16 x 8-inch rectangle. Spread with softened butter or margarine, and, if you like, cinnamon-sugar, jam or other filling. Roll up from the long side, jelly-roll fashion; slice 1-inch thick. Place, cut-sides up, in greased muffin-pan cups.

Quick Cloverleafs: Pinch off pieces of the dough and shape into balls slightly larger than golf balls. Place in greased muffin-pan cups, then with kitchen shears, snip a cross into the top of each roll, forming "four-leaf clovers."

Fan-Tans: Divide the dough into three equal parts and roll each part on a floured board into a 15x9-inch rectangle; cut crosswise into strips 1½ inches wide, then make a stack by piling 6 strips on top of one another. Cut the stack crosswise into squares and place, cut-side down, in greased muffin-pan cups.

Quick Breads

Quick breads, in general, are well named. They rely on baking powder, baking soda and eggs for leavening. There is no waiting for yeast to proof or dough to rise. No kneading is required. Most can be mixed in fewer than 15 minutes. Baking times vary from 15 minutes for muffins to an hour or more for large, dense loaves.

Fruit and nut loaves, vegetable loaves, corn bread, muffins and biscuits—all essentially quick breads—require no special ingredients, techniques or equipment. They may be baked in a variety of interesting shaped pans now on the market. Homemade loaves, presented in their baking pans, covered in clear wrap and tied with a bright bow, make terrific gifts.

Most fruit and vegetable breads may be kept in the refrigerator for up to two weeks and in the freezer for up to six months. Muffins, on the other hand, should be enjoyed soon out of the oven. They may be frozen for up to three months, then reheated and served.

Fruit and vegetable quick breads are moist and full of fiber. Here are tips and hints for no-fail, nutritious quick breads—great all year.

● Mix the dry and liquid ingredients separately. Add the fruit, vegetables and nuts last. Once the leavening agent (the baking powder or baking soda) comes in contact with the liquid, the leavening begins and within a short time will be spent. To prepare the ingredients ahead, mix the dry ingredients and the liquid ingredients separately, then combine before baking.
● Mix the batter thoroughly but gently with a wooden spoon, only until the ingredients are moistened.
● Make the entire recipe for muffins and freeze the extras.
● Freeze quick breads for up to six months. To thaw: Heat in foil wrapping in a slow oven (300°) for 25 minutes, or until heated.
● Allow the breads to cool for 10 minutes in their pans; remove and cool completely on a wire rack before wrapping in aluminum foil or plastic wrap.
● Mash bananas quickly with an electric blender or food processor, pulsing quickly on and off.
● Shred carrots ahead of time and keep in sealed plastic bags in the refrigerator.
● Grate citrus rind and keep in the freezer for use later.
● Grate apples with the skin, because the skin contains more fiber and vitamins and gives more flavor.
● Try adding up to ¼ cup shredded carrot, apple, pear or mashed banana to your favorite muffin or sweet bread recipe for extra flavor.
● Substitute pears for apples in most muffin and quick bread recipes.
● Substitute cranberries for blueberries in most recipes. Cut cranberries in half and roll in granulated sugar before adding to recipe.
● Add grated lemon, orange or lime rind to your favorite bread or muffin recipe for extra zest. Try about two teaspoons per recipe first, then increase to taste.
● Squeeze the juice from a lemon or orange when the fruit is at room temperature to get the most juice.

Apple-Spice Granola Muffins

Apple-Spice Granola Muffins

Bake at 400° for 15 to 20 minutes.
Makes 12 muffins.

Nutrient Value Per Muffin: 213 calories, 4 g protein, 11 g fat, 26 g carbohydrate, 232 mg sodium, 24 mg cholesterol.

**2   cups Homemade Granola Crunch
      (see recipe, page 274)**
1   cup sifted all-purpose flour
¼   cup firmly packed light brown sugar
2   teaspoons baking powder
½   teaspoon ground cinnamon
¼   teaspoon ground nutmeg
¼   teaspoon salt
**1   cup finely chopped, pared cooking
      apples, such as Granny Smith
      (1 medium-size)**
½   cup milk
**⅓   cup margarine, melted and cooled to
      room temperature**
1   egg, slightly beaten
1   teaspoon vanilla

1. Preheat the oven to hot (400°). Grease twelve 2½-inch muffin-pan cups.
2. Combine the granola, flour, sugar, baking powder, cinnamon, nutmeg and salt in a large bowl. Mix well. Stir in the apples. Make a well in the center.
3. Beat together the milk, margarine, egg and vanilla in a small bowl. Pour into the well of granola mixture; stir just to combine. Spoon the batter into the prepared muffin-pan cups.
4. Bake in the preheated hot oven (400°) for 15 to 20 minutes, or until a wooden pick inserted in the centers comes out clean. ▶

Cool the muffins in the pan on a wire rack for 5 minutes. Turn out muffins. Serve warm or cool completely on the wire rack.

Baking Powder Freshness Test

Since the leavening ability of baking powder diminishes with age, always test the powder: Place ½ teaspoon in ¼ cup of hot water. If the powder is fresh, the water will bubble actively.

Buttermilk and Bacon Corn Muffins

Bake at 400° for 20 minutes.
Makes 10 muffins.

Nutrient Value Per Muffin: 190 calories, 5 g protein, 7 g fat, 27 g carbohydrate, 310 mg sodium, 43 g cholesterol.

1½ cups unsifted all-purpose flour
½ cup yellow cornmeal
2 tablespoons sugar
2 teaspoons baking powder
½ teaspoon baking soda
½ teaspoon salt
1 cup buttermilk
¼ cup (½ stick) unsalted butter or margarine, melted
1 egg
1 cup fresh corn kernels or drained, canned whole corn kernels
4 slices cooked bacon, crumbled

1. Preheat the oven to hot (400°). Generously grease ten 2½-inch muffin-pan cups.
2. Mix together the flour, cornmeal, sugar, baking powder, baking soda and salt in a large bowl.
3. Beat together the buttermilk, melted butter and egg in a small bowl. Stir into the flour mixture just until moistened. Do not overmix; batter should be lumpy. Stir in the corn and bacon. Spoon into the prepared muffin-pan cups, filling three-quarters full.
4. Bake in the preheated hot oven (400°) for 20 minutes; or until lightly browned and a wooden pick inserted in the center comes out clean. Let the muffins cool in the pans on a wire rack for 5 minutes. Remove the muffins from the pans to the wire rack to cool completely.

MICROWAVE DIRECTIONS
650 Watt Variable Power Microwave Oven
INGREDIENT CHANGES: Add ¼ teaspoon paprika.
MICROWAVE DIRECTIONS: Grease 6 cups in a microwave-safe muffin baking pan. Set aside. Place the bacon in a single layer between layers of paper toweling on a paper plate. Microwave at full power for 2½ to 3 minutes, or until crisp. Remove from the microwave oven; crumble. Assemble the muffin batter as in the above recipe. Fill the prepared cups about three-quarters full. Sprinkle lightly with paprika. Microwave, uncovered, at full power for 3 minutes, rotating the pan one-quarter turn after 2 minutes. Remove the muffins from the cups to a wire rack. Repeat to make 6 more muffins. Repeat with the remaining batter to make 2 or 3 more muffins; microwave at full power for 2 minutes. Makes about 15 muffins.

Did You Know?

Baking soda (bicarbonate of soda) works only when combined with an acid substance (such as in baking powder mixtures) or when an acidic liquid—buttermilk, sour milk, chocolate, honey, corn syrup or molasses—is used.

Citrus Lime Muffins

Citrus Lime Muffins

Bake at 400° for 20 minutes.
Makes 12 muffins.

Nutrient Value Per Muffin: 192 calories, 3 g protein, 6 g fat, 32 g carbohydrate, 213 mg sodium, 46 mg cholesterol.

2 **cups sifted *all-purpose flour***
1 **cup sugar**
3 **teaspoons baking powder**
½ **teaspoon salt**
¼ **cup milk**
2 **eggs, lightly beaten**
¼ **cup vegetable oil**
1 **teaspoon grated lime rind**
¼ **cup lime juice**

1. Preheat the oven to hot (400°). Grease twelve 2½-inch muffin-pan cups.
2. Sift together the flour, sugar, baking powder and salt into a large bowl.
3. Mix the milk, eggs, oil, lime rind and lime juice in a 2-cup measure. Add all at once to the flour mixture; stir lightly with a fork just until moist. (Batter will be lumpy.) Spoon into the prepared muffin-pan cups, filling each three-quarters full.
4. Bake in the preheated hot oven (400°) for 20 minutes or until golden. Remove the muffins from the cups to a wire rack. Serve warm with butter, if you wish.

Wheat Germ Muffins

Doubly rich with old-fashioned molasses and nut-sweet wheat germ—and good for you, too!

Bake at 400° for 30 minutes.
Makes 12 muffins.

Nutrient Value Per Muffin: 172 calories, 5 g protein, 6 g fat, 25 g carbohydrate, 308 mg sodium, 35 mg cholesterol.

1½ **cups sifted** *all-purpose flour*
¼ **cup sugar**
2 **teaspoons baking powder**
1 **teaspoon salt**
1 **cup wheat germ**
1 **egg, well beaten**
¾ **cup milk**
¼ **cup (½ stick) butter or margarine,**
    melted and cooled
¼ **cup molasses**

1. Preheat the oven to hot (400°). Grease twelve 2½-inch muffin-pan cups.
2. Sift together the flour, sugar, baking powder and salt into a medium-size bowl; stir in the wheat germ.
3. Beat together the egg, milk, melted and cooled butter and molasses in a small bowl. Stir into the flour mixture just until moistened. Do not overmix; batter should be lumpy. Spoon into prepared muffin-pan cups, filling each two-thirds full.
4. Bake in the preheated hot oven (400°) for 30 minutes or until lightly browned, or a wooden pick inserted in the center comes out clean. Let muffins cool in the pan on a wire rack for 5 minutes. Turn out the muffins. Serve warm or cool completely on the wire rack.

Sticky Liquids

To avoid residue when measuring sticky liquids (honey, molasses), rinse measuring cup in hot water first.

Cranberry-Nut Bread

Bake at 325° for 1 hour.
Makes 1 loaf (12 slices).

Nutrient Value Per Slice: 240 calories, 5 g protein, 9 g fat, 36 g carbohydrate, 192 mg sodium, 46 mg cholesterol.

2 **cups sifted** *all-purpose flour*
½ **teaspoon salt**
1½ **teaspoons baking powder**
½ **teaspoon baking soda**
1 **large navel orange**
    Boiling water
2 **tablespoons vegetable shortening**
2 **eggs**
1 **cup sugar**
1 **cup fresh or thawed frozen cranberries,**
    coarsely chopped
1 **cup chopped walnuts**

1. Preheat the oven to slow (325°). Grease a 9 x 5 x 3-inch loaf pan.
2. Sift together the flour, salt, baking powder and baking soda into a medium-size bowl.
3. Grate the rind from the orange. Measure and reserve 1 tablespoon. Squeeze the juice into a 2-cup measure. Add boiling water to make ¾ cup liquid. Stir in the reserved orange rind and shortening until the shortening is melted.
4. Beat the eggs in a large bowl until foamy. Gradually beat in the sugar; continue to beat until the mixture is thick and light.
5. Stir the dry ingredients into the egg mixture alternately with the orange mixture, blending well after each addition. Stir in the cranberries and nuts. Spoon into the prepared pan.
6. Bake in the preheated slow oven (325°) for 1 hour or until the center springs back when lightly touched with fingertip. Cool in the pan on a wire rack for 10 minutes. Turn out the bread from the pan; cool completely. Bread slices best the following day.

Cranberry Availability

Stock up on fresh cranberries when they are available (November through January). They freeze in their plastic bags beautifully for use later.

Whole-Wheat Muffins

Vitamin-rich whole wheat gives these tasty muffins a nutrition boost.

Bake at 400° for 25 minutes.
Makes 12 muffins.

Nutrient Value Per Muffin: 139 calories, 4 g protein, 5 g fat, 20 g carbohydrate, 311 mg sodium, 36 mg cholesterol.

- **1 cup sifted *all-purpose flour***
- **2 teaspoons baking powder**
- **1 teaspoon salt**
- **1 cup unsifted *whole-wheat flour***
- **¼ cup molasses**
- **1 egg, beaten**
- **1 cup milk**
- **¼ cup (½ stick) butter or margarine, melted and cooled**

1. Preheat the oven to hot (400°). Grease twelve 2½-inch muffin-pan cups.

2. Sift together the all-purpose flour, baking powder and salt into a medium-size bowl; stir in the whole-wheat flour. Make a well in the center.

3. Beat together the molasses, egg, milk and melted, cooled butter in a small bowl. Pour into the well in the flour mixture; stir just until moistened. Do not overmix; batter should be lumpy. Spoon into the prepared muffin-pan cups, filling each two-thirds full.

4. Bake in the preheated hot oven (400°) for 25 minutes, or until golden brown or a wooden pick inserted in the center comes out clean. Let muffins cool in the pan on a wire rack for 5 minutes. Turn out the muffins. Serve warm or cool completely on the wire rack.

Coconut Bread

Bake at 375° for 1 hour.
Makes 2 loaves (16 slices each).

Nutrient Value Per Slice: 213 calories, 4 g protein, 10 g fat, 28 g carbohydrate, 171 mg sodium, 46 mg cholesterol.

- **5½ cups sifted *all-purpose flour***
- **1½ cups sugar**
- **2 tablespoons baking powder**
- **2 teaspoons ground cinnamon**
- **1 teaspoon ground nutmeg**
- **½ teaspoon salt**
- **1½ cups fresh coconut milk***
- **¾ cup butter or margarine, melted**
- **4 eggs, slightly beaten**
- **⅔ cup walnuts, chopped**
- **⅔ cup raisins**

1. Preheat the oven to moderate (375°). Grease two 9 x 5 x 3-inch loaf pans.

2. Stir together the flour, sugar, baking powder, cinnamon, nutmeg and salt in a large bowl until well mixed.

3. Combine the fresh coconut milk, butter and eggs in a medium-size bowl; stir to mix. Pour all at once into dry ingredients; stir just to evenly moisten. Stir in the chopped walnuts and raisins. Divide the batter equally into the prepared pans.

4. Bake in the preheated moderate oven (375°) for 1 hour or until a toothpick inserted in the center comes out clean. Remove to a wire rack; let stand for 5 minutes. Remove from the pans; cool to room temperature on the wire rack. This bread slices better if made the day before.

***Note:** To make coconut milk: Pierce the "eyes" of a fresh coconut with a screwdriver; drain off the liquid. Place the coconut on a baking sheet; heat for 20 minutes in a 400° oven. Tap all over to loosen the meat; then crack open with a hammer. Pry the chunks of white meat from the shell; peel off the brown skin. Grate the coconut meat on a hand grater or in a food processor. Place the grated coconut in a small bowl; pour 3 cups boiling water over. Let cool to room temperature. Place a large sieve over a bowl; pour in the coconut mixture. Squeeze the coconut to remove as much of the "milk" as possible. Any leftover coconut milk from the above recipe can be used in making curries, desserts and beverages.

Honey Raisin Bread

![] ![] Honey Raisin Bread

Bake at 325° for 1 hour and 10 minutes.
Makes 1 loaf (12 slices).

Nutrient Value Per Slice: 278 calories, 5 g protein, 10 g fat, 44 g carbohydrate, 182 mg sodium, 25 mg cholesterol.

2¾ cups sifted *all-purpose flour*
 1 teaspoon baking powder
 ½ teaspoon baking soda
 ½ teaspoon salt
 1 egg
 2 tablespoons shortening
 ½ cup honey
 ¾ cup milk
 ¼ cup buttermilk
 1 cup raisins
 1 cup chopped pecans

1. Preheat the oven to slow (325°). Grease a 9 x 5 x 3-inch loaf pan.
2. Sift together the flour, baking powder, baking soda and salt into a medium-size bowl.
3. Beat together the egg, shortening and honey in a large bowl. Stir in the flour mixture alternately with the milk and buttermilk just until the dry ingredients are moistened. Stir in the raisins and pecans. Spoon into the prepared pan.
4. Bake in the preheated slow oven (325°) for 1 hour and 10 minutes or until a wooden pick inserted in the center tests clean. If browning too fast, cover the top with foil. Remove the bread from the pan to a wire rack. Let stand overnight before slicing.

![] ![] Chocolate-Zucchini Tea Bread

Bake at 350° for 1 hour.
Makes 2 loaves (10 slices each).

Nutrient Value Per Slice: 307 calories, 4 g protein, 18 g fat, 35 g carbohydrate, 55 mg sodium, 55 mg cholesterol.

1 square (1 ounce) unsweetened chocolate
 1 cup raisins
 ½ cup hot water
 3 cups unsifted all-purpose flour
 1⅓ cups sugar
 2 teaspoons baking powder
 1 teaspoon baking soda
 ½ teaspoon salt
 1 tablespoon ground cinnamon
 ½ cup chopped walnuts
 4 eggs, well beaten
 2½ cups zucchini, grated
 1¼ cups vegetable oil

1. Melt the unsweetened chocolate in the top of a double boiler over hot, not boiling, water. Set aside.
2. Soak the raisins in hot water in a 1-cup measure for 15 minutes.
3. Preheat the oven to moderate (350°). Grease two 8½ x 4½ x 2½-inch loaf pans.
4. Sift together the flour, sugar, baking powder, baking soda, salt and cinnamon into a large bowl; stir in the walnuts. Make a well in the center and add the eggs, zucchini, oil and melted chocolate.
5. Mix until thoroughly blended; fold in the drained raisins.

6. Spread the mixture evenly into the prepared loaf pans.
7. Bake in the preheated moderate oven (350°) for 1 hour, or until a wooden skewer inserted near the center comes out clean.
8. Cool in the pans; loosen around the edges; wrap in foil; store at room temperature for 24 hours before slicing, then refrigerate rest.

Irish Brown Bread

Whole-wheat flour adds nutty sweetness and extra nutrition to this Irish treat.

Bake at 375° for 40 minutes.
Makes one 9-inch round (10 slices).

Nutrient Value Per Slice: 218 calories, 7 g protein, .9 g fat, 48 g carbohydrate, 468 mg sodium, 1 mg cholesterol.

2 cups whole-wheat flour
1½ cups unsifted all-purpose flour
3 tablespoons light brown sugar
1 tablespoon baking powder
1 teaspoon baking soda
1 teaspoon salt
1 cup dry currants or raisins
1⅓ cups buttermilk

1. Combine the whole-wheat and all purpose flours, brown sugar, baking powder, baking soda and salt in a large bowl. Stir with a wire whip until well blended.
2. Preheat the oven to moderate (375°). Grease a medium-size cookie sheet.
3. Stir in the currants or raisins, then buttermilk all at once, just until the dough forms and leaves the side of the bowl.
4. Turn the dough out onto a lightly floured surface. Knead 8 times, turn right-side up, pat into an 8-inch round.
5. Place on the prepared cookie sheet; cut a cross in the center with a sharp knife. Brush with milk.
6. Bake in the preheated moderate oven (375°) for 40 minutes, or until the bread gives a hollow sound when tapped. Slide off the cookie sheet onto wire rack and cool.
7. Plan to use within one day, or cut and freeze in serving-size pieces.

Country Corn Bread

Bake at 450° for 25 minutes.
Makes two 8 x 8 x 2-inch breads
(16 servings each).

Nutrient Value Per Serving: 74 calories, 2 g protein, 1 g fat, 12 g carbohydrate, 141 mg sodium, 21 mg cholesterol.

1½ cups yellow cornmeal
2 cups sifted all-purpose flour
2 tablespoons sugar
4 teaspoons baking powder
1 teaspoon salt
2 eggs
2 cups milk
2 tablespoons butter or margarine

1. Preheat the oven to very hot (450°). Grease an 8 x 8 x 2-inch baking pan.
2. Combine the cornmeal, flour, sugar, baking powder and salt in a large bowl. Add the eggs and milk. Stir to make a smooth batter; stir in the butter or margarine.
3. Pour into the prepared baking pans.
4. Bake in the preheated very hot oven (450°) for 25 minutes or until crusty and golden brown. Cool slightly in the pans on wire racks; serve warm.

Spoon Bread

Bake at 350° for 40 minutes.
Makes 4 to 6 servings.

*Nutrient Value Per Serving: 270 calories, 12 g protein,
17 g fat, 17 g carbohydrate, 905 mg sodium,
375 mg cholesterol.*

5 eggs
4 teaspoons baking powder
¼ cup white cornmeal
1 tablespoon sugar
½ teaspoon salt
2 cups milk
2 tablespoons butter or margarine, melted

1. Preheat the oven to moderate (350°). Grease a 6-cup baking dish.
2. Beat the eggs with the baking powder until foamy in a medium-size bowl. Stir in the cornmeal, sugar, salt, milk and melted butter. Pour into the prepared dish.
3. Bake in the preheated moderate oven (350°) for 40 minutes or until puffed and golden. Serve hot in the place of potatoes or bread.

Storing Bread

Allow quick breads to stand overnight. When completely cool, wrap them in foil or plastic wrap and store at room temperature.

Completely cooled yeast breads, when properly wrapped in freezer paper, heavy foil or heavy plastic bags, can be frozen for up to 6 months. If the bread is to be used for sandwiches, slice it before freezing. The frozen slices will pull apart easily and thaw quickly.

Flaky Biscuits

Bake at 400° for 15 minutes.
Makes 8 biscuits

*Nutrient Value Per Biscuit: 188 calories, 4 g protein, 8 g fat,
25 g carbohydrate, 256 mg sodium, 3 mg cholesterol.*

2 cups unsifted all-purpose flour
2 teaspoons baking powder
1 teaspoon salt
¼ cup vegetable shortening
¾ cup milk

1. Preheat the oven to hot (400°). Sift together the flour, baking powder and salt into a medium-size bowl; cut in the shortening with a pastry blender. Stir in the milk just until blended.
2. Turn the dough out onto a lightly floured pastry cloth or board and knead several times.
3. Roll or pat the dough out to a ½-inch thickness. Cut into 8 rounds with a 2½-inch floured biscuit cutter. Place the biscuits, 1 inch apart, on an ungreased cookie sheet. Reroll any trimmings and cut into additional biscuits.
4. Bake in the preheated hot oven (400°) for 15 minutes or until golden brown.

Biscuit Trivia

In the United States, the word "biscuit" is used to describe a small, soft, unsweetened cake, considered a quick bread, made from baking powder or soda-leavened dough and served as a hot bread. It was in the late 1700's that these little cakes first appeared here in place of traditional yeast breads. They became popular because they were so quick and easy to make.

Our biscuits are not found in other parts of the world. In fact, the word is French in origin for flour-made cakes that were baked twice to dry them out for use on long trips. The English call sweet biscuits, cream biscuits or water biscuits what Americans term cookies or crackers.

To make tender, flaky biscuits, handle the dough as little as possible. If you want biscuits with soft sides, bake them in a small round pan with the sides of the biscuits touching.

Buttermilk Pancakes

Makes about 12 pancakes

Nutrient Value Per Pancake: 109 calories, 3 g protein, 4 g fat, 15 g carbohydrate, 233 mg sodium, 55 mg cholesterol.

¾ **cup** sifted **unbleached all-purpose flour**
¾ **cup** buckwheat or whole-wheat flour
2½ **to 3 tablespoons sugar***
1 **teaspoon baking soda**
½ **teaspoon salt**
2 **eggs, slightly beaten**
1½ **cups buttermilk**
2 **tablespoons butter or margarine, melted**
   Butter or margarine for frying

1. Sift together the unbleached flour, buckwheat or whole-wheat flour, sugar, baking soda and salt in a medium-size bowl. (If using whole-wheat flour, add any wheat grains that remain in the sifter.)
2. Beat together the eggs, buttermilk and melted butter in a second bowl; gradually stir into the dry ingredients just until blended, but not overmixed. Batter should still be slightly lumpy.)
3. Heat a griddle until it is hot enough for a drop of water to sizzle. Grease with the butter.
4. Using a ladle, pour about 2½ tablespoons of the batter onto the griddle for each pancake. When the edges look dry and bubbly, turn and brown the second side. Serve with butter or margarine and syrup, if you wish.

Note: Vary the amount of sugar according to your family's taste.

Variation: These pancakes can be made with all-purpose flour, with or without the addition of ¼ cup of wheat germ. In that case, add an extra ¼ cup of buttermilk and use only 1½ tablespoons of sugar and 1 tablespoon of butter.

Sour Cream Waffles with Brown Sugar Syrup

Makes 16 four-inch waffles.

Nutrient Value Per Waffle: 204 calories, 3 g protein, 5 g fat, 38 g carbohydrate, 210 mg sodium, 60 mg cholesterol.

1¾ **cups** sifted **all-purpose flour**
3 **teaspoons baking powder**
½ **teaspoon baking soda**
½ **teaspoon salt**
3 **eggs**
1 **cup milk**
1 **container (8 ounces) dairy sour cream**
1 **tablespoon grated lemon rind**
   Brown Sugar Syrup (recipe follows)

1. Sift together the flour, baking powder, baking soda and salt onto wax paper.
2. Beat together the eggs, milk, sour cream and lemon rind in a large bowl. Beat in the flour mixture until smooth.
3. For each waffle, pour about 1 cup waffle mixture into the center of a hot waffle iron. Cook following manufacturer's directions. Serve with the Brown Sugar Syrup.

Brown Sugar Syrup: Combine 2 cups firmly packed light brown sugar with 2 cups water in a medium-size saucepan. Bring to boiling. Lower heat and simmer for 20 minutes or just until mixture thickens. Stir in 1 teaspoon maple extract. Cool slightly. Makes 2 cups.

Louisiana Salad (page 86)

Magnificent Openings

T he first course whets appetites and sets the mood for the entire meal. And you'll get off to a delicious start when you choose from our savory dips, spreads and hot and cold dishes. We've put together an assortment that will delight your taste buds!

If you want to create a truly unforgettable meal, prepare one of our flavorful soups. Take our Iced Buttermilk-Lemon Soup (page 81). It's a cool, refreshing beginning that's surprisingly complementary to a rich, hot entrée like Butterflied Lamb (page 147).

Salads are also a welcome addition to any meal, even if it's just a simple assortment of leafy greens. Try perking up your usual combination with one of our zesty additions, like Chili-Lime Dressing (page 88).

So read on—you'll find everything you need for a delicious start to a great meal. Bon appétit!

 Quick

 Make Ahead

 Entertaining

 Low Cost

 Low Calorie

Smoked Salmon and Caviar Cheese Torte (page 72), Della Robbia Fruit Punch (page 278), Norwegian Seafood Dip topped with sardines (page 73), Open-Faced Flatbread Sardine/Cucumber Sandwich (serving idea), Shrimp Roulade (page 75), Chevre and Prosciutto in Phyllo Cups (page 74)

Cherry Tomato-topped Chicken, Spinach and Gazpacho Pâté (page 74), Open-Faced Flatbread Salmon Sandwich (serving idea), Nacho Mushrooms (page 72), Open-Faced Flatbread Red Caviar/ Sieved Hard-Cooked Egg Yolk Sandwich (serving idea), Red and Green Pepper Phyllo Triangles (page 73)

Appetizers

Nacho Mushrooms

Prepare ahead through Step 3, then broil just before serving.

Makes 24 mushrooms.

Nutrient Value Per Mushroom: 100 calories, 4 g protein, 9 g fat, 2 g carbohydrate, 188 mg sodium, 22 mg cholesterol.

24 large mushrooms, for stuffing
½ cup (1 stick) butter, melted
¼ pound pepperoni, thinly sliced
½ pound Monterey Jack cheese with jalapeño peppers, shredded
⅓ cup chopped green onions
1 jar (4 ounces) pimiento, drained and cut into strips

1. Remove the stems from the mushroom caps (reserve the stems for soup).
2. Place the caps, rounded-side up, in a large broiler pan. Brush with the melted butter. Broil 6 inches from the heat for 1 minute. Remove from the broiler. Turn the mushrooms over.
3. Place a pepperoni slice in the bottom of each mushroom. Top with the shredded cheese.
4. Brush with the remaining melted butter. Broil until cheese melts. Garnish with the green onions and pimiento. Serve warm.

Smoked Salmon and Caviar Cheese Torte

A layered cheese dome, perfect for spreading or dipping. Prepare early in the day.

Makes 16 servings.

Nutrient Value Per Serving: 241 calories, 7 g protein, 23 g fat, 1 g carbohydrate, 715 mg sodium, 98 mg cholesterol.

2 packages (8 ounces each) cream cheese, softenened
½ pound (2 sticks) unsalted butter, softened
1 tablespoon grated lemon rind
1 tablespoon lemon juice
½ cup finely chopped fresh dill
¼ pound smoked salmon, finely chopped
½ cup red lumpfish caviar
Sprigs of fresh dill

1. Beat together the cream cheese and butter in a small bowl until light and fluffy. Add the lemon rind and juice. Divide the mixture into thirds; place one-third in a bowl and the other two-thirds in a second bowl. Blend the chopped dill into the one-third until well blended. Blend the chopped salmon into the other two-thirds.
2. Line a 2½-cup bowl with plastic wrap, leaving a 2-inch overhang.
3. Turn the salmon-cheese mixture into the lined bowl; pack firmly. Spread ¼ cup of the lumpfish caviar evenly over the salmon mixture.
4. Carefully spread the dill-cheese mixture over the caviar; pack firmly. Cover the top with the plastic wrap overhang. Refrigerate for 2 to 3 hours, or until firm.
5. To serve, fold back the plastic wrap. Unmold the torte onto a platter. Carefully remove the plastic wrap. Garnish the top of the torte with the remaining caviar and dill sprigs. Serve with snow peas, zucchini rounds and Belgian endive for dipping and Norwegian flatbread for spreading.

Norwegian Seafood Dip

Makes 16 servings.

Nutrient Value Per Serving: 144 calories, 6 g protein, 13 g fat, 232 mg sodium, 43 mg cholesterol.

2 packages (8 ounces each) cream cheese, softened
1 can (6½ ounces) solid white tuna packed in oil*, drained and flaked
1 tablespoon grated lemon rind
2 tablespoons lemon juice
1 medium-size red onion, chopped
1 medium-size tomato, chopped
½ cup sliced, pitted ripe black olives
1 tablespoon drained capers
1 can (3¾ ounces) Norwegian brisling sardines packed in oil, well drained.

1. Beat the softened cheese in a small bowl until light and fluffy. Beat in the tuna, lemon rind and juice. Turn into a 1-quart clear glass soufflé dish.
2. Spread the chopped onion in an even layer over the cheese mixture, then the tomato. Sprinkle the olive slices and capers over the tomato. Arrange the sardines over the top. Garnish with parsley and serve with flatbread, if you wish.

*Note: You may use tuna packed in water, if you wish.

Capers

The flower buds of a wild Mediterranean shrub which are salted and preserved in vinegar. They are used as a condiment or for a seasoning sauce. Capers are sold in small bottles, usually imported from Spain, France or Italy. Refrigerate them once the bottle is opened and use them to add a unique flavor to mayonnaise sauces and seafood or veal dishes.

Red and Green Pepper Phyllo Triangles

Bake at 350° for 30 minutes.
Makes 16 servings (48 triangles).

Nutrient Value Per Triangle: 358 calories, 14 g protein, 23 g fat, 24 g carbohydrate, 351 mg sodium, 65 mg cholesterol.

Red Pepper Purée:
3 large sweet red peppers, halved, seeded and cut into 1-inch strips
1 clove garlic, finely chopped
1 tablespoon olive oil
½ teaspoon crushed red pepper flakes

Green Pepper Purée:
3 large sweet green peppers, halved, seeded and cut into 1-inch strips
1 clove garlic, finely chopped
1 tablespoon oil
1 teaspoon leaf basil, crumbled

Phyllo Triangles:
1 cup (2 sticks) unsalted butter or margarine, melted
1 package (1 pound) phyllo pastry, thawed according to package directions, if frozen
1 cup grated Parmesan cheese
1 container (15 ounces) ricotta cheese
1 pound mozzarella cheese, thinly sliced

1. Prepare Red Pepper Purée: Purée red peppers in a blender or food processor. Sauté with the garlic in oil in a medium-size skillet over moderate heat until the excess liquid has evaporated. Stir in the red pepper flakes. Sauté for 5 minutes. Remove to a bowl.
2. Prepare Green Pepper Purée: Purée the green peppers in a blender or food processor. Sauté with the garlic in oil in a medium-size skillet over medium heat until the excess liquid has evaporated. Stir in the basil. Sauté for 5 minutes. Remove to a second bowl.
3. Prepare Triangles: Brush a 13 x 9 x 2-inch baking pan with melted butter. Unfold the sheets of phyllo. While working, keep the unused phyllo covered with a damp towel. Arrange 2 sheets of phyllo, each brushed with melted butter, in the bottom of the pan. Sprinkle with 1 tablespoon of the Parmesan. Repeat with 6 more buttered sheets of phyllo, layering with the Parmesan. Spread the green pepper purée over the top sheet of phyllo. Top with half of the ricotta and half of the mozzarella. ▶

4. Repeat layering with another 8 buttered sheets of phyllo and Parmesan. Spread the red pepper purée over the top sheet of phyllo. Cover with ricotta and mozzarella layers. Top with the remaining phyllo sheets, buttered, and Parmesan. Generously brush with butter. Cut the top layer of phyllo with a sharp paring knife into 48 triangles.

5. Bake in a preheated moderate oven (350°) for 30 minutes, or until the top is golden brown. Cool slightly.

6. To serve, cut all the way through to the bottom of the pan. Serve warm or at room temperature.

Phyllo

Phyllo is a paper-thin pastry of flour and water used primarily in Greek and Turkish cooking for both sweet and savory dishes. It is available freshly made and sold by weight or in packages in specialty shops, or frozen in pound packages and sold in supermarkets. Sometimes phyllo is called strudel pastry leaves and used to make apple strudel.

Chevre (Goat Cheese) and Prosciutto in Phyllo Cups

Bake at 350° for 20 minutes.
Makes 40 cups.

Nutrient Value Per Cup: 113 calories, 3 g protein, 8 g fat, 8 g carbohydrate, 165 mg sodium, 31 mg cholesterol.

8 ounces phyllo pastry, thawed if frozen
½ cup (1 stick) butter, melted
12 ounces milk-flavored goat cheese, at room temperature
2 eggs
1 cup heavy cream
1 teaspoon leaf thyme, crumbled
½ pound thinly sliced prosciutto
Parsley sprigs

1. Preheat the oven to moderate (350°).
2. Unfold the sheets of phyllo. While working, keep the unused phyllo covered with a damp towel to prevent drying out. Cut the phyllo pastry into 4-inch squares. Use eight 4-inch squares of phyllo for each cup. Brush the squares with melted butter. Place 4 squares into a mini-muffin-pan cup. Place 4 more

squares, each at a 90° angle to each other, in the cup, forming a tulip-shape. Repeat with the remaining squares. (If you have less than 40 muffin-pan cups, bake as many as possible; then repeat.)

3. Combine the cheese, eggs, heavy cream and thyme in a medium-size bowl. Beat until well blended.

4. Reserve 3 slices prosciutto for garnish. Finely chop the remaining prosciutto. Stir the chopped prosciutto into the cheese mixture. Spoon into the phyllo cups.

5. Bake in the preheated moderate oven (350°) for 20 minutes, or until the phyllo is golden brown and the cheese filling is slightly puffed. Remove from the oven. Let stand for 5 minutes. Carefully remove the cups from the pans.

6. Cut any excess fat from the remaining prosciutto. Cut the slices into 3-inch-long, ½-inch-wide strips. Roll each strip into a small roll. Place the roll upright on top of each cup. Garnish with a small sprig of parsley.

Chicken, Spinach and Gazpacho Pâté

A Christmasy-colored cold pâté, cut into bite-size squares and each square festively topped with a cherry tomato half.

Makes 64 squares.

Nutrient Value Per Square: 17 calories, 2 g protein, 0 g fat, 1 g carbohydrate, 50 mg sodium, 5 mg cholesterol.

Spinach layer:
1 envelope unflavored gelatin
¼ cup cold water
2 packages (10 ounces each) frozen chopped spinach, thawed and drained
½ cup chopped green onions
½ teaspoon ground nutmeg

Chicken Layer:
½ cup chopped onion (1 medium-size)
1 cup chopped mushrooms (¼ pound)
1 pound boneless chicken breasts, cut into ½-inch cubes
1 tablespoon butter
2 teaspoons dry sherry
½ teaspoon leaf basil, crumbled
1 envelope unflavored gelatin
¼ cup cold water

Tomato Layer:

1 envelope unflavored gelatin
¼ cup cold water
2 cups tomato juice
½ cup chopped onion (1 medium-size)
1 sweet red pepper, halved, seeded
   and chopped
1 whole canned green chili, seeded
   and chopped
3 cloves garlic, finely chopped
1 teaspoon prepared horseradish
2 tablespoons lime juice
2 tablespoons red wine vinegar
¼ teaspoon salt
¼ teaspoon pepper
1 pint cherry tomatoes, halved

1. Line a 9-inch square pan with aluminum foil.
2. Prepare the Spinach Layer: Sprinkle the gelatin over the cold water in a measuring cup; let stand to soften for 5 minutes. Combine the drained spinach, green onion, and nutmeg in a bowl; mix well. Place the cup with the gelatin over boiling water; stir to dissolve the gelatin. Stir into the spinach mixture until well combined. Spread the mixture evenly in the bottom of the prepared pan. Refrigerate.
3. Prepare the Chicken Layer: Sauté the onion, mushrooms and chicken in the butter in a medium-size skillet just until tender. Add the sherry and basil; cook for 5 minutes. Sprinkle the gelatin over the cold water in a measuring cup; let stand to soften for 5 minutes. Place the cup with the gelatin over boiling water; stir to dissolve the gelatin. Stir into the chicken mixture. Carefully spread the chicken mixture evenly over the spinach layer. Refrigerate until chilled.
4. Prepare the Tomato Layer: Sprinkle the gelatin over the cold water in a measuring cup; let stand to soften, for 5 minutes. Combine the tomato juice, onion, red pepper, green chili, garlic, horseradish, lime juice, vinegar, salt and pepper in a medium-size bowl; mix well. Place the cup with the gelatin over boiling water; stir to dissolve the gelatin. Stir into the tomato mixture until well combined. Carefully pour over the chicken mixture. Chill in the refrigerator until slightly firm.
5. Place 64 cherry tomato halves, cut-side down, in 8 even rows on top of the tomato mixture. Refrigerate until firm, for about 4 hours.
6. To serve, carefully cut into 64 squares, with a cherry tomato half on each square. Gently remove with a small spatula.

Shrimp Roulade

A creamy shrimp and mushroom mixture wrapped in a Swiss cheese-flavored savory cake.

Bake at 400° for 30 minutes.
Makes 16 servings (2 roulades).

Nutrient Value Per Serving: 187 calories, 11 g protein, 13 g fat, 6 g carbohydrate, 266 mg sodium, 135 mg cholesterol.

Roulade:

¼ cup (½ stick) butter
½ cup sifted all-purpose flour
½ teaspoon salt
¼ teaspoon pepper
2 cups milk
¼ cup shredded Swiss cheese (2 ounces)
4 eggs, separated
¼ teaspoon cream of tartar
   Fine dry bread crumbs

Shrimp Filling:

⅓ cup chopped onion
3 tablespoons butter
1 cup finely chopped mushrooms
   (¼ pound)
1 package (10 ounces) frozen chopped
   spinach, thawed and drained
1 cup chopped, shelled and deveined
   cooked shrimp (¾ pound)
1 tablespoon Dijon-style mustard
½ teaspoon dillweed
2 packages (3 ounces each) cream cheese,
   softened
¼ cup dairy sour cream

1. Preheat the oven to hot (400°). Butter two 15 x 10 x 1-inch jelly-roll pans. Line with wax paper; butter and flour the paper.
2. Prepare the Roulade: Melt the ¼ cup of butter in a medium-size saucepan. Stir in the flour, salt and pepper until smooth. Cook, stirring, until golden brown, for about 3 minutes. Slowly stir in the milk. Cook over medium heat, stirring constantly, until thick and bubbly. Stir in the cheese until melted.
3. Beat the egg yolks in a small bowl. Stir a little of the hot cheese mixture into the yolks. Stir back into the saucepan. Cook over very low heat, stirring constantly, until thickened, for about 2 minutes. Do not let boil. Remove from the heat.
4. Beat the egg whites in a small bowl until frothy. Add the cream of tartar. Beat until stiff, but not dry, peaks form. Stir a little of the beaten whites into the cheese mixture. ▶

Gently fold in the remaining whites. Divide evenly between the prepared pans, spreading the batter evenly.

5. Bake in the preheated hot oven (400°) for 30 minutes, or until lightly browned. Invert onto towels sprinkled with the fine dry bread crumbs. Carefully remove the paper.

6. While the roulade is baking, prepare the Filling: Sauté the onion in the 3 tablespoons of butter in a large skillet until golden brown, for 4 minutes. Add the mushrooms; cook until lightly browned, for 5 minutes. Add the spinach and shrimp. Cook, stirring frequently, until the shrimp turns pink, for 2 to 3 minutes. Stir in the mustard, dillweed, cream cheese and the sour cream.

7. Spread half of the Shrimp Filling evenly over each of the roulade cakes. Roll up gently from a long side, jelly-roll fashion. Let cool thoroughly.

8. To serve, cut crosswise into 1-inch-thick slices. Place on the baking sheet. Heat in the preheated slow oven (250°) just until warm. Serve.

Note: To make a day ahead, wrap the assembled roulades tightly in plastic wrap and refrigerate. To serve, slice and reheat in a preheated slow oven (250°).

Hot Crabmeat Dip

This is an easy way to stretch expensive crabmeat—and just a little of this spread goes a long way. Serve with whole-wheat crackers or thin slices of dark bread.

Bake at 350° for 25 minutes.
Makes 2½ cups.

Nutrient Value Per Tablespoon: 28 calories, 1 g protein, 2 g fat, 0 g carbohydrate, 29 mg sodium, 13 mg cholesterol.

- **1 package (8 ounces) cream cheese, softened**
- **2 tablespoons finely chopped onion**
- **1 tablespoon prepared horseradish**
- **2 tablespoons heavy cream**
  Salt and pepper
- **8 ounces fresh or thawed frozen* crabmeat**

1. Preheat the oven to moderate (350°). Butter a 3- to 4-cup baking dish.

2. Combine the cream cheese, onion, horse-radish, heavy cream, and salt and pepper to taste in a medium-size bowl. Stir in the crab-meat. Spoon into the prepared baking dish.

3. Bake in the preheated moderate oven (350°) for 25 minutes, or until hot. Serve with your favorite cracker or bread.

*Note: If using frozen crabmeat, be sure to pat thoroughly dry on paper toweling to avoid any excess moisture in the dip.

Salmon Spread

With a can of salmon on hand, you'll be ready to whip up this spread in minutes.

Makes 10 servings.

Nutrient Value Per Serving: 125 calories, 7 g protein, 9 g fat, 2 g carbohydrate, 270 mg sodium, 17 mg cholesterol.

- **1 can (16 ounces) red salmon, drained and flaked**
- **½ cup finely chopped onion**
- **⅓ cup finely chopped celery**
- **3 tablespoons sweet pickle relish**
- **⅓ cup mayonnaise**

Combine the red salmon, onion, celery and relish in a medium-size bowl. Add the mayonnaise and stir to mix. Use this spread to fill store-bought hors d'oeuvre cups and homemade croustades or as a spread on crackers. Garnish with a pimien-to diamond and pickle relish leaves, if you wish.

Mango Chutney Cream Cheese

Simple and tasty.

Makes 1½ cups (12 servings).

Nutrient Value Per Serving: 94 calories, 2 g protein, 7 g fat, 8 g carbohydrate, 79 mg sodium, 21 mg cholesterol.

- **½ cup Indian mango chutney**
- **1 package (8 ounces) cream cheese, softened**
- **¼ cup chopped green onions**
  Dash ground curry
  Dash ground ginger

Strain the chutney by forcing through a wire-mesh sieve, pushing gently with the back of a wooden spoon; reserve the juice; finely chop the fruit and stir back in to the juice. Beat the cream cheese, chutney, green onions, curry and ginger with a wooden spoon until smooth and spreadable. Use to fill store-bought hors d'oeuvre cups and home-made croustades or spread on crackers. Garnish with additional chopped green onions, if you wish.

Gorgonzola Toast

These tangy, Christmas tree-shaped cheese toasts are guaranteed to whet the appetite.

Bake at 400° for 5 to 8 minutes.
Makes 18 to 24 servings.

Nutrient Value Per Serving: 69 calories, 2 g protein, 4 g fat, 8 g carbohydrate, 152 mg sodium, 8 mg cholesterol.

18 to 24 slices very thin-sliced bread
¼ cup crumbled Gorgonzola cheese OR: blue cheese
¼ cup (½ stick) butter

1. Preheat the oven to hot (400°).
2. Cut each bread slice into a tree shape, using 3- or 4-inch cookie cutter.
3. Melt together the cheese and butter in a small skillet over low heat. Dip each tree shape quickly into the cheese mixture, coating one side only. Place, cheese-side up, on cookie sheet.
4. Bake in preheated hot oven (400°) for 5 to 8 minutes until toasty and golden. Remove the breads to wire racks to cool.

Note: Use trimmings from bread to make bread crumbs for another use.

Artichoke Vinaigrette Appetizer

Makes 4 servings.

Nutrient Value Per Serving: 403 calories, 2 g protein, 41 g fat, 11 g carbohydrate, 614 mg sodium, 0 mg cholesterol.

1 large clove garlic, finely chopped
1 teaspoon salt
6 tablespoons olive oil
6 tablespoons vegetable oil
8 teaspoons fresh lemon juice
¼ teaspoon pepper
4 medium-size artichokes (about 1¾ pounds)

1. Chop the garlic with ¼ teaspoon of the salt. Place in a medium-size screw-top jar. Add the olive oil, vegetable oil, lemon juice, the remaining ¾ teaspoon of salt and pepper to the jar. Shake well to blend.
2. Combine 1 quart of water and ¼ cup of the vinaigrette mixture in a large saucepan. Bring to boiling.

3. Meanwhile, wash the artichokes well under cold water; make sure to clean the dirt from between the leaves. Cut about a ¾-inch piece from the top of each artichoke and with kitchen shears, trim ½-inch from the top of each leaf. Trim the stems even with the bases so the artichokes stand upright.
4. Add the artichokes to the boiling water. Cook for 20 to 35 minutes, or until the center of the base feels just tender when pierced with a fork. Remove the artichokes from the water with a slotted spoon. Drain upside down.
5. When cool enough to handle, gently spread out the center leaves and pull out the inner leaves with your fingers. With a teaspoon, scrape out the fuzzy inner choke at the cavity's bottom. Stand the artichokes upright in a shallow nonmetal dish.
6. Shake the remaining vinaigrette mixture to blend. Pour over the artichokes; cover; refrigerate for at least 2 hours, or until ready to serve. Serve on lettuce-lined plates.

Note: To eat, pull away the leaves, one at a time, with your fingers and, with the front teeth, scrape off succulent tidbit at the base of each leaf. Quarter and eat the remaining thick base or bottom.

Soups

SOUP—CALORIE CRUNCHER

Eating soup takes more time and concentration than most solid foods.
If the soup is nice and hot, you'll be forced to relax and carefully sip each spoonful no matter how ravenous you are. This process allows plenty of time for satiety signals to reach your brain before you've actually eaten very much. The intestinal hormones that tell your brain you are FULL are released faster, due to the fact that liquids empty more quickly from stomach to intestine.
Soup is high on volume.
Once you've completed a big bowl of soup, your stomach is likely to feel just as full and warm as it would after eating an entire meal of more solid (and more fattening) foods. A cup of soup before a meal will naturally diminish the amount of other foods you eat.
Soups tend to be low on calories and saturated fat.
Especially those which are prepared with a low-fat beef or poultry consommé, seafood or vegetable broth. There are exceptions to this rule—but if you look at the following list of tricks for reducing fat consumption, you'll see how soup can fill the bill every time.
● Serving soup as a main course is an easy way to cut down on your consumption of red meat per sitting and still enjoy the taste. Only one-half pound of meat can flavor enough soup to serve the entire family.
● Soup is a delicious way to enjoy eating leaner cuts of meat and poultry. Trim off all visible fat before cooking or skim all excess fat off the top of the soup before serving.
● The amount of fatty cheese or heavy cream called for in soup recipes can easily be reduced or replaced by low-fat dairy alternatives, e.g. skim milk, grated Parmesan cheese or yogurt. Yogurt can be used to replace the cream in soups, if you stir it in after taking the soup off the stove.
● Soups are a tasty way to combine low-fat vegetable proteins, e.g. grains and legumes. To limit the number of meals which contain animal proteins, prepare soups which combine rice, corn or wheat pasta with peas or beans.
Eating soup is likely to help you change your dietary habits for the better—nutrition-wise.
Examination of the results from two large U.S. Governmental studies has shown that people who consume more soup and dairy products tend to eat the least amount of sugary foods and drinks. They tend to consume an average amount of all foods and show the fewest signs of nutrition problems. By slowing down your dietary pace, soup can help you break the tendency to overeat. It will force you to sit down and concentrate on the fact that you're eating.
Soup is easy to prepare.
This is an advantage, diet-wise, because it cuts down on time in the kitchen where the temptation to nibble can get the best of you. If you use commercially prepared products, making soup is an easy as boiling water. If you make your own, you can prepare large quantities at one time and refrigerate or freeze the rest in small quantities—ideal for quick meals or snacks.

Ruby Red Minestrone

A little pasta thickens this shortcut version of an all-time favorite.

Makes 6 servings.

Nutrient Value Per Serving: 83 calories, 4 g protein, 1 g fat, 14 g carbohydrate, 588 mg sodium, 1 mg cholesterol.

> **1** can (16 ounces) Italian-style tomatoes
> **1** can (10½ ounces) condensed beef broth
> **1⅓** cups water
> **1** package (10 ounces) frozen mixed vegetables
> **3** tablespoons small pasta, such as orzo or pastina
> **2** tablespoons grated Parmesan cheese

1. Place the tomatoes with their juice in the container of an electric blender or food processor. Cover; whirl until puréed. Pour into a medium-size saucepan. Add the beef broth, water, frozen vegetables and pasta. Bring to boiling. Lower the heat and simmer, uncovered, for 15 minutes.
2. Ladle into 6 warmed soup bowls. Sprinkle each with 1 teaspoon Parmesan and serve.

Mexican Corn Soup

Makes 6 servings.

Nutrient Value Per Serving: 280 calories, 8 g protein, 13 g fat, 31 g carbohydrate, 938 mg sodium, 32 mg cholesterol.

2 cans (13¾ ounces each) chicken broth
1 package (16 ounces) frozen corn kernels
1 cup mild taco sauce
1 cup dairy sour cream
¾ cup shredded Cheddar cheese

1. Combine the chicken broth, corn and taco sauce in a medium-size saucepan. Bring to boiling. Lower the heat and simmer, uncovered, for 15 minutes.
2. Place the soup mixture in the container of an electric blender or food processor, working in batches if necessary. Cover; whirl until the mixture is smooth. Pour back into the saucepan.
3. Whisk ¼ cup of the hot soup into the sour cream in a small bowl. Stir the sour cream mixture back into the saucepan. Whisk in ½ cup of the Cheddar cheese. Gently heat through; do not boil.
4. Ladle the soup into 6 warmed soup bowls. Garnish with the remaining cheese and serve.

Green Pea and Onion Soup

Makes 4 servings.

Nutrient Value Per Serving: 162 calories, 6 g protein, 7 g fat, 17 g carbohydrate, 739 mg sodium, 20 mg cholesterol.

1 can (10½ ounces) condensed French onion soup
1⅓ cups water
1 package (10 ounces) frozen green peas
½ teaspoon leaf tarragon, crumbled
½ cup light cream or half-and-half
¼ cup sliced green onion

1. Combine the onion soup, water, green peas and tarragon in a medium-size saucepan. Bring to boiling. Lower the heat and simmer, uncovered, for 15 minutes.
2. Place the soup mixture in the container of an electric blender or food processor, working in batches if necessary. Cover; whirl until smooth. Pour back into the saucepan. Stir in the light cream. Gently heat through.
3. Ladle into 4 warmed soup bowls. Garnish with the green onion and serve.

Cream of Broccoli Soup

Makes 6 servings.

Nutrient Value Per Serving: 172 calories, 5 g protein, 12 g fat, 11 g carbohydrate, 872 mg sodium, 37 mg cholesterol.

1 bunch fresh broccoli (about 1½ pounds)
1 medium-size onion, chopped (½ cup)
2 tablespoons butter or margarine
1 large potato, pared and diced (1 cup)
2 cans (13¾ ounces each) chicken broth
½ teaspoon salt
Dash cayenne
1 cup light cream or half-and-half
⅛ teaspoon ground nutmeg

1. Trim the outer leaves and tough ends from the broccoli. Separate the stalks and cut into 2 or 3 shorter lengths. Parboil in boiling salted water in a large saucepan for 5 minutes; drain well.
2. Sauté the onion in the butter in a large saucepan for 5 minutes, until soft but not browned. Add the potato, chicken broth, salt and cayenne. Heat to boiling; lower the heat; simmer for 15 minutes. Add the broccoli, reserving a few flowerets for garnish; simmer for 5 minutes longer, or until the vegetables are tender.
3. Pour the mixture, half at a time, into the container of an electric blender; cover; whirl until smooth. Return the mixture to the saucepan; add the cream and nutmeg; bring to boiling (if the soup is too thick, add more cream or milk). Taste and add more salt, if needed. Garnish with the reserved flowerets.

Bean and Escarole Soup

Makes 6 servings.

Nutrient Value Per Serving: 155 calories, 10 g protein, 1 g fat, 25 g carbohydrate, 878 mg sodium, 0 mg cholesterol.

2 can (19 ounces each) cannellini beans, drained
1 can (13¾ ounces) chicken broth
½ cup water
¼ teaspoon pepper
2 cups finely shredded escarole
2 tablespoons fresh lemon juice
Garnish (optional):
Lemon slices, quartered
Sweet red pepper strips

1. Purée the beans with the chicken broth, working in batches if necessary, in a blender or food processor until smooth. Pour into a medium-size saucepan. Add the water and pepper. Bring to boiling over medium heat. Cook for 2 to 3 minutes, stirring occasionally.

2. Remove from the heat. Stir in the escarole and lemon juice. Garnish with the lemon slices and pepper strips, if you wish.

Watercress Cream Soup

Makes 6 servings.

Nutrient Value Per Serving: 98 calories, 9 g protein, .47 g fat, 14 g carbohydrate, 868 mg sodium, 5 mg cholesterol.

2 bunches watercress
2 tablespoons flour
6 cups skim milk
2 teaspoons instant minced onion
2 teaspoons salt

1. Wash the watercress and dry on paper toweling. Set aside 6 sprigs for garnish; chop the remaining stems and leaves fine. (You should have about 3 cups.)

2. Combine the flour and about ¼ cup of the milk until smooth in a large saucepan; slowly stir in the remaining milk, onion and salt. Cook, stirring constantly, until the mixture thickens slightly and bubbles for 3 minutes. Remove from the heat. Stir in the chopped watercress.

3. Ladle the soup into heated soup plates; float a watercress sprig on each serving. Serve hot.

Watercress

A perennial aquatic plant, watercress is cultivated in large ponds and grows wild in springs or along streams. A member of the mustard family, watercress has succulent, peppery-tasting leaves. Watercress is eaten raw in salads and sandwiches, or it can be cooked in soups. It is a good source of vitamins A and C.

Believed to be native to the eastern Mediterranean region, watercress is available all year-round, sold in small bunches. Purchase 1 bunch for 3 or 4 salad servings.

Untie each bunch and discard any wilted or yellowing leaves. Wash in ice water. Drain well and dry with paper toweling. Refrigerate wrapped in plastic and use within a few days.

Leek and Potato Soup

Makes 6 servings.

Nutrient Value Per Serving: 82 calories, 2 g protein, 2 g fat, 15 g carbohydrate, 588 mg sodium, 3 mg cholesterol.

1 package (2.4 ounces) dehydrated leek soup mix
3½ cups water
¼ cup dry white wine
¼ cup milk
1 can (16 ounces) whole new potatoes, drained and quartered
⅛ teaspoon pepper
Pinch leaf thyme

Combine all the ingredients in a medium-size saucepan. Bring to boiling. Lower the heat and simmer, uncovered, for 15 minutes. Ladle into 6 warmed soup bowls and serve.

Chilled Zucchini Soup

Makes 8 servings.

Nutrient Value Per Serving: 105 calories, 3 g protein, 7 g fat, 6 g carbohydrate, 778 mg sodium, 24 mg cholesterol.

1 cup chopped green onions
1 cup sliced celery
2 tablespoons butter or margarine
6 medium-size zucchini, washed and sliced (2 pounds)
2 cans (13¾ ounces each) chicken broth
1 teaspoon salt
¼ teaspoon pepper
¼ teaspoon leaf basil, crumbled
¼ teaspoon leaf oregano, crumbled
1 cup light cream or half-and-half

1. Sauté the onions and celery in the butter until soft in a large saucepan.

2. Add the zucchini, chicken broth, salt, pepper, basil and oregano; cover. Cook over medium heat for 10 minutes, or just until tender. Cool slightly.

3. Pour the soup, part at a time, into the container of an electric blender; cover. Whirl until smooth.

4. Pour into a large bowl. Stir in the cream. Cover; chill for several hours.

5. Pour into a chilled serving bowl. Garnish with seasoned croutons.

Iced Buttermilk-Lemon Soup

A quick, cool soup you can put together in 10 minutes, then just chill until dinner.

Makes 6 servings.

Nutrient Value Per Serving: 133 calories, 7 g protein, 3 g fat, 19 g carbohydrate, 196 mg sodium, 98 mg cholesterol.

  2 eggs
  5 tablespoons sugar
  2 tablespoons lemon juice
  2 teaspoons grated lemon rind
  1 quart buttermilk
    Whipped cream (optional)
    Wheat germ (optional)

1. Beat the eggs and sugar in a bowl with an electric mixer at high speed until light and fluffy, for about 5 minutes. Blend in the lemon juice and rind. Gradually beat in the buttermilk with the mixer at low speed.

2. Chill for several hours. Serve in chilled soup bowls; garnish with a dollop of whipped cream and a sprinkling of wheat germ, if you wish.

Gazpacho

Makes 4 servings (about 5 cups).

Nutrient Value Per Serving: 91 calories, 3 g protein, 2 g fat, carbohydrate (not available), 356 mg sodium, 8 mg cholesterol.

  2 medium-size cucumbers (about ¾ pound), peeled and cut into chunks
  1 clove garlic
  ¼ teaspoon pepper
  1 can (18 ounces) tomato juice, chilled
  ⅔ cup dry red wine
  ¼ cup crumbled feta cheese
    Chopped parsley

1. Combine the cucumber, garlic, pepper and ½ cup of the tomato juice in the container of an electric blender or food processor. Cover; whirl until it becomes a smooth purée.

2. Pour into a 1½-quart bowl. Stir in the remaining tomato juice and wine. Top with the feta and parsley.

Cold Cantaloupe Soup

A chilly fruit combination to refresh the palate.

Makes 4 servings.

Nutrient Value Per Serving: 126 calories, 2 g protein, .43 g fat, 30 g carbohydrate, 13 mg sodium, .00 mg cholesterol.

  1 ripe cantaloupe (about 2 pounds)
  3 cups orange juice
  ½ teaspoon ground cinnamon
  2 tablespoons lime juice
    Fresh mint sprigs

1. Pare, seed and cut the melon into chunks. Place in the container of an electric blender or food processor with 1 cup of the orange juice; whirl until puréed.

2. Add the remaining orange juice, cinnamon and lime juice; whirl for 30 seconds.

3. Refrigerate thoroughly before serving. Just before serving, pour into bowls. Garnish with the fresh mint.

Buying and Storing Cantaloupe

Choosing a ripe cantaloupe is no easy task. A ripe melon will have a distinct aroma and be somewhat springy when pressed lightly between your hands. Shaking the melon to hear the seeds slosh is not a good test for ripeness. Look for heavily netted skin and a smooth sunken scar at the stem end. Cantaloupe is in season from May to November, but can be found in some cities year-round. Plan to store cantaloupe for 2 to 3 days at room temperature before serving. This way the flesh will soften and be juicier. Refrigerate the melon when ripe.

  Plan on ¼ to ½ cantaloupe per serving. Half a 5-inch cantaloupe is an excellent source of vitamins A and C, with only 60 calories.

Salads

A Gallery of Salad Greens
From crunchy iceberg to peppery cress, here are the tossings of superb salads. For contrast, toss two together. Better yet, three.

Chicory (or Curly Endive) Sprawling, frilly, green head, sharp flavor, medium-crisp. Season: Year-round.

Sorrel Also known as **Dock.** Bright green, tongue-shaped leaves, pleasantly sour in flavor. Season: Year-round.

Bibb Lettuce Also know as **Limestone Lettuce.** The tiny dark-green heads have buttery leaves. Season: Year-round.

Belgian Endive Small, chunky, ivory-hued heads with mellow to bitter flavor. Softly crisp, but not crunchy. Season: Fall to spring.

Watercress Has peppery, medium-crisp, medium-green leaves branching from slender stalks. Season: Year-round.

Romaine Also know as **Cos Lettuce.** Cylindrical, medium-green head with crisp, delicate leaves. Season: Year-round.

Iceberg Lettuce Compact, crisp head with pale- to medium-green leaves. Season: Year-round.

Chinese Cabbage Also called **Celery Cabbage.** Has tight, long, pale-green to ivory head. Delicate. Season: Year-round.

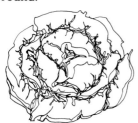

Boston Lettuce Also known as **Butterhead.** Soft, loose head; tender, delicate leaves ranging from yellow to green. Season: Year-round.

Field Salad Also known as **Lamb's Quarter.** Dark-green, small, spoonlike leaves with radish-sharp flavor. Season: Fall, winter.

Leaf Lettuce Also know as **Garden Lettuce.** Has sprawling, ruffled leaves; pale green and delicate. Season: March to July.

Escarole A cross between leaf lettuce and chicory. Curly green leaves, medium-crisp, mildly bitter flavor. Season: Year-round.

Salad of Watercress, Cherry Tomatoes and Boston Lettuce

Makes 8 servings.

Nutrient Value Per Serving: 72 calories, 1 g protein, 7 g fat, 2 g carbohydrate, 48 mg sodium, 0 mg cholesterol.

Basil Dressing:
- ¼ cup vegetable oil
- 3 tablespoons red wine vinegar
- 1 tablespoon water
- 1 teaspoon leaf basil, crumbled
- ⅛ teaspoon salt
- ⅛ teaspoon pepper

- 1 bunch watercress
- 1 large head Boston lettuce
- 1 pint cherry tomatoes

1. Prepare the Basil Dressing: Combine the oil, vinegar, water, basil, salt and pepper in a jar with a tight-fitting lid. Cover; shake to mix.
2. Wash and trim the watercress; wash the lettuce and tear into bite-size pieces; blot dry with paper toweling. Wash the tomatoes. Arrange the lettuce in a salad bowl, with the watercress and tomatoes over the top.
3. To serve, shake the dressing in the jar and pour over the salad; toss to mix.

Salad of Radish, Cucumber and Romaine

Makes 8 servings.

Nutrient Value Per Serving: 70 calories, 2 g protein, 6 g fat, 3 g carbohydrate, 54 mg sodium, 34 mg cholesterol.

Mustard Dressing:
- 1 egg yolk
- 2 tablespoons red wine vinegar
- 1 tablespoon water
- ½ teaspoon Dijon-style mustard
- ⅛ teaspoon salt
- ⅛ teaspoon pepper
- 3 tablespoons vegetable oil
- 1 head romaine lettuce
- 1 large cucumber, pared, halved lengthwise, seeded and sliced crosswise (about 2 cups)
- 8 red radishes, sliced

1. Prepare the Mustard Dressing: Combine the egg yolk, vinegar, water, mustard, salt and pepper in the container of an electric blender

or food processor. Cover; whirl until smooth, for about 5 seconds. With the motor running on low speed, gradually add the oil in a fine stream. Reserve.
2. Wash the lettuce and blot dry with paper toweling. Tear into bite-size pieces. Arrange in a large salad bowl. Add the cucumber and radishes.
3. Pour the dressing over the salad; toss; serve.

Storing Tomatoes

Never, ever refrigerate tomatoes. Cold ruins their delicate flavor. Store in a dark place at a temperature between 50° to 70° F., if possible, for no more than a week.

Special Spinach-Mushroom Salad

Sprinkle the cut mushrooms with lemon juice. Prepare the spinach in advance, then add the mushrooms and dressing at the last minute.

Makes 6 servings.

Nutrient Value Per Serving: 134 calories, 3 g protein, 12 g fat, 5 g carbohydrate, 209 mg sodium, 0 mg cholesterol.

- 1 to 1¼ pounds fresh spinach, washed and stems removed
- ½ pound large mushrooms, sliced
- ½ cup finely chopped green onions
- 1 small clove garlic, crushed
- ¼ teaspoon coarse salt
- 2 teaspoons Dijon-style mustard
- 1 tablespoon lemon juice (½ lemon)
- 2 tablespoons tomato juice
- ⅓ cup olive oil
  Pinch leaf marjoram

1. Pat the spinach dry with paper toweling. Tear into bite-size pieces, if you wish. Place in a large bowl with the mushrooms and onions.
2. Mash the garlic with the salt in a small bowl with the back of a spoon to make a smooth paste. Gradually whisk in the mustard, lemon juice, tomato juice, oil and marjoram. Pour over the salad; toss well.

Pear and Apple Slaw

Pear and Apple Slaw

Two of winter's best fruits team with shredded cabbage and a tangy orange dressing.

Makes 6 servings.

Nutrient Value Per Serving: 321 calories, 3 g protein, 21 g fat, 34 g carbohydrate, 115 mg sodium, 11 mg cholesterol.

- **2 ripe pears**
- **2 large apples**
- **½ cup mayonnaise or salad dressing**
- **⅓ cup orange juice**
- **4 cups shredded cabbage**
- **½ cup chopped walnuts**
- **½ cup raisins**

1. Quarter and core the pears; dice and place in a small bowl. Peel, quarter, and core the apples; dice and place in a second small bowl.
2. Combine the mayonnaise or salad dressing and orange juice in a cup. Drizzle a few tablespoons of the dressing over each bowl of fruit and toss to coat well. Cover each bowl with plastic wrap and refrigerate for at least 1 hour.
3. When ready to serve, layer the shredded cabbage in the bottom of a salad bowl; toss the walnuts with the apples. Spoon the apple-nut mixture into the center of the bowl and spoon the pears around the edges. Top with the raisins and serve remaining orange dressing to pour over and toss well. Serve on chilled glass serving plates.

Onion Salad

Onions and cucumber are marinated with the salad dressing, then tossed with the salad greens at serving time.

Makes 12 servings.

Nutrient Value Per Serving: 167 calories, 2 g protein, 14 g fat, 11 g carbohydrate, 147 mg sodium, .00 mg cholesterol.

- **4 large red onions, thinly sliced**
- **2 large cucumbers, seeded and thinly sliced**
- **2 large green peppers, halved, seeded and cut in slivers**
- **1 can jalapeño peppers, seeded and cubed**
- **6 radishes, thinly sliced**
  Juice and grated rind of 1 lemon
- **½ cup red wine vinegar**
- **1½ tablespoons sugar**
- **¾ cup olive or vegetable oil**
- **1 firm head lettuce, shredded**

1. Combine the onions, cucumbers, green and jalapeño peppers, sliced radishes and lemon juice and rind in a large bowl. Toss well.
2. Sprinkle with the vinegar, sugar and oil. Mix again. Cover and refrigerate until ready to serve.
3. Serve the chilled mixture heaped on the shredded lettuce in a salad bowl. Toss gently just before serving.

Slicing Tomatoes

Slice raw tomatoes vertically so the inner pulp holds its shape for salads.

Mexican Avocado Salad

Cayenne and hot chili pepper turn mild avocado into a fruit with character.

Makes 6 servings.

Nutrient Value Per Serving: 208 calories, 3 g protein, 18 g fat, 12 g carbohydrate, 156 mg sodium, 4 mg cholesterol.

- **1 small onion, chopped (¼ cup)**
- **1 green chili pepper, seeded and chopped**
- **1 clove garlic, minced**
- **3 tablespoons mayonnaise or salad dressing**
- **3 tablespoons lemon juice**

▶

1 teaspoon Worcestershire sauce
¼ teaspoon salt
Dash cayenne
2 large ripe avocados
2 medium-size tomatoes sliced
Shredded iceberg lettuce

1. Combine the onion, chili pepper, garlic, mayonnaise or salad dressing, lemon juice, Worcestershire sauce, salt and cayenne in a small bowl. Cover tightly and refrigerate.
2. When ready to serve, quarter the avocados; pit, peel and slice; arrange with the tomato and lettuce in a salad bowl. Pour the dressing over; toss to coat.

Worcestershire Sauce

A commercially prepared sauce used as a table condiment or recipe ingredient. Worcestershire sauce is an aged blend of soy, vinegar, tamarind, molasses, sugar, anchovies, garlic, shallots and a number of other spices and flavorings. Based on an Indian recipe, it was originally created by a shop in Worcester, England, belonging to Lea and Perrins.

Breadstick Salad

Add the breadsticks just before serving, so they won't lose their crispness.

Makes 8 servings.

Nutrient Value Per Serving: 214 calories, 3 g protein, 20 g fat, 6 g carbohydrate, 207 mg sodium, .56 mg cholesterol.

1 large head romaine lettuce
1 small head radicchio lettuce (optional)
1 bunch watercress
⅔ cup olive or vegetable oil
⅓ cup red wine vinegar
1 teaspoon mixed Italian herbs, crumbled
2 cloves garlic, halved
   Salt and pepper
4 sesame breadsticks, broken up
1 tablespoon grated Parmesan cheese
16 oil-cured black olives

1. Trim the romaine and radicchio lettuces; break into bite-size pieces. Trim the coarse stems from the watercress; cut the sprigs in half. Wash and dry the lettuce and watercress

well; place in paper towels, then in a plastic bag. Refrigerate.
2. Combine the oil, vinegar, Italian herbs, garlic and salt and pepper to taste in a jar with a tight fitting lid. Let stand for several hours. Always shake just before using.
3. Arrange the greens in a salad bowl. Remove the garlic from the dressing; pour the dressing over the greens; top with the breadsticks, Parmesan and olives; toss.

Louisiana Salad

Yellow peppers from Holland add to this colorful salad.

Makes 6 servings.

Nutrient Value Per Serving: 189 calories, 2 g protein, 18 g fat, 6 g carbohydrate, 101 mg sodium, 0 mg cholesterol.

1 small green pepper
1 small red pepper
1 small yellow pepper
¼ pound Chinese snow peas OR:
   1 package (6 ounces) frozen snow peas, thawed
1 large head Boston lettuce
1 head Bibb lettuce
   Chive-Onion Dressing (recipe, page 89)

1. Halve and seed the green, red and yellow peppers. Cut into julienne slices. Trim the snow peas.
2. Wash and dry the Boston and Bibb lettuces. Break the leaves into bite-size pieces; place in a medium-size salad bowl. Scatter the pepper slices and snow peas over the lettuce. Cover and refrigerate.
3. When ready to serve, pour Chive-Onion Dressing over salad; toss.

Lettuce

Although lettuce is available all year long, summer is the prime time to enjoy light, fresh, cool salads. Include a variety of lettuces for intersting texture and flavors. The most common are iceberg, butterhead, romaine, bibb and leaf.

To crispen lettuce, remove all broken, decayed or wilted leaves. Soak leaf lettuce in *warm, not* cold water (70° to 90° F.). The warm water helps to open the pores, allowing more water to be absorbed.

Iceberg lettuce should not be fully immersed. Place iceberg lettuce core down, after trimming, in a tray or sink in about two inches of warm water to remove sand.

All excess water should be drained off and the lettuce placed in a clean plastic bag or container with small holes for drainage. Do not pack too tightly so that the cool air can circulate. Refrigerate a minimum of six hours before using. This allows pores to close, trapping the moisture gained in soaking for added crispness.

Spinach & Citrus Salad

Grapefruit and oranges combine beautifully with tangy spinach leaves.

Makes 8 servings.

Nutrient Value Per Serving: 108 calories, 3 g protein, .40 g fat, 26 g carbohydrate, 336 mg sodium, .00 mg cholesterol.

- 3 **small grapefruit**
- 3 **eating oranges**
- 1 **medium onion, sliced**
- 1 **medium cucumber, scored and thinly sliced**
- 1 **can (6 ounces) water chestnuts, drained and thinly sliced**
- ½ **cup wine vinegar**
- ¼ **cup sugar**
- 1 **tablespoon soy sauce**
- ½ **teaspoon salt**
- 1 **package (10 ounces) fresh spinach, washed thoroughly and dried**

1. Pare and section the grapefruit and oranges over a small bowl to catch all the juice, placing the sections in a large bowl. Separate the onion into rings and add with the cucumber and water chestnuts to the fruit.
2. Add the vinegar, sugar, soy sauce and salt to the fruit juices in a small bowl; stir until the sugar dissolves; refrigerate.

3. Break the spinach into bite-size pieces in a large salad bowl. Spoon the fruits over the spinach. Cover with plastic wrap; refrigerate for at least 1 hour.

Cook's Tip: You can substitute 4 ripe pears, quartered, cored and sliced for the grapefruit and oranges and Boston lettuce for the spinach.

Water Chestnut

A crunchy, white vegetable ingredient in Chinese cooking, the water chestnut is a tuber, or corm, of a tropical plant. The sedge or marsh plant produces the corms in the mud several inches under water. A freshwater chestnut has a chestnut brown skin with a disk-like shape that tapers to a point at one of its flat sides. It's about 1½ inches in diameter. When peeled with a knife, it can be eaten raw or cooked. It has a crisp, white flesh with a starchy sweet taste. When cooked, freshwater chestnuts lose their starchy taste but still remain sweet and crunchy. Commercially canned water chestnuts have lost all of their flavor but have retained their crispness.

Freshwater chestnuts are available in the Chinese markets of major cities from July to September. Store them in a brown bag or unsealed plastic bag. They will keep for several weeks in the refrigerator.

Water chestnuts contain calcium, iron and potassium; 3½ ounces of raw water chestnuts contain 79 calories.

Gazpacho Salad

Inspired by the classic cold soup of Spain, tomatoes and cucumber are flavored with olive oil and garlic.

Makes 6 servings.

Nutrient Value Per Serving: 140 calories, 1 g protein, 12 g fat, 8 g carbohydrate, 189 mg sodium, .00 mg cholesterol.

2   large tomatoes
2   large cucumbers
1   large sweet onion, coarsely chopped
⅓   cup olive or vegetable oil
⅓   cup cider vinegar
1   clove garlic, crushed
1   teaspoon leaf thyme, crumbled
½   teaspoon salt

1. Halve and core the tomatoes; cut into small pieces and place in a medium-size glass or ceramic bowl.
2. Score the cucumbers with a 4-tined fork and cut into small pieces; add the cucumbers and chopped onion to the tomatoes and toss well.
3. Combine the oil, vinegar, garlic, thyme and salt in jar with tight fitting lid. Shake well to blend. Pour over the vegetables and toss well. Cover with plastic wrap and let stand at room temperature for 1 hour to blend flavors.

Chili-Lime Dressing

Makes 1 cup.

Nutrient Value Per Tablespoon: 61 calories, .03 g protein, 7 g fat, .55 g carbohydrate, 140 mg sodium, .00 mg cholesterol.

½   cup olive or vegetable oil
⅓   cup lime juice
2   tablespoons cider vinegar
1   teaspoon salt
½   to 2 teaspoons chili powder
**   Liquid red-pepper seasoning**

Combine the oil, lime juice, cider vinegar, salt, chili powder and liquid red-pepper seasoning to taste in a jar with a tight-fitting lid. Shake well to blend. Let stand for several hours. Always shake just before using.

New Salad Bar Ideas

For party pizzazz, how about an ethnic salad bar? You can develop an Italian theme around an antipasto salad, with salami strips, marinated artichokes, cheese strips, marinated beans, fresh or pickled mushrooms, sliced zucchini, prepared eggplant and pepperoni. Or try an Oriental salad with water chestnuts, bean sprouts, sliced celery, cold cooked rice, pineapple, green pepper, chuntney and chicken strips. A Tex-Mex taco salad can be assembled with corn chips, chilies, hot taco-flavored ground beef, chopped tomato, onion, sour cream and shredded lettuce.

Basic Vinaigrette Dressing

Two parts of oil to one part of vinegar or citrus juice make a simple, standard vinaigrette—a light salad dressing and marinade. Add your favorite fresh herbs, a clove of garlic or a touch of honey, depending on the salad you're tossing with the dressing.

Experiment with the many new oils and vinegars now available, such as the different virgin olive oils, walnut oil, sesame oil, fruit and herb vinegars.

Fruit or Herb Vinegars

Fruit Vinegar: Heat 1 quart of good quality white wine vinegar slightly and pour over one cup of your favorite fresh fruit: strawberries, raspberries, diced peaches, blueberries, blackberries, lemon peel, orange peel, etc. Let stand, covered, for two weeks and decant into hot sterilized bottles; cover. Add additional fruit to the bottles as garnish, if you wish.

Herb Vinegar: Heat good-quality white wine vinegar slightly and pour into individual jars filled with several sprigs of your favorite fresh herb (or combination of herbs): choose from tarragon, basil, dill, chive, garlic, oregano, mint, rosemary, thyme.

Most Common Types of Vinegars

Wine—When wine is stored exposed to air and to the action of microorganisms over a period of time, it turns sour. Red wine vinegar is made from dark or red grapes, while white wine vinegar is made from white grapes or red grapes with the skins removed.
Cider—Made from fermented apple juice or hard cider.
Distilled white—Made from diluted distilled ethyl alcohol. It is inexpensive to produce this crystal-clear vinegar, which adds no color to a food when used, but it has a very sharp taste. It is best used as a preservative in pickels, catsup, relishes and spiced fruits.
Malt—Made from barley, this vinegar is a deep russet color and has a pungent flavor. It's the traditional vinegar for fish and chips but can also be used to season vegetables and seafood salads. It can be used instead of lemon juice in many dishes including sauces for fish.
Tarragon-flavored—A white wine or cider vinegar heated to the boiling point and poured over sprigs of tarragon.
Oriental vinegars—The Chinese white rice vinegar is used to make pickles. Japanese white rice vinegar is sweeter and used for sushi and vegetables. White rice vinegar is similar to distilled vinegar but is not as pungent. Chinese red vinegar is used for sweet and sour sauces. Black vinegar is fermented from black rice.
European vinegars—Raspberry white wine vinegar is made with raspberry juice and honey added to the basic vinegar. Other fruit-flavored vinegars include blueberry, strawberry, black currant and cherry. Parsley and peppercorn red wine vinegar, garlic or onion vinegar are other flavored vinegars which are marketed. The Italian balsamic vinegar is a sweet specialty vinegar.

Yogurt-Mushroom Dressing

Makes 2 cups.

Nutrient Value Per Tablespoon: 5 calories, .42 g protein, .12 g fat, .70 g carbohydrate, 49 mg sodium, .42 mg cholesterol.

1 **container (8 ounces) plain yogurt**
1 **cup sliced mushrooms**
2 **tablespoons lemon juice**
1 **teaspoon seasoned salt**
¼ **teaspoon lemon pepper**

Combine the yogurt and mushrooms in a small

bowl; stir in the lemon juice, seasoned salt and lemon pepper. Cover with plastic wrap and refrigerate to blend the flavors. Garnish with fresh basil just before serving, if you wish.

Chive-Onion Dressing

Makes about ¾ cup.

Nutrient Value Per Tablespoon: 81 calories, .01 g protein, 9 g fat, .25 g carbohydrate, 46 mg sodium, .00 mg cholesterol.

½ **cup olive or vegetable oil**
¼ **cup red wine vinegar**
1 **tablespoon finely chopped red onion**
2 **teaspoons snipped chives**
¼ **teaspoon salt**
   Dash freshly ground pepper

Combine the oil, vinegar, onion, chives, salt and pepper in a jar with a tight-fitting lid. Shake well to blend. Let stand for several hours. Always shake just before using.

Pineapple-Lemon-Mint Dressing

Makes 1 cup.

Nutrient Value Per Tablespoon: 93 calories, .03 g protein, 10 g fat, .65 g carbohydrate, 103 mg sodium, .00 mg cholesterol.

¾ **cup vegetable or salad oil**
¼ **cup unsweetened pineapple juice**
1 **teaspoon grated lemon rind**
2 **tablespoons lemon juice**
1 **teaspoon leaf mint, crumbled**
¾ **teaspoon salt**
½ **teaspoon dry mustard**

Combine the oil, pineapple juice, lemon rind, lemon juice, mint, salt and dry mustard in a large jar with a tight-fitting lid. Shake well to blend. Let stand for several hours. Always shake just beore using.

Dry Mustard

Dry mustard is blended from a number of flavorful varieties of mustard seeds and can be hot or mild.

Rolled Flank Steak (page 93), Parslied New Potatoes (page 194)

Main Courses

The key ingredient of any dinner is, of course, the entrée. Whether it's prepared from meat, fish or vegetables, nothing makes a successful meal like a hearty and delicious main dish.

In this chapter, you'll find beef, veal, pork and lamb recipes that use all kinds of cooking techniques; roasting, grilling, broiling, braising.There are quick and easy family favorites, such as Spicy Ground Beef and Kidney Bean Sauté (page 94), as well as elegant gourmet specialties, like Lemon Roasted Cornish Hens (page 124). Try any one of these recipes the next time you entertain.

Our poultry dishes are always popular. Not only are chicken, turkey and duck delicious, they're very versatile and economical, too. Add an international flair to your menu with Sweet and Sour Chicken (page 119) or Spanish-Style Chicken (page 112).

You're sure to find favorites among our fish and shellfish recipes, especially if you're pressed for time. Preparing dishes like Marjoram Poached Halibut (page 138) is so fast and easy, you'll want to add many of these recipes to your culinary repertoire.

Who can resist a good barbecue? Our barbecue section offers some tantalizing combinations for your grill. And we've included plenty of tips and hints to guarantee success at your next outdoor cookout.

Now that you know about the variety of entrées you can make, it's time for you to pick your next main course. But beware! You may have a tough time choosing.

 Quick

 Make Ahead

 Entertaining

 Low Cost

Low Calorie

Beef & Veal

Choosing Meats

Cost: The most accurate way to determine meat cost is to base your calculations on price per serving, rather than price per pound. Cuts which contain a large amount of bone and fat may not be as economical as higher-priced cuts which contain less waste.

Do not confuse the number of servings with the number of people you can serve. A hearty eater can consume 3 servings at a meal!

To find the cost per serving, divide the price per pound by the number of servings per pound the cut will provide. For example, if a roast costs $1.79 a pound and that cut gives you 2½ servings a pound, your cost per serving would be 71¢.

Cut: Tender cuts come from muscles which are not used in movement and which have the least connective tissue. These muscles are found along the back of the animal and are called rib, loin or sirloin. The remaining muscles are used in movement and are less tender.

Many stores use a standardized meat-labeling system on their prepackaged meats. The label tells you the kind of meat (beef, pork, lamb, etc.), the primal or wholesale cut (chuck, rib, loin, round, etc.) which is where the cut comes from on the animal, and the retail cut (blade, arm, short rib, etc.) which tells you from what part of the primal cut the meat comes.

Ground beef, or hamburger, contains not less than 70% lean. Use it for burgers, chili, sloppy joes and casseroles. Lean ground beef, or ground chuck, has not less than 77% lean. Use it for meatloaf, meatballs and steaks. Extra-lean ground beef, or ground round or sirloin, has not less than 85% lean. Use it as you would ground chuck, or when you're watching calorie and fat consumption.

Meat Selection Tips

• The color of meat is an important indication of tenderness. For example, beef can vary from dark pink to dark red. The lighter the color, the younger the animal and more tender the meat.
• Watch out for liquid in a package. The drier the package, the fresher tasting the meat. The presence of liquid also indicates that the meat may have been frozen or is of a lower grade.

DRY-HEAT COOKING METHODS FOR TENDER CUTS

To Panbroil: For small, tender pieces cut 1 inch thick or less. Place steak or patty in a heavy frying pan. Don't add fat or water and do not cover the pan. Cook slowly, turning often; pour off any fat as it collects. Brown or cook to the desired degree; season and serve.

To Panfry: For very thin, tender cuts or cuts made tender by pounding or cubing. They may be dusted with flour or crumbs. Heat a small amount of fat in a frying pan. Add meat and brown on both sides over high heat, turning occasionally. Stir-frying is a form of panfrying used in Oriental-style cooking. A wok, large pan or electric skillet can be used. Ingredients must be cut into uniform sizes before cooking. Sautéing is the French term for panfrying.

To Broil: For tender steaks or patties at least 1 inch thick. Place the meat on a broiler rack over a pan. Broil the meat, which is 1 inch thick, 2 to 3 inches from the preheated heat source. Broil the thicker cuts 3 to 5 inches from the heat. Turn the meat with tongs rather than a fork as a fork will pierce the meat, releasing the juices. A charcoal, electric or gas grill can be used for broiling.

To Roast: For large, tender roasts. Season with salt, pepper or herbs. Place meat, fat-side up, on a rack in an open, shallow pan. The fat on top bastes the meat and the rack holds it out of the drippings. Insert a meat thermometer in the center of the largest muscle; do not let it touch bone or rest in fat. Do not add water or cover the meat. Roast in a slow oven (300° to 325° F.). When the thermometer reads 5° F. below the desired degree of doneness, remove the roast from the oven and let stand for 15 minutes for easier carving. Rotisserie cooking is a form of roasting. Use large, uniformly shaped cuts. Insert the rotisserie rod lengthwise through the center of the roast; fasten securely. Place a drip pan under the turning meat to prevent flare-ups.

To Microwave: For tender roasts that are compact and uniform in shape. Boneless roasts are ideal. Place the roast on a rack and cover with wax paper. Use a low power setting for a longer cooking time to get the most uniform doneness. If a roast is irregular in shape and a portion is cooking too fast, cover that piece with small strips of foil to retard cooking. To assure even cooking, turn roast or rotate the dish at intervals during the cooking time. To enhance the appearance of meat cooked by microwave, try brushing the surface with soy sauce, Worchestershire or a browning sauce. Or coat the surface with bread crumbs or glaze. You can also prebrown the roast in a frying pan or use the browning dish of the microwave. The cooking time will vary, depending on the shape and size of the meat.

MOIST-HEAT COOKING METHODS FOR LESS-TENDER CUTS

To Braise: Brown beef, which may be coated with flour, in its own rendered fat or in a small amount of added fat in a heavy pan. Brown on all sides slowly; add onion, herbs and about ¼ to ½ cup liquid such as water, broth, vegetable juice or a marinade. Cover and cook over low heat until tender. Braising can be done on top of the range or in a slow oven (300° to 325° F.).

To Cook in Liquid: Coat meat with flour and brown on all sides in its own fat or added fat in a heavy pan. Or, omit the step above; cover the meat with liquid; cover the pan. Cook over low heat until meat is just tender. If you like, add vegetables and cook along with the meat until tender.

To Pressure-Cook: Follow the manufacturer's directions.

To Slow-Cook: Follow the manufacturer's or recipe directions.

Tenderizing Meat

Less-tender cuts may be tenderized, then cooked using dry-heat methods. Tenderize by pounding the meat with a meat mallet, or by using a marinade or commercial tenderizing mixture.

Manually pounding cuts such as round steak with a meat mallet tenderizes by breaking down the fibers and tissue. Cube steak is round steak that a butcher has put through a special machine which tears the fiber structure and creates a flattened steak.

Marinades are usually made of an acidic liquid such as vinegar, wine, citrus or tomato juice. The acid helps soften the meat fibers and connective tissue and adds flavor. Marinades also often contain flavoring ingredients, such as garlic, pepper, etc.

Commercial tenderizing mixtures are sold in various forms and container enzymes which break down the connective tissue. Enzymes such as papain from papaya and bromelain from pineapple are usually used in these tenderizers.

Rolled Flank Steak

The beef is first marinated, then filled with a sweet red pepper and green onion stuffing.

Roast at 450° for 15 minutes;
then at 400° for 20 minutes for rare.
Makes 8 servings.

Nutrient Value Per Serving: 265 calories, 35 g protein, 12 g fat, 2 g carbohydrate, 341 mg sodium, 107 mg cholesterol.

2 flank steaks, about 1½ pounds each
Marinade:
½ teaspoon salt
¼ teaspoon pepper
2 tablespoons vegetable oil
2 tablespoons chopped parsley
2 teaspoons leaf basil, crumbled
1 teaspoon leaf thyme, crumbled
1 clove garlic, crushed
Stuffing:
⅔ cup chopped sweet red pepper
⅔ cup chopped green onions (about 6)
½ cup chopped parsley
2 tablespoons fresh bread crumbs
1 clove garlic, crushed
2 teaspoons leaf basil, crumbled
½ teaspoon salt
¼ teaspoon pepper

1. Trim excess fat from the meat. Cut a pocket lengthwise into each steak with a long, sharp knife to within 1 inch of the edges. (Or ask your butcher to do it for you.)
2. Marinate the steaks: Rub the salt and pepper into only one side of the steaks. Mix together the oil, parsley, basil, thyme and garlic in a small bowl. Spread over the same side as the salt and pepper. Place the steaks in a large, shallow dish and let stand, covered, at room temperature for ½ hour or refrigerated for up to 8 hours.
3. Mix the red pepper, green onions, parsley, bread crumbs, garlic, basil and ¼ teaspoon of the salt in a small bowl. Spread the stuffing evenly into each steak pocket.
4. Preheat the oven to very hot (450°).
5. Roll each steak, beginning with a short end, into a tight roll, so the seasoned side (marinated side) is on the inside of the roll. Tie each with string at 1-inch intervals. Sprinkle each with the remaining salt and pepper.
6. Heat lightly an oiled heavy roasting pan in a preheated very hot oven (450°) for 5 minutes. Place the rolls, seam-side down, in the heated pan. Roast for 15 minutes. Lower the oven to hot (400°). Roast for 20 minutes for rare (meat thermometer inserted in the center of the roll will read 130°), or until desired doneness.
7. Let the meat stand for 20 minutes. Remove the string. Cut into thin slices and arrange on a warmed serving platter.

All About Mustards

● **Dijon and Dijon-type**—French mustards with a wine flavor. You will find many varieties to choose from at gourmet stores.
● **Creole or Louisiana**—Pungent mustards with specks of spices showing in a beige-colored base.
● **English, Dusseldorf and German**—Very hot blends with a deep brown color. Great with sausages or sharp cheese.
Whichever you choose, be sure to serve it in its own jar, so your guests will know which one they wish to try. Serve the mustards at room temperature with a stainless spoon for each. Mustard discolors silver.

Mustard-Crusted Flank Steak

Makes 4 servings.

Nutrient Value Per Serving: 197 calories, 23 g protein, 10 g fat, 3 g carbohydrate, 412 mg sodium, 72 mg cholesterol.

　2　*tablespoons Dijon-style mustard*
　1　*tablespoon olive oil*
　1　*clove garlic, finely chopped*
　½　*teaspoon leaf thyme, crumbled*
　¼　*teaspoon salt*
　⅛　*teaspoon pepper*
　1　*pound flank steak, trimmed of excess fat*
　¼　*cup fresh bread crumbs*

1. Combine the mustard, olive oil, garlic, thyme, salt and pepper in a small bowl. Brush half of the mixture over one side of the steak.
2. Broil the steak, seasoned-side up, 4 inches from the heat for about 4 minutes for medium-rare*.
3. Turn the steak over. Spread with the remaining mustard mixture. Broil for 4 minutes more. Sprinkle the top with the bread crumbs. Broil for 1 or 2 minutes more until the crumbs are brown.
4. Serve on a carving board or platter. Cut the steak crosswise diagonally against the grain into thin slices.

***Note:** Broil for 2 minutes more on each side for medium.*

Spicy Ground Beef and Kidney Bean Sauté

If you like chili, you're sure to like this quick ground beef sauté.

Makes 4 servings.

Nutrient Value Per Serving: 480 calories, 27 g protein, 31 g fat, 25 g carbohydrate, 971 mg sodium, 77 mg cholesterol.

　1　*pound ground beef*
　3　*tablespoons oil, preferably olive oil*
　1½　*cups chopped onion (3 medium-size)*
　1　*cup thinly sliced celery (2 large stalks)*
　2　*cloves garlic, finely chopped*
　1　*can (15 ounces) kidney beans, drained*
　½　*cup thinly sliced pitted black olives*
　½　*cup finely chopped parsley*
　¾　*teaspoon salt*
　¼　*teaspoon pepper*
　¼　*teaspoon liquid red-pepper seasoning*
　　Finely chopped parsley, celery leaves or thinly sliced red onion (optional)
　　Creamed spinach (optional)

1. Brown the beef in a large, heavy skillet, breaking up the meat with a wooden spoon. Remove the meat with a slotted spoon to a bowl. Set aside. Drain and discard the fat from the skillet.
2. Heat the oil in the same skillet. Add the onion, celery and garlic and sauté over medium heat, stirring occasionally, until the vegetables are tender, for about 5 minutes.

3. Stir in the reserved meat, kidney beans, olives, parsley, salt, pepper and red-pepper seasoning. Simmer, covered, stirring occasionally, for about 5 minutes, or until heated through. Garnish with the chopped parsley, celery leaves or onion slices, if you wish. Serve over creamed spinach, if you wish.

Ground Meat Tips

● Buy meat the day you plan to use it whenever possible. If ground meat must be saved until the next day, wrap it in wax paper and store it in the coldest part of your refrigerator.
● To freeze ground meat, wrap it in plastic wrap, aluminum foil or freezer paper soon after purchasing and place in the freezer.

Mole Chili (Medium-Hot)

The Mexican word molli *means a concoction, while the Spanish* mole *means a sauce made with chilies. One variation contains bitter chocolate; hence the name of our recipe.*

Makes 6 servings.

Nutrient Value Per Serving: 710 calories, 35 g protein, 51 g fat, 31 g carbohydrate, 754 mg sodium, 107 mg cholesterol.

$\frac{1}{3}$ *cup raisins (2 ounces)*
$\frac{1}{3}$ *cup blanched almonds (1½ ounces)*
2 *tablespoons sesame seeds*
4 *tablespoons vegetable oil*
5 *tablespoons chili powder*
$\frac{1}{2}$ *cup water*
1 *medium-size onion, sliced*
4 *cloves garlic*
2 *teaspoons ground coriander*
2 *teaspoons ground cinnamon*
$\frac{1}{2}$ *teaspoon ground cloves*
1 *pound lean ground beef*
1 *pound lean ground pork*
1 *can (16 ounces) whole tomatoes, drained and chopped*
1 *cup beef broth*
2 *tablespoons red wine vinegar*
1 *can (15¼ ounces) red kidney beans, drained and rinsed*
$\frac{1}{2}$ *of a 1-ounce square unsweetened chocolate, chopped*
$\frac{1}{4}$ *teaspoon salt*

1. Sauté the raisins, almonds and sesame seeds in 2 tablespoons of the oil in a medium-size saucepan over medium heat. Cook, stirring constantly, until the raisins are puffy and the sesame seeds are slightly browned, for about 3 minutes. Add the chili powder; cook, stirring, for 1 minute longer. Remove from the heat. Add the water.

2. Transfer the mixture to the container of an electric blender or food processor. Cover; whirl until the mixture is the consistency of coarse peanut butter; add a little more water, if needed. Add the onion and garlic. Whirl until a smooth purée. Mix in the coriander, cinnamon and cloves.

3. Sauté the beef and the pork, working in batches if necessary, in the remaining 2 tablespoons of oil in a large saucepan over high heat until lightly browned, for about 5 minutes; break up the meat with a wooden spoon.

4. Add the chili powder mixture, tomatoes and beef broth. Bring to boiling. Lower the heat. Simmer, uncovered, stirring frequently, for 1 hour, or until thickened. The mixture should not be too dry; add a little water if the chili becomes too dry.

5. Add the vinegar and beans. Cook, stirring occasionally, until the beans are heated through, for about 10 minutes. Stir in the chocolate and salt. Cook, stirring, until the chocolate is melted, for about 2 minutes. Serve.

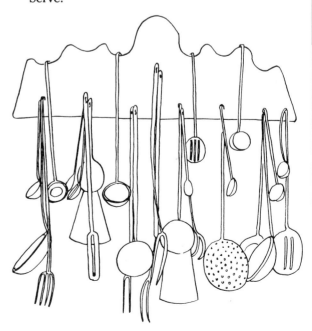

Beef Turnovers

Beef Turnovers

Pimiento-stuffed olives flavor the beef filling in these flaky turnovers.

Bake at 375° for 15 minutes.
Makes 6 servings.

Nutrient Value Per Serving: 444 calories, 13 g protein, 29 g fat, 29 g carbohydrate, 506 mg sodium, 126 mg cholesterol.

  1 small onion, chopped
  2 cloves garlic, finely chopped
  1 teaspoon vegetable oil
  ½ pound ground round
  ½ teaspoon leaf oregano, crumbled
  ⅛ teaspoon pepper
  5 pimiento-stuffed green olives, chopped
  1 hard-cooked egg, chopped
  1 tablespoon tomato sauce
  1 box (11 ounces) piecrust mix
  1 egg, slightly beaten

1. Sauté the onion and garlic in the oil in a medium-size skillet until the onion is tender, for about 3 minutes. Add the beef, oregano and pepper; cook, breaking up with the wooden spoon, until the meat is no longer pink. Stir in the olives, egg and tomato sauce. Remove from the heat; reserve.

2. Preheat the oven to moderate (375°).

3. Prepare the piecrust mix, following the package directions. Divide into 6 equal pieces.

4. Roll out one piece on a lightly floured surface to a ⅛-inch thickness. Cut into a 5½- to 6-inch circle. Place about ⅓ cup of the beef mixture on one-half of the circle. Moisten the edges of the pastry with the beaten egg. Fold over to make a crescent. Press the edges together with your fingers or a fork to seal. Lift onto an ungreased cookie sheet. Repeat to make a total of 6 turnovers.

5. Reroll the trimmings. Cut into small decorative shapes with a pastry wheel or small knife. Brush the top of the pastries with the beaten egg. Decorate with pastry cutouts; brush with the egg. Make 2 steam vents with a fork in the top of each.

6. Bake in the preheated moderate oven (375°) for 15 to 20 minutes, or until pale golden. Remove to a wire rack to cool slightly. Serve warm or at room temperature.

Beef Tomato and Rice Soup

Makes 8 servings (about 2 quarts).

Nutrient Value Per Serving: 213 calories, 21 g protein, 5 g fat, 22 g carbohydrate, 665 mg sodium, 56 mg cholesterol.

1½ pounds top round, cut into 1-inch cubes
2 quarts water
1 can (35 ounces) tomatoes
3 beef bouillon cubes
½ teaspoon pepper
½ teaspoon leaf thyme, crumbled
¼ teaspoon leaf marjoram, crumbled
5 carrots, pared and sliced ½-inch thick
5 stalks celery, sliced ½-inch thick
1 onion, coarsely chopped
½ cup uncooked white rice

1. Brown the beef in a large saucepan. Add the water. Bring to boiling. Lower the heat; simmer for 20 minutes, or until the meat is almost tender.
2. Stir in the tomatoes with their liquid, breaking up the chunks with a spoon. Add the bouillon, pepper, thyme and marjoram. Simmer for 1 hour. Add the carrots, celery, onion and rice during the last 30 minutes of cooking.

Soup Slimmer

Make soups a day ahead, then refrigerate. Before reheating, skim the congealed fat off the top.

Beef Tomato and Rice Soup

Oriental Beef Salad

Makes 6 servings.

Nutrient Value Per Serving: 531 calories, 31 g protein, 41 g fat, 10 g carbohydrate, 531 mg sodium, 89 mg cholesterol.

1½ pounds top round steak OR: 1¼ pounds roasted or broiled beef, cut into ¼-inch-wide strips
1 small sweet red pepper, cored and seeded
2 large celery stalks
3 green onions
1 medium-size clove garlic, finely chopped
1 tablespoon chopped fresh gingerroot OR: 1½ teaspoons ground ginger
¼ cup orange juice
½ cup peanut or other vegetable oil
2 tablespoons soy sauce
¼ teaspoon cayenne pepper
¼ pound dry-roasted unsalted cashews or peanuts

1. Wipe the steak with damp paper toweling. Place on the rack in a broiler pan. Broil 4 inches from the heat, for about 6 minutes on each side; the meat should be pink inside. Let cool. Cut diagonally into ¼-inch-thick slices across the grain. Cut each slice into ¼-inch-wide strips.*
2. Cut the red pepper into ¾ x ¾-inch pieces. Cut the celery diagonally into ¼-inch-thick slices. Thinly slice the green onions, including part of the tender green leaves.
3. Combine the garlic, gingerroot, orange juice, oil, soy sauce and cayenne pepper in a large bowl. Add the beef, red pepper, celery, onion and cashews; toss well.
4. Refrigerate, covered, for at least 2 hours or overnight, tossing once or twice. Toss just before serving.

*****Note:** If using leftover beef, omit Step 1.

Reuben Brunch Casserole

● Bake at 350° for 55 minutes.
Makes 10 servings.

Nutrient Value Per Serving: 513 calories, 32 g protein, 35 g fat, 18 g carbohydrate, 932 mg sodium, 265 mg cholesterol.

10 slices rye bread, cut into ¾-inch cubes
1½ pounds cooked corned beef
2½ cups shredded Swiss cheese (10 ounces)
6 eggs, lightly beaten
3 cups milk
¼ teaspoon pepper

1. Grease a 13 x 9 x 2-inch glass baking dish. Arrange the bread cubes on the bottom of the dish.
2. Coarsely shred the corned beef with a knife. Layer the meat over the bread. Sprinkle with the cheese.
3. Beat the eggs, milk and pepper in a bowl until well blended. Pour over the corned beef mixture. Cover with foil. Refrigerate overnight.
4. When ready to bake, preheat the oven to moderate (350°).
5. Bake the casserole, covered, in the preheated moderate oven (350°) for 45 minutes, then uncovered for 10 minutes, or until bubbly and puffed. Serve immediately.

Reuben Brunch Casserole

Reduced Calorie

We've lowered calories by using a reduced-calorie sausage, less cheese and skim milk.

Bake at 350° for 55 minutes.
Makes 10 servings.

Nutrient Value Per Serving: 328 calories, 21 g protein, 19 g fat, 19 g carbohydrate, 686 mg sodium, 187 mg cholesterol.

1 pound Light Breakfast Pork and Rice Bulk Sausage, thawed and crumbled
10 slices rye bread, cut into ¾-inch cubes
2 cups shredded Swiss cheese (8 ounces)
6 eggs, lightly beaten
3 cups skim milk
¼ teaspoon pepper

1. Panfry the sausage in a medium-size nonstick skillet, without adding oil, for 4 minutes. Drain. Reserve.
2. Spray a 13½ x 8½ x 2-inch glass baking dish with nonstick vegetable cooking spray. Arrange the bread cubes in the bottom of the prepared dish. Sprinkle the sausage over the top; sprinkle with the cheese.
3. Beat together the eggs, milk and pepper in a medium-size bowl until well blended. Pour over the sausage mixture. Cover with aluminum foil; refrigerate overnight.
4. Bake, covered, in a preheated moderate oven (350°) for 45 minutes. Uncover and bake another 10 minutes, or until puffed and bubbly. Serve immediately.

Grilled Open-Face Club Sandwich

Grilled Open-Face Club Sandwich

Broil for 2 to 3 minutes.
Makes 4 servings.

Nutrient Value Per Serving: 468 calories, 31 g protein, 26 g fat, 29 g carbohydrate, 643 mg sodium, 107 mg cholesterol.

- **¼ cup (½ stick) unsalted butter, softened**
- **1 tablespoon drained bottled horseradish**
- **2 teaspoons Dijon-style mustard**
- **8 slices rye bread, lightly toasted**
- **½ pound thinly sliced deli roast beef**
- **1 large ripe tomato, cut into 8 slices**
- **8 slices cooked bacon OR: ¼ cup real bacon bits**
- **½ cup shredded Swiss cheese (2 ounces)**

1. Adjust the oven rack 6 inches from the broiling element, if using a conventional oven. Preheat the broiler; preheating a toaster oven is not necessary.
2. Combine the butter, horseradish and mustard in a small bowl; blend well. Spread evenly on one side of each bread slice.
3. Place the roast beef over the mustard-coated side of each bread slice, dividing equally. Top them with 1 slice each of tomato and bacon.
4. Place 4 of the bread slices on top of the other 4 slices, making 4 open-face double-decker sandwiches.
5. Sprinkle the shredded cheese over the top of each sandwich, dividing equally. Place the sandwiches on the broiler or toaster oven pan.
6. Broil the sandwiches in the oven or toaster oven for 2 to 3 minutes, or until the cheese is melted.

Sandwich Tip

When the supermarket is having a special on roast beef, fresh ham or turkey this summer, don't pass it by and say that it's too hot to serve roast meat. Rather, buy a roast and cook late in the evening, or early in the morning, when it is cooler. Then you'll have a week's worth of cold meat to slice and serve in sandwiches or salad, or add to a quick stir-fry skillet dish with a variety of vegetables. You'll find you'll be saving money on cold cuts and the flavor will be much better in each case.

Grilled Open-Face Sandwich

Reduced Calorie

We've substituted diet margarine for the butter, eliminated the bacon, used part-skim milk cheese and reduced the serving size.

Broil for 1 to 2 minutes.
Makes 4 servings.

Nutrient Value Per Serving: 239 calories, 22 g protein, 10 g fat, 16 g carbohydrate, 394 mg sodium, 57 mg cholesterol.

- **3 tablespoons diet margarine**
- **1 tablespoon drained bottled horseradish**
- **2 teaspoons Dijon-style mustard**
- **4 slices rye bread, lightly toasted**
- **8 leaves romaine lettuce**
- **½ pound thinly sliced roast beef**
- **1 large ripe tomato, cut into 8 slices**
- **¼ cup shredded part-skim milk Swiss or Mozzarella cheese (1 ounce)**

1. Adjust the oven rack 6 inches from the broiling element, if using a conventional oven. Preheat the broiler; preheating a toaster oven is not necessary.
2. Combine the margarine, horseradish and mustard in a small bowl; blend well. Spread sparingly on one side of each bread slice. Top with the lettuce.
3. Place the roast beef over the lettuce, dividing equally. Top each with 2 tomato slices.
4. Sprinkle the cheese over the top of each sandwich, dividing equally. Place them on the broiler or toaster oven pan.
5. Broil the sandwiches in the oven or toaster oven for 1 to 2 minutes, or until the cheese is melted and golden.

Roast Beef and Onion Sandwich

Adjust the horseradish in this recipe to suit your own taste.

Makes 4 servings.

Nutrient Value Per Serving: 457 calories, 32 g protein, 24 g fat, 30 g carbohydrate, 435 mg sodium, 112 mg cholesterol.

8 slices caraway rye bread
4 ounces soft cream cheese
6 to 12 teaspoons bottled horseradish
12 ounces thinly sliced roast beef from the deli
¼ teaspoon pepper
4 outer leaves iceberg lettuce
½ cup thinly sliced onion
4 thin slices tomato

1. Layer the following ingredients on one slice of the bread to make one sandwich: 1½ tablespoons of cream cheese, 1 to 2 teaspoons of horseradish, 3 ounces of roast beef, a dash of pepper, 1 lettuce leaf, 1 slice of bread, 1½ tablespoons of cream cheese, 1 to 2 teaspoons of horseradish, ¼ cup of thinly sliced onions, 2 slices of tomato, 1 slice of bread, 1½ tablespoons of cream cheese, 1 to 2 teaspoons of horseradish, 3 ounces of roast beef, a dash of pepper, 1 lettuce leaf and 1 slice of bread.
2. Repeat with the remaining ingredients to make a second sandwich.
3. Cut each sandwich in half and serve.

Veal and Rice Gremolata

Veal and Rice Gremolata

Makes 10 servings.

Nutrient Value Per Serving: 456 calories, 31 g protein, 22 g fat, carbohydrate (not available), 497 mg sodium, 103 mg cholesterol.

3 pounds boneless veal shoulder, cut into 2-inch cubes
⅓ cup all-purpose flour for coating, or as needed
1 teaspoon salt
¼ teaspoon pepper
¼ cup olive oil, or as needed
2 tablespoons butter or margarine
1 teaspoon leaf rosemary, crumbled
2 medium-size onions, chopped
2 carrots, chopped
2 stalks celery, sliced
1 cup dry white wine
1 cup chicken broth
2 tablepoons tomato paste
1 package (10 ounces) frozen peas
   Grated rind of 2 medium-size lemons
3 tablespoons finely chopped parsley
1 large clove garlic, crushed
4 cups cooked rice

1. Pat the veal dry with paper toweling. Combine the flour, salt and pepper on wax paper. Lightly coat the veal with the flour mixture, shaking off the excess.
2. Heat 2 tablespoons of the oil and the butter in a large flameproof casserole. Lightly brown the veal in batches, adding more oil as necessary. As the meat browns, remove to a plate. Sprinkle with the rosemary.
3. Sauté the onion, carrot and celery in the oil remaining in the casserole, stirring often, until tender but not browned, for about 5 minutes. Stir in the wine and chicken broth, scraping up any browned bits from the bottom of the casserole with a wooden spoon. Stir in the tomato paste.
4. Return the veal to the casserole. Bring to boiling. Lower the heat; cover; simmer for 45 minutes to 1 hour, or until the veal is almost tender. Add the peas; cook for 10 minutes.
5. Combine the lemon rind, parsley and garlic. Stir into the casserole. Serve with rice. Garnish with thin strips of lemon rind, if you wish.

Veal

The most delicate meat of all, veal is bland, thus making it ideal for cooking with sauces. The best veal comes from young milk-fed calves less than 3 months old, and the meat shows virtually no pink at all. Veal is fine-grained, with no marbling and only a thin external layer of fat. It has a large amount of connective tissue which requires cooking at low to moderate temperatures. Veal should not be broiled. It is best panfried, braised or roasted.

Veal scaloppine, sometimes called scallops, is the most expensive cut and comes from the leg. They are thin, boneless slices that are pounded to break some of the connective tissue. Scaloppine may also be made from the loin or shoulder. The less-expensive cuts include breast of veal, shoulder and shanks. The cuts of veal are similar to beef but they're smaller in size.

Vealballs with Dilled Fettuccine

Bake Vealballs at 400° for 15 minutes.
Makes 4 servings.

Nutrient Value Per Serving: 283 calories, 15 g protein, 9 g fat, 33 g carbohydrate, 454 mg sodium, 77 mg cholesterol.

Vealballs:
- **6½ ounces finely ground veal (14% fat)**
- **1 tablespoon dry bread crumbs**
- **1 tablespoon finely chopped onion**
- **1 tablespoon water**
- **¼ teaspoon grated lemon rind**
- **¼ teaspoon salt**
- **¼ teaspoon pepper**

Dill Sauce:
- **¼ cup plain yogurt**
- **2 tablespoons dairy sour cream**
- **1 teaspoon lemon juice**
- **1 tablespoon firmly packed snipped fresh dill**
- **½ teaspoon salt**
- **⅛ teaspoon white pepper**
- **6 ounces egg fettuccine**

1. Preheat the oven to hot (400°).

2. Prepare the Vealballs: Combine the veal, bread crumbs, onion, water, lemon rind, salt and pepper in a medium size bowl. Shape into about 20 meatballs, using a rounded measuring teaspoon for each. Arrange the meatballs on a rack in a small pan.

3. Bake in the preheated hot oven (400°) for 15 minutes, or until no longer pink in the center.

4. Meanwhile, prepare the Dill Sauce: Combine the yogurt, sour cream, lemon juice, dill, salt and white pepper in a medium-size bowl.

5. Cook the fettuccine in a large pot of salted boiling water, following the package directions. Drain. Turn into a serving bowl. Add the Dill Sauce; toss to coat well. Add the Vealballs. Serve immediately. Garnish with fresh dill sprigs, if you wish.

New Mexican Pork Chili (right), Vegetarian Chili (page 164), Tortilla Cups (page 201), Carrot Cake (page 226)

Chile (also chili, chilli or chilie)

To say chile is synonymous with Mexican cooking is not entirely correct. A lot of chiles are used in dishes from Mexico, but chiles are also used in Africa, India, Southeast Asia, China, Japan, some Pacific Islands, Spain and Italy. It is used fresh or dried and ground.

Chile is a species of *Capsicum* (the pepper family) which includes the green pepper (sometimes called bell or sweet pepper). A variety of the small red chile when dried and ground is called ground red pepper or cayenne.

Identifying chiles is a problem because there are so many varieties; moreover, one variety which is mild when grown in certain soil may become a hot chile when grown elsewhere. Basically, we can divide chiles into two categories: mild and hot. Mild green chiles include the 6-inch-long *Anaheim* or *California* chili, and the longer *Mild New Mexico* chile. Hot chiles include Jalapeño, Serrano, Poblano, Mulato, Guero and Fresno. *Jalapeño* is dark green and about 2½ inches long. *Serrano* is also dark green but only 1½-inches long. *Poblano* is shaped like a small, triangular green pepper but is black-green in color. *Mulato* is shaped like Poblano but is larger and darker in color. *Guero* is yellow, about 3 inches long. *Fresno* is bright green and looks like Jalapeño but is wider and bigger. Other vegetables on the market may look like chiles but may actually be sweet frying peppers.

Chiles may be dried when ripe. They are sold whole or can be ground. *Ancho* or dried *pasilla* is the most popular, sold whole or ground. *Ground chile* should not be confused with *chili powder,* which is a blend of spices. *Chipotle* is a 2-inch chile that's very hot in flavor. Chile *tepin,* which are ¼-inch-round chiles, and chile *pequin,* which are tiny oval-shaped chiles, are extremely hot. *Hapaka* is a very hot dried Japanese chile. Also on the market are crushed red peppers, used in Italian or Chinese recipes, and whole small red peppers, used primarily for pickling.

Buying and Storing: When buying fresh chiles, select firm, plump unblemished ones. Store in plastic bags and refrigerate. Store all dried chiles in a very cool dry place or refrigerate.

Mild green chiles and Jalapeños are usually canned in a mild brine or pickled. Refrigerate canned chiles when opened.

To Prepare: When handling fresh or canned chiles, you may want to wear rubber gloves. Capsaicin, the substance which gives the chile its hotness, is found concentrated in the tissue to which the seeds are attached. When cleaning chiles, handle that part carefully. Chiles should be seeded and deveined before use. Usually only the long, mild chiles are peeled before use. To peel, heat the chiles over a gas flame or under a broiler until the skin blisters and browns. Drop them into a plastic bag; when cool, peel, seed, devein and rinse in water before using.

New Mexican Pork Chili (Hot)

Serve beans on the side with this chunky pork chili, along with sour cream and chopped onions for garnish, if you wish. For a "hot" chili, add the maximum number of jalapeño peppers indicated in the recipe.

Makes 6 servings.

Nutrient Value Per Serving: 723 calories, 35 g protein, 50 g fat, 33 g carbohydrate, 818 mg sodium, 121 mg cholesterol.

- **2 tablespoons vegetable oil**
- **4 strips bacon, cut into small dice (¼ cup)**
- **2 pounds stewing pork (shoulder or butt), cut into ½-inch cubes**
- **½ cup all-purpose flour**
- **1 medium-size onion, finely chopped (about 1 cup)**
- **3 cloves garlic, finely chopped (about 1 tablespoon)**
- **3 tablespoons chili powder**
- **1 to 3 pickled jalapeño peppers, stemmed, seeded and finely chopped**
- **2 cups chicken broth**
- **¼ teaspoon salt**
- **3½ cups cooked pinto beans OR: 2 cans (15¼ ounces each) pinto beans, drained and rinsed**

1. Heat the oil in a 10-inch skillet over medium-high heat. Add the bacon; cook until crisp, for about 5 minutes. Remove with a slotted spoon to paper toweling to drain; set aside. Reserve the skillet with the drippings.
2. Shake the pork with the flour in a paper bag until coated. Remove the pork and shake off any excess flour.
3. Working in batches, sauté the pork in the bacon drippings in the skillet until evenly browned, for about 5 minutes; remove the pork to a plate as it browns.
4. Lower the heat to medium. Return all the pork and bacon to pan. Add the onion and garlic; cook until the onion is softened and transparent, about 8 minutes. Add the chili powder, jalapeño peppers and chicken broth. Bring to boiling. Lower the heat; simmer, uncovered, stirring occasionally, for 2 hours, or until the meat is very tender and the sauce is thickened. If the sauce becomes too thick, thin with a little water. Stir in the salt.
5. To serve, heat the beans in a little water in a medium-size saucepan. Drain. Serve separately. Each person can spoon chili over his own beans.

Chili Pie

Bake at 425° for about 40 minutes.
Makes 6 servings.

Nutrient Value Per Serving: 438 calories, 29 g protein, 16 g fat, 47 g carbohydrate, 1,550 mg sodium, 106 mg cholesterol.

- **5 cups cooked chili***
- **1 cup cornmeal**
- **2 teaspoons baking poder**
- **1 teaspoon salt**
- **1 teaspoon sugar**
- **⅔ cup milk**
- **1 egg**

1. Preheat the oven to hot (425°).
2. Spoon the chili into the bottom of an 8 x 8 x 2-inch square or 9 x 9 x 2-inch-square baking pan.
3. Bake in the preheated hot oven (425°) until hot and bubbly, for 10 to 15 minutes.
4. While the chili is heating, sift together the cornmeal, baking powder, salt and sugar into a medium-size bowl. Beat together the milk and egg in a small bowl. Stir into the cornmeal mixture until smooth. Pour evenly over the hot chili.
5. Bake in the hot oven (425°) until the top is set and golden, for 25 to 30 minutes. Serve in squares.

***Note:** Use any of our recipes for the chili. For example, the New Mexican Pork Chili, or our Mole Chili, page 95.

Temperature and Time for Roasting Pork

Cut	Approximate Pound Weight	Oven Temperature	Internal Meat Temperature When Done	Minutes Per Pound Roasting Time
Loin				
Center	3 to 5	325° to 350°F.	170°F.	30 to 35
Half	5 to 7	325° to 350°F.	170°F.	35 to 40
Blade Loin or Sirloin	3 to 4	325° to 350°F.	170°F.	40 to 45
Rolled	3 to 5	325° to 350°F.	170°F.	35 to 45
Picnic Shoulder	5 to 8	325° to 350°F.	170°F.	30 to 35
Rolled	3 to 5	325° to 350°F.	170°F.	35 to 40
Cushion Style	3 to 5	325° to 350°F.	170°F.	30 to 35
Boston Shoulder	4 to 6	325° to 350°F.	170°F.	40 to 45
Leg (Fresh ham)				
Whole (Bone in)	12 to 16	325° to 350°F.	170°F.	22 to 26
Whole (Rolled)	10 to 14	325° to 350°F.	170°F.	24 to 28
Half (Bone in)	5 to 8	325° to 350°F.	170°F.	35 to 40
Spareribs	3	325° to 350°F.	Well done	1½ to 2½ hrs. (total)

Temperature and Time for Roasting Cured and Smoked Pork

Cut	Approximate Pound Weight	Oven Temperature	Internal Meat Temperature When Done	Total Roasting Time
Ham (cook before eating)				
Bone in, half	5 to 7	325°F.	160°F.	2½ to 3 hours
Ham (fully cooked)				
Bone in, half	5 to 7 lbs.	325°F	140°F.	1½ to 2¼ hours
Boneless, half	3 to 4 lbs.	325°F	140°F.	1¼ to 1¾ hours
Arm Picnic Shoulder				
Bone in	5 to 8 lbs.	325°F	170°F.	2½ to 4 hours
Shoulder				
Boneless roll	2 to 3 lbs.	325°F	170°F.	1½ to 1¾ hours

Pork Chops in Beer

A hearty, flavorful dish with apples and a beer sauce that will warm the spirit on a cool autumn evening.

Makes 4 servings.

Nutrient Value Per Serving: 461 calories, 30 g protein, 25 g fat, 29 g carbohydrate, 717 mg sodium, 113 mg cholesterol.

- 8 **very thin pork loin chops (1¾ pounds), trimmed of fat**
- 1 **tablespoon vegetable oil**
- 1 **teaspoon salt**
- ½ **teaspoon pepper**
- 3 **tablespoons butter or margarine**
- 2 **medium-size onions, thinly sliced (2 cups)**
- 2 **medium-size tart apples, pared, cored and thinly sliced (2½ cups)**
- 2 **large cloves garlic, crushed**
- 1 **can (12 ounces) beer**
- 2 **tablespoons brown sugar**
- 1 **tablespoon cornstarch**
- 1 **tablespoon red wine vinegar Chopped parsley for garnish**

1. Brown the pork chops in the oil in a large, heavy skillet over high heat; remove the chops as they brown to a large platter. Sprinkle with the salt and pepper.
2. Melt the butter in the same skillet. Add the onions, apples and garlic. Sauté over medium-high heat, stirring occasionally, until the onions and apples are tender, for about 10 minutes. Stir in the beer and brown sugar until well combined. Add the pork chops along with any juices that have accumulated on the platter. Spoon the beer mixture over the chops. Bring to boiling. Lower the heat. Cover and simmer, for about 10 minutes, or until the chops are cooked through. Remove the chops, onions and apples with a slotted spoon to a serving platter.
3. Mix together the cornstarch and red wine vinegar in a small bowl; stir to dissolve the cornstarch. Stir into the beer mixture in the skillet. Cook until slightly thickened, for about 1 minute. Spoon over the pork chops. Garnish with the parsley.

Champagne Choucroute with Smoked Meats

Makes 12 servings.

Nutrient Value Per Serving: 631 calories, 25 g protein, 43 g fat, 29 g carbohydrate, 2,825 mg sodium, 97 mg cholesterol.

- 4 **pounds sauerkraut**
- 1 **medium-size onion, thinly sliced**
- 4 **tablespoons butter or margarine**
- ½ **pound slab bacon, halved**
- 1 **large carrot, cut in 1-inch chunks**
- 3 **whole cloves**
- 1 **bay leaf**
- ⅓ **cup gin**
- 1 **can (13¾ ounces) chicken broth**
- 1 **cup Champagne or white wine**
- 1 **pound Canadian bacon, in one piece Boiled New Potatoes and Onions (recipe follows)**
- 4 **fully cooked knockwurst (about 1 pound)***
- 5 **to 6 fully cooked weisswurst or bockwurst (white veal sausage)* (about 1 pound)**
- ½ **pound fully cooked cocktail sausage**

1. Rinse the sauerkraut well; drain. Squeeze dry.
2. Sauté the sliced onion in 3 tablespoons of the butter in a large, heavy kettle or Dutch oven until golden brown. Add the sauerkraut. Cook, stirring often, for 5 minutes longer.
3. Add the bacon, carrot with a clove stuck into 3 of the chunks, bay leaf, gin and chicken broth. Bring to boiling. Lower heat; simmer, covered, for 1½ to 2 hours, or until the bacon is tender.
4. Add the Champagne and Canadian Bacon. Cook, covered, for 30 minutes longer or until heated through.
5. Prepare the Boiled New Potatoes and Onions.
6. Meanwhile, brown the knockwurst, weisswurst and cocktail sausages on all sides in the remaining tablespoon of butter in a large skillet over medium heat. Add to the kettle with the sauerkraut mixture. Cook, covered, for 5 to 10 minutes longer, or until the sausage is heated through.
7. To serve, remove the meats and sausage to a cutting board. Slice or dice the Canadian bacon and cut up the sausages, if you wish. Arrange the sauerkraut and meats on a heated deep platter. Serve the potatoes and onions separately. ▶

Boiled New Potatoes and Onions: Cook 16 red new potatoes, with their skins on, in boiling salted water for 20 minutes, or until tender. Drain. Keep warm. Cook 8 medium-size yellow onions in boiling salted water for 30 minutes, or just until tender. Drain and cut in half. Keep warm. (If red new potatoes are not available, use red potatoes, halved or quartered.)

*Note: Any variety of fully cooked or smoked sausage may be substituted, pound for pound, for knockwurst, weisswurst or bockwurst, or cocktail sausages. You may be able to find lower-sodium meats and sausages in your area.

Knockwurst

Also known as knackwurst, this German sausage looks like a fat frankfurter. It's made of finely chopped pork and beef and is seasoned like a frankfurter but with a touch of garlic. It is fully cooked and smoked so it needs only to be reheated in water or panfried, broiled or grilled until browned.

⚡ 💲

Sausage and Garbanzo Beans with Tomato Sauce

Makes 6 servings.

Nutrient Value Per Serving: 419 calories, 22 g protein, 27 g fat, 22 g carbohydrate, 1,224 mg sodium, 65 mg cholesterol.

**1½ pounds sweet Italian sausage
    Water
2 tablespoons oil, preferably olive oil
1 medium-size sweet green pepper, halved, seeded and cut into thin strips
½ cup very thinly sliced onion (1 small)
1 clove garlic, crushed
1 can (15 ounces) tomato sauce
¼ cup finely chopped parsley
½ teaspoon leaf basil, crumbled
¼ teaspoon pepper
1 can (19 ounces) garbanzo beans (chick-peas), drained
    Grated Parmesan cheese** (optional)

1. Prick the sausages in several places with a fork. Place in a large, heavy skillet. Add enough water to cover. Bring to boiling. Lower the heat and simmer for 1 minute. (This draws out the excess fat from the sausages and heats them, reducing cooking time.) Remove the sausages to a platter and pour off the water.
2. Heat the oil in the same skillet over medium heat. Return the sausages to the skillet and cook, turning occasionally, for about 15 minutes, or until the sausages are nicely browned and cooked through.
3. Remove the sausages to the platter. Set aside. Drain off all but 2 tablespoons of the fat. Add the green pepper, onion and garlic. Sauté over medium heat, stirring occasionally, for 5 to 7 minutes, or until the vegetables are tender.
4. Stir in the tomato sauce, parsley, basil, pepper, garbanzo beans and reserved sausages. Bring to boiling. Lower the heat and simmer, uncovered, stirring frequently, for 5 to 10 minutes, or until the mixture is heated through and flavors are blended. Serve with the Parmesan cheese, if you wish.

⚡ 💲

Italian Stack Cakes

Bake at 350° for 10 minutes.
Makes 4 servings.

Nutrient Value Per Serving: 439 calories, 17 g protein, 26 g fat, 36 g carbohydrate, 1,210 mg sodium, 54 mg cholesterol.

**½ pound sweet Italian sausage, casings removed and discarded, and meat crumbled
1 package (10 ounces) frozen chopped spinach, thawed and squeezed dry
1 cup complete pancake and waffle mix
¾ cup water
¼ teaspoon pepper
½ cup shredded mozzarella cheese (2 ounces)
1 cup bottled spaghetti sauce with mushrooms, warmed**

1. Sauté the sausage in a medium-size nonstick skillet for 2 minutes, or until no longer pink. Stir in the spinach. Cool slightly.
2. Stir together the pancake mix and water in a medium-size bowl until smooth. Add the sausage mixture and pepper.

3. Wipe the skillet clean. Pour about ¼ cup of the batter into the skillet, spreading to make a 3-to 3½-inch pancake. Cook, without adding oil, over very low heat until bubbles appear on top of the pancake and the edges begin to brown, for about 2 minutes. Turn over; cook until golden. Continue with the remaining batter to make a total of 8 pancakes.

4. For each serving, prepare the following stack and arrange on a baking sheet. Sprinkle one pancake with 1 tablespoon of the cheese; top with a second pancake. Spoon ¼ cup of sauce over the top and sprinkle with another tablespoon of cheese. Prepare another 3 stacks.

5. Bake in a preheated moderate oven (350°) for 10 minutes, or until the cheese melts. Serve immediately.

Chorizo Sausage

A spicy Spanish-style sausage.

Makes 2 pounds (16 patties).

Nutrient Value Per Pattie: 144 calories, 9 g protein, 11 g fat, carbohydrate (not available), 37 mg sodium, 39 mg cholesterol.

2 pounds boneless pork, preferably pork shoulder butt, 75% lean (not smoked), cut into 1-inch cubes
2 tablespoons paprika, preferably sweet
2 tablespoons chili powder
1 teaspoon leaf oregano, crumbled
1 teaspoon ground cumin
1 teaspoon pepper
½ teaspoon ground cinnamon
½ teaspooon ground cloves
¼ teaspoon coriander seeds
¼ teaspoon ground ginger
3 tablespoons red wine vinegar
3 tablespoons brandy
Vegetable oil for cooking

1. Grind the pork with a meat grinder fitted with a coarse plate. Or, working in batches, coarsely grind the pork in a food processor fitted with a metal blade, with on-and-off pulses; do not over grind.

2. Combine the ground pork with the paprika, chili powder, oregano, cumin, pepper, cinnamon, cloves, coriander, ginger, vinegar and brandy in a bowl. Mix thoroughly with your hands to distribute the spices evenly.

3. Place the chorizo in a heavy plastic bag; seal tightly. Refrigerate in the very cold section of the refrigerator for at least 24 hours but no more than 3 days, to allow the sausage to cure; the flavor will become stronger the longer the sausage cures. For longer storage, freeze for up to 2 months.

4. To cook fresh or thawed frozen sausage: Shape into 16 equal patties. Lightly oil the bottom of a large skillet. Add just enough water to cover the bottom. Add the patties to the skillet, making sure they do not touch. Cook, uncovered, over medium heat, turning once, until browned and cooked through, for 10 to 15 minutes.

Lamb Burgundy

Temperature and Time for Roasting Lamb

Cut	Approximate Pound Weight	Oven Temperature	Internal Meat Temperature When Done	Minutes Per Pound Roasting Time
Leg	5 to 9	300° to 325°F.	140°F. (rare)	20 to 25
			160°F. (med.)	25 to 30
			170° to 180°F. (well)	30 to 35
Leg, shank half	3 to 4	300° to 325°F.	140°F. (rare)	25 to 30
			160°F. (med.)	30 to 35
			170° to 180°F. (well)	35 to 40
Rib	2 to 3	375°F.	140°F. (rare)	25 to 30
			160°F. (med.)	30 to 35
			170° to 180°F. (well)	35 to 40

Time Saver's Tip

To cook casseroles more quickly, spoon the mixture into individual casseroles and arrange the dishes on a large cookie sheet. Reduce the baking time by one-quarter.

Lamb Burgundy

The French favorite with a twist—chunks of lamb, instead of beef, simmer in a deep-red wine sauce.

Bake at 375° for 30 minutes.
Makes 6 servings.

Nutrient Value Per Serving: 333 calories, 26 g protein, 15 g fat, 24 g carbohydrate, 743 mg sodium, 95 mg cholesterol.

1½ pounds lean lamb shoulder, cubed
  3 tablespoons butter or margarine
  ⅓ cup all-purpose flour
  ½ teaspoon salt
  1 can condensed beef broth
  1 cup red Burgundy wine
  2 large yellow squash
  1 bunch leeks
  1 package (10 ounces) frozen snow peas

1. Brown the lamb cubes, one-third at a time, in the butter or margarine in a medium-size skillet; remove with a slotted spoon to an 8-cup casserole.
2. Blend the flour and salt into the drippings in the skillet; stir in the beef broth until smooth, then the wine; bring to boiling, stirring constantly.
3. Tip the yellow squash; cut into ½-inch-thick slices on the diagonal. Wash the leeks in a bowl of warm salted water.
4. Cook the squash, leeks and snow peas separately, part at a time, in boiling water in a large skillet for 3 minutes, or just until crisp-tender; drain. Spoon into the casserole with the lamb. Pour the wine sauce over the lamb and vegetables.
5. Bake in a moderate oven (375°) for 30 minutes, or until bubbly hot. Serve with French bread, if you wish.

Suggested Variation: For Chicken Burgundy, substitute 1½ pounds of chicken fillets and cut into cubes and use white Burgundy wine.

Lamb Pilaf Seville

Coriander and cumin combine to give this dish a real Spanish flavor.

Bake at 350° for 1 hour.
Makes 4 servings.

Nutrient Value Per Serving: 377 calories, 37 g protein, 13 g fat, 26 g carbohydrate, 1,258 mg sodium, 119 mg cholesterol.

1½ pounds lean lamb shoulder, cubed
  ½ teaspoon crushed coriander seeds
  ½ teaspoon crushed cumin seeds
  ½ teaspoon basil
  ⅛ teaspoon pepper
  1 large onion, chopped (1 cup)
  ¾ cup wheat pilaf (from a 12-ounce package)
  1 cup diced celery
1½ teaspoons salt
  2 cups water
  1 cup chopped parsley

1. Brown the lamb cubes, a third at a time, in a medium-size skillet; spoon into a 6 cup casserole; stir in the coriander, cumin seeds, basil and pepper.
2. Sauté the onion until golden in the drippings in the skillet; stir in the wheat pilaf, celery, salt and water; heat to boiling. Pour over the meat mixture; toss lightly to mix; cover.
3. Bake in a moderate oven (350°) for 1 hour, or until the lamb is tender and the liquid is absorbed; stir in the parsley. A simple mixed green salad goes well with this casserole.

Poultry

A domesticated bird raised for food, poultry includes chicken, turkey, Rock Cornish game hen, duckling and goose. Chicken is the all-American favorite, although turkey is a close second. Rock Cornish game hens are gaining in popularity, especially among white-meat fanciers, as these tender, plump-breasted little birds are nearly all white meat. Ducklings and geese are neither as plentiful nor as popular as chicken, turkey or game hen, but they are very good and not exorbitantly priced.

CHICKEN—NUTRITIOUS AND ECONOMICAL

Chicken has been on the menu of mankind for over 4,000 years. Historically, chicken was gourmet fare, saved for only the finest occasions. It is only in recent years that the modern broiler-fryer industry has made chicken an economical family dish. What we know today are most often "spring chickens," first grown by housewives on small farms and sold young and tender—a far cry from the older birds good only for stewing.

No matter how economical, chicken is still gourmet and the basis of many a famous international dish. Chicken Kiev dates back to the czarist days of Russia. Napoleon's chef, Dumand the Younger, created Chicken Marengo to celebrate the Emperor's victory over the Austrians at Marengo in 1800. To honor a popular Italian coloratura soprano, Chicken Tetrazzini was born. And Chicken Divan made Divan Parisien one of the most popular restaurants in New York City.

Chicken: Nutritious and Delicious

Chicken is well suited to most all dietary needs, providing complete protein at a moderate cost. It is a short-fibered meat and is easy to digest. Calorie-conscious consumers concerned with nutrition naturally think of chicken when trying to diet. And here's why:
● Chicken contains fewer calories than most meats. A 3½-ounce serving of broiled chicken (without the skin) has only about 136 calories. That same 3½-ounce serving, however, provides 31.2 grams of protein or 52% of the average adult daily requirements. Plus you get vitamin A, thiamine, riboflavin, niacin, iron and phosphorous.
● More heartening news is that chicken also is lower in fats than most red meats. Three ounces of broiled chicken with skin yields about 9 grams of fat; that amount is doubled or tripled in an equal portion of other meats. Chicken skin contains only about 17% fat, a small amount compared to the flavor it offers. Interestingly, the fat that is present is two-thirds unsaturated. This is good news, especially for people watching their cholesterol intake.

If you're cooking slim, chicken is the perfect choice.
● For calorie-wise eating, rely on the addition of herbs and spices such as rosemary, tarragon or dill to enhance flavor.
● Team chicken with low-calorie vegetables—broccoli, tomatoes, zucchini—instead of starchy fillers.
● Cook chicken in low-cal ways—poached in broth, sautéed in a non-stick pan instead of frying in oil.
● If you're really counting calories, don't eat the skin.

The Thrifty Chicken

● Whole birds are about 6¢ to 10¢ less per pound than cut-up chicken. It pays to buy a whole bird and cut it up yourself. Turn to page 120 for illustrated easy step-by-step directions. Deboning your own chicken breast, for example, yields tremendous savings.
● Buy chicken breast quarters (wings attached) when available. They are less expensive than breast halves, and you can easily remove the wings to freeze until you have enough for a bonus dish. As a main course, allow about four wings per person.
● Save the backs, giblets and bones removed during the deboning. Add water and seasoning and simmer for stock.
● Keep a container in the freezer for chicken livers. This way you can save them up until you have enough for a meal.
● Substitute deboned chicken breasts for veal in your favorite Parmesan and scallopini recipes.
● Chicken is a versatile meat that's compatible with many other foods. A little chicken will go a long way when you combine it with economical extenders like rice, pasta, dried beans and sauce for a hearty hot casserole.

Chicken Suits Single Households

Single households are an important part of today's lifestyle, and chicken fits their special food needs. It can be bought in small quantities, it's nutritious and easy to prepare, it's economical, and it's versatile.

The National Broiler Council recommends the following cooking times for baking individual chicken servings. Dip the chicken first in melted butter, turn and baste once during cooking. (Note: Cooking in a toaster oven will save energy and cleanup.)

Cooking Time For Chicken Parts

Part	Temperature	Time
4 Chicken Wings	350°F	20 minutes
1 Half breast	350°F	25 to 27 minutes
2 Chicken Thighs	375°F	22 minutes
1 Leg-thigh Combination	375°F	35 minutes

Storing Chicken
● Refrigerate tray-wrapped chicken from the supermarket for only two days from the time of purchase.
● Multiple-bagged chickens should be rinsed, separated into the desired portions and repacked in clean plastic wrap or heavy plastic bags.
● Freeze chickens in moisture-vapor-resistant materials such as heavy-duty aluminum foil, freezer paper or plastic freezer bags. Press air out of package before sealing.
● Small families or single people will find it convenient and economical to wrap and freeze chicken parts in sizes that are just enough for one meal.
● Storage time for home-frozen fresh chicken is 4 to 6 months.
● Cooked chicken can be safely refrigerated for no more than 2 to 3 days in the coldest part of your refrigerator. It can also be frozen and packaged the same way as fresh chicken, but the recommended freezing period is only 2 months.
● Commercially frozen chicken, wrapped and stored under the most favorable conditions, can be safely stored in the freezer for up to 12 months.
● Always refrigerate broth or gravy in separate containers.
● Remove all stuffing from the bird; store separately, in an oven-safe casserole, in the refrigerator. Reheat at 350° for 30 minutes.

How To Defrost Frozen Birds
It's best to thaw chicken in the refrigerator. Don't unwrap it, because the skin tends to dry out and toughen when exposed to air. Allow 12 to 16 hours for thawing whole birds under 4 pounds, 4 to 9 hours for thawing chicken parts. For more rapid thawing, place chicken, still wrapped, in cold water. Refreezing chicken is not recommended. Do not refreeze thawed raw chicken. Instead, cook the chicken, then freeze.

Types of Chicken
Poultry is graded by the Government to insure quality. This grading system, U.S. Grade A (or No. 1), U.S. Grade B (or No. 2) and U.S. Grade C (or No. 3), is based on such factors as health, pep, fleshing and feathering. Animals that rate below these grades are rejected.

Here are the types of chickens available today.

A **Broiler-Fryer** is a meaty, tender, all-purpose chicken that tastes good when cooked by any method. Broiler-fryers weigh around 2½ to 3½ pounds and are marketed when they're about 7 to 8 weeks old.

A **Roaster** is a slightly larger and older chicken. It weighs between 4½ to 6 pounds and is best roasted as its name implies.

A **Stewing Chicken** or **Bro-Hen** is a plump, meaty bird, a year or more old. It weighs around 4½ to 6 pounds. Because it is older, this chicken is tougher than either the roaster or broiler-fryer and is best stewed.

A **Capon** is a young male chicken that has been desexed. Capons are fleshy and tender with a high proportion of white meat. They can weigh from 6 to 9 pounds and can be cooked many ways but are superb roasted.

A **Rock Cornish Game Hen** is a special breed developed by crossing a Cornish game cock with a white Rock hen. It is marketed at 4 to 6 weeks old and weighs 1½ pounds or less. It's popular with white-meat lovers.

Chicken in Parts is available in most markets today, making it possible to buy only those parts you prefer— breasts, drumsticks, wings, thighs or combinations of any of the above. Skinned and boned breasts and chicken for scallopini are also available.

New Chicken Products are showing up more and more in the supermarkets. For example, chicken nuggets are available uncooked or fully cooked. Other cooked varieties of chicken range from whole barbecued chickens to chicken frankfurters.

Buying Chicken—What To Look For
Look for chicken that has moist skin without any dry spots. Avoid packages where blood or juice has accumulated in the bottom—a sign that the chicken has been out for too long, or may have been frozen. Chicken should smell fresh. This can mean no smell at all or a pleasant chicken aroma. If upon opening the package at home you find a slight chicken odor, rinse the chicken under cold water and rub with a lemon half or dip briefly in vinegar-water.

Amount To Buy
Chicken for frying: Allow ¾ to 1 pound per serving.
Chicken for roasting: Allow ¾ to 1 pound per serving.
Chicken for broiling or barbecuing: Allow ½ a chicken or 1 pound per serving.
Chicken for stewing: Allow ½ to 1 pound per serving.
Chicken livers: Allow ¼ pound per serving.
Rock Cornish Game Hen: Allow 1 game hen per person.

Spanish-Style Chicken and Rice

Spanish-Style Chicken and Rice

Use small chicken legs for quick cooking. Round out the meal with cooked broccoli and individual caramel flans.

Makes 6 servings.

Nutrient Value Per Serving: 303 calories, 22 g protein, 11 g fat, 28 g carbohydrate, 366 mg sodium, 93 mg cholesterol.

Quick-cooking rice for 6 servings
¼ teaspoon turmeric
¼ cup all-purpose flour
6 small chicken drumsticks (1¼ pounds)
2 tablespoons olive oil
2 cloves garlic, crushed
1 can (8 ounces) tomato sauce
¼ cup dry white wine
1 tablespoon lemon juice
1 sprig parsley
1 teaspoon leaf thyme, crumbled
⅛ teaspoon salt
⅛ teaspoon pepper
½ pound medium-size shrimp, peeled and deveined
Lemon slices (optional)

1. Prepare the rice, following the package directions, adding the turmeric to the water.
2. Place the flour in a medium-size paper or plastic bag. Shake 3 drumsticks at a time in the bag to coat with the flour.
3. Heat the oil in a skillet over high heat. Add the chicken and garlic. Brown the chicken quickly on all sides, for about 4 minutes.
4. Lower the heat to medium. Stir in the tomato sauce, white wine, lemon juice, parsley, thyme, salt and pepper. Cook, covered, for 8 minutes (the mixture should be gently boiling).
5. Add the shrimp. Cook, uncovered, for 2 minutes longer. Serve over the rice. Garnish with the lemon slices, if you wish.

Creole-Style Chicken Stew

Use a large, shallow saucepan to bring the liquids in this stew to a quick boil. Serve with corn muffins, a green salad and chocolate-fudge cake for dessert.

Makes 4 servings.

Nutrient Value Per Serving: 431 calories, 41 g protein, 16 g fat, 31 g carbohydrate, 1,075 mg sodium, 91 mg cholesterol.

1 can (13¾ ounces) chicken broth
1 can (14½ ounces) stewed tomatoes
1 bag (16 ounces) frozen vegetables for stew
1 teaspoon leaf thyme
¼ teaspoon liquid red-pepper seasoning
Pinch pepper
4 sprigs parsley
2 tablespoons oil
4 boneless, skinned chicken breast halves (1¼ pounds), each cut into 6 pieces
5 brown-and-serve sausage links (½ package; wrap and freeze remainder for another use), each cut in half
2 cloves garlic, pressed
1 tablespoon all-purpose flour
1 package (10 ounces) frozen cut okra
1 tablespoon chopped parsley (optional)

1. Combine chicken broth, tomatoes, frozen vegetables, thyme, red-pepper seasoning, pepper and parsley in large saucepan. Bring to boiling over high heat. Lower heat. Cook, covered, over medium heat 5 minutes (mixture should be gently boiling).
2. Meanwhile, heat oil in medium-size skillet over high heat. Add chicken, sausage and garlic and stir-fry until chicken turns white on all surfaces, about 2 minutes. Remove from heat. Sprinkle flour over chicken, stirring to coat chicken.
3. When vegetable mixture has cooked 5 minutes, add okra, breaking up gently with fork. Cover and cook 3 minutes.
4. Stir chicken and sausage into stew. Cover and simmer 5 minutes or until vegetables are tender. Garnish with chopped parsley, if you wish.

Braising Poultry

To braise poultry brown it first in a little fat in a heavy skillet or kettle, then cook it, covered, in a small amount of wine, broth, tomato juice or water in the oven or on a surface burner.

Sautéed Chicken Breasts with Oranges

Serve with steamed broccoli flowerets.

Makes 4 servings.

*Nutrient Value Per Serving: 218 calories, 27 g protein,
7 g fat, 10 g carbohydrate, 269 mg sodium,
81 mg cholesterol.*

- **2 whole boneless, skinned chicken breasts (about 1 pound), halved**
- **¼ teaspoon leaf thyme, crumbled**
- **¼ teaspoon salt**
- **⅛ teaspoon pepper**
- **¼ cup finely chopped shallots OR: chopped green onion, white part only**
- **2 tablespoons butter**
- **2 large navel oranges, peeled and sectioned**

1. Place the chicken breasts between 2 sheets of dampened wax paper. Pound to ¼-inch thickness with a rolling pin or the flat side of meat mallet. Sprinkle with the thyme, salt and pepper.
2. Sauté the chicken and shallots in the butter in a large nonstick skillet until the chicken is brown, for 2 to 3 minutes on each side. Add the orange sections. Cook, turning the chicken breasts, for 1 to 2 minutes more or until the juices are slightly thickened.

Sautéed Chicken Breasts with Oranges

Chicken with Hazelnuts Sublime

Wrap boned chicken breasts around sticks of cheese, dust them with ground hazelnuts and then sauté them to a golden brown.

Bake at 350° for 40 to 45 minutes.
Makes 4 servings.

*Nutrient Value Per Serving: 530 calories, 41 g protein,
39 g fat, 6 g carbohydrate, 275 mg sodium,
131 mg cholesterol.*

- **2 whole boneless, skinned chicken breasts (each about 9 ounces), halved**
- **4 ounces Jarlsburg or Swiss cheese, cut into 4 sticks, each about 3½ x ½-inch**
- **¼ cup (½ stick) butter**
- **2 tablespoons dry sherry**
- **1 cup ground hazelnuts or almonds (4 ounces)**

1. Preheat the oven to moderate (350°).
2. Pound the chicken breasts between sheets of wax paper with the side of a wooden meat mallet until the chicken is thin and as even as possible.
3. Place one stick of cheese in the middle of each breast on the bone side. Starting with a short end, roll up, jelly-roll fashion, tucking in the sides. Secure with a wooden pick or tie with kitchen twine.
4. Melt the butter in a small saucepan. Stir in the sherry. Remove from the heat. Dip the chicken in the butter mixture and roll in the hazelnuts. Pour any remaining butter mixture into a 9-inch pie plate. Place the chicken rolls in a single layer in the pie plate.
5. Bake, uncovered, in the preheated moderate oven (350°) for 40 to 45 minutes, or until the chicken is no longer pink and the nuts are toasted. Serve immediately, with sautéed vegetables, if you wish.

Chicken Jarlsburg

We lowered calories by using less cheese, eliminating the butter and replacing the ground nuts with bread crumbs.

Bake at 350° for 40 minutes.
Makes 4 servings.

Nutrient Value Per Serving: 314 calories, 39 g protein, 10 g fat, 15 g carbohydrate, 293 mg sodium, 163 mg cholesterol.

> 2 **whole boneless, skinned chicken breasts (about 9 ounces each), halved**
> 3 **ounces Jarlsburg or other low-fat cheese, shredded (about ¾ cup)**
> 1 **egg, beaten**
> 3 **tablespoons water**
> ¾ **cup unseasoned dry bread crumbs**

1. Preheat the oven to moderate (350°). Line a 9-inch pie plate with aluminum foil.
2. Pound the chicken breasts between 2 sheets of parchment or wax paper, with the side of a wooden meat mallet until ⅛ inch thick and as even as possible.
3. Arrange the cheese in the middle of each breast, dividing equally. Starting at a short end, roll up each breast, jelly-roll fashion. Secure with several wooden picks or tie in two places with string.
4. Beat the egg with the water in a shallow bowl. Place the crumbs on wax paper. Dip the chicken rolls into the egg mixture, then roll in the bread crumbs to coat evenly. Arrange the rolls in the prepared pie plate.
5. Bake, uncovered in the preheated moderate oven (350°) for 40 minutes until the chicken is no longer pink. Serve immediately.

Chicken Grill with Hash Brown Potatoes

This tasty mixed grill of chicken thighs, sausage and tomatoes is sparked with a piquant mustard and currant jelly sauce. Serve with cole slaw and rice pudding.

Broil for 13 minutes.
Makes 4 servings.

Nutrient Value Per Serving: 629 calories, 28 g protein, 36 g fat, 48 g carbohydrate, 650 mg sodium, 103 mg cholesterol.

> 2 **tablespoons dry white wine or water**
> 3 **tablespoons currant jelly**
> 1 **tablespoon Dijon-style mustard**
> ½ **teaspoon leaf rosemary, crumbled Pinch pepper**
> 1 **bag (16 ounces) frozen hash brown potatoes**
> ¼ **cup vegetable oil**
> 1 **sweet green pepper, halved, seeded and cut into ½-inch pieces**
> 4 **boneless chicken thighs (1 pound)**
> 4 **brown-and-serve sausage links (freeze the remainder for another use)**
> 2 **tomatoes, halved crosswise Grated Parmesan cheese (optional)**

1. Preheat the broiler. Lightly grease the broiler pan.
2. Combine the wine, jelly, mustard, rosemary and pepper in a small saucepan. Bring to boiling; boil, stirring, for 1 minute. Remove the sauce from the heat.
3. Meanwhile, cook the hash brown potatoes, following the package directions, using the ¼ cup of oil. Add the green pepper for the final 5 minutes of cooking time.
4. Place the thighs, skin-side down, in the lightly greased broiler pan. Brush with the sauce.
5. Broil 3 to 4 inches from the source of heat for 6 minutes.
6. Turn the thighs over. Arrange the sausages and tomatoes, cut-side up, on the broiler pan. Brush with the sauce. Sprinkle the tomatoes with the Parmesan, if you wish.
7. Broil for about 7 minutes longer or until the chicken is no longer pink near the bone and the sausages are heated through. Turn the sausages after 3 minutes; brush the sausages and chicken with the sauce, if needed. Serve with the hash browns.

Chicken and Vegetable Brochettes

Serve with hot cooked rice.

Broil for 10-12 minutes.
Makes 6 servings.

Nutrient Value Per Serving: 146 calories, 20 g protein, 4 g fat, 9 g carbohydrate, 516 mg sodium, 44 mg cholesterol.

Soy Marinade:
  2 **tablespoons fresh lemon juice**
  2 **tablespoons soy sauce**
  1 **tablespoon vegetable oil**
  1 **teaspoon fresh gingerroot, pared and finely chopped**
  1 **clove garlic, finely chopped**

  2 **whole boneless, skinned chicken breasts (about 1 pound), cut into 1½-inch cubes**
  1 **package (10 ounces) frozen artichoke hearts, thawed and drained**
  6 **large mushrooms, trimmed and quartered**
  2 **sweet red or green peppers, halved, cored and cut into 1-inch pieces**
  1 **medium-size red onion, cut into 1-inch pieces**

1. Prepare the Soy Marinade: Combine the lemon juice, soy sauce, vegetable oil, ginger and garlic in a medium-size bowl. Add the chicken; stir to coat. Cover and refrigerate for several hours or overnight.
2. Thread the chicken, artichoke hearts, mush-rooms, pepper and onion on 6 metal skewers.
3. Broil or grill 4 inches from the heat, basting with the marinade, for 10 to 12 minutes, turning.

Soy Sauce

Chicken absorbs a piquant flavor when it marinates in a soy sauce-based blend. Soy sauce is an excellent salt substitute when seasoning Chinese dishes.

Chicken and Vegetable Brochettes

Tips for Microwaving Chicken

To Microwave: Chicken cooks quickly on the high power setting and retains its natural juices. In general, a 3-pound whole chicken takes 1 to 1½ hours to roast in a regular oven, but it will cook in less than 30 minutes in a microwave. Here are some tips for cooking chicken in a microwave oven:

● To brown chicken, coat it with butter (not margarine), or use soy sauce, paprika, herbs or a commercial browning sauce.

● Do not salt chicken before cooking. Add salt during the standing time.

● Chicken parts cook best on high power, but use medium power for whole birds.

● Choose chicken pieces (breasts, thighs or drumsticks) of equal size so that they will cook evenly.

● When cooking parts, place the larger, thicker parts near the outside and the thinner parts toward the center of the baking dish. Place giblets under the breast.

● Place whole chicken, breast-side down, on a microwave-safe roasting rack in a shallow pan.

● Cover the chicken lightly with wax paper to prevent spattering.

● Microwave on medium, 9 minutes per pound, turning the chicken breast-side up after half the cooking time, or until a drumstick moves easily.

● When in doubt about whether the chicken is done, undercook rather than overcook. It's easy to return the chicken to the microwave oven for more cooking. Remember, chicken will continue to cook during the standing time.

● Allow to rest 10 minutes, then carve.

● Because chicken cooks so quickly, added flavors are absorbed more fully if chicken is marinated before cooking.

Special Creamed Chicken on Toast Points

This extra-creamy chicken may also be spooned over noodles or rice. Serve with a green salad and fresh fruit.

Makes 4 servings.

Nutrient Value Per Serving: 521 calories, 44 g protein, 23 g fat, 32 g carbohydrate, 1,051 mg sodium, 123 mg cholesterol.

1 **package (9 ounces) frozen artichoke hearts**
4 **boneless, skinned chicken breast halves (1¼ pounds), cut into ¾-inch pieces**
¼ **cup frozen chopped onions**
2 **tablespoons butter**
3 **tablespoons all-purpose flour**
1 **can (10¾ ounces) condensed chicken broth**
1 **teaspoon lemon juice**
½ **teaspoon leaf tarragon, crumbled**
  Pinch pepper
1 **jar (4.5 ounces) whole mushrooms, drained**
2 **tablespoons chopped pimiento**
¾ **cup half-and-half**
3 **tablespoons mayonnaise**
1 **tablespoon chopped parsley**
6 **slices toast, each cut into 4 triangles**

1. Cook the artichoke hearts, following the package directions, omitting the salt.

2. Meanwhile, sauté the chicken and onion in the butter in a large skillet, for 4 minutes, or until the chicken is lightly browned.

3. Stir in the flour. Cook, stirring, for 30 seconds. Then add the chicken broth, lemon juice, tarragon and pepper. Cook, stirring, until thickened, for 1 to 2 minutes.

4. Drain the artichokes. Add to the chicken along with the mushrooms and pimiento. Reduce the heat to low; simmer for 1 minutes.

5. Whisk the half-and-half into the mayonnaise in a bowl. Stir into the skillet; simmer until heated. Stir in the parsley; serve on the toast points.

MICROWAVE DIRECTIONS FOR SPECIAL CREAMED CHICKEN

650 Watt Variable Power Microwave Oven
Ingredient Changes: Omit the butter. Reduce the condensed chicken broth to 1 cup; reduce the tarragon to ¼ teaspoon.
Directions: Place the artichoke hearts and 2 tablespoons of water in a microwave-safe 1-quart casserole. Cover. Microwave at full power for 6 minutes, stirring once. Drain; reserve. Combine the chicken, onions, ½ cup of chicken broth in a microwave-safe 2-quart casserole. Cover. Microwave at full power for 7 minutes, stirring after 4 minutes. Mix the remaining ½ cup of broth and flour in a small cup until smooth; stir into the chicken mixture. Cover. Microwave at full power for 2 minutes, or until boiling. Mix the half-and-half, mayonnaise, lemon juice, tarragon and pepper until smooth; stir into the casserole. Add the mushrooms, pimiento and artichoke hearts. Cover. Microwave at full power for 2 minutes. Let stand for 2 minutes. Sprinkle with the parsley and serve over the toast. *Nutrient Value Per Serving: 464 calories, 43 g protein, 17 g fat, 32 g carbohydrate, 870 mg sodium, 107 mg cholesterol.*

Chicken in a Bun with Special Sauces

Try this tempting version of a popular fastfood restaurant treat with your choice of dill or chili sauce. Serve with raw vegetables (great dipped in our special sauces), potato salad, and apples and Gorgonzola cheese.

Makes 6 servings.

Nutrient Value Per Serving with Dill Sauce: 890 calories, 57 g protein, 25 g fat, 103 g carbohydrate, 596 mg sodium, 150 mg cholesterol.
Nutrient Value Per Serving with Chili Sauce: 877 calories, 57 g protein, 25 g fat, 107 g carbohydrate, 817 mg sodium, 144 mg cholesterol.

6 boneless, skinned, chicken breast halves (about 1¾ pounds), flattened slightly
⅓ cup all-purpose flour
1 egg, slightly beaten
1 tablespoon water
⅛ teaspoon pepper
1 cup packaged unseasoned bread crumbs
¼ cup grated Parmesan cheese
3 tablespoons olive oil
6 individual-size Italian bread rolls (grinders or hero rolls), split
1 ripe avocado
Dill Sauce (recipe follows)
Chili Sauce (recipe follows)

1. To quickly flatten the chicken breasts, place between pieces of wax paper. Firmly smack 2 or 3 times with the bottom of a large, heavy saucepan or skillet.
2. Place the flour on wax paper. Combine the egg, water and pepper in a shallow dish.

Combine the bread crumbs and Parmesan on another piece of wax paper.
3. Turn the chicken in the flour to coat both sides evenly. Dip the floured chicken in the egg mixture, then the crumb mixture, turning to coat all sides.
4. Heat 2 tablespoons of the oil in a large skillet over medium-high heat. Sauté 3 chicken breasts at a time, turning once, until golden and firm to the touch, for about 6 minutes. Remove to a plate. Add the remaining oil to the skillet and sauté the remaining chicken.
5. Place a cooked cutlet in each roll. Cut the avocado in half; pit, peel and slice into 6 wedges. Place 2 wedges on each cutlet. Spoon on the Dill Sauce or Chili Sauce.

Dill Sauce: Combine ½ cup of dairy sour cream, 2 tablespoons of snipped fresh dill and 1 teaspoon of lemon juice. Makes ½ cup. Nutrient Value Per Tablespoon: 31 calories, 0 g protein, 3 g fat, 1 g carbohydrate, 8 mg sodium, 6 mg cholesterol.

Chili Sauce: Combine ½ cup of bottled chili sauce, 1 teaspoon of bottled grated white horseradish and 1 teaspoon of lemon juice. Makes ½ cup. Nutrient Value Per Tablespoon: 18 calories, 0 g protein, 0 g fat, 4 g carbohydrate, 229 mg sodium, 0 mg cholesterol.

Chicken Substitution

Thighs and other less expensive chicken parts may be substituted in many recipes calling for chicken breasts.

Stir-Fried Chicken and Vegetables in Oyster Sauce

Stir-Fried Chicken and Vegetables in Oyster Sauce

Makes 4 servings.

Nutrient Value Per Serving: 292 calories, 30 g protein, 15 g fat, 8 g carbohydrate, 818 mg sodium, 66 mg cholesterol.

- **1 pound mixed salad bar vegetables (about 6 cups), such as cauliflower flowerets, broccoli flowerets, sweet red pepper and mushrooms**
- **1 tablespoon soy sauce**
- **1 tablespoon dry sherry**
- **1 pound boneless, skinned chicken breasts, cut into ½-inch cubes**
- **4 tablespoons vegetable oil**
- **3 to 4 tablespoons chicken broth**
- **½ teaspoon sugar**
- **2 tablespoons bottled oyster sauce***

1. Slice any large vegetables into bite-size pieces and reserve. Stir together the soy and sherry in a medium-size bowl; add the chicken cubes; cover and let marinate for 30 minutes.
2. Stir-fry the chicken and marinade in 2 tablespoons of the oil in a 10-inch skillet for 2 to 3 minutes, or until firm. Transfer with a slotted spoon to bowl.
3. Stir-fry the salad bar vegetables in the remaining 2 tablespoons of the oil in the skillet for 1 minute. Add the chicken broth and sugar. Cover the pan; cook over low heat until the vegetables are crisp-tender, for 1 to 2 minutes. Check the skillet occasionally to make sure the vegetables don't burn; add an additional tablespoon of chicken broth, if necessary.
4. Return the chicken to the skillet. Stir in the oyster sauce. Cook for 1 minute longer to reheat the chicken. Serve immediately with hot cooked rice, if you wish.

*Note: Oyster sauce is available in the Oriental section of your supermarket.

MICROWAVE DIRECTIONS FOR STIR-FRIED CHICKEN
650 Watt Variable Power Microwave Oven
Ingredient Changes: Increase the soy sauce to 4 teaspoons; decrease the vegetable oil to 1 tablespoon; eliminate the broth and sugar.
Directions: Stir together 3 teaspoons of the soy sauce, the sherry and the 1 tablespoon of oil in a microwave-safe dish, about 12x8 inches. Add the chicken; stir to mix well. Cover with wax paper. Let stand at room temperature for 30 minutes. Microwave, uncovered, at full power for 4 minutes, stirring after 2 minutes. Remove the chicken with a slotted spoon to a bowl. Scatter the vegetables into the same dish. Cover with wax paper. Microwave at full power for 4 minutes, stirring after 2 minutes. Stir in the chicken, oyster sauce and the remaining 1 teaspoon of soy sauce. Cover with wax paper. Microwave at full power for 1 minute. Let stand for 2 minutes. Nutrient Value Per Serving: 199 calories, 30 g protein, 5 g fat, 8 g carbohydrate, 888 mg sodium, 66 mg cholesterol.

Sweet and Sour Chicken

An Oriental favorite, served with fried noodles and Duck Sauce. Ice cream sprinkled with toasted almonds completes the meal.

Makes 4 servings.

Nutrient Value Per Serving: 461 calories, 39 g protein, 9 g fat, 54 g carbohydrate, 545 mg sodium, 82 mg cholesterol.

Quick-cooking rice for 4 servings
1 medium-size onion
1 small sweet green pepper, halved, cored and seeded
1 carrot, pared
2 tablespoons vegetable oil
1 can (8 ounces) pineapple chunks in pineapple juice
1¼ cups chicken broth
2 tablespoons catsup
1½ tablespoons distilled white vinegar
2 tablespoons sugar
4 boneless, skinned chicken breast halves (1¼ pounds), cut into 1¼-inch pieces
¼ cup water
1 teaspoon soy sauce
2 tablespoons cornstarch
1 package (6 ounces) frozen snow peas

1. Cook the rice, following the package directions.
2. Meanwhile, cut the onion into very thin wedges. Cut the green pepper into thin strips. Thinly slice the carrot using the slicing edge of a grater for fast slicing.
3. Meanwhile, heat the oil in a wok or large skillet over high heat. Add the onion, green pepper and carrot and stir-fry until softened, for about 2 minutes.
4. Meanwhile, drain the juice from the pineapple into the bowl, reserving the pineapple. Add the chicken broth, catsup, vinegar and sugar to the juice; stir well to mix.
5. Remove the vegetables with a slotted spoon from the skillet to a plate. Add the chicken to the skillet. Stir-fry over high heat until it turns white, for about 2 minutes.
6. Add the stir-fried vegetables and pineapple juice mixture to the skillet. Lower the heat to medium. Cover and cook for 3 minutes, or until the chicken is just firm to the touch.
7. Stir together the water, soy sauce and cornstarch in a small bowl until smooth. Add to the chicken. Cook, stirring, until the cornstarch turns clear, for about 1 minute. Add the reserved pineapple and snow peas. Cook just until heated through. Serve with the rice.

MICROWAVE DIRECTIONS FOR SWEET AND SOUR CHICKEN
650 Watt Variable Power Microwave Oven
Ingredient Changes: Omit the oil and water; reduce the chicken broth to 1 cup.
Directions: Combine the onion, green pepper, carrot, chicken and the 1 cup of chicken broth in a microwave-safe 2-quart casserole. Cover. Microwave at full power for 9 minutes, stirring once. Drain the pineapple, reserve the juice. Stir together the juice and cornstarch until smooth. Stir in the catsup, vinegar, sugar and soy sauce. Stir the cornstarch mixture into the casserole. Cover. Microwave at full power for 4 minutes, or until boiling. Stir in the pineapple and snow peas. Cover. Microwave for 2 minutes. Serve with the quick–cooking rice. Nutrient Value Per Serving: 399 calories, 38 g protein, 3 g fat, 54 g carbohydrate, 496 mg sodium, 82 mg cholesterol.

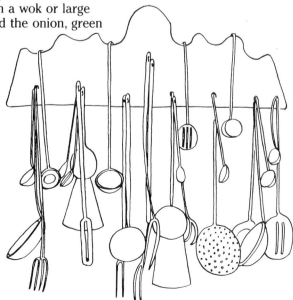

HOW TO CUT AND BONE A CHICKEN

1. Place the chicken breast-side up. Using a sharp knife, make a lengthwise slit through the skin and flesh from the neck to the cavity. Turn the bird over and repeat the cut.

2. Using poultry shears (a) or kitchen shears (b), cut right through the bones (ribs). Cutting to one side of the breast-bone is easier than cutting through it.

3. Turn the chicken over. Cut through the bones, cutting to one side of the backbone. You may remove the backbone. A small bird is cut this way for serving.

4. To quarter the chicken, continue using the shears. Cut across half the bird, following the natural division just below the rib cage and the breastbone.

5. The thigh may be left attached to the leg for broiling; but for frying, bend the leg joint. Cut through the joint with a sharp knife, separating the leg from the thigh.

6. To separate the wing from the breast, bend the joint. Cut through the joint with a sharp knife. The chicken will now be in eight pieces and is ready for frying.

7. If your recipe calls for skinned chicken breasts, use a sharp, small paring knife to start, then slip your fingers between the skin and flesh and peel the skin.

8. To bone the chicken breast, use a small paring knife. Cut the meat away from the rib bones with quick little strokes, feeling your way along with your fingers.

Economical Soup Base

Freeze assorted parts such as necks, gizzards and trims from different chickens in a plastic container with a tight cover, until you have about 4 cups. Use in place of turkey carcass for a soup base starter.

Creole Gumbo with Rice

Our delicious gumbo is the answer to a busy cook's prayers—a hearty, simple, one-pot meal that can be made ahead.

Makes 6 servings.

Nutrient Value Per Serving: 560 calories, 45 g protein, 23 g fat, 40 g carbohydrate, 1,838 mg sodium, 121 mg cholesterol.

1 **broiler-fryer (about 3 pounds), cut up**
  About ¼ cup all-purpose flour for
    dredging
1 **teaspoon salt**
¼ **teaspoon pepper**
2 **tablespoons vegetable oil**
2 **tablespoons butter or margarine**
1 **large onion, chopped**
1 **large sweet green pepper, chopped**
2 **stalks celery, chopped**
2 **cups cubed cooked ham (about**
    10 ounces)
3 **cups chicken broth**
1 **can (8 ounces) tomato sauce**
1 **package (10 ounces) frozen, cut okra,**
    thawed
1 **cup long-grain white rice**
1 **tablespoon Worcestershire sauce**
⅛ **to ¼ teaspoon cayenne pepper**
  Few drops liquid red-pepper seasoning
1 **tablespoon filé powder***
2 **tablespoons chopped fresh parsley**

1. Pat the chicken dry with paper toweling. Coat with the flour, shaking off the excess. Sprinkle with the salt and pepper.
2. Heat the oil and butter in a large flameproof casserole. Working in batches, brown the chicken until golden on all sides. Transfer to paper toweling to drain.
3. Pour off most of the fat from the casserole; sauté the onion, green pepper and celery until tender but not browned, for about

5 minutes. Add the ham; sauté for 1 minute.
4. Return the chicken to the casserole; add the chicken broth and tomato sauce. Bring to boiling; add the okra, rice, Worcestershire sauce, cayenne and liquid red pepper seasoning. Cover; reduce the heat and simmer for 25 to 35 minutes, or until the chicken and rice are tender.
5. Remove from the heat; stir in the filé powder. Sprinkle with the parsley and serve immediately.

Note: This dish may be made ahead, but add the filé powder and parsley just before serving.

***Filé powder** is made from the young leaves of the sassafras tree. These leaves contain a certain amount of mucilage which is both appetizing and healthy. When added to any mixtures containing water, it binds and thickens. The art of making gumbo involves the measuring and mixing of the filé. It is not cooked but added to the gumbo immediately before serving. Filé powder is available at supermarkets in the spice section, and at specialty and gourmet stores.

Smoke Eliminator

For smoke-free sautéeing or frying of poultry, use equal parts of butter or margarine and vegetable oil or olive oil. While butter adds great flavor, the addition of the oil increases the smoking temperature of the butter, giving you a more golden skin.

To Saute Chicken

Heat about ¼ cup of vegetable or peanut oil, butter or margarine or butter flavored vegetable shortening in a large skillet. Place the chicken pieces, coated with seasoned flour or plain, skin-side down and brown for 5 minutes, or until beads of blood appear in the bones. Turn and brown for 5 minutes longer on second side, then follow the recipe directions.

Chicken Chili (Medium-Hot)

Makes 6 servings.

Nutrient Value Per Serving: 327 calories, 35 g protein, 15 g fat, 13 g carbohydrate, 583 mg sodium, 106 mg cholesterol.

2 pounds skinless, boneless chicken, preferably light and dark meat, cut into ½-inch cubes (about 4½ pounds on the bone)
¼ cup vegetable oil
1 medium-size onion, finely chopped (about 1 cup)
3 cloves garlic, finely chopped
1 sweet red pepper, halved, seeded and diced (about 1 cup)
1 can (4 ounces) mild green chilies, drained and chopped
1 can (16 ounces) whole tomatoes, with their liquid, chopped
1½ tablespoons tomato paste
3 tablespoons chili powder
1 teaspoon leaf oregano, crumbled
1 cup chicken broth
2 tablespoons cornmeal
¼ teaspoon salt

1. Sauté the chicken in the oil in a large saucepan, working in batches if necessary, over medium-high heat, stirring frequently, for 4 minutes, or until white and firm to the touch.

2. Lower the heat to medium. Add the onion and garlic; cook stirring frequently, until the onion is softened and transparent, for about 8 minutes.

3. Add the sweet red pepper, chilies, tomatoes, tomato paste, chili powder, oregano, chicken broth and cornmeal; stir well to combine. Bring to boiling. Lower the heat; simmer, uncovered, stirring occasionally, for 30 minutes, or until the chicken is tender. Stir in the salt. Serve.

Just What Is Chili?

Nowadays "real chili" is difficult to find. Each region of the U.S. has its own version—and you'll encounter a wide range of recipes clear across the country.

Many people think of chili as a spicy ground meat sauce or a pinto bean stew with meat and chili powder. But originally, a steaming hot bowl of chili was made of diced or coarsley chopped beef—not ground beef—simmered with onion, garlic, oregano, cumin and ground dried red chile, not chili powder.

Most of the chili powder sold in this country is a mixture of such spices as cumin, garlic powder, oregano and ground chili.

The actual translation of *chili con carne* is "chili with meat," so if you want authenticity, there should not be any beans in the recipe. However, beans may be served alongside.

Over the years, there have been many delicious and different variations of chili, including those made with chicken and pork. Each has its own special flavor, well worth trying. Chili can range from mild to firey hot—season according to your tastes.

Chicken Sandwiches Olé

Bake at 375° for 8 minutes; broil 2 minutes.
Makes 4 servings.

Nutrient Value Per Serving: 452 calories, 27 g protein, 25 g fat, 30 g carbohydrate, 424 mg sodium, 75 mg cholesterol.

1 large onion, chopped (1 cup)
1 clove garlic, finely chopped
2 tablespoons vegetable oil
2 cups chopped, cooked, skinless chicken breasts*
½ cup mild to medium-hot salsa
4 slices white bread, lightly toasted
1 medium-size ripe avocado, peeled, pitted and thinly sliced
2 tablespoons fresh lemon juice
½ cup shredded Monterey Jack cheese (2 ounces)
   Salsa for garnish (optional)

1. Preheat the conventional oven to moderate (375°), if using; preheating the toaster oven is not necessary.
2. Sauté the onion and garlic in the oil in a skillet until tender but not browned, for 5 minutes.
3. Combine the onion mixture, chicken and salsa in a medium-size mixing bowl.
4. Spread the chicken mixture over the bread slices. Place on the broiler or toaster oven pan.
5. Bake in the moderate oven (375°) or toaster oven for 8 to 10 minutes, or until golden. Remove from the oven. Increase the temperature to broil.
6. Toss the avocado with the lemon juice in a bowl. Top each sandwich with the avocado and about 2 tablespoons of cheese. Return the sandwiches to the broiler or toaster oven for 2 minutes, or until the cheese is melted. Serve with the salsa on the side, if you wish.

***Note:** About 1½ pounds of uncooked bone-in chicken breast will yield about 2 cups of chopped cooked chicken.*

Chicken Sandwiches Olé

Reduced Calorie

For the chicken, we've specified chicken breast meat rather than fattier dark meat. And we've eliminated the oil, substituted orange sections for high-fat avocado and reduced the amount of cheese.

Bake at 375° for 2 to 3 minutes;
broil 1 to 2 minutes.
Makes 4 servings.

Nutrient Value Per Serving: 287 calories, 26 g protein, 5 g fat, 31 g carbohydrate, 352 mg sodium, 67 mg cholesterol.

1 small red onion, finely chopped
2 cups chopped, cooked, skinned chicken breast*
½ cup mild to medium-hot salsa
4 thin slices white bread, lightly toasted
2 cups orange sections (2 navel oranges)
¼ cup shredded Monterey Jack cheese (1 ounce)
   Salsa for garnish (optional)

1. Preheat the conventional oven to moderate (375°), if using; preheating the toaster oven is not necessary.
2. Combine the onion, chicken and salsa in a medium-size mixing bowl.
3. Spread the chicken mixture over the bread slices, dividing equally. Place on the broiler or toaster oven pan.
4. Bake in the preheated moderate oven (375°) or toaster oven for 2 to 3 minutes, or until the filling is warm. Remove the sandwiches from the oven. Increase the oven temperature to broil.
5. Top each sandwich with the orange sections and about 1 tablespoon of the cheese. Return the sandwiches to the broiler or toaster oven for 1 to 2 minutes, or until the cheese is melted and golden. Remove from the oven with a spatula and transfer to a serving plate. Serve additional salsa on the side, if you wish.

***Note:** About 1½ pounds of uncooked bone-in chicken breasts will yield about 2 cups of chopped cooked chicken.*

Lemon-Roasted Cornish Hens

Roast at 375° for 50 minutes.
Makes 4 servings.

Nutrient Value Per Serving: 584 calories, 50 g protein, 40 g fat, 8 g carbohydrate, 977 mg sodium, 177 mg cholesterol.

2 lemons
3 tablespoons butter or margarine
1 teaspoon salt
¼ teaspoon pepper
2 teaspoons chopped fresh mint OR:
   ½ teaspoon dried mint, crumbled
4 Rock Cornish Hens (¾ to 1 pound each)
Lemon Sauce:
1 small onion, sliced
2 tablespoons vegetable oil
1 clove garlic, crushed
1 cup chicken broth
2 teaspoons cornstarch
1 tablespoon water
   Chopped fresh mint or parsley

1. Grate enough lemon rind to make 1 teaspoon. Peel the thin yellow rind from the remaining lemon; cut into thin julienne strips to make 2 tablespoons. Squeeze enough lemon juice to make ¼ cup. Reserve the strips and juice for the sauce.
2. Combine the butter, grated lemon rind, salt, pepper and mint in a small bowl. Rub the mixture over the hens. Place the hens in a shallow, small roasting pan.
3. Roast in a preheated moderate oven (375°), basting often, for about 50 minutes, or until the hens are golden and the juices run clear when the skin is pierced. Arrange on a heated platter; keep warm.
4. Meanwhile, prepare the Lemon Sauce: Sauté the onion in the oil in a medium-size saucepan for 5 minutes. Stir in the reserved lemon peel strips and garlic; cook, stirring, for 1 minute. Add the broth. Bring to boiling. Stir together the cornstarch and water in a small cup until smooth. Quickly stir into the boiling sauce; boil for 1 minute. Stir in the reserved lemon juice; remove from the heat.
5. Spoon some of the sauce over each hen. Sprinkle with the mint or parsley. Garnish with watercress, if you wish. Pass the remaining sauce.

Cornish Game Hens with Savory Stuffing

Bake at 425° for 15 minutes; then at 375° for 50 minutes.
Makes 8 servings.

Nutrient Value Per Serving: 359 calories, 35 g protein, 23 g fat, 1 g carbohydrate, 463 mg sodium, 124 mg cholesterol.

   Savory Stuffing (recipe follows)
8 teaspoons butter or margarine, softened
4 Cornish game hens (about 1¼ pounds each), giblets removed and livers reserved for Savory Stuffing
½ teaspoon salt
¼ teaspoon white pepper
   Pan Gravy (recipe follows)

1. Prepare the Savory Stuffing.
2. Preheat the oven to hot (425°).
3. Stuff 1 teaspoon of the butter under the skin of each breast of each hen. Stuff the body cavity of each hen loosely with the stuffing. Tuck the wings under the body; tie the legs to the tail with kitchen twine. Sprinkle the outside of each hen with the salt and pepper. Place in a flameproof roasting pan.
4. If preparing ahead, prepare through Step 3, cover and refrigerate. Allow to come to room temperature before proceeding with Step 5.
5. Roast the hens in the preheated hot oven (425°) for 15 minutes. Lower the oven temperature to moderate (375°). Roast for 50 minutes, or until tender and the juices run clear. Remove to the platter. Remove the string. Keep warm while preparing the Pan Gravy.

Pan Gravy: Pour off all the fat from the roasting pan. Place the pan over low heat. Add ¼ cup of dry white wine or water, scraping up any browned bits from the bottom of the pan. Remove from the heat; set aside. Melt 1 tablespoon of butter in a medium-size saucepan. Stir in 1 tablespoon of all-purpose flour until smooth. Cook over low heat, stirring, for about 3 minutes. Add 1 can (13¾ ounces) of chicken broth and liquid from the roasting pan. Bring to boiling, stirring constantly. Lower the heat and simmer for 5 minutes. Add a pinch of pepper. Pour into a warmed gravy boat and serve.

Savory Stuffing

Makes 8 servings.

Nutrient Value Per Serving: 95 calories, 7 g protein, 3 g fat, 9 g carbohydrate, 453 mg sodium, 79 mg cholesterol.

- **3 cups fresh bread crumbs**
- **Livers from 4 Cornish game hens, rinsed, trimmed and chopped fine (about ⅓ cup)**
- **4 ounces fully cooked ham, finely chopped (about ¾ cup)**
- **¼ cup chopped parsley**
- **1 teaspoon leaf marjoram, crumbled**
- **½ teaspoon salt**
- **¼ teaspoon pepper**
- **1 egg**
- **3 tablespoons milk**

Combine the bread crumbs, liver, ham, parsley, marjoram, salt and pepper in a medium-size bowl. Mix the egg and milk together in a small measuring cup; add to the bread mixture, stirring just until moistened.

To Make Fresh Bread Crumbs

Tear slices of bread into small pieces with your fingers. Or place one slice at a time, quartered, in the container of an electric blender or food processor; cover; whirl at high speed for 15 seconds.

Chicken Livers

Keep a container in the freezer for chicken livers. This way, you can save them up until you have enough for a meal.

Duckling and Goose

The elegant duckling has dark moist meat that goes well with fruity sauce. Duckling usually comes individually packaged and quick-frozen, although some areas sell fresh, ice-chilled ducklings. Weights range from 4 to 6 pounds. Duckling parts, quick-frozen, are also beginning to appear in supermarkets.

How Much To Buy: Allow about one-quarter to one-half duckling per person. Each bird cuts neatly into quarters with poultry or kitchen scissors. Prick the skin when roasting a whole bird to release excess fat.

Goose is less frequently seen in markets than chicken, turkey or duckling, but quick-frozen geese are beginning to appear in big-city areas with some regularity. And, of course, they can always be ordered. Geese are tender and rich and can weigh from 6 to 14 pounds. The ones in the 8- to 10-pound range are best for roasting. Goose is self-basting, thanks to a thick layer of fat between the skin and meat. Cook the stuffing in a baking dish, not in the bird. Allow ½ to ¾ pound per person.

For Serving Half or Quarter of a Duck

You can use this method to cut Rock Cornish hens or even small chickens.
1. Let roasted duckling rest for at least 15 minutes. Cut with poultry shears, starting at opening and ending at the neck.
2. Turn the bird over and start cutting with shears on either side of the back bone to separate into halves.
3. Follow the natural line between the breast and thigh and cut into even quarters.

Easy Roast Ducklings

Ducklings used to be raised only on Long Island from birds first brought from China. Today most ducklings are raised in the Midwest, so they shouldn't be called "Long Island Ducklings."

Roast at 350° for 1 hour, 45 minutes.
Makes 4 servings.

Nutrient Value Per Serving: 1,352 calories, 66 g protein, 98 g fat, 51 g carbohydrate, 798 mg sodium, 290 mg cholesterol.

- **2 frozen ducklings (about 4 pounds each), thawed**
  Salt and pepper
- **1 cup chopped celery**
- **1 cup chopped carrot**
- **¾ cup orange marmalade**
- **¼ cup Grand Marnier**
- **2 oranges, cut into wedges**
  Strawberries

1. Season the ducklings with the salt and pepper; secure the neck skin; tie the wings and legs with string.
2. Sprinkle the celery and carrots on the bottom of a shallow roasting pan.
3. Roast in a moderate oven (350°), pricking the ducklings with a two-tined fork several times, to drain fat, for 1 hour, 15 minutes, or until richly golden.
4. Pour off all the fat from the pan. Combine the orange marmalade and Grand Marnier in a small saucepan. Heat until bubbly. Brush generously over the ducklings in the roasting pan.
5. Roast for 30 minutes longer, brushing several times, or until richly glazed. Serve on a heated serving platter and garnish with the orange segments and strawberries, if you wish.

Jiffy Stuffing

For stuffing in minutes to serve with any poultry dish, look at the assortment of packaged stuffing mixes on the supermarket shelf. For a distinctive touch, stir in 1 tablespoon of orange rind, 1 teaspoon of lemon rind, ¼ cup of chopped walnuts, almonds or peanuts or 2 tablespoons of chopped celery leaves or parsley.

Crisply Roasted Goose

In days of old, a roast goose was the festive bird of Christmas. Today it's eaten year-round.

Roast at 325° for 2 hours, 30 minutes.
Makes 8 servings, plus leftovers.

Nutrient Value Per Serving: 745 calories, 61 g protein, 53 g fat, 3 g carbohydrate, 185 mg sodium, 218 mg cholesterol.

- **1 frozen goose (8 to 10 pounds), thawed**
  Salt and pepper
- **1 small onion, chopped (¼ cup)**
- **2 large carrots, pared and diced**
- **2 stalks celery, diced**
  Pan Gravy (recipe, page 124)
  Sugared Grapes (recipe follows)

1. Remove the neck and giblets from the goose and cook immediately for goose broth. Remove the excess fat from the body cavity and neck skin. Season with the salt and pepper; stuff with the chopped onion, carrots and celery; truss the goose with string.
2. Place the goose, breast-side up, on a rack in a large roasting pan. Insert a meat thermometer into the inside thigh muscle, if you wish.
3. Roast in a slow oven (325°) for 2 hours, 30 minutes, removing the fat and pricking with a two-tined fork while roasting, or until the temperature on the meat thermometer reaches 165° and the drumstick moves easily. Serve with the Perfect Pan Gravy; garnish the platter with the Sugared Grapes, if you wish.

Sugared Grapes: Wash and dry 1 bunch of green and 1 bunch of red seedless grapes and 1 bunch of dark grapes; break into small bunches. Arrange on a cookie sheet or jelly-roll pan. Beat 2 egg whites and 2 tablespoons sugar in a small cup. Brush the grapes generously with the egg mixture. Sprinkle generously with 2 tablespoons granulated sugar, let dry for 30 minutes. Sprinkle with additional granulated sugar. Allow to dry at most 2 hours.

Crisply Roasted Goose

Types of Turkey

A **Roaster,** the traditional big bird, comes in sizes that range from about 10 pounds to 30 pounds. Big birds look most festive on the groaning board and are the most economical in cost per serving; however, they take longer to roast, and if you have a family that goes for drumsticks and wings, you might consider substituting with two smaller turkeys, and you'll double the number of drumsticks and wings.

A **Fryer-Roaster** is a small, meaty turkey weighing from 4 to 9 pounds. Perfect for smaller families.

A **Boneless Turkey Roast** is plump roast weighing from 2 to 5 pounds and provides an easy-to-carve combination of white and dark meat. Ideal to slice for sandwiches.

A **Frozen Prestuffed Turkey** can go directly from the freezer to the oven with no thawing. Available in a broad range of sizes.

A **Frozen Self-Basting Turkey** is injected with butter before being frozen and bastes itself as it cooks. Available in a wide range of sizes.

A **Frozen Boneless Turkey Roll** can come raw, fully cooked or smoked, and also as all-dark or all-white meat, or as a combination. Sizes range from 3 to 10 pounds.

Frozen Turkey Steaks are turkey minute steaks that come either plain or breaded.

Turkey Parts—drumsticks, wings, thighs and breasts—are marketed just like chicken parts. Legs and wings especially offer good eating at relatively low cost.

Smoked Turkey is a gourmet item, ready to slice and eat.

How Much To Buy

When buying turkeys under 12 pounds, allow ¾ to 1 pound per serving; when buying birds weighing more than 12 pounds, allow ½ to ¾ pound per serving. Remember, the bigger the bird, the more meat there will be in proportion to bone. Half of a 20-pound bird, for example, will be meatier than a 10-pound bird—and less expensive per serving.

Ground Turkey Mix

You'll find ground turkey in the fresh turkey parts section of your grocer's meat case.

Makes two 6-serving recipes.

Nutrient Value Per 1 Six-Serving Recipe: 3,778 calories, 368 g protein, 213 g fat, 93 g carbohydrate, 9,347 mg sodium, 2,334 mg cholesterol.

- **4 pounds ground turkey**
- **6 slices white, whole-wheat or rye bread, crumbled (3 cups)**
- **4 eggs**
- **1 large onion, grated**
- **½ cup milk**
- **1 tablespoon salt**
- **½ teaspoon pepper**

Combine the ground turkey with the bread crumbs, eggs, onion, milk, salt and pepper in a very large bowl. Mix lightly, just until blended. Divide the mixture into thirds; proceed with the Scandinavian Meatballs, or your favorite recipes.

Cook's Tip: Ground beef or pork can be substituted for the turkey.

Scandinavian Meatballs

Fresh or dried dill adds a delightful touch to creamed meat or fish dishes.

Bake and microwave directions below.
Makes 6 servings.

Nutrient Value Per Serving: 447 calories, 34 g protein, 28 g fat, 15 g carbohydrate, 1,053 mg sodium, 225 mg cholesterol.

- **½ Ground Turkey Mix (recipe, above)**
- **1 tablespoon chopped fresh dill OR: 1 teaspoon dry dillweed**
- **¼ cup (½ stick) butter or margarine**
- **¼ cup all-purpose flour**
- **1¾ cups milk**
- **⅓ cup water**
- **1 envelope or teaspoon instant chicken broth**
- **2 tablespoons chopped fresh dill OR: 2 teaspoons dry dillweed**

1. Combine the Ground Turkey Mix (above), and the 1 tablespoon of the chopped fresh dill or 1 teaspoon of the dillweed in a large bowl until blended; shape into 24 small meatballs.

2. Brown the meatballs, part at a time, in the butter or margarine in a large skillet.

3. To freeze: Line a 6-cup shallow casserole, following the instructions in How To Prepare Casseroles For The Freezer, *right.* Transfer the meatballs to the casserole.

4. Sprinkle the flour over the pan drippings and cook, stirring constantly, until the mixture bubbles; stir in the milk, water and instant chicken broth. Cook, stirring constantly, until the sauce thickens and bubbles for 3 minutes. Stir in the 2 tablespoons of the chopped fresh dill. Taste and season with salt, if you wish. Pour the sauce over the meatballs. Cool the meatballs and sauce completely. Continue with the freezing directions.

5. To bake: Fifty minutes before serving, remove the foil from the frozen food and return to the same casserole.

6. Bake in a moderate oven (350°) for 45 minutes, or until bubbly hot. Serve with fluffy hot rice.

How To Prepare Casseroles For The Freezer

Line a recipe-size casserole with heavy-duty aluminum foil, allowing enough overlap to cover the food and make a tight seal. Fill the foil-lined casserole, following the individual recipes. Cover with the overlap of foil; seal tightly, label, date and freeze for up to 3 months. When frozen solid, remove the foil-wrapped food from the casserole; return the food to the casserole.

To Bake: Remove the foil from the frozen food; return to the original casserole. Bake, following the individual recipes.

Microwave: Be sure to use a microwavable casserole in the directions above.

Note: When choosing which casserole to use for freezer meals, remember that the shallower the dish, the quicker the frozen food will heat.

Stuffed Turkey Breasts (page 132), Zucchini Boats with Red Pepper Bulgur Pilaf (page 197), Boiled New Potatoes and Onions (page 106)

Holiday Punch (page 279), Gorgonzola Toast (page 77), Champagne Choucroute with Smoked Meats (page 105), Pear Ginger Pudding with Lemon and Nesselrode Sauces (page 262), Cranberry Linzer Torte (page 261)

Stuffed Turkey Breast

The turkey breast is wrapped around a prosciutto and Fontina cheese stuffing.

Roast at 325° for 2 hours and 15 minutes.
Makes 10 servings.

Nutrient Value Per Serving: 573 calories, 65 g protein, 30 g fat, 8 g carbohydrate, 712 mg sodium, 220 mg cholesterol.

- **1 fresh or frozen bone-in turkey breast (6 to 6½ pounds), thawed if frozen**
- **2 cups fresh bread crumbs**
- **1½ cups chopped parsley**
- **1 egg, slightly beaten**
- **1 leek, washed and sliced (¾ cup)**
- **2 teaspoons finely chopped garlic**
- **½ cup (1 stick) butter or margarine**
- **6 ounces thinly sliced prosciutto**
- **1 cup shredded Fontina cheese**
- **1 can (13¾ ounces) chicken broth OR: 2 cups water**
- **4 teaspoons cornstarch**
- **2 tablespoons cold water**
  Salt and pepper to taste

1. To bone the turkey breast, place, skin-side down, on a cutting board. Using a thin-bladed knife, cut between the bone and flesh, keeping the point of the knife close to the bone so as not to pierce the meat; pull the bone away as you loosen it. When you get to the base of the breastbone, be careful not to cut through the skin. (Save the bone for soup).

2. Place the boned turkey breast, skin-side down, on a work surface. Trim off the excess fat. Cut away the pointed oval fillet from each side of the breast; set aside. Make horizontal slits in the thickest part of the breasts, without cutting all the way through. Open the slits toward the top of the breast; pound slightly with the base of your hand or the mallet to make the meat an even thickness. Set aside.

3. Combine the bread crumbs, parsley and egg in a large bowl.

4. Sauté the leek and garlic in 2 tablespoons of the butter in a small skillet until soft, for 5 minutes. Add to the bread crumb mixture.

5. Overlap half of the prosciutto slices over turkey. Sprinkle with the Fontina. Distribute the bread crumb stuffing over the cheese. Top with the remaining prosciutto; press down gently to compact. Lay the reserved breast fillets, end to end, lengthwise down the center. Roll the breast up from one long side; fasten with skewers to hold its shape. Bring the skin up and over the turkey from both ends; fasten with skewers. Wrap the turkey in a double thickness of cheesecloth. Tie in 4 or 5 places with string. Place, seam-side down, in a small roasting pan. Melt the remaining 6 tablespoons of the butter in a saucepan. Pour over the turkey to soak the cheesecloth. The turkey can be prepared to this point, 3 hours in advance, and refrigerated.

6. Roast in a preheated moderate oven (325°), basting often with the pan drippings, for 2 hours and 15 minutes, or until after a meat thermometer inserted into the thickest part registers 185°. Remove turkey to a cutting board. Let stand for 20 minutes before unwrapping and slicing. Reserve the pan drippings for the gravy. Serve the turkey hot or warm with the pan gravy.

7. Meanwhile, prepare the gravy: Tilt the roasting pan carefully and pour off the fat. Add the chicken broth to the pan. Stir over low heat, scraping up the browned bits from the bottom of the pan. Strain into a small saucepan. Skim off and discard any fat. Bring to boiling. Mix the cornstarch with the cold water in a small cup until smooth. Stir into the saucepan. Return to boiling. Cook, stirring, for 1 minute until thickened and smooth. Add the salt and pepper to taste.

Turkey Cutlets with Fresh Tomato and Coriander Sauce

Makes 4 servings.

Nutrient Value Per Serving: 205 calories, 28 g protein, 8 g fat, 6 g carbohydrate, 491 mg sodium, 86 mg cholesterol.

4 turkey cutlets (4 ounces each)
½ teaspoon plus ⅛ teaspoon salt
     Pinch pepper
2 tablespoons butter
1 clove garlic, finely chopped
3 large tomatoes, peeled, seeded and
     chopped (about 2 cups)
½ teaspoon ground cumin
½ cup chopped fresh coriander OR: parsley

1. Pound the turkey cutlets between 2 sheets of dampened wax paper to ¼-inch thickness. Sprinkle both sides with the ⅛ teaspoon of salt and a pinch of pepper.

2. Sauté the cutlets in the butter in a large nonstick skillet for 2 minutes on each side until light brown. Remove from the skillet; set aside.

3. Add the garlic to the skillet; sauté for 30 seconds. Add the tomatoes, cumin, the ½ teaspoon of salt and a pinch of pepper. Cook for 5 minutes. Stir in the coriander. Return the turkey to the skillet and cook for 1 minute longer.

TURKEY TALK

Storing
Fresh turkeys Refrigerate at all times. Cook within 1 to 2 days of purchase.
Frozen whole turkeys Store in its original wrapper for up to 12 months at 0° F. or lower.

Thawing
Conventional (Long) Method
Thawing time: 3 to 4 days, about 24 hours for each 5 pounds of whole frozen turkey.
● Leave the turkey in its original wrapper.
● Place the frozen turkey on a tray in the refrigerator.

Cold Water (Short) Method
Thawing time: about 30 minutes per pound of whole frozen turkey.
● Leave the turkey in its original wrapper.
● Place the turkey in the sink or a large pan.
● Completely cover with cold water.
● Change the water every 30 minutes.
● Keep immersed in cold water at all times.
Note: Never thaw at room temperature. Once thawed, cook or refrigerate immediately.

Stuffing
When? Just before you roast your turkey is the time to stuff it. You run the risk of food poisoning if you do this earlier.
How much? Allow ¾ cup stuffing per pound of bird for turkeys weighing more than 10 pounds; ½ cup stuffing per pound for smaller birds.
Note: Never freeze stuffing that is in a cooked or raw bird. Remove all the stuffing from the cooked bird, wrap separately and refrigerate.

Cooking a Turkey
Cooking that big bird may be intimidating, but don't get "turkey trauma." Today's turkeys are marketed at a young age so they are meaty and tender; it's no longer necessary to cook them to tenderize.

The best way to cook a turkey is in an open pan. Spread butter, margarine, solid shortening or vegetable oil lightly over the skin before roasting to prevent cracking and promote a mouthwatering golden brown color. Once the turkey is brown, cover the breast loosely with a tent of aluminum foil to prevent further browning. Try to use a pan no more than 2″ deep so it doesn't shield the heat from the drumstick area and increase the roasting time.

Timetable for Roasting Turkey (325°)

Bird Weight (pounds)	Stuffed (hours)	Unstuffed (hours)
6 to 8	3 to 3½	2½ to 3½
8 to 12	3½ to 4½	3 to 4
12 to 16	4 to 5	3½ to 4½
16 to 20	4½ to 5½	4 to 5
20 to 24	5 to 6½	4½ to 5½

For Microwave Cooking Chart, see page 134.

Testing for Doneness
● Meat thermometer inserted in meatiest part of thigh next to the body but not touching the bone reads 180°F to 185°F. If the turkey is stuffed, insert the thermometer in the center of stuffing. It should read 150° to 155°F.
● Turkey juices run clear.
● Drumsticks move up and down easily.

Resting Period
Let turkey stand at room temperature for 20 minutes. This allows the juices to settle and the meat to firm up for easier carving.

MICROWAVE COOKING DIRECTIONS FOR TURKEY

If frozen, thaw turkey as directed on page 133. Thawing in the microwave is not recommended.

First Steps

1. Free the legs from the tucked position. Do not cut the band of skin.

2. Remove the neck and giblets from the neck and body cavities. To microwave, place 3 cups of water, ½ teaspoon of salt, the neck, gizzard and heart in a 2-quart microwave-safe casserole and cover. Microwave at Half Power (50%) for 35 minutes. Add the liver, cover and microwave for 10 minutes more. The cooked neck, giblets and stock may be used in making gravy or stuffing.

3. Rinse the turkey and drain well.

4. If desired, stuff the neck and body cavities lightly. Cover the exposed stuffing with plastic wrap.

5. Turn the wings back to hold the neck skin in place. Return the legs to the tucked position. No trussing is necessary.

6. Make Browning Sauce: Microwave ½ stick of butter in a microwave-safe bowl at Full Power (100%) for 30 to 40 seconds until melted. Blend in ¼ teaspoon paprika and ⅛ teaspoon browning and seasoning sauce. Stir well before each use.

To Cook

1. Place the turkey, breast down, in a microwave-safe dish. If the turkey tips, level with a microwave-safe item to cook evenly.

2. Brush the back of the turkey with 1 tablespoon of the Browning Sauce.

3. See the Microwave Cook Schedule for cooking time. Use the Cook Schedule closest to the weight of the turkey. Follow Part I and Part II Cook Times without any delay interruptions.

4. Microwave at Full Power (100%) for Time 1. Rotate the turkey ½ turn. Microwave for Time 2. Remove and discard the drippings.

5. Turn the turkey, breast up. If stuffed, remove the plastic wrap. Brush with the Browning Sauce. Level if the turkey tips.

6. Microwave at Half Power (50%) for Times 3, 4 and 5. At the end of each time, rotate the turkey ¼ turn; discard the drippings; brush the turkey with the Browning Sauce. If over-browning occurs, shield with small pieces of foil after Time 5, check for doneness. A meat thermometer inserted in the thickest part of the thigh (not touching bone) should register 180° to 185°F; in the thickest part of the breast, 170°F; in the center of the stuffing, 160° to 165°F. If *all* these temperatures have not been reached, cook for Time 6. Recheck the temperatures; cook longer if necessary.

7. Cover the turkey with foil. Let stand for 15 minutes before carving.

Microwave Cooking Schedule for Stuffed or Unstuffed Turkey

Approximate cooking time in 625- to 700-watt microwave ovens

Times	4 lb.	5 lb.	6 lb.	7 lb.	Weight 8 lb.	9 lb.	10 lb.	11 lb.	12 lb.
			Part I—Breast down at Full Power (100%)						
1	8 min.	10 min.	12 min.	14 min.	16 min.	18 min.	20 min.	22 min.	24 min.
2	8 min.	10 min.	12 min.	14 min.	16 min.	18 min.	20 min.	22 min.	24 min.
			Part II—Breast up at Half Power (50%)						
3	8 min.	10 min.	12 min.	14 min.	16 min.	18 min.	20 min.	22 min.	24 min.
4	8 min.	10 min.	12 min.	14 min.	16 min.	18 min.	20 min.	22 min.	24 min.
5*	8 min.	10 min.	12 min.	14 min.	16 min.	18 min.	20 min.	22 min.	24 min.
6	8 min.	10 min.	12 min.	14 min.	16 min.	18 min.	20 min.	22 min.	24 min.
Total Cook Time	48 min.	1 hr.	1 hr., 12 min.	1 hr., 24 min.	1 hr., 36 min.	1 hr., 48 min.	2 hrs.,	2 hrs., 12 min.	2 hrs., 24 min.

*Check for doness after Time 5.

Black Bean Chili with Ham and Turkey (Medium-Hot)

Makes 6 servings.

Nutrient Value Per Serving: 386 calories, 30 g protein, 16 g fat, 32 g carbohydrate, 1,254 mg sodium, 67 mg cholesterol.

1 **medium-size onion, finely chopped (1 cup)**
4 **cloves garlic, finely chopped**
6 **ounces boiled ham, cut into 1/4-inch dice (1 cup)**
2 **tablespoons vegetable oil**
1 **pound ground turkey, thawed if frozen**
2 1/2 **tablespoons chili powder**
1 **can (35 ounces) whole tomatoes, drained and chopped (2 1/2 cups)**
1 1/2 **teaspoons cumin powder**
2 **bay leaves**
2 **cans (15 ounces each) black beans, drained and rinsed**
1/4 **teaspoon salt**

1. Sauté the onion, garlic and ham in the oil in a large saucepan over medium heat until the onion is softened and transparent, for about 8 minutes.
2. Add the turkey. Raise the heat to medium high. Brown the turkey for 2 minutes. Add the chili powder. Cook, stirring for 1 minute longer. Add the tomatoes, cumin and bay leaves. Cook for 20 minutes.
3. Add the beans. Cook until heated through, for about 10 minutes. Remove the bay leaves. Stir in the salt. Serve.

Herbed Turkey and Swiss Cheese Puffs

Bake at 375° for 8 minutes.
Makes 4 servings.

Nutrient Value Per Serving: 459 calories, 29 g protein, 31 g fat, 16 g carbohydrate, 491 mg sodium, 87 mg cholesterol.

2 **cups chopped cooked turkey**
1/2 **cup finely chopped celery**
1 **small red onion, finely chopped (about 1/3 cup)**
1/4 **teaspoon leaf basil, crumbled**
1/4 **teaspoon leaf thyme, crumbled**
1/8 **teaspoon pepper**
1/2 **cup mayonnaise**
1/2 **cup shredded Swiss cheese**
1/4 **cup grated Parmesan cheese**
4 **slices rye bread, lightly toasted**

1. Preheat the conventional oven to moderate (375°), if using; preheating the toaster oven is not necessary.
2. Combine the turkey, celery, onion, basil, thyme and pepper in a medium-size bowl. Add the mayonnaise, Swiss cheese and 1 tablespoon of the Parmesan cheese; stir to mix well.
3. Spread the mixture over the bread slices, dividing equally. Sprinkle with the remaining Parmesan. Place on a baking sheet or toaster oven pan.
4. Bake in the preheated moderate oven (375°) or toaster oven for 8 minutes, or until the tops are lightly golden and puffed.

Fish and Shellfish

For Fresh Fish, Look For
- Firm flesh that springs back when pressed with your fingertip.
- Shiny scales that adhere firmly to the skin (they should not be slimy).
- Reddish-pink gills, free of odor or discoloration.
- Bulging, clean and clear eyes.
- Sweet-smelling odor.

The forms of fresh fish available:

Whole Fish—This is, of course, the entire fish, no different than it was when just pulled from the water. Hence, the most work has to be done with this form before it is cooked. It must be cleaned, dressed, scaled and finned.

Drawn Fish—This form of fish has already been eviscerated, but it still must be scaled and finned before it is cooked.

Pan-dressed Fish—This is completely cleaned and dressed fish, so all you have to do is cook it.

Fish Fillets—These are the sides of the fish, skinned and boned, that are ready to cook.

Fish Steaks—Crosscut slices of large fish containing the backbone and vertebrae, they are ready to cook.

How much to buy? As a general rule, allow 1 pound of whole or drawn fish for 1 serving or ½ pound of pan-dressing fish, fillets or steaks for 1 serving.

To Freeze Fish

Fresh fish is highly perishable. It should be used within one day. Keep it refrigerated. For freezing, wrap the fish in moisture-proof paper and store it for up to 6 months at 0°F.

Thaw frozen fish in the refrigerator, but remember that it is really better to cook the fish frozen. This takes a little longer, but there is less loss of liquid, which means better flavor and texture. Store-bought frozen fish should be solidly frozen when purchased. If thawed, use immediately. Do not refreeze.

To Cook

Fresh or frozen fish may be cooked in a number of ways. But whichever way you choose, keep in mind that it takes very little time to cook. Most often, people overcook fish. You need only to cook it until the flesh is firm and has lost its translucent appearance.

To test for doneness, insert a fork into the thickest part and gently separate the flesh. It should fall into thick flakes or layers; with whole fish, the flesh should easily be freed from the backbone.

Most fresh or frozen fish can be baked, panfried, broiled, grilled, poached or steamed.

Vegetable Fish Chowder

Vegetable Fish Chowder

Filled with the rich goodness of the sea, this meal-in-a-bowl is ready in less than 30 minutes.

Makes 4 servings.

Nutrient Value Per Serving: 251 calories, 27 g protein, 2 g fat, 34 g carbohydrate, 1,268 mg sodium, 62 mg cholesterol.

   1 **can (1 pound, 12 ounces) tomatoes**
   1 **bottle (8 ounces) clam broth**
   1 **teaspon salt**
   1 **teaspoon leaf thyme, crumbled**
   ¼ **teaspoon freshly ground pepper**
   2 **ears corn, cut in 2-inch pieces**
   1 **cup frozen lima beans
       (from a 1-pound bag)**
   2 **carrots, cut in 2-inch pieces**
   1 **cup sliced celery**
   1 **cup cut-up green beans**
   1 **package (1 pound) frozen fillet of
       flounder or cod, cut into 1-inch pieces**

1. Combine the tomatoes and clam broth in a large saucepan; stir in the salt, thyme and pepper; bring to boiling.
2. Add the corn, lima beans, carrots, celery and green beans; return to boiling; lower the heat; simmer for 10 minutes, or until crisp-tender.
3. Add the frozen fish cubes and simmer for 10 minutes, or until the fish flakes easily.

Flounder and Salmon Roulade

Makes 8 servings.

Nutrient Value Per Serving: 398 calories, 37 g protein, 25 g fat, 4 g carbohydrate, 395 mg sodium, 157 mg cholesterol.

1 **fresh or thawed frozen salmon steak (about 1 pound)**
4 **fresh or thawed frozen fillets of flounder or sole fillets (about 8 ounces each)**
2 **teaspoons lemon juice**
¼ **teaspoon pepper**
½ **cup water**
½ **cup dry white wine**
2 **shallots, thinly sliced**
½ **teaspoon salt**
1 **teaspoon leaf tarragon**
 Lobster or Crab Sauce (recipe follows)
 Fresh dill sprigs

1. Skin and bone the salmon; halve crosswise; cut each half into 4 strips.
2. Halve each flounder fillet lengthwise; sprinkle with the lemon juice and pepper. Place a strip of salmon on each fillet. Roll up; secure with wooden picks.
3. Combine the water, wine, shallots and salt in a large skillet. Tie the tarragon in a small piece of cheesecloth; drop into the skillet. Stand the fish rolls in the skillet.
4. Heat to boiling; lower the heat; cover; simmer for 5 minutes, or until the fish loses its translucency, becomes white and feels firm. Remove to a platter; keep warm. Cook the pan liquid rapidly until reduced to ½ cup; reserve.
5. Prepare the Lobster or Crab Sauce; spoon over the fish; garnish with the dill.

Lobster or Crab Sauce: Cook 1½ cups of heavy cream rapidly in a large saucepan until reduced to 1 cup. Add the reserved fish liquid, ¼ teaspoon of salt, ⅛ teaspoon of paprika and 1 can (6½ ounces) of drained, boned and coarsely shredded lobster or crab meat. Heat, stirring, until hot.

Flounder

A saltwater flatfish, which is related to sole, fluke (known also as summer flounder), halibut and turbot. Winter flounder is the most abundant and popular East Coast species. It is usually sold fresh or frozen in fillets, or in fresh whole, small sizes.

Flounder has a delicate, fine-textured white meat. Whole flounder can be prepared by panfrying; fillets can be broiled, baked, fried or poached.

Seafood Stew

Makes 4 servings.

Nutrient Value Per Serving: 213 calories, 21 g protein, 8 g fat, 16 g carbohydrate, 287 mg sodium, 138 mg cholesterol.

2 **jars (6 ounces each) marinated artichoke hearts**
1 **pound fresh mushrooms, sliced**
1 **pound medium-size shrimp, shelled and deveined**
1 **cup chopped parsley**
¼ **cup fresh lemon juice**
 Salt and pepper to taste

1. Drain the artichoke marinade into the skillet; reserve the hearts.
2. Cook the mushrooms in the marinade until tender, for 3 minutes. Add the shrimp, ½ cup of the parsley and the lemon juice. Cook, turning often, until the shrimp are pink and firm, for about 2 minutes. Stir in the artichoke hearts; cook until heated through.
3. Garnish with the remaining ½ cup of parsley. Serve warm over rice as a main dish or at room temperature in lettuce cups as the appetizer. Season with the salt and pepper.

MICROWAVE DIRECTIONS FOR SEAFOOD STEW
650 Watt Variable Power Microwave Oven
Directions: Drain the liquid from the artichoke hearts into a 12 x 7½ x 2-inch microwave-safe baking dish. Add the mushrooms; stir well. Microwave, uncovered, at full power for 4 minutes, stirring once. Add the shrimp, artichokes, lemon juice and ½ cup of the parsley. Cover with wax paper. Microwave at full power for 7 minutes, stirring twice to bring the less-cooked shrimp to the sides of the dish. Sprinkle with the remaining ½ cup of parsley.

Baked Red Snapper

Bake at 350° for 35 minutes.
Makes 8 servings.

*Nutrient Value Per Serving: 204 calories, 25 g protein,
8 g fat, 8 g carbohydrate, 712 mg sodium, 73 mg cholesterol.*

> *1 whole red snapper (about 4 pounds),
> cleaned and ready to cook*
> *2 teaspoons salt*
> *1 cup chopped green onions*
> *2 tablespoons vegetable oil*
> *¼ cup chopped fresh parsley*
> *1 teaspoon grated lemon rind*
> *½ teaspoon leaf oregano, crumbled*
> *⅛ teaspoon pepper*
> *2 tablespoons lemon juice*
> *½ cup saltine cracker crumbs*
> *2 tablespoons butter or margarine*
> *¾ cup dry white wine*
> *1 lemon, sliced*
> *1 medium-size onion, sliced*
> *2 small tomatoes, sliced*

1. Wash the fish; pat dry with paper toweling.
   Sprinkle the fish inside and out with the salt.
   Preheat the oven to 350°.
2. Sauté the green onions in the oil in a small
   skillet for 2 minutes; stir in the parsley, rind,
   oregano, pepper and juice.
3. Spread half of the onion mixture in the
   bottom of a baking pan to hold the fish
   snugly. Place the fish on the onion mixture;
   spread the remaining mixture on top.
   Sprinkle with the cracker crumbs; dot with
   the butter. Pour the wine into the pan.
4. Bake in the preheated moderate oven (350°)
   for 15 minutes. Arrange the lemon and onion
   slices alternately on top of the fish and
   tomato slices on both sides; brush with the
   pan juices. Bake for 20 minutes longer, or
   until the fish flakes easily.

Red Snapper

A saltwater fish found in the south Atlantic and
the gulf of Mexico and usually caught off the
coasts of North Carolina and Florida. This is the
best-known species of snapper, distinguished
by its rose-red skin color. In California fish
markets, a red-skinned fish called red rockfish
is sometimes mislabeled as red snapper.
Rockfish is not comparable in quality to red
snapper. Red snapper is considered a lean
fish with a delicate flavor. Rockfish has a
coarser texture.

Red snapper is marketed from 2 to 6 pounds
in size, usually left whole. It can be cooked by
any method for cooking fish, but is ideal for
stuffing and baking.

Marjoram Poached Halibut

*A tasty marjoram-flavored sauce transforms and
enhances the fish flavor; even fish-haters will
like this dish.*

Makes 4 servings.

*Nutrient Value Per Serving: 223 calories, 27 g protein,
5 g fat, 19 g carbohydrate, 1,056 mg sodium,
64 mg cholesterol.*

> *2 leeks, chopped, OR: 2 large onions,
> chopped (2 cups)*
> *2 cloves garlic, minced*
> *1 tablespoon butter or margarine*
> *1 can (35 ounces) plum tomatoes*
> *1 tablespoon chopped fresh marjoram OR:
> 1 teaspoon leaf marjoram, crumbled*
> *1 teaspoon salt*
> *¼ teaspoon pepper*
> *4 halibut steaks (4 ounces each)*

1. Sauté the leeks and garlic in the butter in a
   large skillet until soft. Drain the liquid from
   the tomatoes into the skillet; cook, stirring
   often, until the liquid is reduced by half.
2. Stir in the tomatoes, marjoram, salt and
   pepper breaking up the tomatoes with the
   back of a wooden spoon.
3. Place the fish on the tomato mixture,
   spooning part of the sauce over the fish;
   lower the heat. Cover the skillet; simmer for
   10 minutes, or until the fish flakes easily.
   Serve with boiled potatoes, if you wish.

Halibut

The common name of four species of flounders which are all saltwater flatfish. Halibut is the largest. Like other flatfish which lie on the bottom of the ocean, the halibut has two eyes on one side of its head. They flourish in the deep, cold waters of the north Pacific and the north Atlantic Oceans.

Halibut has firm, delicate, sweet, white flesh and can be prepared in a variety of ways. It is usually sold as steaks or fillets.

Cooking with Herbs

Give herbs time to season foods. If the cooking time is short, let the herbs soak in part of the cooking liquid or a little white wine while preparing the other ingredients.

Sole

Although a number of flat fish in the market bear the name "sole," such as "gray sole," "lemon sole," or "white sole," they are not true soles. Gray or white sole is actually witch flounder; lemon sole is winter flounder. The true soles in the western Atlantic are too small to be commercially marketed. The Dover sole, available frozen or air-freighted fresh from Europe, is the only true sole obtainable. The Dover sole is found from the Mediterranean to Denmark. It is about 12 inches long, oval and flat in shape. Its flesh is lean, firm and fine textured.

The other fish which are marketed as "sole" belong to other families of flat fish. Their body shape is round rather than elliptical. They are sold whole or in fillets, fresh or frozen. They are a lean, delicately flavored fish. They can be poached and sauced, sautéed, broiled or baked.

Poached Sole with Oranges

Grapes and oranges turn frozen fish fillets into something special.

Makes 6 servings.

Nutrient Value Per Serving: 194 calories, 26 g protein, 3 g fat, 14 g carbohydrate, 690 mg sodium, 81 mg cholesterol.

> 2 packages (1 pound each) frozen sole, flounder or other white fish fillets
> 1 cup dry white wine
> 2 tablespoons lemon juice
> 1½ teaspoon salt
> ½ teaspoon white pepper
> 2 large oranges
> 1½ tablespoons cornstarch
> 1 tablespoon butter or margarine
> 1 cup seedless green grapes

1. Cut the fish into 6 pieces. Place the fish in a large skillet; add the wine, lemon juice, salt and pepper. Cover the skillet, bring to boiling; lower the heat, then simmer for 8 minutes, or just until the fish flakes easily.
2. Transfer the cooked fish carefully to a hot serving platter. Cover the platter; keep warm.
3. Pare and section the oranges over a small bowl to catch the juices.
4. Pour the liquid from the fish into a small saucepan. Combine the cornstarch with the juice from the oranges in a 1-cup measure. Stir into the fish liquid. Cook over low heat, stirring constantly, until the sauce thickens and bubbles, for 1 minute. Add the butter or margarine, orange segments and grapes. Heat and spoon over the fish.

Cook's Tip: You can substitute frozen halibut for the frozen white fish in this recipe. Arrange 6 frozen halibut steaks in the skillet and add the wine, lemon juice and seasonings. After bringing to boiling, lower the heat and simmer for 12 minutes, basting with the poaching liquid several times.

Seafood Tortillas

Bake at 375° for 25 to 30 minutes.
Makes 4 servings.

Nutrient Value Per Serving: 740 calories, 30 g protein, 31 g fat, 79 g carbohydrate, 1,417 mg sodium, 92 mg cholesterol.

> **White Sauce (recipe follows)**
> 1 large onion, finely chopped
> 3 tablespoons unsalted butter
> ⅓ cup finely chopped parsley
> ½ cup shredded Monterey Jack cheese (2 ounces) ▶

1 **pound surimi (imitation shellfish from crab and pollock) coarsely chopped**
½ **teaspoon ground coriander**
¼ **teaspoon cayenne pepper**
8 **flour tortillas (7-inch)**
1 **jar (8 ounces) mild or hot salsa or taco sauce**

1. Prepare the White Sauce.
2. Preheat the oven to moderate (375°). Grease on 11¾x7½x1¾-inch glass baking dish.
3. Sauté the onion in the butter in a skillet, for 3 minutes. Stir in the parsley, cheese and 1 cup of the White Sauce. Stir in the surimi, coriander and cayenne.
4. Divide the filling among the tortillas. Roll up and arrange, seam-side down, in the prepared dish. Pour the remaining sauce over. Cover with foil.
5. Bake in the preheated moderate oven (375°) for 25 to 30 minutes, or until bubbly hot. Just before serving, spoon the salsa over the tortillas.

White Sauce: Melt 2 tablespoons of unsalted butter in a saucepan. Stir in 2 tablespoons of all-purpose flour; cook, stirring, for 1 minute. Gradually stir in 2 cups of milk; cook, stirring constantly, until bubbly thick. Stir in ¼ cup of shredded Monterey Jack cheese and a dash of cayenne pepper.

Seafood Tortillas

Grilled Tuna Rolls with Bacon

Broil for 1 to 2 minutes; bake at 375° for 8 to 10 minutes; broil for 2 to 3 minutes.
Makes 4 servings.

Nutrient Value Per Serving: 563 calories, 28 g protein, 40 g fat, 23 g carbohydrate, 886 mg sodium, 130 mg cholesterol.

2 **cans (6½ ounces each) tuna, drained and flaked**
¼ **cup finely chopped celery**
1 **tablespoon finely chopped sweet green pepper**
1 **tablespoon finely chopped pimiento**
2 **green onions, finely chopped**
1 **clove garlic, finely chopped**
1 **hard-cooked egg, sieved**
⅓ **cup mayonnasie**
1 **tablespoon fresh lemon juice Cayenne pepper**
4 **frankfurter rolls, split**
2 **tablespoons unsalted butter, melted**
2 **tablespoons shredded Gruyère or Swiss cheese**
8 **strips bacon, partially cooked**

1. Adjust an oven rack 6 inches from the broiling element, if using a conventional oven. Preheat the broiler; preheating the toaster oven is not necessary.
2. Combine the tuna, celery, green pepper, pimiento, green onions, garlic and egg in a bowl; mix well. Set aside.
3. Combine the mayonnaise, lemon juice and cayenne pepper to taste in a small bowl. Fold into the tuna mixture.
4. Brush the insides of the rolls with the melted butter. Toast under the broiler or in the oven until lightly browned, for 1 to 2 minutes. Reduce the temperature to moderate (375°).
5. Spread the tuna mixture over the toasted rolls, dividing equally. Place on the broiler or toaster oven pan.
6. Bake in the preheated moderate oven (375°) or toaster oven for 8 to 10 minutes, or until lightly golden. Remove sandwiches from the oven. Increase the oven temperature to broil.
7. Top each sandwich with 1½ teaspoons of the cheese and 1 slice of the bacon. Return the sandwiches to the broiler for 2 to 3 minutes, or until the bacon is crisp.

Grilled Tuna Rolls with Bacon Bits

To lower calories in this recipe, we've used tuna packed in water and reduced-calorie mayonnaise and omitted the cheese. And we've substituted whole-wheat English muffins for frankfurter rolls and imitation bacon bits for real bacon.

Broil for 1 to 2 minutes; bake at 375° for 2 to 3 minutes.
Makes 4 servings.

Nutrient Value Per Serving: 196 calories, 16 g protein, 7 g fat, 17 g carbohydrate, 708 mg sodium, 96 mg cholesterol.

1 **can (7 ounces) tuna packed in water, drained and flaked**
¼ **cup finely chopped celery**
2 **tablespoons finely chopped sweet green pepper**
1 **tablespoon finely chopped pimiento**
2 **green onions, finely chopped**
1 **clove garlic, finely chopped**
1 **hard-cooked egg, coarsely chopped**
3 **to 4 tablespoons reduced-calorie mayonnaise**
1 **tablespoon fresh lemon juice**
   Cayenne pepper
2 **whole-wheat English muffins, split**
¼ **cup imitation bacon bits**

1. Adjust an oven rack 6 inches from the broiling element if using a conventional oven. Preheat the broiler; preheating the toaster oven is not necessary.
2. Combine the tuna, celery, green pepper, pimiento, green onion, garlic and eggs in a bowl; mix well. Set aside.
3. Combine the mayonnaise, lemon juice and cayenne pepper to taste in a small bowl; blend well. Stir into the tuna mixture until well blended.
4. Toast the muffin halves under the broiler or in the toaster oven until lightly browned, for 1 to 2 minutes.
5. Reduce the oven temperature to moderate (375°).
6. Mound the tuna mixture on the toasted muffin halves, dividing equally. Place the muffins on the broiler or toaster oven pan. Top each half with 1 tablespoon of the bacon bits.
7. Bake in the preheated moderate oven (375°) for 2 to 3 minutes, or until the tuna mixture is warm.

Canned Tuna

Canned *light* meat tuna comes from yellowfin, skipjack or small bluefin tuna. The *white* meat tuna comes only from albacore tuna. Use light tuna for mayonnaise-dressed salads, casseroles or any recipe where appearance is not important. Use the more expensive white tuna for antipasto platters and in vinaigrette salads. Both are equally nutritious, although tuna packed in water contains about half the calories of tuna packed in oil. Tuna is packed in 3 styles: solid, chunk and flake. Solid-packed tuna has large pieces of tuna; chunk tuna has about 3 chunks of tuna, filled in with small bits; flake tuna is entirely small bits or fragments.

Scallops and Vegetables in Foil Packets

Bake at 350° for 15 minutes.
Makes 4 servings.

Nutrient Value Per Serving: 174 calories, 19 g protein, 6 g fat, 11 g carbohydrate, 522 mg sodium, 55 mg cholesterol.

2 **tablespoons finely chopped shallots OR: chopped white part of green onion**
2 **tablespoons butter**
2 **cups thinly sliced mushrooms (7 ounces)**
1 **cup julienne carrots (2 carrots)**
1 **cup julienne celery (2 medium-size stalks)**
1 **tablespoon chopped fresh dill OR: 1 teaspoon dillweed**
¼ **teaspoon salt**
   Pinch pepper
1 **pound sea scallops, halved or quartered if large**
4 **teaspoons fresh lemon juice**

1. Preheat the oven to moderate (350°).
2. Sauté the shallots in the butter in a large skillet for 1 minute. Add the mushrooms, carrots and celery. Cook, stirring constantly, for 1 minute more. Sprinkle with the dill, ⅛ teaspoon of the salt and the pepper. Set aside. ▶

3. Cut a sheet of aluminum foil into four 12-inch squares. Arrange the scallops near the middle of each sheet. Sprinkle with the lemon juice, ⅛ teaspoon of salt and a pinch of pepper. Top each with the sautéed vegetables. Fold half of the foil over to form a triangle. Fold the edges over twice to seal. Place the packages on a cookie sheet.

4. Bake in the preheated moderate oven (350°) for 15 minutes. To serve in foil, cut an "X" opening with scissors in the top of each package.

MICROWAVE DIRECTIONS FOR SCALLOPS AND VEGETABLES
650 Watt Variable Power Microwave Oven

Directions: Place the butter in a 10-inch microwave-safe pie plate. Microwave, uncovered, at full power for 1 minute to melt. Add the shallots, mushrooms, carrots and celery. Microwave, uncovered, at full power for 2 minutes. Set aside. Divide the scallops among four 1½-cup microwave-safe casseroles. Sprinkle with the dill, salt, pepper and lemon juice. Top with the vegetable mixture. Cover tightly with the plastic wrap, pleated to allow for steam expansion. Microwave, one casserole at a time, at half power, for 3 minutes, or until the scallops are opaque. Let stand, covered, for 3 minutes.

Scallops

There are two varieties: the tiny bay scallops, usually ½ inch in diameter; and the larger, less expensive sea scallops that can measure up to 2 inches across. Bay scallops, which have a more delicate flavor and a more tender texture, are not as readily available as sea scallops. The larger sea scallops, which are best for broiling, have a somewhat stronger flavor and firmer texture. There are color differences among scallops harvested from different water. Color of the flesh can range from white to cream to yellow-orange.

Scallops are low in calories (81 calories for 3½ ounces raw) but rich in iodine and phosphorous as well as in protein. They cook quickly and there is no waste in preparation. **Buying and Storing:** Fresh sea scallops are available in fish markets along the coasts of the United States, or major inland cities if they are flown in. They are also sold frozen, either plain or breaded and fried. In the northeastern part of this country, bay scallops are marketed fresh from mid-September until mid-April.

The freshness of scallops can be judged by smell and sight. Scallops should have a sweet aroma. Their surface should be moist and shiny, and they should not be swimming in liquid. Fresh scallops should be stored in the coldest part of the refrigerator and used within 2 days.

Barbecue

To barbecue is to cook foods over an open or covered fire or gas grill, using direct or indirect heat.

In open brazier or barbecue cooking, an uncovered grill is used to cook foods such as burgers, steaks and chops that require quick searing.

A covered fire is similar to oven roasting—the food is cooked by heat reflected down from the grill cover as well as by heat from the coals underneath. This method is more suitable for roasts, whole poultry, whole fish and vegetables.

With direct heat, hot coals are spread directly under the food to be cooked.

With indirect heat, the hot coals are spread to either side of the grill, and a drip pan is placed directly under the food. A cover is placed over the grill.

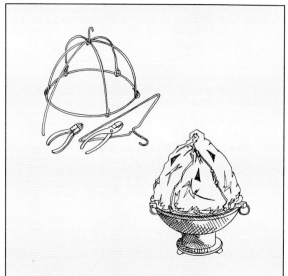

To Make A Grill Cover or Dome for a Barbecue Grill

When the recipe calls for a covered grill, an open-style grill may be used by constructing your own dome from a wire coat hanger frame and then covering it with aluminum foil. Snip the hooks off of several hangers and open them out into straight pieces. With pliers, twist together the ends of 2 or 3 hanger pieces to make a ring the size of your grill. Use 5 or 6 more to fashion a dome. Twist the ends of the hangers, forming the dome around the ring base *(left)*. Then cover the dome with several sheets of overlapping aluminum foil, gathering the foil at the top of the dome and twisting it together to form a topknot for a handle. Cut several flaps for vents near the top *(right)*.

Grilling Tips

Proper grilling techniques are important for succulent, crusty, charcoal-flavored—not smothered—barbecued food. Here are a dozen pointers for no-fail, no-burn barbecues.

• Store the charcoal in its tightly closed package in a cool, dry place. Charcoal is difficult to light if it gets wet or absorbs a lot of moisture from the air.

• For easy cleanup, line the fire pan with heavy-duty aluminum foil.

• Heap the charcoal in the center of the grill or around the drip pan (if you're using one) and set aflame.

• To start the fire, use charcoal starter or an electric starter. Chemical charcoal starter may cause "off" flavors in foods, but the electric starter imparts no odor. If using liquid starter, wait for 2 minutes for the starter to soak in before igniting.

• Start a charcoal fire at least 30 to 40 minutes before you start to cook, to allow the coals to burn and become covered with a gray ash. The heat will be radiant and will cook the food gradually without burning.

• When the coals are hot, separate them into an even layer on the bottom of the grill. To add coals, start them burning in another pan and transfer them to the grill when they are gray.

Temperature Guide for Grilling

Testing by Thermometer
Low: about 300°
Medium: about 350°
Hot: about 400°

Testing by Hand*
Low: 4 to 5 seconds
Medium: 3 to 4 seconds
Hot: less than 3 seconds

*The length of time you can hold your hand over the coals before you have to remove it determine the distance your grill should be from the coals.

• Sprinkle the charcoal with fresh herbs such as marjoram, rosemary, thyme or mint, or dried herbs such as bay leaf or fennel, soaked in water, to give the grilled meat a subtle flavor. Additional flavorings such as hickory, apple, cherry, alder and mesquite may be obtained in the form of soaked aromatic wood chips. Sprinkle the chips over the glowing coals before grilling.

• Brush the grill with fat or oil or use vegetable cooking spray just before cooking to prevent food from sticking.

• When grilling fatty foods, make a drip pan of foil and place directly under the food to prevent fat flare-ups.

• To maintain an even temperature, place the grill in a sheltered place away from drafts. On a windy day, cover the grill with a hood or a tent of foil.

• When grilling foods that need slow cooking, set the grill rack at its highest position and lower it during cooking as the coals get cooler.

• When you use a gas grill, the same principles apply. Preheat the grill to allow the ceramic element to become radiantly hot. Use marinades and barbecue sauces that contain as little sugar as possible, but if you have a favorite sweet sauce, keep the grill rack as high as possible, turn foods every five minutes and brush with sauce every time food is turned. Use tongs for turning to prevent piercing food and releasing juices.

• If any marinade or basting sauce remains, heat it in a saucepan on the grill rack and serve it.

• The last glowing embers can be used to keep coffee hot, toast marshmallows or pound cake, heat fudge or butter-pecan sauce for ice cream, warm cookies, rolls, apple pie, or grill orange or pineapple slices.

Cooking Hints For Barbecue

• If your firebox is not adjustable, cook food on a hinged grill that you can raise and lower manually.

• When wrapping food to be cooked in aluminum foil, place the shiny side of the foil toward the food.

• Marinate less tender cuts of meat like chuck, rump and shoulder and round steaks to tenderize them.

• Trim all excess fat from meat to prevent drippings from flaring up.

• Score fat around edges of meat such as steaks or chops at 1-inch intervals, cutting just to the edge of the meat to prevent curling.

• For best results, cook thin steaks close to the coals, about 3 inches for a higher heat, and thicker steaks further from the coals, about 5 inches, for medium heat.

• Salt meat after the juices have been sealed in by searing.

• To make hamburgers hold together while cooking, add one egg and ¼ cup of bread crumbs to each pound of meat. Or broil hamburgers on foil: Punch holes in the foil at 2-inch intervals to let the fat drip down and the smoke flavor the meat.

• When placing meat on a spit for rotisserie cooking, be sure to balance it properly so it will rotate evenly.

Barbecue Safety Tips

- Don't use kerosene to start a fire. Besides being dangerous, it will make the food taste of kerosene.
- Never use gasoline to start a fire—you can end up in the hospital.
- Do not add more liquid starter once the charcoal has ignited—it can flare up dramatically.
- Keep children and pets away from the grill while lighting and cooking.
- Keep the grill away from where people are sitting so a change in wind won't blow smoke or sparks on them.
- Keep a sprinkler bottle of water handy for dousing occasional flames.
- Wear clothes without dangling scarves, strings or shirttails.
- Always use pot holders and long-handled implements.
- Use your grill in a well-ventilated area—not in your garage.

Grill Cleanup

To clean the grill once it has cooled down, use a stiff, narrow wire or special grill brush to scrape the rack and inside of the grill—no water needed!

How to Grill The Perfect Steak

Below are the best four cuts of beef steak, plus pork and lamb suggestions—all great grilled outdoors.

1. Bone-in Chuck Steak is a delicious way to serve the family steak often and keep within the budget. Be sure to treat with instant meat tenderizer, or marinade for up to 24 hours, before grilling to assure that beef is fork-tender.

2. Strip or **New York-Cut Steak** is the most deluxe individual-size steak. Perfect when you want to grill each guest's steak to desired doneness. Look for supermarket specials that offer a whole shell of beef on sale and have cut to order.

3. Cured Ham Steak is an ideal change of pace on the barbecue. Since the meat is already cooked, it just needs basting and heating. Buy half a ham and ask the butcher to cut 1½-inch-thick center slice—and you will still have a Sunday roast for a little more than the cost of a precut ham steak.

4. Fresh Pork Steak is a cut that you might not have considered before. It too is cut from the center half of a fresh ham. However, since the pork is uncooked, it requires longer, slower grilling.

5. Lamb Steak is one of the most delicious steaks you can offer guests. It is also cut from the center half of a leg of lamb. Cook just to rare. You can always return it to the grill, if desired.

6. T-Bone Steak is the perfect choice when you want a steak to serve two. This very tender cut of beef should be at least 1½ to 2 inches thick, for a well-charred surface, yet rare beef on the inside.

7. Sirloin Steak is the tender, juicy answer when you wish to serve four to six guests. Unless it is cut from prime meat, treat with instant meat tenderizer or marinate.

Vino Round Steak

Wine is a great meat tenderizer as well as a flavor enhancer for barbecued meats.

Grill for 15 to 30 minutes.
Makes 6 servings.

Nutrient Value Per Serving: 385 calories, 35 g protein, 25 g fat, 3 g carbohydrate, 826 mg sodium, 102 mg cholesterol.

- **1 round steak, cut 1 inch thick (about 2½ pounds)**
- **1 cup dry red wine**
- **½ cup lemon juice**
- **½ cup vegetable oil**
- **2 teaspoons salt**
- **1 teaspoon leaf oregano, crumbled**
- **2 cloves garlic, crushed**

1. Trim the excess fat from the steak; score the remaining fat at 1-inch intervals; score the surface of the meat in a diamond pattern ⅛ inch deep with a sharp knife; place the meat in a large plastic bag or shallow glass baking dish.
2. Combine the wine, lemon juice, oil, salt, oregano and garlic in a small saucepan; bring to boiling; lower the heat; simmer for 10 minutes; cool the marinade.
3. Pour the marinade over the steak; seal in the plastic bag or cover the dish with plastic wrap. Refrigerate for 6 to 8 hours, or overnight. Let the steak stand at room temperature for 1 hour before grilling. Remove the steak from the marinade and reserve the marinade to baste the steak.
4. Build a medium-hot fire, or set a gas or electric grill to medium-high, following the manufacturer's directions.
5. Grill the steak, 3 inches from the heat, for 8 minutes for rare, 12 minutes for medium and 15 minutes for well done; brush with the reserved marinade; turn the steak with tongs; grill for 7 minutes for rare, 12 minutes for medium, 15 minutes for well done, or until the steak is done as you like it. Let rest for 10 minutes; cut into thick slices.

Key West Ribs

Lime juice add a distinctive flavor to barbecued spareribs—or try the glaze with lamb or veal riblets.

Grill for 1 hour, 30 minutes.
Makes 4 servings.

Nutrient Value Per Serving: 819 calories, 53 g protein, 54 g fat, 29 g carbohydrate, 1,851 mg sodium, 214 mg cholesterol.

- **4 pounds fresh spareribs**
- **½ cup catsup**
- **¼ cup lime juice**
- **¼ cup soy sauce**
- **¼ cup honey**

1. Build a medium fire, arranging the coals around a drip pan, or set a gas or electric grill to medium, following the manufacturer's directions.
2. Grill, 6 inches from the heat, turning several times, for 1 hour, or until the meat is almost tender.
3. Mix the catsup, lime juice and soy sauce in a small metal saucepan with a flameproof handle; heat to bubbling over the grill; brush part of the sauce over the ribs. Continue grilling, turning and brushing several times with the sauce mixture, for 20 minutes.
4. Blend the honey into the remaining sauce; brush over the ribs. Grill, turning and brushing once or twice with the remaining honey mixture, for 10 minutes, or until the ribs are tender and richly glazed.
5. Remove the ribs to a carving board; cut into serving-size pieces.

Amount of Ribs to Buy

Pork ribs shrink slightly in cooking, so plan on ¾ to 1 pound per serving.

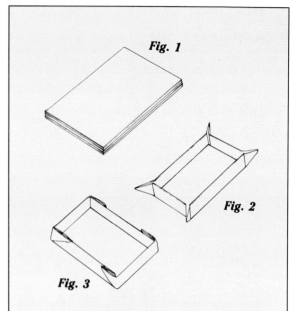

Kettle-Roasting

This technique can be used to cook large cuts of meat such as pork shoulder or beef eye round roast or leg of lamb, or turkey, large chickens or ducklings. Try also to cook or heat casseroles by this method.

To Grill Meat: Arrange gray coals around a drip pan; place the meat, fat side up, directly on the grill, directly over the drip pan. *(See drawing.)* Cover the kettle and arrange the vents, following the manufacturer's directions; follow the individual recipe directions for cooking times.

To Cook Casseroles: Arrange gray coals in a ring around the edge of the barbecue; place the casserole inside the ring on the grill. Cover the kettle and arrange the vents, following the manufactuer's directions, and follow the individual recipes for cooking times.

How To Make A Drip Pan

Fat flare-ups will be a problem of the past when you place a custom-size drip pan under the meat you are kettle-grilling or roasting on the rotisserie. Tear off three 24-inch pieces of 18-inch-wide heavy-duty aluminum foil. Fold in half to make a double thickness (Fig. 1). Turn up the edges 2 inches on each side and press the edges firmly together to form mitered corners (Fig 2). Press the mitered corners inward, toward pan sides, to make a firm pan (Fig. 3). *Note:* This will give you an 8 x 14-inch drip pan. If this is not the right size for your needs, begin with the size pan you will need and then add 4 inches to both the length and the width and then double the measurement of the width.

Times & Temperatures for Rotisserie Cooking Beef Roasts on Charcoal Grills

Important! The grilling times below may differ according to the amount of coals used, weather conditions and type of grill. We recommend these times be used only as a guide. For best results, use a meat thermometer and remove the roast when the thermometer reaches 10° below desired doneness.

Cut of Meat	Rare 130°F.	Medium 145°F.	Well-Done 160°F.
Beef Rib, 6½ pounds	1½ to 1¾ hrs.	2 to 2½ hrs.	2⅓ to 3 hrs.
Rib Eye Roast, 6 pounds	1½ to 1¾ hrs.	2 to 2½ hrs.	3 to 3½ hrs.
Tenderlion Roast, 4 pounds	45 minutes	1 hour	1¼ to 1½ hrs.
Beef Round Tip Roast, 6 pounds	1½ to 1¾ hrs.	2 to 2½ hrs.	2¾ to 3½ hrs.
Eye Round Roast, 6 pounds	1½ to 1¾ hrs.	2 hours	2½ hours
Cross Rib Pot Roast (boneless) or **Rump Roast**	1¾ to 2¼ hrs.	2½ to 3 hrs.	3¼ to 3¾ hrs.

Butterflied Lamb

Talk to the butcher ahead of time and request a boned leg of lamb. It makes carving so much easier.

Grill for 1 hour, 30 minutes to 2 hours.
Makes 8 servings.

Nutrient Value Per Serving: 493 calories, 56 g protein, 27 g fat, 3 g carbohydrate, 412 mg sodium, 198 mg cholesterol.

1 **leg of lamb, boned (have butcher do it), about 7 pounds**
½ cup olive or vegetable oil
½ cup dry white wine or vermouth
¼ cup fresh lemon juice
2 cloves garlic, minced
1 teaspoon leaf oregano, crumbled
1 bay leaf
1 large onion, chopped (1 cup)
1 teaspoon salt
½ teaspoon pepper
Fresh mint

1. Tie the meat into a neat rectangle with kitchen twine.
2. Mix the oil, wine, lemon juice, garlic, oregano, bay leaf, onion, salt and pepper in a bowl large enough to hold the lamb.
3. Add the lamb; spoon the marinade over; cover the bowl with plastic wrap. Marinate in the refrigerator for 24 hours. Turn two or three times.
4. Build a medium fire in a kettle grill, arranging the coals around a drip pan *(see page 146)*, or set the gas or electric grill to medium, following the manufacturer's directions.
5. Grill the lamb, 8 inches from the heat, with a cover on the kettle or grill and basting with the reserved marinade, for 1 hour, 30 minutes for rare, 1 hour, 45 minutes for medium or 2 hours for well done. Cover lightly with aluminum foil. Allow the meat to "rest" for 20 minutes before carving.
6. Place the lamb on a heated serving platter; garnish with the fresh mint leaves, if you wish.

When Buying a Half Leg of Lamb

Choose a 4-pound or more shank half. A smaller one would have a higher proportion of bone and less meat.

Peppery Grilled Chicken

Red pepper and garlic give character to charcoal-broiled chicken quarters.

Grill for 40 minutes.
Makes 8 servings.

Nutrient Value Per Serving: 430 calories, 34 g protein, 31 g fat, 1 g carbohydrate, 732 mg sodium, 130 mg cholesterol.

2 broiler-fryers, quartered (about 2½ pounds each)
⅓ cup butter or margarine
¼ teaspoon dried red pepper, crushed
¼ cup olive or vegetable oil
1 small onion, chopped (¼ cup)
1 clove garlic, minced
¼ cup chopped parsley
¼ cup lemon juice
2 teaspoons salt

1. Wipe the broiler-fryers with damp paper towels; remove any excess fat. Let the chicken stand at room temperature for at least 1 hour before grilling.
2. Melt the butter or margarine with the red pepper in a small saucepan; add the oil, onion, garlic, parsley, lemon juice and salt; simmer for 5 minutes. Brush generously over the chicken pieces.
3. Build a medium-hot fire or set an electric or gas grill to medium-high, following the manufacturer's directions.
4. Grill, 6 inches from the heat for 20 minutes, brushing with the reserved marinade several times; turn and grill for 20 minutes, brushing with the marinade, or until the chicken is tender.

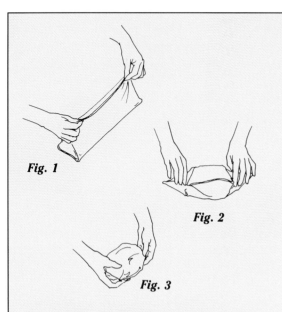

Fig. 1

Fig. 2

Fig. 3

The Drugstore Wrap

This is a great way to wrap and seal packets of food for the barbecue (or meats for the freezer). It is essential that the seal be tight, so that the juices of the cooking food won't spill over into the fire (and the air won't get into the meat and cause freezer-burn). Start by placing the item to be wrapped in the center of a piece of heavy-duty aluminum foil that is large enough to go around the food and allow for folding at the top and sides. Bring the two long sides up and over the food and fold them over about 1 inch (Fig. 1). Make a crease the entire length; make one more tight fold to bring the wrapping down to the level of the food surface. Press out the air toward the ends (Fig. 2). Fold the ends up and over, pressing out the air and shaping to the contours of the food (Fig. 3).

Corn 'N' Chicken

Chicken quarters and colorful vegetables cook to moist tenderness in individual aluminum foil packets.

Grill for 1 hour.
Makes 4 servings.

Nutrient Value Per Serving: 510 calories, 45 g protein, 29 g fat, 17 g carbohydrate, 1,019 mg sodium, 154 mg cholesterol.

- **1 broiler-fryer, quartered (about 3 pounds)**
- **1 can (12 ounces) whole-kernel corn, drained**
- **1 can (1 pound) tomatoes, drained and chopped**
- **1 small onion, grated**
- **1 large green pepper, cut into rings**
- **2 tablespoons butter or margarine**
- **1 teaspoon salt**
- **¼ teaspoon seasoned pepper**
- **¼ cup shredded American cheese**

1. Build a medium fire, or set an electric or gas grill to medium, following the manufacturer's directions.
2. Grill the chicken quarters, skin-side down, 4 inches from the heat, for 10 minutes; turn with tongs; grill for 5 minutes longer, or until golden.
3. While the chicken browns, combine the corn, tomatoes, onion and green pepper in a small bowl. Tear four 18-inch squares of heavy-duty aluminum foil and spoon the vegetable mixture into the center of the foil squares; dot vegetables with the butter or margarine.
4. Place a chicken quarter in each foil square; season with the salt and pepper and sprinkle with the American cheese. Wrap the foil with drugstore wrap, following the directions at left.
5. Grill, 4 inches from the heat, turning every 10 minutes, for 45 minutes, or until the chicken is tender.

Scallops en Coquille

You can use sea shells, metal au gratin dishes or individual foil pans to serve this definitely French dish.

Grill for 20 minutes.
Makes 6 servings.

Nutrient Value Per Serving: 304 calories, 25 g protein, 16 g fat, 15 g carbohydrate, 896 mg sodium, 69 mg cholesterol.

- **2 pounds fresh or frozen sea scallops**
- **⅔ cup dry white wine**
- **¼ cup peanut or vegetable oil**
- **¼ cup lemon juice**
- **2 tablespoons chopped chives**
- **1 teaspoon salt**
- **¼ teaspoon white pepper**
  Buttered Bread Crumbs (recipe follows)

1. Build a medium fire in a grill with a cover, or set an electric or gas grill to medium, following the manufacturer's directions.
2. Thaw the scallops, if necessary. Divide the

scallops among 6 scallop shells, au gratin dishes or individual almuminum foil pans. Drizzle first with the wine, then the oil and lemon juice. Sprinkle with the chives, salt and pepper. Top with the Buttered Bread Crumbs.

3. Grill, 6 inches from the heat in the covered grill, for 20 minutes, or until the crumbs are golden. Serve with buttered Italian green beans and yellow squash.

Buttered Bread Crumbs: Makes 2 cups. Place 4 slices of white bread, quartered, 1 slice at a time in the container of an electric blender; cover; process on high for 15 seconds; empty into a medium bowl. Drizzle 3 tablespoons of melted butter or margarine over the bread crumbs; add 1 teaspoon of paprika. Toss with a fork until the crumbs are evenly coated.

Chives

Chives grow from tiny bulbs in grass-like clumps. They are noted for their delicate onion flavor and fresh, spring-green color. Most supermarkets now sell them in the spring or summer in little flowerpots. When they are 6 to 8 inches high, snip them off with scissors and add to salads, soup, scrambled eggs, salad dressing, mashed or baked potatoes and cottage cheese. The plant will continue to grow, providing you with another crop to harvest.

If chives are allowed to flower, the result will be clover-like rose-colored buds. The flowers can be cut and tossed into a green salad.

Another different variety of chives found in some markets is called "garlic," or "Chinese chives." They look much like other chives, but their leaves are flatter and wider. Garlic chives have a milk garlic flavor. Their flowers are white.

Fresh chives can be preserved by drying or freezing. To dry in a microwave oven, place the washed and cut chives on a piece of doubled paper toweling. Microwave for 1½ minutes on high power, or until dry. Store in a jar at room temperature. To freeze, wash, cut and put chives in small, airtight containers. Label, date and freeze. Commercially frozen chopped chives and freeze-dried chives are readily available.

Curried Swordfish

Simmer swordfish steaks in a skillet over your barbecue for a gourmet treat.

Grill for 15 minutes.
Makes 4 servings.

Nutrient Value Per Serving: 244 calories, 33 g protein, 10 g fat, 3 g carbohydrate, 643 mg sodium, 94 mg cholesterol.

1½ pounds swordfish OR: 2 packages
(12 ounces each) frozen halibut steaks
  2 cups water
  1 teaspoon salt
  ¼ teaspoon pepper
  1 tablespoon lemon juice
  1 bay leaf
  1 tablespoon vegetable oil
  1 tablespoon chopped onion
  1 tablespoon chopped green pepper
  1 to 2 teaspoons curry powder
  1 tablespoon cornstarch

1. Build a medium-hot fire or set an electric or gas grill to medium-high, following the manufacturer's directions.

2. Cut the fish into 4 pieces. Heat the water to boiling in a large skillet with a flameproof handle; add the fish, salt, pepper, lemon juice and bay leaf; simmer for 15 minutes on the grill, or until the fish flakes easily when tested with a fork; remove the fish to a metal au gratin dish; cover with aluminum foil and push to the back of the grill to keep warm.

3. Strain the cooking liquid into a 2-cup measure. Add the oil to the skillet; sauté the onion and green pepper for 2 minutes; add the curry powder and cook for 1 minute.

4. Pour 1 cup of the strained cooking liquid into the skillet and bring to boiling. Combine the cornstarch and 2 tablespoons of the cold water in a cup; stir into the skillet. Cook stirring constantly, until the sauce thickens and bubbles, for 3 minutes; pour over the fish and garnish with chopped green onion and parsley.

BARBECUING VEGETABLES

Vegetables should be grilled 6 inches above coals that have been allowed to burn until they are covered with white ash (about 30 to 45 minutes); if using a gas grill, preheat on medium setting. Cooking times for grilling will vary depending on the size and type of vegetable. Eggplant, for instance, will cook in 30 minutes; root vegetables, like carrots and potatoes, need at least 45 minutes. Cooked directly on the grill, sliced vegetables or vegetable kabobs will take approximately 15 minutes. Vegetables wrapped in foil are thoroughly cooked when they yield to gentle pressure. Vegetable slices and kabobs are done when easily pierced with a fork.

Foil Grilling

First, rinse the vegetables thoroughly and *do not* dry. The water that clings will help steam-cook them in their packets. Place no more than four servings of vegetables on a single sheet of heavy-duty aluminum foil. When combining vegetables either in foil packets or on kabobs, cut them into similar sizes for even cooking. Corn on the cob should be wrapped separately. Dot vegetables evenly with butter or margarine, or sprinkle with vegetable or olive oil or Italian dressing before sealing the foil. Most vegetables are done when just fork-tender.

Direct Grilling

Grilling vegetables directly imparts that wonderful barbecue flavor, though it is a bit trickier than foil-roasting. Zucchini, summer squash, eggplant and onion should be sliced 1 inch thick and brushed with basting sauce, melted butter or margarine or oil. Vegetables prepared for kabobs should be cut into equal sizes so that they cook evenly. Lightly grease the grill and turn the vegetables occasionally to prevent sticking.

Coal Roasting

Hearty vegetables like potatoes, carrots and onions may be wrapped whole in foil and cooked in the coals—great for campfire cooking. Place the foil-wrapped vegetables on the edge of the fire or place directly into a low, low flame.

The cooking time varies greatly, depending on the intensity of the heat.

Here is a quick glimpse at vegetables that can take to the grill and tips for carefree barbecuing. See the Vegetable Grilling Chart (page 152) for more specific information on preparation, cooking times and suggested seasoning.

Mushrooms, peas, asparagus, beans and sweet bell peppers share approximate cooking times and make delicious foil companions. They will cook in 15 to 20 minutes. Mushrooms and bell peppers can also hold their own when kabobed and cooked directly on the grill for about 15 minutes, turning occasionally.

Broccoli, carrots, cauliflower and summer squash are best cooked in foil. Cooking times are 20 to 25 minutes and make colorful combinations.

Eggplants, onions, potatoes, tomatoes and winter squash do well in foil or directly on the grill. Slice all 1 inch thick for grilling and baste with melted butter or margarine or vegetable oil. Cook directly on the grill for 20 to 25 minutes or combine cubed vegetables on kabobs for a colorful side dish. All except tomatoes may also be wrapped in foil and roasted whole on the grill. Allow about 30 to 50 minutes depending on the temperature and size of the vegetable. A little overcooking does no harm. Potatoes, winter squash or onions may be foil-wrapped and roasted in a low fire or coal bed. Allow 45 to 50 minutes.

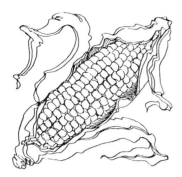

Corn comes with its own special packet—the husk. Strip the husk back, but do not detach from the stalk. Remove the corn silk. Reassemble the husk by returning each leaf back to its original position.

Secure the husk around the cob by tying string around the loose tips. Soak the tied ears of corn in cold water for 10 minutes. Drain and cook on the grill for 20 to 25 minutes. Corn is done when the husks are brown all over.

Whole corn may also be cooked husked and then wrapped in foil.

- Foil packets and kabobs may be prepared up to one day ahead to save time when entertaining. (Cover the kabobs with foil or plastic wrap.)
- Marinating time for vegetables may range from 1 to 3 hours. Brush the marinade on vegetables cooked directly on the grill.
- Rotate foil packets and kabobs frequently to be sure the heat is dispersed evenly throughout.
- Try grilling meat separately from vegetables on kabob skewers. The meat usually needs a longer cooking time and the vegetable kabobs may be added during the last period of cooking to prevent them from becoming over done. Baste the meat and vegetables with the same marinade.

- Garden fresh herbs add exciting flavors, naturally. Strong herbs, like oregano, tarragon and thyme may be added to the foil packet before cooking. Delicate flavors such as mint, dill and basil should be added a few minutes before serving.

- Sprinkle vegetables with the juice and rind of lemons, limes and oranges just after grilling, for zest.
- Prepared or homemade salad dressings make quick seasonings for foil packets, marinades and basting sauces. Test your favorite combinations with low-cal or regular dressings.
- Add a little chopped bacon or salt pork to foil packets before cooking. Wrap a strip of bacon around a corn cob after soaking. Reassemble the husk and roast for 20 minutes, or until almost done. Remove 1/3 of the husk and continue to grill to crisp the bacon.

- Experiment: Try different combinations of vegetables and seasoning. For example, fresh peas and fresh mint, carrots and fresh dill, tomatoes and fresh basil...the only limit is one of imagination.
- Grilling vegetables needn't be limited to the summer months. For those who long for a taste of summer in February and are willing to brave the weather, several winter vegetables make good candidates for the grill. Turnips, parsnips and beets, cooked in foil for 25 to 30 minutes, help summertime chefs span the season.

VEGETABLE GRILLING CHART

Vegetable	Serving Size (about 4 oz.)	Preparation Tips	Grilling Time	Suggested Seasonings
Asparagus	4 to 6 medium-size spears.	Snap off and discard tough ends, remove scales with vegetable scraper, plunge in cold water and drain.	15 to 20 minutes or until just tender.	Butter or margarine, tarragon, lemon, dill.
Beans (Green, Italian, Wax)	10 to 15 green or wax, about 8 to 12 Italian.	Rinse, snap off and discard ends. Leave whole or cut in half.	15 to 20 minutes or until fork-tender.	Butter or margarine, chives, fresh dill, lemon, Italian dressing; add a little to the foil packet before grilling.
Broccoli	About 2 stalks, ½ cup flowerets.	Rinse, cut and discard base; leave whole and slash through bottom inch of stalks or slice stalk and cut into flowerets.	20 to 25 minutes or until fork-tender.	Butter or margarine, lemon, dill, fresh ginger, curry.
Carrots	2 to 5, depending on size.	Trim tops and root ends and scrub or peel with a vegetable peeler.	20 to 25 minutes or until fork-tender.	Butter or margarine, mustard, horseradish mixed with mayonnaise, fresh mint and nutmeg.
Cauliflower	½ cup flowerets.	Trim away green leaves, core and cut or break into flowerets.	20 to 25 minutes or until fork-tender.	Butter or margarine, tarragon, lemon juice, soy, dill.
Corn on the Cob	1 ear.	Remove the husk and silk, wrap in aluminum foil; or peel back husk, remove silk, and replace husk to cover cob. Do not wrap in foil.	15 to 20 minutes until just tender.	Butter or margarine and bacon.
Eggplant	¼ large or ½ medium.	Slice into ½-inch slices or 1-inch cubes.	15 to 20 minutes per side, or until brown, or use on kabobs.	Italian dressing or olive oil with oregano, parsley, garlic.
Mushrooms	5 to 7, depending on size.	Wipe with damp towel or mushroom brush, trim stem end, leave whole.	10 to 15 minutes.	Italian dressing, olive oil with oregano, lemon, butter, dill.
Onions (Dry)	¼ to ½ medium or 1 small, depending on size and strength.	Peel away dry skin and slice; or chop and use with other vegetables; or leave skin on and use directly on grill.	20 to 25 minutes, sliced; cubed for kabobs; 45 to 50 minutes, whole unskinned.	Butter or margarine, Italian dressing, or olive oil with oregano, lemon butter, basil or nutmeg.
Peppers (Red or Green Bell)	½ large or 1 whole medium.	Core and remove seeds. Cut in half; or in cubes for kabobs; or leave whole.	15 to 20 minutes until tender.	Italian dressing, olive oil with oregano, lemon butter, basil.
Potatoes	1 large or 2 to 3 small.	Scrub and pierce with a fork. Leave whole or slice lengthwise or horizontally.	50 to 60 minutes or until tender, or 15 minutes per side, until brown.	Butter or margarine, chives, dill sour cream, yogurt, cheese. Baste with oil and seasonings or Italian dressing.
Squash (Summer)	½ medium or 1 small.	Slice lengthwise or horizontally.	20 to 25 minutes or until tender.	Butter or margarine, chives, basil, Italian dressing.
Squash (Winter)	¼ to ½, depending on size.	Remove seeds, place cut-side down on grill.	40 to 45 minutes until tender.	Butter or margarine, nutmeg, brown sugar.
Tomatoes (Whole, Cherry)	1 medium or ½ large; 3 to 5 cherry.	Cut leaves from stem and core. Quarter or use cherry tomatoes for kabobs.	20 to 25 minutes or until soft.	Drizzle with salad oil or olive oil and basil, dill, oregano; add grated cheese 5 minutes before removing from grill.

Athenian Vegetable Bake

Eggplant, zucchini and yellow squash star in a
show-stopping casserole

Grill for 40 minutes.
Makes 8 servings.

Nutrient Value Per Serving: 187 calories, 6 g protein, 13 g fat,
15 g carbohydrate, 340 mg sodium, 11 mg cholesterol.

    1 **large eggplant**
    8 **tiny zucchini**
    8 **tiny yellow squash**
 1/3 **cup olive or vegetable oil**
    1 **teaspoon salt**
    1 **teaspoon leaf oregano, crumbled**
 1/4 **teaspoon pepper**
    2 **large tomatoes, sliced**
    1 **cup shredded mozzarella cheese**
       (4 ounces)

1. Trim the eggplant; cut into ½-inch-thick
slices; trim the zucchini and squash.
2. Build a medium fire, or set a gas or electric
grill to medium, following the manufacturer's
directions.
3. Combine the oil, salt, oregano and pepper in
a 1-cup measure. Brush the seasoned oil over
one side of the eggplant and on the zucchini
and yellow squash.
4. Grill, 6 inches from the heat, basting with the
oil and turning often, for 30 minutes, or just
until crisp-tender.
5. Arrange the vegetables in a flameproof
10-cup casserole. Top with the tomato slices
and sprinkle with the cheese. Cover the
casserole with heavy-duty aluminum foil.
6. Grill, 6 inches from the heat, for 10 minutes,
or until the cheese melts and the tomatoes
are heated through.

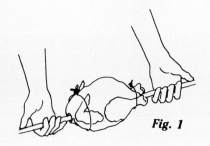

Fig. 1

To Truss Poultry

Secure the neck skin with a metal skewer;
push the tail into the cavity and secure with a
metal skewer. Press the wings against the side
of the breast and wrap a long piece of cotton
twine twice around the bird and tie securely;
loop a second long piece of twine several
times around the drumsticks and tie. If the
poultry is stuffed, be sure to secure the
opening with small metal skewers and lace
it closed with twine.

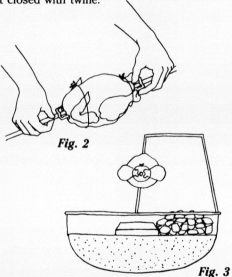

Fig. 2

Fig. 3

Points On Rotisserie Cooking

Roasts, chickens, turkeys and Rock Cornish
hens are more moist and flavorful when
cooked over the coals, turning slowly on a
rotisserie. In Fig. 1 you see how the roast or
poultry should balance evenly on the rotisserie
rod for even cooking. Fig. 2 shows how the
holding forks should be inserted securely to
prevent the meat from slipping while roasting.
Fig. 3 illustrates how the gray coals should be
piled at the back of the grill with the drip pan
directly under the grilling meat or poultry to
prevent flare-ups that give a burnt, rather than
a charcoal, taste to foods.

*Vealballs with Dilled Fetuccine (page 101), Cheese Ravioli with Red-Pepper and Tomato Sauce (page 156),
Confetti Primavera with Mozzarella (page 157)*

More Main Courses

Thanks to today's healthier way of eating, a whole new arena for recipe creativity and experimentation has opened up. In this chapter, we bring you main dishes that make use of meal-stretching staples—like pasta, cheese, eggs and legumes—in delicious combinations. For example, you can indulge in something unusual, such as Spicy Noodles with Pork (page 161), a zesty meal for four. Or, go meatless with a more familiar dish—Pasta with Broccoli (page 158).

Dried beans are more than an excellent way to save on your budget. Add them to soups, casseroles and salads, like our Bean and Potato Salad with Ham (page 162), and they create scrumptious main dishes that are packed with protein, too.

Eggs and cheese are two of nature's simplest and versatile—not to mention tasty!—foods. Eggs Au Gratin (page 165), for instance, combines hard-cooked eggs with macaroni and is baked under a layer of Parmesan—delicious! And don't forget that eggs are a terrific source of complete protein—that is, they contain all of the eight essential amino acids necessary for good health.

Main dishes using fresh vegetables and fruits can also be a delightful change of pace. Fresh oranges and leftover chicken go together in Chicken, Orange and Beet Salad (page 181) for a cool main-dish salad that doesn't require cooking.

Flip through this chapter and you'll find yet more fabulous ways to spark your culinary creativity!

 Quick

 Make Ahead

 Entertaining

$ Low Cost

Low Calorie

Pasta

Buy pasta in well-wrapped packages and avoid those packages with too many broken pieces.

Cooking time varies with the size, shape and type of pasta, as well as its freshness. Be sure to read individual package directions and test after minimum time; *do not overcook.*

How much pasta should you cook and serve? It's a matter of personal preference. One pound of spaghetti is sufficient for 6 to 8 first-course or accompaniment servings but makes only 3 to 4 main-dish servings.

Different shapes of pasta are interchangeable in most recipes, but if the size or thickness is different, the amount of pasta needed may have to be adjusted. Dry or uncooked pasta should be substituted by weight, not measurement, because pastas of different shapes will not have the same volume. A cupful of one pasta may differ in weight from a cupful of a differently shaped pasta. Cooked pasta can be substituted cup for cup.

How to Cook Pasta

1. Use a large kettle because the pasta needs plenty of room to bubble if it's to cook without sticking.

2. Do not cook more than 1 pound of pasta at a time in the same kettle. It will clump or stick together.

3. Fill a large kettle with water, leaving about 4 inches at the top (for 1 pound of pasta, you should use at least 12 cups of water). Add a drop of olive or vegetable oil (this helps keep pasta from sticking), set the kettle over high heat and bring to a boil. Salt the water, if you wish.

4. When cooking long macaroni or spaghetti, slowly lower a handful at a time into the rapidly boiling water until it softens enough to fit into the kettle. Stir once or twice to separate strands, if necessary.

5. Boil rapidly, uncovered, until a strand of pasta cut in half shows no raw starch in the center—it shows up as a white dot—or until the pasta has no raw starch taste, but *does* feel a bit firm between the teeth (*al dente* is the Italian term for this firm tenderness).

6. Drain pasta in a large colander the instant it's *al dente.* But do not rinse in cool water unless the pasta is for a salad.

7. If pasta must wait for a few minutes before being served, toss with a little oil, set the colander over a kettle containing about 1 inch of simmering water and cover.

Ravioli with Red Pepper and Tomato Sauce

Makes 4 servings.

Nutrient Value Per Serving: 253 calories, 12 g protein, 8 g fat, 35 g carbohydrate, 509 mg sodium, (Cholesterol not available.)

1 *small onion, chopped*
1 *clove garlic, chopped*
1 *tablespoon olive oil*
2 *medium-size sweet red peppers (6 ounces), halved, seeded and cut into 1/2-inch pieces*
1 *cup drained canned whole tomatoes*
1/2 *teaspoon salt*
1/4 *teaspoon leaf basil, crumbled*
1/4 *teaspoon crushed red pepper flakes*
12 *ounces mini-round frozen cheese ravioli*
16 *very small asparagus spears*

1. Sauté the onion and garlic in the oil in a medium-size nonstick saucepan until the onion is softened, for about 3 minutes. Add the sweet red peppers; sauté over low heat, stirring constantly, until the peppers begin to blister, for about 3 minutes.

2. Add the tomatoes, salt, basil and red pepper flakes. Simmer, covered, for 10 to 15 minutes, or until the red peppers are very soft.

3. Turn the tomato mixture into the container of a food processor or blender, working in batches, if necessary. Cover; whirl with on-and-off pulses until the sauce is as coarsely textured or as fine as you wish.

4. Meanwhile, cook the ravioli in a large pot of lightly salted water according to the package directions.

5. Steam the asparagus spears until crisp-tender, for 1 to 2 minutes.

6. Drain the ravioli. Transfer to 4 serving bowls or plates, dividing evenly. Spoon the red pepper sauce over each. Garnish each with 4 asparagus spears.

Confetti Primavera with Mozzarella

Makes 4 servings.

Nutrient Value Per Serving: 294 calories, 12 g protein, 10 g fat, 38 g carbohydrate, 298 mg sodium, 11 mg cholesterol.

- **4 ounces zucchini**
- **4 ounces yellow squash**
- **4 ounces pared carrots**
- **6 ounces vermicelli or thin spaghetti**
- **2 cloves garlic, finely chopped**
- **2 tablespoons olive oil**
- **1 to 2 tablespoons chopped fresh basil**
- **¼ teaspoon salt**
- **⅛ teaspoon pepper**
- **3 ounces part-skim milk lite mozzarella cheese, cut into ½-inch cubes**

1. Cut the zucchini, yellow squash and carrots into 2½ x ¼-inch sticks; you should have about 4 cups. Set aside.
2. Cook the pasta in a large pot of boiling salted water, according to the package directions. During the last 2 minutes of cooking time, add the vegetable sticks. Raise the heat to maintain boiling, if necessary. Drain in the colander; rinse. Transfer to a serving bowl; keep warm.
3. While the pasta is cooking, sauté the garlic in the oil in a small skillet until lightly browned; do not let burn. Remove from heat.
4. Add the basil, salt and pepper to the pasta; toss gently to mix.
5. Divide the pasta equally among 4 individual plates or bowls. Place the mozzarella over the top of each. Spoon the garlic and oil over each and serve.

Quick Pasta Fagioli

Serve this thick, stew-like pasta in large, shallow soup bowls.

Makes 6 servings.

Nutrient Value Per Serving: 330 calories, 18 g protein, 8 g fat, 45 g carbohydrate, 1,089 mg sodium, 6 mg cholesterol.

- **2 cloves garlic, halved**
- **2 tablespoons olive oil**
- **1 large carrot, pared and coarsely chopped**
- **1 large onion, coarsely chopped**
- **1 stalk celery with leaves, coarsely chopped**
- **1 teaspoon leaf rosemary, crumbled**
- **2 tablespoons tomato paste**
- **2 cans (20 ounces each) white kidney beans (cannellini), undrained**
- **1 can (10½ ounces) condensed chicken broth**
- **1 soup can (10½ ounces) water**
- **4 ounces small pasta, such as elbows, ditali or small shells**
- **½ cup grated Parmesan cheese**
- **¼ cup finely chopped parsley**
- **1 tablespoon red wine vinegar**

1. Sauté the garlic in the oil in a 10-inch skillet or Dutch oven with at least a 2-quart capacity, until the garlic is lightly browned. Remove the garlic and discard.
2. Add the chopped carrot, onion and celery; sauté until they begin to color, for 3 to 5 minutes.
3. Add the rosemary and tomato paste. Add the beans with their liquid, the chicken broth and water. Simmer, uncovered, for 2 minutes.
4. Add the pasta, stirring to distribute the ingredients evenly. Cover and simmer, stirring occasionally, for 8 minutes, or until pasta is *al dente,* firm but tender. Remove the pan from the heat. Let stand, covered, for 10 minutes. Add the salt, if necessary.
5. Combine the cheese and parsley in a small serving bowl.
6. Stir the vinegar into the soup, and ladle into warmed soup bowls. Serve with the cheese-parsley mixture.

MICROWAVE DIRECTIONS FOR PASTA FAGIOLI
650 Watt Variable Power Microwave Oven
Ingredient Changes: Reduce the rosemary to ½ teaspoon.
Directions: Combine the garlic and oil in a 4-quart microwave-safe casserole. Microwave, uncovered, at full power for 2 minutes. Remove the garlic. Add the carrot, onion and celery. Microwave, uncovered, for 3 minutes. Add the rosemary, tomato paste, undrained beans, chicken broth and water. Cover. Microwave at full power for 14 to 16 minues, or until boiling. Stir in the pasta. Cover. Microwave at half power for 12 minutes. Stir in the vinegar. Add the salt, if necessary. Let stand, covered, for 10 minutes. Serve with the cheese and parsley mixture.

Pasta with Broccoli

A quick, meatless entrée.

Makes 4 servings.

Nutrient Value Per Serving: 464 calories, 14 g protein, 23 g fat, 54 g arbohydrate, 413 mg sodium, 52 mg cholesterol.

1½ **pounds broccoli**
2 **large cloves garlic, finely chopped**
2 **tablespoons olive oil**
1 **tablespoon butter**
1 **tomato, cut into ½-inch cubes, OR: 1 cup**
    drained canned tomatoes, chopped
2 **tablespoons anchovy paste OR:**
    6 anchovies canned in oil, mashed
½ **teaspoon crushed red pepper flakes**
    (optional)
½ **teaspoon salt**
¼ **teaspoon black pepper**
8 **ounces penne, rigatoni or ziti pasta**
3 **cups boiling water**
½ **cup heavy cream**
    Grated Romano or Parmesan cheese

1. Trim the flowerets from the broccoli; cut into bite-size pieces. Reserve the stems for soup or other use.
2. Sauté the garlic in the oil and butter in a 10-inch skillet with at least a 2-quart capacity, for 30 seconds. Stir in the tomato, anchovy paste, red pepper flakes, if using, salt and black pepper. Sauté, stirring, for 1 minute.
3. Add the pasta and boiling water, stirring to distribute the ingredients evenly. Cover and cook for the least amount of time suggested in the package directions. After 3 minutes, arrange the broccoli evenly over the top of the pasta. Cover and simmer for the remaining time, or until the broccoli is tender and the pasta is *al dente*, or firm but tender.
4. Stir in the cream and heat for 30 seconds. Toss and serve immediately with the cheese.

Pasta with Broccoli

In this recipe we've reduced the amount of cooking fat and anchovy paste, substituted half-and-half for the heavy cream and eliminated the cheese.

Makes 4 servings.

Nutrient Value Per Serving: 286 calories, 11 g protein, 5 g fat, 49 g carbohydrate, 341 mg sodium, 10 mg cholesterol.

1 **pound broccoli**
2 **large cloves garlic, finely chopped**
1 **tomato, cut into ½-inch cubes**
1 **to 2 teaspoons olive oil**
1 **tablespoon anchovy paste**
¼ **teaspoon crushed red pepper flakes**
    (optional)
½ **teaspoon salt**
¼ **teaspoon black pepper**
8 **ounces penne, rigatoni or ziti pasta**
3 **cups boiling water**
⅓ **cup half-and-half**

1. Trim the flowerets from the broccoli; cut into bite-size pieces. Reserve the stems for soup or other use.
2. Sauté the garlic and tomato in the oil in a large nonstick saucepan for 1 minute, adding only as much oil as necessary to prevent sticking. Add the anchovy paste, pepper flakes if using, salt and black pepper; sauté for 1 minute.
3. Add the pasta and boiling water, stirring to distribute the ingredients evenly. Cover and cook for the least amount of time suggested in the package directions. During the last 5 minutes of cooking time, stir in the broccoli and cook, uncovered, for the last 5 minutes. Remove from the heat.
4. Stir in the half-and-half. Cover the saucepan and let stand for 5 minutes, or until the sauce thickens slightly. Serve.

Reduced Calorie

Pasta with Broccoli

Pasta with Mushrooms and Prosciutto

Makes 6 servings.

Nutrient Value Per Serving: 447 calories, 18 g protein, 18 g fat, 53 g carbohydrate, 670 mg sodium, 54 mg cholesterol.

   1   **clove garlic, halved**
   2   **tablespoons butter**
   1   **tablespoon olive oil**
   1   **pound mushrooms, coarsely chopped**
  1/4 **pound prosciutto, coarsely chopped**
   1   **large onion, coarsely chopped**
  1/2 **teaspoon salt**
  1/4 **teaspoon crushed red pepper flakes**
  1/2 **cup dry white wine**
  12   **ounces penne, ziti or mostaccioli pasta**
   4   **cups boiling water**
  1/2 **cup grated Parmesan cheese**
  1/4 **cup finely chopped parsley**
   1   **cup frozen peas, thawed**
  1/2 **cup heavy cream**

1. Sauté the garlic in the butter and oil in a 10-inch skillet with at least a 2-quart capacity, until the garlic is lightly browned, for about 1 minute. Remove the garlic and discard. Add the mushrooms, prosciutto and onion. Sauté just until the mixture begins to color, for about 5 minutes. Add the salt, red pepper flakes and wine. Continue to cook just until the wine has evaporated.
2. Stir in the pasta and the boiling water. Cover and simmer, stirring occasionally, for the least amount of time suggested in the package directions, or until the pasta is *al dente*, firm but tender. Check halfway through the cooking time; add a little more water, if necessary.
3. Combine the cheese and parsley in a small serving bowl.
4. Stir the peas and cream into the pasta mixture. Heat gently for 30 seconds. Serve immediately. Pass the cheese-parsley mixture.

Pasta with Eggplant and Black Olives

Makes 4 servings.

Nutrient Value Per Serving: 335 calories, 9 g protein, 10 g fat, 54 g carbohydrate, 805 mg sodium, 0 mg cholesterol.

- **1 long, thin eggplant (about 1 pound), pared and cut into ½-inch dice**
- **2 tablespoons olive oil**
- **1 clove garlic, finely chopped**
- **¼ teaspoon crushed red pepper flakes**
- **1 can (14 ounces) Italian-style whole tomatoes with their liquid, chopped**
- **¼ cup Italian or Greek black olives, pitted and chopped**
- **1 teaspoon salt**
- **¼ teaspoon black pepper**
- **8 ounces spaghetti, vermicelli or other pasta strands broken into 3-inch pieces**
- **3 cups boiling water**
- **½ teaspoon leaf oregano, crumbled**
- **¼ cup finely chopped parsley Grated Parmesan cheese**

1. Sauté the eggplant in the oil in a 10-inch skillet with at least a 2-quart capacity, until it begins to soften, for about 5 minutes.

2. Add the garlic and red pepper flakes; cook for 1 minute. Add the tomatoes with the liquid, olives, salt and peppper. Cover and simmer for 5 minutes.

3. Add the pasta and boiling water, stirring to distribute the ingredients evenly. Cover and cook, stirring occasionally, for the least amount of time suggested in the package directions, or until the pasta is *al dente*, firm but tender. Check halfway through the cooking time; add a little more water, if necessary.

4. Add the oregano and toss. Remove from the heat. Sprinkle with the parsley and serve. Pass the cheese.

Pasta with Sausage and Peppers

Makes 4 servings.

Nutrient Value Per Serving: 664 calories, 24 g protein, 40 g fat, 50 g carbohydrate, 1,448 mg sodium, 86 mg cholesterol.

- **1 pound Italian sausage, sweet, hot or a combination, casings removed and meat cut into 1-inch pieces**
- **1 tablespoon olive oil**
- **1 large onion, cut into ½-inch dice**
- **1 large sweet green pepper, cut into ½-inch dice**
- **1 large sweet red pepper, cut into ½-inch dice**
- **2 tablespoons tomato paste**
- **1 teaspoon salt**
- **¼ teaspoon black pepper**
- **8 ounces small pasta, such as small shells or wagon wheels**
- **3 cups boiling water Grated Parmesan cheese**

1. Brown the sausage in the oil in a 10-inch skillet with a 2-quart capacity, for 5 minutes. Add the onion and peppers; sauté for 2 minutes. Add the tomato paste, salt and pepper.

2. Add the pasta and boiling water, stirring to distribute the ingredients evenly. Cover and cook, stirring occasionally, for the least amount of time suggested in the package directions, or until the pasta is *al dente*, firm but tender. Check halfway through the cooking time; add a little more water, if necessary.

3. Serve immediately with the grated cheese.

Pasta with Quick Bolognese Sauce

Makes 6 servings.

Nutrient Value Per Serving: 524 calories, 23 g protein, 25 g fat, 49 g carbohydrate, 543 mg sodium, 60 mg cholesterol.

- 1 **large onion, finely chopped**
- 1 **stalk celery, finely chopped**
- 1 **large clove garlic, finely chopped**
- 2 **bay leaves**
- 1 **teaspoon leaf rosemary, crumbled**
- 2 **tablespoons olive oil**
- 1 **pound lean ground beef**
- 1 **can (10½ ounces) condensed beef broth**
- ½ **cup dry red wine**
- 3 **tablespoons tomato paste**
- ¼ **teaspoon pepper**
  Salt (optional)
- 12 **ounces rigatoni, rotelle, penne or ziti pasta**
- 4 **cups boiling water**
- ½ **cup dairy sour cream**
- ¼ **cup finely chopped parsley**
  Grated Parmesan cheese

1. Sauté the onion, celery, garlic, bay leaves and rosemary in the oil in a 10-inch skillet with a 2-quart capacity, until the vegetables just begin to color, for 3 minutes.
2. Add the beef. Sauté, breaking up with a spoon, until no longer pink, for 5 minutes.
3. Stir in the broth, wine, tomato paste, pepper and salt to taste. Cook over medium heat until thick, for 5 minutes.
4. Add the pasta and boiling water, stirring to distribute the ingredients. Cover and cook, stirring occasionally, for the least amount of time suggested in the package directions, or until the pasta is *al dente*, firm but tender. Check halfway through the cooking time; add more water, if necessary.
5. Stir in the sour cream; heat gently without boiling for 30 seconds. Remove the bay leaves. Sprinkle with the parsley and serve immediately. Pass the Parmesan.

Spicy Noodles with Pork

Makes 4 servings.

Nutrient Value Per Serving: 657 calories, 27 g protein, 40 g fat, 46 g carbohydrate, 1,400 mg sodium, 136 mg cholesterol.

- 2 **tablespoons finely chopped garlic (about 6 cloves)**
- 1 **tablespoon finely chopped, pared fresh gingerroot**
- 1 **bunch green onions, trimmed, white and green parts separated, and chopped fine**
- 2 **tablespoons vegetable oil**
- 1 **pound ground pork**
- ¼ **cup soy sauce**
- 1 **tablespoon Oriental sesame oil***
- ¾ **teaspoon crushed red pepper flakes**
- ½ **pound wide egg noodles**
- 3 **cups boiling water**

1. Sauté the garlic, ginger and white part of the green onions in the oil in a 10-inch skillet with a 2-quart capacity, for 30 seconds. Add the pork; sauté, breaking up with a spoon, until no longer pink, for 5 minutes.
2. Add the soy sauce, sesame oil and red pepper flakes. Bring to boiling, stirring.
3. Add the noodles and boiling water, stirring to distribute the ingredients. Cover and cook over medium heat until the noodles are *al dente*, firm but tender, for 7 minutes.
4. Top with the green part of the onions. Serve.

*__Note:__ Oriental sesame oil can be found in the Oriental food section of your supermarket or in a specialty food store.

Dried Beans

Bean and Potato Salad with Ham

Makes 4 servings.

Nutrient Value Per Serving: 582 calories, 27 g protein, 26 g fat, 6 g carbohydrate, 617 mg sodium, 33 mg cholesterol.

- 1 **pound new potatoes*, unpeeled**
- 1 **can (15½ ounces) chick-peas**
- 1 **can (15½ ounces) kidney beans**
- ¼ **cup Dijon-style mustard**
- 2 **tablespoons apple cider vinegar**
- ⅓ **cup vegetable oil**
- ¼ **teaspoon salt**
- ½ **teaspoon pepper**
- ½ **pound cooked ham, cut into ¼-inch-thick cubes**
- 1½ **tablespoons finely chopped onion**
- 2 **tablespoons coarsely chopped flat-leaf (Italian) parsley**

1. Place the potatoes in a saucepan with water to cover. Bring to boiling, covered, over high heat. Lower the heat. Simmer, covered, for 30 minutes, or until the potatoes are easily pierced with a fork. Drain in a colander. Run cold water over the potatoes. When cool, cut into quarters.
2. Drain the chick-peas and kidney beans in a colander. Rinse under cold water. Drain.
3. For dressing, whisk together the mustard, vinegar, oil, salt and pepper until blended.
4. Combine the potatoes, chick-peas, kidney beans, ham, onion and parsley in a large serving bowl. Pour the dressing over; toss to mix well. Let stand, covered, for at least 1 hour or overnight. Toss before serving.

*Note: Or use 1¼ pounds of all-purpose potatoes. Simmer, in their skins, for about 40 minutes, or until fork-tender. Drain. Peel while still warm. Cut into 1¼-inch pieces.

Chick–Pea Salad

Chick-Pea Salad

Makes 8 servings.

Nutrient Value Per Serving: 410 calories, 14 g protein, 17 g fat, 54 g carbohydrate, 310 mg sodium, .00 mg cholesterol.

- 1 **bag (1 pound) dried chick-peas (garbanzos)**
- 1 **pound potatoes (3 medium-size), pared, cut into ½-inch cubes**
- 3 **large carrots, pared, cut diagonally into ½-inch-thick slices**
- 4 **large onions, sliced into ½-inch-thick rounds**
- ¼ **cup chopped garlic***
- ½ **cup olive oil**
- ⅓ **cup red wine vinegar**
- 1 **teaspoon salt**
- 1 **teaspoon pepper**
- ½ **cup chopped fresh dill OR: 2 tablespoons dried dillweed***

1. Pick over, sort and wash the beans. Cover with water in a bowl. Refrigerate overnight.
2. Drain the chick-peas. Cook in boiling salted water in a kettle for 35 minutes. Add the potatoes and carrots; boil for 10 minutes, or until the chick-peas are tender. Drain into a large bowl.
3. Sauté the onions and garlic in the olive oil until tender, for 3 minutes; add to the warm chick-peas.
4. Stir in the vinegar, salt, pepper, dill. Serve warm or at room temperature over the greens.

*Note: The original recipe called for 6 cloves of garlic. In Family Circle's Test Kitchen, we preferred the extra garlic, and we added the dill.

Falafel

Makes 8 servings.

Nutrient Value Per Serving: 506 calories, 13 g protein, 25 g fat, 61 g carbohydrate, 1,160 mg sodium, .62 mg cholesterol.

- **1 can (20 ounces) chick-peas**
- **1 large onion, finely chopped (1 cup)**
- **2 tablespoons chopped parsley**
- **2 cloves garlic**
- **1 tablespoon ground coriander**
- **1 teaspoon salt**
- **1 teaspoon red pepper flakes**
- **1 cup unseasoned bread crumbs**
  Vegetable oil for frying
- **8 whole-wheat pita breads**
- **2 cups shredded lettuce**
- **1 large tomato, cored and diced (1 cup)**
  Tahini Dressing (recipe follows)

1. Drain the chick-peas; reserve ¼ cup of liquid.

2. Combine the chick-peas, the reserved ¼ cup of liquid, onion, parsley, garlic, coriander, salt and red pepper flakes in an electric blender or food processor; cover; whirl until smooth, scraping down the sides of the container once or twice.

3. Turn the mixture into a medium-size bowl; add the bread crumbs, mixing thoroughly.

4. Form into walnut-size balls using 1 tablespoon of the mixture. Arrange on a jelly-roll pan.

5. Pour oil to a 1½-inch depth in a medium-size saucepan. Heat the oil to 365° on a deep-fat frying thermometer. Fry the falafel, a few at a time, until golden brown, for about 3 minutes. Remove with a slotted spoon; drain on paper toweling; keep warm. (Frying temperature should remain at 365°, or the falafel will fall apart in the oil.)

6. To serve, warm the pita breads. Cut a ½-inch slice off to open the pocket. Drop in 3 or 4 falafel; mash slightly against the side of the pita with a fork; top with the lettuce and tomato; spoon the Tahini Dressing over all.

Tahini Dressing: Combine ¾ cup of water, ⅓ cup of vegetable oil, 3 tablespoons of lemon juice, 1 jar (2.6 ounces) of sesame seeds, 1 clove garlic and ¾ teaspoons of salt in the container of an electric blender. Cover; whirl at high speed for 1 minute, or until the seeds are crushed and the mixture is smooth. Pour into a small bowl; stir in ¼ cup of chopped parsley. Cover with plastic wrap. Chill for at least 1 hour. Makes 1½ cups.

Salad Bar Minestrone

Salad Bar Minestrone

Makes 4 servings (2 quarts).

Nutrient Value Per Serving: 498 calories, 22 g protein, 26 g fat, 45 g carbohydrate, 1,844 mg sodium, 43 mg cholesterol.

- **1¼ pounds mixed salad bar vegetables (about 7 cups), such as sweet green and red pepper, broccoli flowerets, cauliflower flowerets, carrots, shredded cabbage, celery, onion and chick-peas**
- **½ pound sweet Italian sausage, casings removed and meat crumbled**
- **1 clove garlic, finely chopped**
- **2 tablepoons olive or vegetable oil**
- **1 can (8 ounces) tomato sauce**
- **1 can (10¾ ounces) condensed beef broth**
- **3 soup cans (10¾ ounces each) water**
- **1 can (19 ounces) white kidney beans (cannellini), undrained**
- **½ teaspoon leaf oregano, crumbled**
- **½ teaspoon salt (optional)**
- **½ teaspoon pepper**
- **⅓ cup orzo or other small pasta**
  Grated Parmesan cheese

1. Slice any large salad bar vegetables into bite-size pieces; reserve.

2. Sauté the sausage and garlic in the oil in a large saucepan until the meat is no longer pink. Add the vegetables. Sauté for 2 to 5 minutes, or until the vegetables just begin to brown. Stir in the tomato sauce, broth, water, beans, oregano, salt, if using, and pepper.

3. Simmer, uncovered, for 15 minutes. Sprinkle the pasta over the soup; simmer for 15 minutes, or until the pasta is tender. Serve with the Parmesan.

◤ ⫷ 💲
Vegetarian Chili (Medium-Hot)

Makes 6 servings.

Nutrient Value Per Serving: 407 calories, 19 g protein, 15 g fat, 55 g carbohydrate, 1,177 mg sodium, .0 mg cholesterol.

- ½ **cup (3½ ounces) dried pinto beans**
- ½ **cup (3½ ounces) dried red kidney beans**
- 8 **cups cold water**
- 1 **large onion, finely chopped (about 1½ cups)**
- 4 **cloves garlic, finely chopped**
- 1 **small carrot, diced (⅓ cup)**
- 1 **small rib celery, diced (⅓ cup)**
- ⅓ **cup vegetable oil**
- 1 **cup (6½ ounces) dried lentils, picked over and washed**
- 4 **tablespoons chili powder**
- 1 **tablespoon leaf oregano, crumbled**
- 2 **teaspoons ground coriander**
- 2 **tablespoons sweet paprika**
- 1 **can (16 ounces) whole tomatoes, with their liquid, chopped**
- 1 **sweet red pepper, halved, seeded and diced (about 1 cup)**
- ½ **pound mushrooms, quartered (about 2½ cups)**
- ¼ **cup soy sauce**
- ¼ **teaspoon salt**

1. Pick over and wash the pinto and red kidney beans. Combine the beans in a large bowl. Cover with 5 cups of the cold water; soak overnight. Rinse and drain. Set aside.
2. Sauté the onion, garlic, carrot and celery in the oil in a large saucepan over medium heat until the onion is softened and transparent, for about 8 minutes.
3. Add the drained beans, lentils, chili, oregano, coriander, paprika, tomatoes and the remaining 3 cups of water; stir. Bring to boiling. Lower the heat; simmer, uncovered, stirring occasionally, for 1½ hours.
4. Add the sweet red pepper, mushrooms and soy sauce. Continue simmering, adding more water as needed if the chili becomes too dry, until the beans are very tender and the lentils are falling apart, for about 2 hours longer. Stir in the salt. Serve.

Eggs and Cheese

Eggs

Eggs are graded by the U.S. Department of Agriculture according to appearance. Grade AA or Fresh Fancy Eggs are the highest quality.

Eggshell color is determined by the breed of the hen and has no effect on the quality, taste or nutrient value of the egg.

Eggs should be stored in the refrigerator, large end up (this keeps the yolks centered), in their original carton for up to one week. Soiled eggs should be wiped clean with a dry cloth before storing. A wet cloth would wash off the natural protective film.

Keep eggs away from strong-smelling foods, as the shell is porous and will absorb odors.

If you're in doubt about an egg's freshness, break it into a saucer. A super-fresh egg has a cloudy white and a highstanding yolk. Older eggs will have less cloudy whites and flatter yolks. A "bad" egg will have a definite odor or chemical smell when sniffed.

◤ 💲
Egg, Bacon and Cheese Monster Muffin

*Make your own **giant** version at home of the popular fast-food breakfast.*

Makes 4 servings.

Nutrient Value Per Serving: 402 calories, 20 g protein, 24 g fat, 25 g carbohydrate, 900 mg sodium, 320 mg cholesterol.

- **Top and bottom slice a 9-inch round loaf white bread, each about ½ inch thick (reserve center for fresh bread crumbs, stuffing, croutons or dried bread crumbs)**
- 1 **tablespoon mayonnaise**
- 2 **teaspoons Dijon-style mustard**
- 4 **slices Canadian bacon (2 ounces)**
- 2 **tablespoons butter or margarine**
- 4 **eggs**
- 4 **slices smoked or plain provolone cheese (4 ounces)**

1. Wrap the bread in aluminum foil. Heat in a preheated moderate oven (350°) while preparing the filling, for about 10 minutes.
2. Mix the mayonnaise and mustard in a small cup; set aside.
3. Sauté the bacon in the butter in a large skillet on both sides until heated through. Set aside and keep warm.
4. Break each egg into the skillet. Cook over the low heat until the yolks are beginning to set. Place a slice of cheese over each egg. Cover the skillet with a tight-fitting lid. Cook for 1 minute, or until the cheese has melted. Remove from the heat.
5. Remove the bread from the oven. Spread the cut sides with the mayonnaise mixture. Place the eggs on the bottom slice of bread. Top with the bacon and cover with the top slice of bread.
6. Cut into 4 equal wedges and serve immediately.

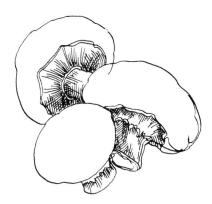

Egg on a Muffin

Makes 1 serving.

Nutrient Value Per Serving: 288 calories, 17 g protein, 12 g fat, 27 g carbohydrate, 646 mg sodium, 233 mg cholesterol.

 1 **whole-wheat English muffin, split**
 1 **small egg, slightly beaten**
 1 **slice Muenster, Swiss or American cheese***
 1 **slice (½ ounce) lean deli-style ham**

1. Toast the English muffin. Arrange the halves on a toaster oven tray or small cookie sheet.
2. Scramble the egg, using no butter, in a small ungreased nonstick skillet. Spoon the egg onto one muffin half; cover with the cheese. Place the ham on the other muffin half.
3. Broil until the cheese melts and ham is warm, for 1 minute. Sandwich the halves together. Serve at once, or wrap in foil to eat on the run within 30 minutes.

Note: Substituting low-salt or low-fat cheese will reduce salt, cholesterol, fat and/or calories. For other breakfast sandwich variations, spread ¼ cup of cottage cheese or 2 tablespoons of peanut butter over a toasted whole-wheat English muffin.

Eggs Au Gratin

Hard-cooked eggs and macaroni bake under a layer of Parmesan cheese.

Bake at 350 for 30 minutes.
Makes 4 servings.

Nutrient Value Per Serving: 364 calories, 18 g protein, 20 g fat, 28 g carbohydrate, 859 mg sodium, 447 mg cholesterol.

 2 **tablespoons butter or margarine**
 2 **tablespoons all-purpose flour**
 2 **cups milk**
 6 **hard-cooked eggs, shelled**
 2 **cups cooked elbow macaroni**
 ½ **cup chopped celery**
 2 **tablespoons finely chopped onion**
 1½ **teaspoons leaf basil, crumbled**
 1 **teaspoon salt**
 ¼ **teaspoon pepper**
 1 **tomato, thinly sliced**
 3 **tablespoons grated Parmesan cheese**

1. Melt the butter or margarine in a large skillet; blend in the flour. Cook, stirring constantly, until the mixture bubbles. Stir in the milk; bring to boiling, stirring constantly; cook for 3 minutes.
2. Chop the eggs; stir the chopped eggs, macaroni, celery, onion, basil, salt and pepper into the white sauce. Pour into a greased 8-cup casserole; arrange the tomato slices on top; sprinkle the Parmesan cheese over the top. Cover with plastic wrap.
3. Refrigerate for up to 24 hours; 45 minutes before serving, remove from the refrigerator; uncover. Meanwhile, preheat the oven to moderate (350°).
4. Bake in the moderate oven (350°) for 30 minutes, or until bubbly hot.

Cheese

There are literally hundreds of different kinds of cheeses in the world, yet all have the same main ingredient—milk. Milk is curdled by the action of heat or rennet (or other bacteria) or both, then the watery part, called whey, is separated from the curd. The curd, sometimes the whey, is made into cheese.

The origin of cheese-making is lost in antiquity. It was probably discovered by chance. Records show that cheese was know to the Sumerians in 4000 B.C. We do know that cheese existed in Biblical times. Roman conquerors probably introduced cheese to England. Cheese was made by monks during the Middle Ages.

The word "cheese" comes from *cese* or *cyse* in Old English. To the French, cheese is *fromage;* Italians call it *fromaggio.*

Cheese is divided into two categories. The first is *natural cheeses.* The other category is *cheese blends*, in which natural cheeses are used to make new products.

Natural cheeses may be subdivided by texture or consistency and degree or kind of ripening. The amount of whey drained from the curd generally determines the consistency of the cheese. Examples:

- Very hard—Parmesan, Romano
- Hard—Cheddar, Swiss
- Semi-soft to hard—Colby, Gouda
- Semi-soft—blue, brick, Muenster, Roquefort
- Soft—Brie, Camembert, cottage cheese, cream cheese, Limburger, Neufchâtel, ricotta.

Cheese blends can be subdivided into three products:

- Pasteurized process cheese is a blend of shredded fresh and aged natural cheese heated with water and an emulsifier to a homogeneous mixture. It is shaped into loaves or wheels. Buy it by the piece, or presliced or cut up and packaged. Popular-priced, it is perfect for cooking or making sandwiches. American cheese is an example.
- Pasteurized process cheese food is made the same way as process cheese, but with nonfat dry milk added. The moisture content is higher so it is softer and spreads more easily. It will melt faster than process cheese. It is packaged as loaves, rolls or links.
- Pasteurized process cheese spread is similar to process cheese food but spreads more easily because it contains more moisture. The milk-fat content is lower. It's packaged in jars, tubes and pressurized cans. Some may be flavored with pimiento, olives or onions. Cheese spreads can be used for appetizers and sandwiches.

Storing Cheese: The softer the cheese, the more perishable it is. The harder the cheese, the longer it will keep. Keep cheese chilled, the same as milk. Use soft cheeses—cottage, cream, ricotta, Brie—within a week. Hard cheeses will keep for weeks if left in their original wrapper or rewrapped tightly with plastic wrap. Should the surface of a hard cheese get moldy, simply cut off the affected area. Cheese mold is harmless and should not affect the cheese's quality. Some pasteurized cheese products do not need refrigeration, but once they are opened, they should be refrigerated if labels direct. Freeze cheese only if you must. Cheese loses flavor and becomes crumbly when frozen.

Cooking Cheese: Cheese is very heat sensitive and can curdle or become rubbery with excessive heat. Cook cheese over low or moderate heat. Since it melts quickly, you really don't need much heat. When making a cheese sauce, add the cheese last and cook just to melt it.

Cheese Nutrition: Cheese is a good source of high quality protein (as that in meat, poultry and eggs). It contains most of the nutrients of milk, including calcium and riboflavin.

Cheese Tart with Tomato

Bake crust at 425° for 15 minutes; bake tart at 350° for 55 to 65 minutes.
Makes 6 servings.

Nutrient Value Per Serving: 452 calories, 21 g protein, 31 g fat, 21 g carbohydrate, 776 mg sodium, 244 mg cholesterol.

½ **recipe Flaky Pastry (see recipe, page 251) OR: ½ of 11-ounce package piecrust mix**
8 **ounces ripe Brie cheese including rind, cut into chunks, OR: 8 ounces sharp Cheddar, cut into chunks (2 cups), OR: 6 ounces imported bleu, cut into chunks (1½ cups)**
1½ **cups whole-milk cottage cheese**
4 **eggs**
1 **medium-size onion, chopped (½ cup)**
⅛ **teaspoon cayenne pepper**
2 **medium-size tomatoes, peeled and thinly sliced**
1 **tablespoon olive oil**
1 **tablespoon salt**
1½ **tablespoons each of chopped fresh basil, chives and parsley**

1. Prepare ½ recipe of the Flaky Pastry or ½ package of the piecrust mix, following the label directions.
2. Preheat the oven to hot (425°).
3. Roll out the dough on a lightly floured surface to a 12-inch round. Fit into a 9-inch pie plate. Fold the edge under to make a stand-up edge; flute. Line the crust with aluminum foil. Fill with pie weights or dried beans.
4. Bake the crust in the preheated hot oven (425°) for 10 minutes. Remove the aluminum foil and weights. Bake for 5 minutes longer. Remove from the oven. If any bubbles have formed in the pastry, flatten gently with a wooden spoon. Lower the oven temperature to moderate (350°).
5. Place the cheese, cottage cheese, eggs,

onion and cayenne pepper in the container of an electric blender or food processor. Cover; whirl until puréed. Pour evenly into the partly baked shell.

6. Bake on a cookie sheet in the preheated moderate oven (350°) for 25 to 30 minutes, or until partially set.

7. Meanwhile, place the sliced tomatoes on paper toweling to absorb as much moisture as possible.

8. Remove the tart from the oven. Arrange the tomato slices, overlapping slightly, in the border around the edge of filling.

9. Return the tart to the oven and bake for 30 to 35 minutes, or until a knife inserted near the center comes out clean.

10. Lightly brush the tomato slices with the olive oil and sprinkle with the salt. Sprinkle with the basil, chives and parsley. Cool for 20 minutes before serving.

Cheese Tart with Tomato

We've developed a lower-calorie pie pastry, used fewer eggs and eliminated the oil. We've replaced the high-fat, high-calorie cheeses with a smaller amount of lower-fat feta, and we've maintained the volume by using more low-fat cottage cheese.

Bake pastry at 425° for 5 minutes;
bake pie at 350° for 25 to 30 minutes.
Makes 6 servings.

Nutrient Value Per Serving: 127 calories, 14 g protein, 6 g fat, 5 g carbohydrate, 539 mg sodium, 148 mg cholesterol.

Slim Pie Pastry (recipe follows)
1 **container (16 ounces) 1% low-fat cottage cheese**
2 **ounces feta cheese, crumbled**
3 **eggs**
1 **small onion, chopped**
¼ **teaspoon salt**
⅛ **teaspoon cayenne pepper**
1 **medium-size tomato, thinly sliced**
¼ **cup chopped fresh basil, chives or parsley**

1. Preheat the oven to hot (425°). Prepare the Slim Pie Pastry.
2. Line the crust with aluminum foil and fill with pie weights or dried beans. Bake the crust for 3 minutes; remove the foil and beans. Bake for 2 minutes until light golden. Remove to a wire rack. Reduce the oven temperature to moderate (350°).

3. Purée the cottage cheese, feta, eggs, onion, salt and cayenne in a food processor or blender until very smooth. Pour into the crust.

4. Bake in the preheated moderate oven (350°) for 20 minutes; cover the crust with foil if the pastry browns too quickly.

5. Meanwhile, drain the tomatoes on paper toweling. Remove the tart from the oven after 20 minutes. Arrange the tomato, overlapping slightly, around the edge.

6. Bake for 5 to 10 minutes longer, or until a knife inserted near the center comes out clean. Sprinkle with the basil. Cool for 10 to 15 minutes before slicing.

Slim Pie Pastry: Stir together 1 cup of *un*sifted all-purpose flour and ½ teaspoon of salt in a medium-size bowl. Add 3 tablespoons of vegetable oil and 3 tablespoons of water. Stir until well blended. Add up to 1 more tablespoon of water, if necessary, to form a ball of dough. Refrigerate for 5 minutes. Roll the dough between 2 sheets of wax paper into a 12-inch circle. Remove the top sheet of paper and turn the dough over the top of a 9-inch pie plate; fit into the plate; remove the wax paper. Turn the pastry edge under and seal with the tines of a fork. Prick the shell all over with the fork before baking. Makes one single 9-inch crust.

Reduced Calorie

Fresh Vegetable Lasagne

Bake at 350° for 45 minutes.
Makes 8 servings.

Nutrient Value Per Serving: 379 calories, 26 g protein, 24 g fat, 17 g carbohydrate, 636 mg sodium, 171 mg cholesterol.

- **4 large tomatoes (about 2 pounds), cored and cut into ¼-inch-thick slices**
- **1 medium-size eggplant (about 1½ pounds), trimmed and cut lengthwise into ¼-inch-thick slices**
- **2 medium-size zucchini (about 12 ounces), trimmed and cut lengthwise into ¼-inch-thick slices Vegetable oil**
- **1 container (15 ounces) ricotta cheese**
- **1 cup grated Parmesan cheese**
- **3 eggs**
- **¼ cup chopped fresh parsley**
- **2 or 3 cloves garlic, finely chopped**
- **1 teaspoon leaf oregano, crumbled**
- **1 teaspoon leaf basil, crumbled**
- **½ teaspoon salt**
- **¼ teaspoon pepper**
- **⅛ teaspoon crushed red pepper flakes**
- **2 packages (8 ounces each) mozzarella cheese, shredded**

1. Preheat the oven to moderate (350°). Grease a shallow 2-quart baking dish.
2. Drain the tomato slices between sheets of paper toweling.
3. Lightly brush the eggplant and zucchini slices with the oil. Heat a large nonstick skillet over medium-high heat. Cook the eggplant and zucchini slices in batches, for about 4 minutes on each side, or until lightly browned. Remove to paper toweling.
4. Combine the ricotta, Parmesan, eggs, parsley, garlic, oregano, basil, salt, pepper and red pepper flakes in a bowl.
5. Layer half the eggplant, ricotta mixture, tomato slices, mozzarella cheese and all the zucchini in the prepared dish. Continue to layer, ending with the mozzarella cheese.
6. Bake in the preheated moderate oven (350°) for 45 minutes, or until bubbly hot and lightly browned on top.

Zesty Avocado, Bacon and Swiss Cheese Melts

Bake at 375° for 8 to 10 minutes;
broil for 2 to 3 minutes.
Makes 4 servings.

Nutrient Value Per Serving: 280 calories, 10 g protein, 19 g fat, 20 g carbohydrate, 271 mg sodium, 19 mg cholesterol.

- **1 large ripe avocado, peeled, pitted, sliced and cut into chunks**
- **3 tablespoons lime juice**
- **1 small tomato, finely chopped**
- **1 small onion, finely chopped**
- **1 clove garlic, finely chopped**
- **½ teaspoon ground cumin Salt to taste Liquid red-pepper seasoning to taste**
- **4 slices whole-wheat bread, lightly toasted**
- **4 slices cooked bacon, crumbled**
- **½ cup shredded Swiss cheese**

1. Preheat the conventional oven to moderate (375°), if using; preheating the toaster oven is not necessary.
2. Combine the avocado, lime juice, tomato, onion, garlic, cumin, salt and red-pepper seasoning to taste in a bowl. Mix until well blended but still slightly chunky. Spread over the bread slices. Place on the broiler or toaster oven pan.
3. Bake in the moderate oven (375°) or toaster oven for 8 to 10 minutes, or until golden. Remove from the oven. Increase the temperature to broil.
4. Sprinkle each sandwich with the bacon and cheese. Broil for 2 to 3 minutes, or until the bacon is crisp and the cheese melted.

Blue Cheese and Roasted Pepper Sandwich

A strongly flavored sandwich for blue cheese lovers.

Makes 4 servings.

Nutrient Value Per Serving: 471 calories, 15 g protein, 32 g fat, 34 g carbohydrate, 1,184 mg sodium, 32 mg cholesterol.

1 jar (8 ounces) marinated mushrooms
6 ounces blue cheese, crumbled (about 1 cup)
1 oval loaf (8x4 inches) pumpernickel bread, unsliced or 6 slices pumpernickel bread
1 jar (7 ounces) roasted red peppers, drained
4 large leaves romaine lettuce

1. Drain the mushrooms, reserving the marinade. Chop fine.
2. Mix the mushrooms, blue cheese and 1 tablespoon of the marinade in a small bowl.
3. Cut the bread with a serrated knife in 3 equal horizontal slices. Brush a third of the reserved marinade over the bottom slice of the bread. Layer the remaining ingredients in the following order: half of the blue cheese-mushroom mixture, half of the roasted red peppers, 2 leaves of the lettuce, the middle slice of bread, another third of the reserved marinade, the remaining blue cheese mixture, the remaining roasted red peppers and 2 lettuce leaves. Brush the remaining marinade on the cut side of the top slice of bread; place on top of the sandwich. (If using sliced pumpernickel bread, make two sandwiches with the same layering.)
4. Slice the loaf into 4 equal portions and serve.

Vegetable and Feta Cheese Pie

This meatless pie is a perfect luncheon.

Bake crust at 425° for 25 minutes; bake pie at 350° for 45 minutes.
Makes 8 servings.

Nutrient Value Per Serving: 410 calories, 11 g protein, 29 g fat, 24 g carbohydrate, 627 mg sodium, 104 mg cholesterol.

1 package (10 ounces) piecrust mix
1¼ teaspoons dried dillweed
1 teaspoon leaf oregano, crumbled
⅛ teaspoon cayenne pepper
1 medium-size zucchini (about 6 ounces) halved crosswise, then cut lengthwise into ⅛-inch-thick sticks
3 tablespoons vegetable oil
1 medium-size onion, cut in half lengthwise, then cut crosswise into thin slices
1 small sweet green pepper, cored, seeded and cut into thin strips
1 small sweet red pepper, cored, seeded and cut into thin strips
½ teaspoon salt
¼ teaspoon pepper
4 ounces feta cheese, crumbled (1 cup)
4 ounces Swiss or Gruyère cheese, coarsely grated (1 cup)
1 cup milk
2 eggs

1. Preheat the oven to hot (425°).
2. Prepare the piecrust mix according to the package directions, blending in ¼ teaspoon of the dillweed, ½ teaspoon of the oregano and a pinch of cayenne. Roll the dough out on a floured surface into a ⅛-inch-thick round. Fit the dough into a 10 x 1-inch fluted quiche pan, leaving a ½-inch overhang. Fold the overhang over, and press the dough inside the pan to form an edge. Line the crust with aluminum foil. Fill with dry beans or pie weights.
3. Bake the crust in the preheated hot oven (425°) for 15 minutes, or until lightly golden. Remove the beans; prick the crust with a fork. Bake for 10 minutes longer, or until the pastry is baked through. Remove to a wire rack. Lower the oven temperature to moderate (350°).
4. Brush the zucchini with 1 tablespoon of the oil. Heat a large nonstick skillet over medium-high heat. Cook the zucchini in batches, for ▶

4 minutes on each side, or until lightly browned. Remove to a bowl.

5. Add the remaining oil to the skillet. Lower the heat to low. Add the onion, green and red peppers, the remaining 1 teaspoon of dillweed, ½ teaspoon of oregano, a pinch of the cayenne, salt and pepper. Sauté, stirring for 5 minutes, or until softened. Add to the zucchini.

6. Layer half the feta cheese, Swiss cheese and vegetables over the crust. Cover with the remaining cheese. Combine the milk and eggs in a small bowl. Pour over the vegetable cheese mixture. Top with the remaining vegetables.

7. Bake in the preheated moderate oven (350°) for 45 minutes, or until the top of the pie is puffed and browned and a knife inserted in the center comes out clean. Let stand on the wire rack for about 15 minutes before cutting.

MICROWAVE DIRECTIONS FOR VEGETABLE AND FETA CHEESE PIE
650 Watt Variable Power Microwave Oven
Ingredient Changes: Use a frozen deep-dish 9-inch pie shell. Reduce the dillweed to ¾ teaspoon; the oregano to ½ teaspoon; the cayenne to a few grains and the oil to 2 tablespoons. Coarsely chop the zucchini, red and green peppers and onion.
Microwave Directions: Remove the frozen pie shell from the foil pan and place, still frozen, in a 9-inch microwave-safe pie plate. Microwave at full power for 1 minute. Press the pastry gently to fit the pie plate exactly; prick the bottom and sides with a fork. Recrimp the edges and brush with browning liquid, if you wish. Microwave at full power for 2 minutes. Set aside. Place the zucchini, onion, red and green peppers and oil in a 10-inch microwave-safe pie plate. Microwave, uncovered, at full power for 5 minutes, stirring once. Combine the feta and Swiss cheeses; sprinkle half over the bottom of the pastry shell. Cover with the vegetable mixture; sprinkle with the remaining cheese. Combine the milk, eggs, dillweed, oregano, cayenne, salt and pepper; pour into the pastry shell. Microwave, uncovered, at full power for 11 minutes, rotating a quarter turn after 5 to 8 minutes. The filling should look set but not dry. Let stand for 10 minutes before cutting. Nutrient Value Per Serving: 395 calories, 11 g protein, 27 g fat, 24 g carbohydrate, 627 mg sodium, 104 mg cholesterol

Croque Monsieur

Makes 6 servings.

Nutrient Value Per Serving: 391 calories, 24 g protein, 21 g fat, 25 g carbohydrate, 1,179 mg sodium, 118 mg cholesterol.

1 **round 9-inch loaf unsliced white bread**
¼ **pound thinly sliced baked ham**
¼ **pound thinly sliced Swiss cheese**
¼ **pound thinly sliced prosciutto or capocollo**
¼ **pound thinly sliced hot-pepper cheese**
½ **cup milk**
1 **egg**
2 **tablespoons butter**

1. Cut 2 horizontal ½-inch-thick slices with a serrated knife from the center of the loaf. Reserve the top and bottom for fresh bread crumbs, stuffing, croutons or dried bread cubes.

2. Layer the ham, Swiss cheese, prosciutto and hot-pepper cheese between the slices. Cut into 4 equal wedges.

3. Mix the milk and egg in a pie plate. Dip both sides of the sandwich in the egg mixture. Set aside.

4. Heat the butter in a large skillet. Sauté the sandwiches over medium heat, turning once, until golden brown on both sides. Serve immediately.

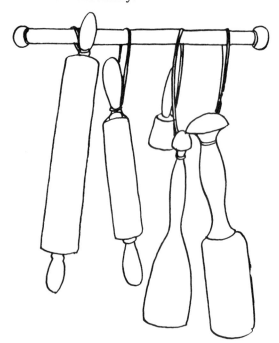

POPULAR CHEESES

Kind	Description	Flavor	Uses
American	Process cheese of uniform texture made from domestic Cheddar; comes in slices and loaves.	Mild. Very popular with children.	A favorite for sandwiches and casseroles.
Bel Paese	Mellow, semi-soft Italian cheese.	Mildly nutty.	Team with fresh fruit as dessert, or with cocktails.
Blue, Gorgonzola, Roquefort	Medium-soft with blue to blue-green veins, crumbles easily.	Mild to tangy, slightly peppery.	These give a gourmet touch to appetizers, salads, dressings, desserts.
Brie, Camembert	Rounds and wedges with an edible gray-white crust; soft inside.	Mild to pungent, depending on age.	Favorites for desserts and appetizers. Serve at room temperature.
Cheddar	Semi-hard, cream to orange color. Sold as wedges, cubes, slices or shredded.	Mild to very sharp, depending on aging—check the package.	America's choice for sandwiches, cooked dishes, salads, snacks, desserts.
Cottage, Ricotta, Cream	Cottage and ricotta are creamy-white curd-like, low-calorie. Cream cheese is smooth and calorie-rich.	All are delicately mild; easily spoonable and spreadable.	Perfect for appetizers, sandwiches, cooked dishes, desserts, cake fillings or frostings.
Edam, Gouda	Creamy orange with red-wax coat. Edam is round; Gouda, flattish.	Mellow, slightly salty, with a nut-like taste.	Excellent for appetizer and dessert trays. Good snack cheeses, too.
Gruyère	Smooth, firm, pale, cream-colored cheese; process Gruyère is often sold in foil-wrapped triangles.	Nut-like, faintly caramel.	An all-purpose cheese, excellent for sauces, toppings. Also good in salads, soufflés and omelets.
Liederkranz, Limberger	Soft, bacteria-ripened cheese.	Strong to overpowering; acquired tastes.	Best eaten out-of hand or on crackers.
Mozzarella	Soft and white with a ball-like shape. Also comes shredded.	Mild and a bit chewy to eat, especially when heated.	Known as the pizza-lasagne cheese. Use in salads or on appetizer platters.
Muenster, Brick	Creamy-yellow to white; semisoft; tiny holes.	Muenster is mild; brick, mild to sharp.	Appetizers, sandwiches, salads, desserts.
Parmesan, Romano, Sapsago	The grating cheeses—very hard. White to light green. Sold in blocks, as well as grated.	Parmesan is pungent, but milder than Romano. Sapsago has herb-like flavor.	Topper for casserole dishes and spaghetti. Also popular for sauces and vegetable seasoners.
Port du Salut	Firm, smooth French cheese, the color of cream.	Fairly sharp.	A good cocktail or dessert cheese.
Provolone	Light brown outside; light yellow inside. Sometimes lined with rope marks.	Mellow to sharp, smoky and salty.	Try it in macaroni, spaghetti dishes, for sandwiches, snacks or appetizer trays.
Swiss	Light to creamy-yellow; large uneven holes. Buy sliced or in cuts.	Mild, with nut-like sweetness. One of our most popular cheeses.	Same as Cheddar, but in cooked dishes it may string somewhat.

Main Dish Salads and Vegetables

Broccoli, Mushroom and Sweet Pepper Pie

Bake at 375° for 35 to 40 minutes.
Makes 6 servings.

Nutrient Value Per Serving: 466 calories, 17 g protein, 34 g fat, 24 g carbohydrate, 854 mg sodium, 225 mg cholesterol.

- **½ recipe Flaky Pastry (see recipe, page 251) OR: ½ of 11-ounce package piecrust mix**
- **½ pound fresh broccoli flowerets and stalks, coarsely chopped**
- **1 large sweet green pepper, coarsely chopped (1 cup)**
- **1 large sweet red pepper, coarsely chopped (1 cup)**
- **1 large onion, coarsely chopped (1 cup)**
- **1 clove garlic, finely chopped**
- **¼ cup olive oil**
- **¼ pound mushrooms, sliced (1¼ cups)**
- **1 teaspoon salt**
- **⅛ teaspoon cayenne pepper**
- **4 eggs, slightly beaten**
- **½ cup milk or half-and-half**
- **¾ cup grated Parmesan cheese**
- **¾ cup shredded Gruyère cheese**

1. Prepare ½ recipe of the Flaky Pastry or ½ package of the piecrust mix, following the label directions.
2. Roll out the dough on a lightly floured surface to a 12-inch round. Fit into a 9-inch pie plate. Fold the edge under to make a stand-up edge; flute.
3. Preheat the oven to moderate (375°).
4. Bring a large saucepan of salted water to boiling. Add the broccoli and cook for 3 minutes. Drain; rinse under cold water to stop the cooking. Place in a large bowl.
5. Sauté the peppers, onion and garlic in the olive oil in a large skillet over moderate heat until slightly softened, for about 4 minutes. Add the mushrooms and cook for 4 minutes. Remove the vegetables with a slotted spoon to the bowl with the broccoli. Stir in the salt and pepper; set aside.
6. Combine the eggs, milk and cheeses in a medium-size bowl. Pour about one-third of the egg mixture into the prepared pie shell. Spoon over one-half of the vegetable mixture. Pour over half of the remaining egg-cheese mixture and repeat the process with the remaining egg and vegetable mixtures.
7. Bake the pie on a cookie sheet in the preheated moderate oven (375°) for 35 to 40 minutes, or until a knife inserted near the center comes out clean. Cool on a wire rack for 15 minutes. Serve immediately or serve at room temperature.

Half-and-Half

A dairy product made by blending equal amounts of light cream and milk. It contains 10% to 12% milk fat, almost half the fat of light cream. It can be used as a table cream for coffee, cereal and desserts or used in cooking. Ultra-pasteurized half-and-half is specially processed so that it will keep for weeks in the refrigerator.

Broccoli, Mushroom and Sweet Pepper Pie (page 172), Browned Cabbage and Mushroom Pirog (page 174), Vegetable Pasties (page 175)

Broccoli, Mushroom and Sweet Pepper Custard Pie

In this pie we've eliminated practically all the cheese and oil, reduced the amount of eggs and substituted skim milk for whole.

Bake at 350° for 25 to 30 minutes.
Makes 6 servings.

Nutrient Value Per Serving: 89 calories, 7 g protein, 4 g fat, 6 g carbohydrate, 436 mg sodium, 140 mg cholesterol.

  1 **package (10 ounces) frozen broccoli stalks, thawed**
 ½ **cup coarsely chopped sweet green pepper**
 ½ **cup coarsely chopped sweet red pepper**
 ½ **cup coarsely chopped onion**
  1 **clove garlic, finely chopped**
  1 **teaspoon olive or vegetable oil**
 ½ **cup sliced mushrooms**
 ¾ **cup skim milk**
  3 **eggs**
  1 **teaspoon salt**
 ¼ **teaspoon leaf basil, crumbled**
 ⅛ **teaspoon cayenne pepper**
  2 **tablespoons shredded part-skim milk cheese, such as Swiss**

1. Slice the broccoli into 1-inch pieces; drain on paper toweling. Arrange in a well-greased 9-inch pie plate.

2. Preheat the oven to moderate (350°).

3. Sauté the green and red peppers, onion and garlic in the oil in a nonstick skillet over medium to low heat for 3 minutes. Add the mushrooms; cook until tender and most of the liquid has evaporated, for 2 minutes. Spoon the vegetables over the broccoli in the pie plate.

4. Beat together the milk, eggs, salt, basil and cayenne pepper in a 2-cup glass measure; pour over the vegetables.

5. Bake in the preheated moderate oven (350°) for 25 to 30 minutes, or until a knife inserted near the center comes out clean. Sprinkle with the cheese. Broil until golden brown. Cool on a wire rack for 10 minutes before slicing.

Reduced Calorie

Browned Cabbage and Mushroom Pirog

The roasted kasha adds a nutty flavor to these individual pies. Substitute cooked brown rice if you can't find the kasha in the grain or ethnic section of your supermarket or in a specialty food shop.

Bake at 375° for 35 minutes.
Makes 10 servings.

Nutrient Value Per Serving: 623 calories, 11 g protein, 43 g fat, 48 g carbohydrate, 867 mg sodium, 200 mg cholesterol.

½ **cup roasted kasha**
1   **egg, well beaten**
1   **cup chicken broth**
1   **large onion, coarsely chopped (1 cup)**
6   **tablespoons butter or margarine**
2½ **cups coarsely chopped mushrooms (about 8 ounces)**
8   **cups finely chopped green cabbage (about 1½ pounds)**
4   **hard-cooked eggs, coarsely chopped**
3   **tablespoons chopped fresh dill OR: 3 teaspoons dried dillweed**
1   **teaspoon salt**
¼   **teaspoon pepper**
2   **recipes Flaky Pastry (see recipe, page 251) OR: 2 packages (11 ounces each) piecrust mix**
¾   **cup dairy sour cream**
1   **green onion, finely chopped**

1. Toss the kasha with half of the beaten egg in a small saucepan until the grains are well coated. Cook over medium-high heat, stirring constantly, until the grains are dry and separate. Gradually stir in the chicken broth. Reduce the heat to low; cover and cook for 10 minutes, or until all the liquid is absorbed. Set aside.
2. Sauté the onion in the butter in a large skillet for 2 minutes. Add the mushrooms and sauté for 3 minutes more. Add the cabbage and sauté for 8 to 10 minutes, stirring occasionally (skillet will be quite full), until the cabbage is wilted and the mixture is lightly browned. Remove from the heat. Stir in the chopped egg, 2 tablespoons of the chopped dill or 2 teaspoons of the dillweed, the salt, pepper and kasha.
3. Spoon the cabbage mixture equally into ten 1-cup aluminum-foil baking tins or casseroles.
4. Prepare the 2 recipes of the Flaky Pastry or the 2 packages of the piecrust mix, following label directions. Divide each recipe of the pastry into 5 equal portions. Keep all the portions wrapped in plastic wrap and refrigerated except the one that is to be rolled. Roll out one piece of dough on a lightly floured surface into a circle 1 inch larger than the top of the baking dish. Cut decorative designs or vents in the top for steam to escape.
5. Preheat the oven to moderate (375°).
6. Fit the pastry over the filling. Trim the overhang to 1 inch, if necessary; fold under to make a stand-up edge, allowing just enough overlap to grip the edge of the casserole; flute. Brush the top with a little of the remaining egg. Repeat with the remaining dough and tins.
7. Bake in the preheated moderate oven (375°) for 35 minutes, or until the crust is golden brown. Cool for 10 minutes beore serving.
8. Meanwhile, combine the sour cream, remaining dill or dillweed and the green onion in a small bowl until well blended and smooth. Serve with the pirogs.

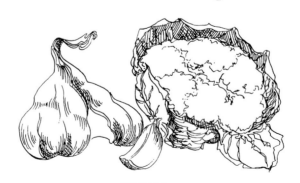

Vegetable Pasty

These individual Cornish pies are excellent without the usual beef or pork. Serve with dill pickles and a splash of catsup. Simple, but delicious.

Bake at 400° for 45 minutes.
Makes 6 servings.

Nutrient Value Per Serving: 441 calories, 6 g protein, 29 g fat, 41 g carbohydrate, 598 mg sodium, 41 mg cholesterol.

- **1** **recipe Flaky Pastry (see recipe, page 251) OR: 1 package (11 ounces) piecrust mix**
- **3** **medium-size all-purpose potatoes (about 1 pound), pared and cut into ¼-inch cubes (about 1¼ cups)**
- **1** **small to medium-size rutabaga (⅓ pound), pared and cut into ¼-inch cubes (about ¾ cups)**
- **¾** **cup chopped onion**
- **¼** **cup finely chopped carrot**
- **½** **teaspoon salt**
- **½** **teaspoon poultry seasoning**
- **¼** **teaspoon pepper**
- **2** **tablespoons butter**

1. Prepare the Flaky Pastry or piecrust mix, following the label directions.

2. Combine the potatoes, rutabaga, onion, carrot, salt, poultry seasoning and pepper in a medium-size bowl; mix well.

3. Preheat the oven to hot (400°).

4. Divide the dough into 6 equal portions. Keep all the portions wrapped in plastic wrap and refrigerated except the one that is to be rolled. Roll out each piece of dough on a lightly floured board into an 8x5-inch rectangle.

5. Place about ½ cup of the filling along one-half of one rectangle. Top with 1 teaspoon of the butter. Moisten the edges with water. Fold the dough in half over the filling; press the edges firmly together. (Be careful not to tear the dough on the pointed corners of vegetables; pasties will be very plump with the filling.) Trim with scissors to make a neat edge. Crimp to make a decorative edge. Repeat with the remaining dough and filling. Place the pasties on a large cookie sheet.

6. Bake in the preheated hot oven (400°) for 45 minutes, or until the vegetables are tender and the crust is golden brown. (If the pasties brown too quickly, cover loosely with foil.)

Deep-Dish Vegetable Pie

The soy sauce makes for a "meaty" taste.

Bake at 400° for 10 minutes; then at 350° for 10 minutes.
Makes 6 servings.

Nutrient Value Per Serving: 346 calories, 7 g protein, 17 g fat, 43 g carbohydrate, 1,133 mg sodium, 26 mg cholesterol.

- **3** **cups water**
- **½** **cup dry vermouth**
- **¼** **cup soy sauce**
- **2** **large all-purpose potatoes (about 1 pound), pared and cut into 1-inch chunks**
- **3** **slender carrots, pared and cut diagonally into ½-inch slices (about 1⅓ cups)**
- **½** **medium-size head cauliflower, cut into bite-size pieces (about 2 cups)**
- **¼** **pound large mushrooms, quartered (about 1¼ cups)**
- **1** **large onion, coarsely chopped (about 1 cup)**
- **4** **cups bok choy or Chinese cabbage, cut into 1-inch pieces**
- **2** **medium-size onions finely chopped (about 1 cup)**
- **2** **tablespoons butter or margarine**
- **1** **small clove garlic, finely chopped**
- **¼** **cup all-purpose flour**
- **½** **recipe Flaky Pastry (see recipe, page 251) OR: ½ package (11 ounces) piecrust mix**

1. Combine the water, vermouth and soy sauce in a large saucepan. Bring to boiling. Add the potatoes; cook for 2 minutes. Add the carrots; cook for 1 minute. Add cauliflower, mushrooms and coarsely chopped onions; cook for 4 minutes. Remove the pan from the heat; stir in the bok choy and set aside for 1 minute, or just until the bok choy has wilted slightly. Transfer the vegetables with a slotted spoon to a 2-quart round casserole dish.

2. Measure the remaining broth. If more than 2 cups, place over moderate heat and boil to reduce to 2 cups; if less than 2 cups, add additional water or vermouth to yield 2 cups. Reserve.

3. Sauté the finely chopped onions in the butter in a medium-size skillet or saucepan until golden. Add the garlic and sauté for 1 minute. Add the flour and cook, stirring constantly, for 2 minutes. Stir in the ▶

reserved broth until smooth. Cook, stirring, until thickened and bubbly. Pour over the vegetables in the casserole; stir to mix.

4. Prepare the ½ recipe of the Flaky Pastry or the ½ package of the piecrust mix, following the label directions.
5. Preheat the oven to hot (400°).
6. Roll out the dough on a lightly floured surface to a diameter 1-inch larger than the diameter of the casserole. Cut decorative designs or vents for steam to escape.
7. Fit the pastry over the filling. Trim the overhang to 1 inch, if necessary. Fold the pastry under to make a stand-up edge, allowing just enough overlap to grip the edge of the casserole; flute.
8. Bake in the preheated hot oven (400°) for 10 minutes. Reduce the oven heat to moderate (350°) and bake for 10 more minutes, or until the mixture is bubbly and crust is golden brown. (If the crust browns too quickly, loosely cover with aluminum foil.)

Tomatoes Stuffed with Ham Salad

A sour cream-mayonnaise dressing spiked with horseradish and mustard adds zip to this ham salad.

Makes 4 servings.

Nutrient Value Per Serving: 279 calories, 18 g protein, 19 g fat, 11 g carbohydrate, 1,419 mg sodium, 58 mg cholesterol.

Horseradish Mayonnaise:
- ⅓ cup dairy sour cream
- 2 tablespoons mayonnaise
- 3 teaspoons bottled horseradish
- 1 teaspoon Dijon-style mustard
- ⅛ teaspoon pepper

- ¾ pound deli baked ham, cut into small dice (about 2 cups)
- 1 cup chopped celery
- ¼ cup chopped black Greek olives*
- ¼ cup finely chopped dill pickle
- ¼ cup chopped parsley
- 4 medium-size ripe tomatoes
- 8 leaves Boston lettuce
- 8 whole black Greek olives for garnish

1. Prepare the Horseradish mayonnaise: Combine the sour cream, mayonnaise, horse-radish, mustard and pepper in a large bowl.
2. Add the ham, celery, olives, pickle and

3 tablespoons of the parsley; toss gently until all ingredients are evenly coated.
3. Cut each tomato vertically into 6 wedges to within ½ inch of the bottom. Carefully spoon out the center membranes and seeds; save for another use. Stuff tomatoes with the ham mixture. Serve on a platter lined with Boston lettuce leaves. Garnish with the olives and the remaining chopped parsley.

*Note: For best flavor, use black Greek olives packed in brine. Regular black ripe olives may be substituted.

Shrimp with Cilantro Mayonnaise

A cooling salad that will satisfy equally well for lunch or a light supper. If you can't find fresh cilantro in your market, substitute a little ground coriander and chopped fresh parsley.

Makes 4 servings.

Nutrient Value Per Serving: 338 calories, 17 g protein, 27 g fat, 12 g carbohydrate, 307 mg sodium, 93 mg cholesterol.

- 8 ounces frozen, cooked, shelled and deveined shrimp, thawed
Cilantro Mayonnaise:
- ¼ cup mayonnaise
- ¼ cup chopped fresh cilantro*
- 2 tablespoons fresh lime juice
- ¼ teaspoon salt
- ⅛ teaspoon pepper
- 4 drops liquid red-pepper seasoning
- 2 ripe avocados
- ½ lemon
- 8 romaine lettuce leaves
- 4 sprigs fresh cilantro
- 4 lime wedges

1. Drain the thawed shrimp thoroughly between several layers of paper toweling in the refrigerator for at least 30 minutes.
2. Prepare the Cilantro Mayonnaise: Combine the mayonnaise, cilantro, lime juice, salt, pepper and red-pepper seasoning in a medium-size bowl. Add the shrimp; toss until evenly coated.
3. Halve, pit and peel the avocados. Rub the cut edges with the lemon to prevent browning.
4. Spoon the shrimp mixture into the avocado halves. Serve on a platter lined with the romaine leaves. Garnish with the fresh cilantro sprigs and lime wedges.

Note: Cilantro, or Chinese parsley, is a pungent herb used in Southwestern, Mexican and Middle Eastern cuisines.

Avocado

The avocado, or alligator pear, is a fruit with buttery-textured, nutty-tasting flesh.

The California Fuerte variety, available from October to May, is green, thin-skinned, weighing 8 to 16 ounces. The Hass variety, sold from May to October, has a dark, pebbly skin. Florida varieties are generally larger than California avocados. They are light green and smooth-skinned, sold from July to January.

Tips for Buying: Hold an avocado in your hands and gently press the ends. If it yields to gentle pressure, it's ripe and ready. It's best to plan ahead and buy several unripe avocados. Let them stand at room temperature until they ripen. Then refrigerate and use within a few days. You can freeze the pulp if it has been mashed with a little lemon juice to prevent discoloration.

Avocado Nutrition: Avocados have a high fat content, most of which is unsaturated. One-half of an 8-ounce avocado has 150 calories and provides vitamin C, riboflavin, magnesium and potassium.

To Prepare: Cut the avocado lengthwise around the pit in the center. Rotate the halves in opposite directions to separate. Remove the pit. Brush the cut surfaces with lemon juice, diluted vinegar or an ascorbic-acid mixture to reduce discoloration. Serve on the half shell, or peel and slice or cube.

Coriander

Fresh coriander (also called Chinese or Japanese parsley and cilantro) is a fragrant herb with a pungent flavor native to southern Europe. The leaves are oval and flat with a toothed edge. The tiny, beige seeds are similar in taste to anise and cumin. The seeds are sold both whole and ground.

Fresh coriander is sold by the bunch. If possible, buy coriander with the roots intact. Store in the refrigerator with the roots in water and the leaves covered with damp paper toweling. Rinse thoroughly just prior to using.

Use coriander as you would parsley, although more sparingly, to flavor beans, stews and sausages.

Cucumber Surprise

Leftover chicken, ham and rice may be used in this recipe. A food processor will quickly slice the onion and carrots, and chop the chicken and ham.

Makes 4 servings.

Nutrient Value Per Serving: 314 calories, 20 g protein, 12 g fat, 32 g carbohydrate, 696 mg sodium, 126 mg cholesterol.

4 large cucumbers (8 to 9 inches)
1 cup finely chopped cooked chicken (about 4 ounces)
1 cup finely chopped cooked ham (about 4 ounces)
1 cup cooked white rice
1 egg, slightly beaten
½ teaspoon leaf thyme, crumbled
¼ teaspoon ground nutmeg
¼ teaspoon salt
Pinch pepper
1 large onion, thinly sliced
2 medium-size carrots, thinly sliced
2 tablespoons butter or margarine
3 medium-size tomatoes, peeled, seeded and coarsely chopped
½ cup dry white wine

1. Pare the cucumbers; cut a thin slice from each end and discard. Halve the cucumbers lengthwise. Scoop out the seeds with a small spoon and discard.
2. Combine the chicken, ham, rice, egg, thyme, nutmeg, salt and pepper in a bowl.
3. Spoon the chicken-ham stuffing into the cucumber shells, dividing equally and pressing the mixture flat.
4. Reform the stuffed halves to make four "whole" cucumbers. Tie each in four places with kitchen string to hold together.
5. Sauté the onion and carrots in the butter in a large skillet or Dutch oven for 5 minutes, or until tender, but not browned.
6. Add the cucumbers to the skillet; roll gently in the butter to coat. Add the tomatoes and wine. Bring to boiling. Lower the heat; cover; simmer for 30 minutes, or until the cucumbers are just tender when pierced with a fork.
7. Place the cucumbers on a serving plate and carefully remove the string. Place the vegetables and cooking liquid left in the pan into the container of an electric blender or food processor. Purée to make a sauce. Pour the sauce over cucmbers.

Note: For an attractive presentation, slice cucumbers and serve over the sauce.

Spinach-Prosciutto Roll Lasagne

For an attractive presentation, arrange the rolls so that they stand up on a serving platter.

Bake at 375° for 45 to 50 minutes.
Makes 4 servings.

Nutrient Value Per Serving: 767 calories, 41 g protein, 47 g fat, 49 g carbohydrate, 897 mg sodium, 205 mg cholesterol.

- 8 curly-edge lasagne noodles
- 3 cups loosely packed shredded Fontina cheese (½ pound)
- 4 packages (10 ounces each) chopped frozen spinach, thawed and squeezed dry
- 8 ounces thinly sliced prosciutto
- ½ cup (1 stick) unsalted butter, melted

1. Preheat the oven to moderate (375°). Grease a 9 x 9 x 2-inch-square baking dish.
2. Cook the lasagne, according to the package directions. Rinse and drain on paper toweling.
3. Reserve ½ cup of the cheese. Mix together the remaining cheese and spinach in a medium-size bowl.
4. Lay out the noodles separately on wax paper on a flat surface. Layer the prosciutto over each noodle, dividing equally. Spread about ⅔ cup of the spinach filling evenly over each strip. Starting at a short end, roll up each noodle, jelly-roll fashion. Place in the prepared baking pan, seam-sides down. Generously brush the butter over the curly edges of the lasagne. Pour the remaining butter over the tops of the rolls. Cover tightly with aluminum foil.
5. Bake in the preheated moderate oven (375°) for 45 to 50 minutes, or until the rolls are heated through. Just before serving, sprinkle the top with the reserved ½ cup of the cheese.

MICROWAVE DIRECTIONS FOR SPINACH-PROSCIUTTO ROLL LASAGNE
650 Watt Variable Power Microwave Oven
Ingredient Changes: Reduce the butter to 2 tablespoons.
Directions: Cook the lasagne noodles and fill as above. Place, seam-side down, in a 9x9x2-inch-square microwave-safe baking dish. Place the 2 tablespoons of butter in a microwave-safe 1-cup measure. Microwave, uncovered, at full power for 1 minute, or until melted. Brush over the rolls. Cover. Microwave at full power for 7 minutes, rotating the dish one-quarter turn after 4 minutes. Let stand for 3 minutes. Nutrient Value Per Serving: 614 calories, 41 g protein, 30 g fat, 49 g carbohydrate, 895 mg sodium, 158 mg cholesterol.

Spinach Ricotta Rolls

Reduced Calorie

Substituting part-skim-milk ricotta cheese for higher-fat cheese and eliminating the prosciutto reduces calories in this recipe.

Bake at 400° for 25 minutes.
Makes 4 servings.

Nutrient Value Per Serving: 415 calories, 24 g protein, 13 g fat, 53 g carbohydrate, 1,124 mg sodium, 149 mg cholesterol.

- 1¾ cups part-skim milk ricotta
- 1 package (10 ounces) frozen chopped spinach, thawed and squeezed dry
- 1 egg
- 1 clove garlic, finely chopped
- 8 curly-edge lasagne noodles
- 1 can (15 ounces) plain tomato sauce*
- ½ teaspoon salt
- ¼ teaspoon pepper
- ¼ teaspoon leaf basil, crumbled
- ¼ teaspoon leaf thyme, crumbled

1. Combine the ricotta, spinach, egg and garlic in the container of the food processor. Cover; whirl until smooth. Reserve.
2. Preheat the oven to hot (400°).
3. Cook the lasagne noodles according to the package directions. Rinse and drain on paper toweling. Lay out the noodles onto a flat surface. Spread the ricotta-spinach filling along the lengths of the strips, dividing equally. Roll up the noodles, jelly-roll fashion.
4. Combine the tomato sauce, salt, pepper, basil and thyme in a small saucepan. Heat over medium heat until bubbly. Remove from the heat.
5. Spoon a thin layer of the sauce over the bottom of a 9 x 9 x 2-inch-square baking pan or other small, shallow baking dish. Arrange the lasagne rolls, seam-side down, in the prepared dish. Cover *tightly* with foil.
6. Bake in the preheated hot oven (400°) for 10 minutes. Pour the remaining sauce over the rolls. Bake, uncovered, for 15 minutes longer, or until heated through. Serve immediately.

***Note:** We used a plain tomato sauce with 70 calories per cup.

Steak Salad with Spinach and Red Onion

Steak Salad with Spinach and Red Onion

Makes 4 servings.

Nutrient Value Per Serving: 622 calories, 26 g protein, 54 g fat, 10 g carbohydrate, 1,085 mg sodium, 107 mg cholesterol.

1 pound boneless sirloin or blade steak
1 teaspoon salt
1 teaspoon pepper
1½ pounds salad bar vegetables (about 9 cups), including 5 cups spinach leaves and 4 cups mixture of mushroom slices, red onion slices and cherry tomatoes
1 cup blue cheese dressing*

1. Sauté the steak without oil in a small non-stick skillet for about 3 minutes on each side for medium rare, or longer for desired doneness. Transfer to a cutting board. Season both sides with the salt and pepper. Cut across the grain into ½-inch-thick strips.

2. Line a large, shallow salad bowl with the spinach leaves. Arrange the mushrooms, red onion, meat and tomatoes in a circular pattern.

3. To serve, pour the blue cheese dressing over the salad; toss well to coat. Serve immediately.

***Note:** Purchase the blue cheese dressing from the salad bar or prepare your own: Combine ½ cup (2 ounces), crumbled blue cheese, ½ cup of mayonnaise and 1 teaspoon of Dijon-style mustard.

Turkey Salad with Corn and Green Beans

Turkey Salad with Corn and Green Beans

All-American ingredients make this colorful salad a great choice for lunch or dinner. Serve it with crusty bread or corn chips.

Makes 4 servings.

Nutrient Value Per Serving: 397 calories, 30 g protein, 22 g fat, 24 g carbohydrate, 676 mg sodium, 78 mg cholesterol.

¾ **pound cooked turkey breast**
1 **package (10 ounces) frozen whole-kernel corn**
½ **pound fresh green beans, trimmed**
2 **medium-size carrots, pared and trimmed Salt**
⅓ **cup mayonnaise**
⅓ **cup dairy sour cream**
1 **tablespoon lemon juice**
½ **teaspoon liquid red-pepper seasoning**
2 **tablespoons chopped fresh cilantro OR: chopped fresh parsley**

1. Cut the turkey into 1 x ¼ x ¼-inch strips.
2. Place the frozen corn and 2 tablespoons of water in a small saucepan. Bring to boiling over high heat. Cover. Lower the heat and simmer for 3 minutes. Drain and cool.
3. Cut the beans into 1½-inch lengths. Halve the carrots lengthwise. Cut into ¼-inch-thick slices.
4. Bring 2 quarts of water and 1 teaspoon of the salt to boiling in a medium-size saucepan. Add the beans and carrots. Cook, uncovered, at a rapid boil for 5 minutes. Drain. Cool under cold running water. Drain.
5. To prepare the dressing, combine the mayonnaise, sour cream, lemon juice, liquid red-pepper seasoning and ¾ teaspoons of the salt in a small bowl.
6. Combine the turkey and the cooled, well-drained vegetables, cilantro and dressing in a large serving bowl. Toss to mix well. Cover and refrigerate for at least 1 hour or overnight. Stir lightly before serving.

Note: For an attractive buffet presentation, arrange the turkey, corn, green beans and carrots in separate mounds on a large serving platter. Spoon the dressing in ribbons over the salad. Toss just before serving.

Chicken, Orange and Beet Salad

Makes 4 servings.

Nutrient Value Per Serving: 244 calories, 23 g protein, 6 g fat, 26 g carbohydrate, 405 mg sodium, 62 mg cholesterol.

Cumin Dressing:
½ **cup orange juice**
1 **tablespoon ground cumin**
2 **teaspoons grated orange rind**
2 **teaspoons sugar**
¼ **teaspoon salt**
⅛ **to ¼ teaspoon cayenne pepper**

2 **large oranges**
½ **pound fresh spinach, stemmed, washed and drained**
2 **cups cooked chicken***
1 **can (16 ounces) sliced beets, drained**
½ **cup red onion slices**

1. Prepare the Cumin Dressing: Mix the orange juice, cumin, orange rind, sugar, salt and cayenne in a small bowl until the sugar is dissolved.
2. Cut off the peel and white membrane from the oranges. Cut out the sections and seed. Set aside.
3. Arrange the spinach, chicken, orange sections and beets on a serving platter. Garnish with the red onion slices.
4. Pour the dressing over the salad just before serving.

Note: We used a rotisserie chicken from the deli. Leftover cooked chicken or canned chicken can also be used.

Chicken with Lemon Yogurt Dressing

Serve this tangy, refreshing dish with sliced pumpernickel or other dark bread.

Makes 4 servings.

Nutrient Value Per Serving: 339 calories, 39 g protein, 16 g fat, 9 g carbohydrate, 417 mg sodium, 104 mg cholesterol.

1 **cucumber (½ pound), peeled**
½ **cup sliced blanched almonds**
2 **teaspoons grated lemon rind (1 lemon)**
3 **tablespoons lemon juice (1½ lemons)**
½ **small clove garlic, finely chopped**
1 **container (8 ounces) low-fat**
   plain yogurt
½ **teaspoon salt**
¼ **teaspoon white pepper**
4 **cups cooked chicken cut into**
   1-inch pieces (1 pound boneless
   cooked chicken)

1. Preheat the oven to hot (400°).
2. Cut the cucumber in half lengthwise; scoop out the seeds with a tablespoon. Cut the cucumber halves crosswise into ¼-inch-thick slices. Set aside.
3. Spread the almonds evenly on a cookie sheet.
4. Toast in the preheated hot oven (400°) for 5 minutes, or until golden brown, stirring once. Watch carefully to prevent burning.
5. Combine the grated lemon rind, lemon juice, garlic, yogurt, salt and pepper in a small bowl. Stir with a wire whisk.
6. Combine the chicken, cucumber, half the almonds and the yogurt dressing in a large bowl. Reserve the remaining almonds. Cover; refrigerate for at least 1 hour or overnight.
7. To serve, sprinkle the remaining toasted almonds over the salad.

How to Poach Chicken

The method is the same, if you are cooking the whole bird or particular parts. It takes only 1 cup water to 1 chicken, or 2 pounds of parts, to gently steam the bird until tender. Add more water, only if you want broth for a sauce, or are making chicken soup. Place the chicken in a large saucepan. Add boiling water, vegetables and seasoning. Bring to boiling; lower the heat to simmer; cover the pan. Simmer for 20 minutes, or just until the chicken is tender. Turn off the heat and allow the chicken to cool in the broth until comfortable temperature to handle. Strain the broth and use to finish the recipe, or pour into a jar and refrigerate; use within 3 days.

Curried Turkey-Rice Salad

This attractive salad includes green peas and is flavored with sour cream and chutney.

Makes 6 servings.

Nutrient Value Per Serving: 521 calories, 28 g protein, 25 g fat, 46 g carbohydrate, 534 mg sodium, 79 mg cholesterol.

1 **cup uncooked long-grain white rice**
1 **package (10 ounces) frozen green peas**
1 **medium-size onion, finely chopped**
   (½ cup)
¼ **cup vegetable oil**
1 **tablespoon curry powder**
3 **tablespoons lemon juice**
1½ **cups dairy sour cream**
1 **teaspoon salt**
¼ **teaspoon pepper**
3 **cups diced cooked turkey**
1 **cup finely chopped carrots**
3 **tablespoons chutney**
   Lettuce leaves
1 **tomato, sliced**

1. Cook the rice, following the label directions. Remove from the heat. Cool; spoon into a large bowl.
2. Cook the peas, following the label directions. Drain; add to the rice.
3. Sauté the onion in the oil in a small skillet until soft. Add the curry powder and lemon juice and cook, stirring, for several seconds. Remove from the heat and mix with the sour cream, salt and pepper. Add to the rice and

peas; mix well. Add the turkey, carrots and chutney; mix well. Refrigerate, covered, for 2 hours or longer.

4. To serve, spoon the salad over the lettuce leaves on a round platter to form a mound. Top with the tomato slices.

Rice

Rice is standard fare for most of the world's population. Added in the form of flour to breads, cakes and cookies, it's also eaten as side dishes, salads and cereals.

Varieties

Although there are over 6,000 varieties of rice in a myriad of colors, only white and brown are available to us. Both come in long and short grains. Use long grains for salads, curries, stews and side dishes—whenever you want plump and fluffy results; short grains are highly absorbent and slow-cooking—use them in creamy Italian risottos and molded rings.

White rice comes in regular Carolina-style (processed before milling), quick (parboiled) and minute-type (packaged precooked). Choose the type that suits your particular cooking needs.

Salami Pepper and Rice Salad

Italians treat rice very much the same way they treat pasta. They dress it up and make a meal of it. Here is a light version of a traditional favorite.

Makes 4 servings.

Nutrient Value Per Serving: 656 calories, 17 g protein, 45 g fat, 46 g carbohydrate, 954 mg sodium, 48 mg cholesterol.

- **¼ cup finely chopped onion**
- **1 medium-size clove garlic, finely chopped**
- **½ cup olive oil**
- **1 medium-size sweet red pepper**
- **2 medium-size sweet green peppers OR: 1 sweet green pepper and 1 sweet yellow pepper**
- **6 ounces sliced Genoa salami**
- **2 teaspoons lemon juice**
- **½ teaspoon Dijon-style mustard**
- **½ teaspoon pepper**
- **1 recipe Cooked Rice (recipe follows)**
- **½ cup grated Parmesan cheese**
- **Oil-cured Italian or Greek olives**

1. Sauté the onion and garlic in ¼ cup of the olive oil in a medium-size skillet until softened, for about 5 minutes.
2. Cut the peppers in half lengthwise; remove the stems, seeds and ribs. Slice into strips ¼-inch wide, 2 inches long.
3. Cut the salami into ½-inch wide strips.
4. Combine the remaining ¼ cup of the olive oil, the lemon juice, mustard and pepper in a small bowl.
5. Combine the rice, Parmesan, onion mixture, peppers, salami and dressing in a large bowl; toss to mix well. Refrigerate, covered, for several hours or overnight. Garnish with the olives.

Cooked Rice: Bring 2½ cups of water to boil in a medium-size saucepan. Add 1 cup of long-grain white rice. Lower the heat. Cover and simmer for 20 minutes. Remove from the heat and let stand until all the water is absorbed. Let cool slightly before using. Makes about 4 cups.

Eggplant Rollatini

Bake at 350° for 30 minutes.
Makes 8 servings.

Nutrient Value Per Serving: 416 calories, 16 g protein, 30 g fat, 24 g carbohydrate, 690 mg sodium, 132 mg cholesterol.

- **1 large eggplant (1½ pounds) Salt**
- **2 eggs, lightly beaten**
- **1 cup unseasoned bread crumbs**
- **¼ cup (½ stick) butter or margarine**
- **¼ cup olive or vegetable oil**
- **1 medium-size onion, finely chopped (½ cup)**
- **½ pound sweet Italian sausage, removed from casings and broken up**
- **1 clove garlic, finely chopped Homemade Tomato Sauce (recipe page 184)**
- **½ pound mozzarella cheese, shredded**
- **¼ teaspoon black pepper**
- **3 tablespoons grated Parmesan cheese**

1. Peel the eggplant and cut lengthwise into ¼-inch-thick slices. Place in a single layer on paper toweling. Sprinkle with the salt. Let stand for 30 minutes.
2. Brush the salt from the eggplant slices with damp paper toweling. Dip each slice ▶

into the beaten egg, then coat with the bread crumbs.

3. Heat 3 tablespoons of the butter with 3 tablespoons of the oil in a large skillet over medium-high heat. Sauté the eggplant slices, a few at a time, until golden on both sides. Add more butter and oil as needed. Drain the sautéed eggplant on the paper toweling.

4. Pour off the grease from the skillet and wipe out the skillet with paper toweling. Add 1 tablespoon of the butter to the skillet; sauté the onion in the butter over medium heat for 1 minute. Stir in the sausage and garlic, breaking up the clumps with a wooden spoon, until lightly browned.

5. Preheat the oven to moderate (350°).

6. Spoon 1 tablespoon of the Homemade Tomato Sauce over each eggplant slice. Sprinkle with the mozzarella cheese and sausage mixture. Roll each slice from the short end; place in a lightly buttered 13 x 9 x 2-inch baking dish. Spoon the remaining sauce over the top. Sprinkle with the pepper and Parmesan.

7. Bake in the preheated moderate oven (350°) for 30 minutes, until bubbly hot.

Homemade Tomato Sauce

Makes 2 cups.

Nutrient Value Per Serving: 443 calories, 9 g protein, 25 g fat, 56 g carbohydrate, 400 mg sodium, 62 mg cholesterol.

2 tablespoons butter or margarine
4 large ripe tomatoes, peeled, seeded and chopped (about 4 cups)
1 medium-size onion, chopped (½ cup)
1 stalk celery, finely chopped (1 cup)
1 clove garlic, finely chopped
1 tablespoon sugar
½ teaspoon leaf basil or 1 teaspoon chopped fresh
¼ teaspoon leaf oregano or 1 teaspoon chopped fresh
¼ teaspoon finely grated orange rind Pinch thyme

Melt the butter in a medium-size saucepan over low heat. Add the remaining ingredients. Increase the heat to medium-low; cook, stirring occasionally, until the tomatoes are tender and the sauce thickened, for about 45 minutes.

Soup 'n' Sandwich Tips

● Many supermarket bakeries produce excellent unsliced loaves of bread in a variety of sizes, shapes and flavors—12-ounce or 1-pound loaves are perfect for these "monster" sandwiches.

● If you have time, weight the sandwiches for easier slicing. Cover round loaves with a 10-inch pie plate and oval loaves with a jelly-roll pan. Balance heavy canned goods on top.

● Use a long serrated knife for easy bread slicing.

● If you're preparing both sandwich and soup for a quick meal, start the soup first. Then assemble the sandwich while the soup is simmering.

● Substitute alfalfa sprouts or "spicy" radish sprouts for the lettuce.

Giant Club Sandwich

Makes 6 servings.

Nutrient Value Per Serving: 612 calories, 33 g protein, 36 g fat, 43 g carbohydrate, 1,317 mg sodium, 82 mg cholesterol.

1 oval or round 9-inch loaf whole-wheat bread
½ cup mayonnaise
1 small head Boston lettuce, separated into leaves
½ pound chicken salad from deli
½ pound thinly sliced Swiss cheese
2 ripe tomatoes, thinly sliced
½ pound thinly sliced baked ham

1. Cut the loaf horizontally with serrated knife into 4 equal slices. Spread the bottom slice with one-third of the mayonnaise. Cover with some lettuce; spread with the chicken salad.

2. Layer the remaining ingredients in the following order: On the second slice of bread, spread with one-third of the mayonnaise, cheese and lettuce; on the third slice of bread, spread with the remaining mayonnaise, tomato, ham, lettuce and the top of the loaf.

3. Cut into 6 equal slices.

Giant Club Sandwich

Asparagus with Mustard–Cream Sauce (page 189)

Savory Accompaniments

**D**on't let old routines and habits leave you in a rut when it comes to dressing up your meals. Accompanying dishes can add a lot of flavor and enjoyment to your main course. You can either choose vegetables and fruits from the list of familiar favorites such as green beans, carrots, apples and pears, or take a chance on some of the new and exotic varieties that pop up every day on your local produce stand.

Since most vegetables and fruits are so versatile, you can combine them with other foods to create such great flavor treats as Vegetable Curry with Fruit (page 195). But they also stand alone deliciously, whether boiled, steamed, stir-fried or baked (just not overcooked), as in Oven-baked Carrots (page 190).

For another kind of accompaniment, why not add some tasty stuffing like our Brandied Chestnut Stuffing (page 199), to your next meal? Not only is it a scrumptious side dish—it's a serving stretcher as well. And if you're feeling particularly creative, check out your pantry for a variety of ways to invent your own stuffings!

Take a good look at our recipes on the following pages, and try something new. There's a whole arena of colorful and flavorful food just waiting to be savored.

 Quick

 Make Ahead

 Entertaining

$ *Low Cost*

 Low Calorie

Vegetables

Fresh Fruit and Vegetable Availability
The following fruits and vegetables (thanks to refrigeration and efficient transportation) are usually available all year:

Apples	Cucumbers	Parsley and herbs
Artichokes	Eggplant	Parsnips
Avocados	Escarole	Pears
Bananas	Garlic	Peas, green
Beans, green	Grapefruit	Peppers, sweet
Beets	Grapes	Pineapples
Broccoli	Greens	Plantains
Brussels Sprouts	Lemons	Potatoes
Cabbage	Lettuce	Radishes
Carrots	Limes	Spinach
Cauliflower	Mushrooms	Squash
Celery	Onions	Strawberries
Chinese cabbage	Onions, green	Sweet potatoes
Coconuts	Oranges	Tomatoes
Corn, sweet	Papayas	Turnips-rutabagas

The following are widely available in the markets during the months indicated, although a variety of fruits may be imported from other countries, making them available during "off" seasons.

Apricots—June to August
Asparagus—March to July
Blueberries—June to August
Cantaloupes—April to October
Cherries—May to August
Cranberries—September to December
Honeydews—February to October
Mangoes—March to August
Nectarines—January and February/June to September
Okra—April to November
Peaches—May to September
Persimmons—October to February
Plums and Prunes—June to October
Pomegranates—September to December
Pumpkins—September to December
Tangelos—October to February
Tangerines—November to March
Watermelons—April to September

Selecting Fresh Fruits and Vegetables
● Take time to look for the freshest of the fresh. Select fruits and vegetables that are of characteristic color, shape and size. Misshapen fruits and vegetables are often inferior and difficult to prepare.

● Use fruits and vegetables as soon as possible. Avoid buying too much at once.
● Enjoy the fresh produce of the season for flavor and price. When supplies are abundant, prices are low.

Refrigeration of Fresh Fruits and Vegetables
Fruits and vegetables may be stored in the refrigerator for several days. The longer they are refrigerated, the greater the vitamin loss, so it is best to eat them as soon after purchase as possible.

Asparagus, broccoli, cabbage, cauliflower, celery, cucumbers, green beans, green onions, green and red peppers, radishes and greens (kale, spinach, turnip greens, chard and salad greens) should be promptly refrigerated in a covered container, moisture-proof bag or a vegetable crisper.

Apples, apricots, berries, cherries, corn (in husks), grapes, nectarines, peaches, pears, peas (in shell) and plums should be refrigerated loosely covered or in a plastic produce bag with air holes.

Vegetable Preparation Techniques
● **Don't overcook!** Vegetables should be cooked only until tender.
● **Boil:** Use a small amount of water, cover with a tight-fitting lid and cook over low heat to minimize loss of vitamins and minerals. Cook until tender.
● **Blanch:** Bring plenty of water to a rolling boil, immerse vegetables and bring water back to a boil for 2 to 4 minutes. Refresh vegetables under icy water and use in salads.
● **Steam:** Place a steaming basket, colander or bamboo steamer over 1½ to 2 inches of boiling water, place the prepared vegetables on the rack. Cover the pan, reduce the heat but keep the water boiling and cook until just tender.
● **Stir-Fry:** Place the wok or wide skillet over high heat; when hot, add salad oil and the cut-up vegetables. Cook uncovered, stirring constantly, just until the vegetables have been lightly coated and slightly cooked (approximately 1 to 2 minutes). Add approximately ¼ cup of broth to 4 cups of vegetables; then cover and cook, stirring occasionally, until tender. Add more broth if necessary.
● **Microwave:** Cook all vegetables on 100% HIGH power, following the manufacturer's directions. Cover the cooking dish with a casserole lid or heavy-duty plastic wrap. Cooking time depends on the freshness, moisture content and maturity of the vegetable. Remove the vegetables from the microwave after the shortest recommended time, let stand and test for doneness. If the vegetables are still too crisp, microwave further in one-minute segments.

● **Sauté:** Melt butter, margarine or oil in a large skillet. Try a combination of butter and corn oil or olive and corn oil. (Butter or olive oil impart flavor, and the corn oil allows for cooking over high heat.) Add the prepared vegetables and cook, stirring constantly, until the vegetables are coated lightly, then cover, reduce the heat and cook just until tender.

● **Bake:** Prepare and cut the vegetables into thick slices, arrange in a single layer in a baking pan or casserole, or place on foil. Dot with butter or oil and bake uncovered until tender.

Try tucking vegetables (i.e., onions, squash and any of the root vegetables) in with the roast, increase the cooking time accordingly.

● **Testing for Doneness:** Cooking time depends on the freshness or maturity of the vegetables. They should be cooked until just tender, that is, until they give slightly but remain firm when pierced. The color of the vegetable becomes intense when it is cooked until just tender.

● **Serving Suggestions:** Season vegetables after they have been cooked, do not salt the water first.

Snip fresh garden herbs over vegetables before serving or sprinkle with fresh lemon or lime juice.

Asparagus with Mustard-Cream Sauce

Makes 8 servings.

Nutrient Value Per Serving: 106 calories, 4 g protein, 7 g fat, 8 g carbohydrate, 363 mg sodium, 19 mg cholesterol.

Mustard-Cream Sauce:
  2 **tablespoons butter or margarine**
  3 **tablespoons all-purpose flour**
  1 **cup chicken broth**
  1 **cup half-and-half**
  ½ **cup Dijon-style mustard**
  2 **teaspoons lemon juice**
     Pinch white pepper
2½ **pounds fresh asparagus, tough stalks trimmed**

1. Melt the butter in a saucepan. Stir in the flour and cook, for 1 minute. Add the chicken broth and half-and-half, stirring constantly with a whisk. Bring to boiling. Lower the heat; simmer for 5 minutes, stirring occasionally. Remove from the heat. Whisk in the mustard, lemon juice and pepper. Keep warm, but do not let boil.

2. Bring 2 quarts of water in a large skillet or Dutch oven to boiling. Add the asparagus. Cook for 3 to 5 minutes until tender-crisp. Drain in colander.

3. Arrange on warmed serving platter. Serve with the Mustard-Cream Sauce.

Asparagus with Mustard-Cream Sauce

Replacing the butter with diet margarine, the half-and-half with skim milk and making the chicken broth from a bouillon cube all help to lower the calories in this sauce.

Makes 8 servings.

Nutrient Value Per Serving: 61 calories, 4 g protein, 2 g fat, 8 g carbohydrate, 418 mg sodium, 1 mg cholesterol.

  2 **tablespoons diet or reduced-calorie margarine**
  3 **tablespoons all-purpose flour**
  1 **cup chicken broth, made from 1 chicken bouillon cube**
  1 **cup skim milk**
  ¼ **cup Dijon-style mustard**
  1 **teaspoon lemon juice**
     Dash white pepper
2½ **pounds fresh asparagus, trimmed**

1. Melt the margarine in a medium-size saucepan. Stir in the flour and cook for 1 minute. Add the chicken broth and skim milk, stirring constantly with a whisk. Bring to boiling. Lower the heat and simmer for 5 minutes, stirring occasionally. Remove from the heat and whisk in the mustard, lemon juice and pepper. Keep warm while cooking the asparagus; do not let boil.

2. Bring 2 quarts of water in a large skillet or Dutch oven to boiling. Add the asparagus. Cook for 3 to 5 minutes, or until tender-crisp. Drain in a colander.

3. Arrange on a warmed serving platter. Serve with the Mustard-Cream Sauce.

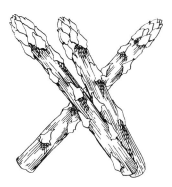

Broccoli and Red Pepper with Herb Cheese

Bake at 500° for 9 minutes.
Makes 4 servings.

Nutrient Value Per Serving: 136 calories, 5 g protein, 11 g fat, 7 g carbohydrate, 67 mg sodium, 31 mg cholesterol.

3 cups 3-inch-long broccoli flowerets
1 cup sweet red pepper strips
1 tablespoon water
¼ cup prepared garlic herb cheese
2 tablespoons unsalted butter or margarine, at room temperature

1. Preheat the oven to very hot (500°).
2. Tear off four 14 x 12-inch sheets of regular-weight aluminum foil.
3. Arrange a quarter of the broccoli and red pepper in the center of the lower half of each foil sheet. Sprinkle with 1 tablespoon water, dividing equally.
4. Mash the cheese and butter together in a small dish. Dot the vegetables with the mixture. Seal the packets tightly.
5. Place a large baking sheet in the very hot oven for about 2 minutes.
6. Bake the packets on the hot baking sheet in the preheated very hot oven (500°) for 9 minutes. Serve immediately.

Oven-Baked Carrots

You'll keep all the vitamins when you cook vegetables this way.

Bake at 350° for 40 minutes.
Makes 6 servings.

Nutrient Value Per Serving: 52 calories, .89 g protein, 2 g fat, 8 g carbohydrate, 413 mg sodium, 5 mg cholesterol.

1 bag (1 pound) carrots, sliced
½ cup water
1 small onion, thinly sliced
1 clove garlic, minced
1 teaspoon salt
1 tablespoon butter or margarine

1. Combine the carrots, water, onion, garlic and salt in a 4-cup casserole; dot with the butter or margarine; cover.
2. Bake in a moderate oven (350°) for 40 minutes, or until crisp-tender.

Snow Peas and Cucumber Medley

Makes 4 to 6 servings.

Nutrient Value Per Serving: 98 calories, 2 g protein, 7 g fat, 8 g carbohydrate, 554 mg sodium, .00 mg cholesterol.

½ pound fresh snow peas
1 cucumber
2 tablespoons peanut oil
1 small onion, finely chopped (¼ cup)
¼ teaspoon crushed red pepper
1 tablespoon cider vinegar
½ teaspoon sugar
1 teaspoon salt
⅛ teaspoon ground ginger

1. Snip off the tips and remove the strings from the snow peas; if large, cut each in half diagonally.
2. Peel the cucumber; cut in half lengthwise; scoop out and discard the seeds. Cut crosswise into about ¼-inch-thick slices.
3. Heat the oil in a large skillet or wok. Stir in the onion; stir-fry for 2 minutes; stir in the crushed pepper; cook for 5 seconds. Add the cucumber slices; stir-fry for 1 minute. Stir in the snow peas; stir-fry for 2 minutes, or just until crisp-tender. Stir in the vinegar, sugar, salt and ginger; serve at once.

Spinach Bake

Bake at 400° for 20 minutes.
Makes 4 servings.

Nutrient Value Per Serving: 245 calories, 17 g protein, 17 g fat, 9 g carbohydrate, 790 mg sodium, 256 mg cholesterol.

3 eggs
2 packages (10 ounces each) frozen chopped spinach, thawed and drained well, OR: 2 pounds fresh spinach, cooked, drained and chopped
1 package (8 ounces) feta cheese, crumbled
¼ cup chopped green onions
¼ teaspoon dried dillweed

1. Preheat the oven to hot (400°). Grease a 2-quart shallow casserole or baking dish.
2. Beat the eggs in a medium-size bowl until frothy. Stir in the spinach, feta cheese,

green onions and dillweed. Turn into the prepared casserole.

3. Bake in the preheated hot oven (400°) for 20 minutes, or until a knife inserted in the center comes out clean. Cool on a wire rack for 5 minutes before serving.

Green and Orange Sticks

Carrots and green beans are simmered in chicken broth and vinegar.

Makes 8 servings.

Nutrient Value Per Serving: 40 calories, 2 g protein, .20 g fat, 9 g carbohydrate, 182 mg sodium, .00 mg cholesterol.

1 **package (1 pound) carrots**
1 **pound green beans**
½ **cup chicken broth**
¼ **cup cider vinegar**
1 **teaspoon salt**
1 **teaspoon caraway seeds, crushed**
¼ **teaspoon seasoned pepper**

1. Pare the carrots and cut into thin sticks; trim and wash the green beans. Arrange the vegetables in separate piles in a large skillet.
2. Add the chicken broth, vinegar, salt, caraway seeds and pepper.
3. Bring to boiling; lower the heat; cover the skillet; simmer for 10 minutes, or until the vegetables are crisp-tender. Drain.

Cheesed Cauliflower & Beans

Cauliflower and beans are perfect vegetables to bake.

Bake at 350° for 50 minutes.
Makes 6 servings.

Nutrient Value Per Serving: 187 calories, 11 g protein, 10 g fat, 16 g carbohydrate, 725 mg sodium, 14 mg cholesterol.

1 **small cauliflower**
½ **pound green beans, tipped**
½ **pound wax beans, tipped**
1 **cup boiling water**
1 **teaspoon salt**
1 **teaspoon dill weed**
¼ **teaspoon lemon pepper**
1 **small can evaporated milk**
4 **slices process American cheese, diced**
1 **tablespoon prepared mustard**

1. Trim the cauliflower and soak in salted hot water for 5 minutes.
2. Arrange the cauliflower and beans in an 8-cup casserole. Add the boiling water, salt, dill weed and lemon pepper.
3. Bake in a moderate oven (350°) for 50 minutes, or until crisp-tender when pierced with a two-tined fork. Put in a shallow casserole; keep warm.
4. Heat the evaporated milk in a small saucepan until very warm. Stir in the cheese and mustard until the cheese melts. Spoon over the cauliflower and garnish with chopped tomato and sliced green onions, if you wish.

Cheesed Cauliflower & Beans (page 191)

Green Pea and Mushroom Timbales

These individual molds of pea purée, mushrooms and heavy cream are a colorful vegetable accompaniment.

Bake at 375° for 45 minutes.
Makes 8 servings.

Nutrient Value Per Serving: 241 calories, 8 g protein, 18 g fat, 13 g carbohydrate, 372 mg sodium, 156 mg cholesterol.

2 packages (10 ounces each) frozen green peas
¼ cup water
1 teaspoon leaf basil, crumbled
1 cup heavy cream
¼ cup milk
3 eggs
¾ teaspoon salt
¼ teaspoon white pepper
¾ pound fresh mushrooms
3 tablespoons butter

1. Cook the green peas in the water with the basil in a large saucepan over medium heat until tender and all the water has evaporated, for about 5 minutes.
2. Purée the peas and cream, working in batches if necessary, in a blender or food processor. Strain the purée through a fine sieve placed over a bowl, forcing through with a wooden spoon or rubber spatula.
3. Combine the milk and eggs in a small bowl. Add to the pea mixture along with ½ teaspoon of the salt and the pepper; stir to combine.
4. Preheat the oven to moderate (375°). Butter 8 ovenproof custard cups or eight 6-ounce ramekins. Line the bottoms with wax paper.
5. Slice 3 or 4 of the mushrooms lengthwise into ⅛-inch-thick slices. Set aside 16 of the prettiest slices. Coarsely chop the remaining slices and whole mushrooms.
6. Sauté the chopped mushrooms and the remaining ¼ teaspoon of salt in 2 tablespoons of the butter in a skillet until all the liquid has evaporated, for about 5 minutes. Add to the green pea purée; stir to mix.
7. Divide the purée equally among the custard cups. Place the cups in a large roasting pan. Fill the pan with 1 inch of warm water. Cover the whole pan loosely with aluminum foil.
8. Bake in the preheated moderate oven (375°) for 45 minutes.

9. Just before the end of the cooking time, sauté the reserved mushroom slices in the remaining tablespoon of butter in a skillet until lightly browned. Set aside. Run a knife around the edge of each timbale. Turn out onto a serving platter; carefully peel off the wax paper. Garnish each timbale with 2 mushroom slices. Serve immediately.

Note: Timbales are delicious with Cornish game hens. To bake the timbales and Cornish game hens at the same time, place the hens on the bottom oven rack and the timbales on the top oven rack.

MICROWAVE DIRECTIONS FOR GREEN PEA AND MUSHROOM TIMBALES
650 Watt Variable Power Microwave Oven
This is an easier version to make than the recipe to the left, since the mixture is not strained. This timbale is also a little denser.
Ingredient changes: Reduce the basil to ½ teaspoon and increase the milk to ½ cup.
Directions: Place the frozen peas and water in a 2-quart microwave-safe casserole. Cover. Microwave at full power for 9 minutes, stirring once. Drain off the liquid. While the peas are cooking, slice, chop and sauté the mushrooms as in Steps 5 and 6 to the left. Combine the peas and cream in the container of a food processor. Whirl until the mixture is very smooth. Add the ½ teaspoon of basil, ½ cup of milk, the eggs, salt and pepper; whirl until blended. Stir in the cooked chopped mushrooms. Divide the mixture among eight 6-ounce microwave-safe custard cups on a large microwave-safe plate. Cover the cups with a sheet of wax paper. Microwave at full power for 2 minutes. Rotate the cups a quarter turn. Microwave, covered with wax paper, at half power for 4 minutes, rotating the cups a quarter turn after 2 minutes. Let stand for 5 minutes before unmolding. Repeat with the remaining 4 timbales. Sauté the mushroom slices and garnish the timbales as in Step 9 to the left.
Nutrient Value Per Serving: 245 calories, 8 g protein, 18 g fat, 14 g carbohydrate, 376 mg sodium, 157 mg cholesterol.

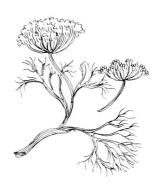

Green Pea Purée in Mushroom Caps

Reduced Calorie

In this recipe we've made a pea purée which is baked in mushroom caps. A little half-and-half replaces the heavy cream, milk and eggs in the original recipe (see previous page) and diet margarine replaces the butter.

Bake at 350° for 10 to 15 minutes.
Makes 8 servings.

Nutrient Value Per Serving: 49 calories, 3 g protein, 2 g fat, 7 g carbohydrate, 139 mg sodium, 2 mg cholesterol.

- **8 large mushrooms**
- **1 package (10 ounces) frozen peas**
- **1 tablespoon diet margarine**
- **2 tablesponns half-and-half**
- **½ teaspoon leaf basil, crumbled**
- **¼ teaspoon salt**
- **¼ teaspoon white pepper**
- **1 tablespoon grated Parmesan cheese**

1. Preheat the oven to moderate (350°). Remove the stems from the mushrooms. (Reserve for other use.)
2. Cook the peas until very tender, following the package directions. Drain well. Turn into the container of the electric blender or food processor. Add the margarine, half-and-half, basil, salt and pepper. Cover; whirl until puréed.
3. Spoon about 2 tablespoons of the purée into each mushroom cap. Sprinkle each with the Parmesan. Arrange the stuffed mushrooms on a cookie sheet.
4. Bake in the preheated moderate oven (375°) for 10 to 15 minutes, or until the mushrooms are crisp-tender and the filling is set and heated through.

Parsleyed New Potatoes

Makes 8 servings.

Nutrient Value Per Serving: 177 calories, 4 g protein, 6 g fat, 28 g carbohydrate, 138 mg sodium, 16 mg cholesterol.

- **3 pounds small red new potatoes**
- **¼ cup (½ stick) butter or margarine, melted**
- **¼ teaspoon salt**
- **⅛ teaspoon pepper**
- **2 tablespoons chopped parsley**

1. Cover the potatoes in a large pot with cold water. Bring to boiling. Cook 10 to 15 minutes, or until fork-tender. Drain.
2. Cut the potatoes in half and place in a large bowl. Sprinkle with the melted butter, salt, pepper and parsley; toss gently to mix.

MICROWAVE DIRECTIONS FOR PARSLEYED NEW POTATOES
650 Watt Variable Power Microwave Oven
Ingredient changes: Cook the potatoes in ¼ cup water.
Directions: Prick the potatoes with a fork. Place in a 3-quart microwave-safe casserole, placing the larger potatoes at the sides of the casserole. Pour in the ¼ cup water. Cover. Microwave at full power for 15 to 17 minutes until tender, rearranging the potatoes after 8 minutes to place the less-cooked potatoes at the sides of the casserole. When finished cooking, let the potatoes stand, covered, for 3 minutes. Drain. Place the butter in a 1-cup microwave-safe measure. Microwave, uncovered, at full power for 45 to 60 seconds to melt. Cut the potatoes in half. Lightly toss with the butter, salt, pepper and parsley.

Whipped Winter Squash

Any winter squash, such as Hubbard, can be used in this cold-weather favorite.

Bake at 325° for 1 hour, 30 minutes.
Makes 8 servings.

Nutrient Value Per Serving: 69 calories, .98 g protein, 3 g fat, 11 g carbohydrate, 308 mg sodium, 8 mg cholesterol.

- **1 butternut squash (about 2 pounds)**
- **2 tablespoons butter or margarine**
- **1 teaspoon salt**
- **¼ teaspoon freshly ground pepper**
  Ground cinnamon

1. Wash the squash, wipe dry and place in a large baking pan.
2. Bake in a slow oven (325°) for 1 hour, 30 minutes, or until the squash is soft when pierced with a two-tined fork.
3. Allow the squash to cool until easy to handle. Cut in half and remove the seeds with a large spoon. Scrape the squash with a spoon into a large bowl.
4. Beat the squash with a potato masher until smooth; beat in the butter or margarine, salt and pepper. Place in a heated serving dish and sprinkle with ground cinnamon before serving.

Baked Turnip

Treat your family to a vegetable they may not have tasted before.

Bake at 350° for 30 minutes.
Makes 6 servings.

Nutrient Value Per Serving: 103 calories, 3 g protein, 4 g fat, 14 g carbohydrate, 490 mg sodium, 10 mg cholesterol.

1   **large yellow turnip (2 pounds)**
2   **tablespoons butter or margarine**
¼   **cup wheat germ**
2   **tablespoons brown sugar**
1   **teaspoon salt**
¼   **teaspoon pepper**
¼   **teaspoon ground nutmeg**

1. Cut the turnip into ½-inch slices; pare the slices; dice. Cook in salted boiling water in a large saucepan for 45 minutes, or until tender when pierced with a two-tined fork. Drain the turnip and return to the saucepan.
2. Mash the turnip until smooth with a potato masher; beat in the butter or margarine until melted; beat in the wheat germ, sugar, salt, pepper and nutmeg. Spoon into a 6-cup casserole.
3. Bake in a moderate oven (350°) for 30 minutes, or until golden.

Vegetable Curry with Fruit

Vegetable Curry with Fruit

Serve with hot cooked rice.

Nutrient Value Per Serving: 325 calories, 6 g protein, 24 g fat, 28 g carbohydrate, 168 mg sodium, 23 mg cholesterol.

1¼ **pounds mixed salad bar vegetables (about 7 cups), such as broccoli and cauliflower flowerets, sweet green pepper, celery, onion, mushrooms and hot Italian or cherry peppers**
3   **tablespoons butter**
3   **tablespoons vegetable oil**
1   **teaspoon finely chopped pared gingerroot**
1   **teaspoon finely chopped garlic**
1   **to 2 tablespoons curry powder**
¼   **cup chicken broth**
½   **pound salad bar fruit OR: fresh or drained canned fruit pieces or sections, such as orange, grapefruit, pineapple, mandarin orange**
¼   **cup raisins**
¼   **cup unsalted cashews**
    Hot cooked rice (optional)
    Chutney (optional)

1. Slice any large vegetables into bite-size pieces. Finely chop the hot peppers. Reserve.
2. Heat the butter and oil in a large skillet. Add the ginger and garlic; stir-fry for 30 seconds. Add the vegetables; stir-fry for 1 minute. Sprinkle the vegetables with the curry; stir to blend well.
3. Pour the chicken broth into skillet. Reduce heat to low; cover the skillet and steam for 2 minutes, or until broccoli and cauliflower are crisp-tender.
4. Remove from the heat. Add the fruit. Cover for 1 minute to heat through. Mix in the raisins and cashews. Serve immediately over the hot rice with the chutney, if you wish.

MICROWAVE DIRECTIONS FOR VEGETABLE CURRY WITH FRUIT
650 Watt Variable Power Microwave Oven
Ingredient changes: Reduce butter and oil to 1 tablespoon each. Use 1 tablespoon curry powder. Add ¼ teaspoon salt.
Directions: Place butter and oil in a microwave-safe pan, about 13 x 9 inches. Sprinkle gingerroot and garlic over bottom of pan. Microwave, uncovered, at full power for 1 minute. Add vegetables and curry; stir to mix well. Pour in chicken broth. Cover. Microwave at full power for 2 minutes. Stir in fruit, raisins and cashews. Cover. Microwave at full power for 2 minutes. Sprinkle with salt. Serve over hot rice with chutney, if you wish. Nutrient Value Per Serving: 211 calories, 5 g protein, 11 g fat, 27 g carbohydrate, 243 mg sodium, 8 mg cholesterol.

A ROSTER OF RICE

White Rice It's dubbed "regular" because it is the most familiar and popular. Hull, bran and polishings have been removed, leaving a snow-white grain. The size regulates the price: *Short-grain* or *medium-grain* rice are the thriftiest. These cook moist and tender and are an ideal choice for casseroles, puddings and croquettes. *Long-grain* rice, at a few pennies more a pound, cooks fluffier and flakier and is preferred for serving as a vegetable or as a base for curry. Most white rice is enriched, but let the label be your guide.

Processed White Rice The term *"parboiled"* or *"converted"* on the package of rice simply means that the grains have been partly cooked before milling, with special care taken to protect the vitamins and minerals in the outer layer. This rice is long grain with a light golden color; it cooks the same as regular rice.

Precooked White Rice It's called *"instant"* because it needs only the briefest cooking. It is milled from special long-grain rice, is enriched and comes plain and seasoned.

Brown Rice This is whole grain rice with only the outer hull removed. The cooking time for brown rice is longer than for regular rice and its savory, nut-like flavor makes it a perfect partner for meat or game.

Wild Rice This is not a true rice, but is the seed of a water grass native to some of our northern states. When cooked, these long, slender, gray-brown grains have a sweet, nut–like flavor. Wild rice is available as is or mixed with long-grain white rice.

Seasoned Rice These are quick-to-fix, convenience foods. The seasonings are mixed with the rice before packaging. Take your pick of beef, chicken, chili, cheese, curry, herb, pilaf or saffron (yellow) rice flavors. Frozen seasoned rice is the easiest to fix; just heat and serve.

HOW TO COOK RICE PERFECTLY

To Boil: Measure 2 to 2½ cups of water (as the label directs), 1 tablespoon of butter or margarine and 1 teaspoon of salt into a heavy, medium-size saucepan. Bring to boiling. Stir in 1 cup of uncooked long-grain or processed (converted) white rice; let return to a boil, then adjust the heat so the water bubbles gently. Cover the pan snugly and cook for 14 to 25 minutes (following the label directions) until the rice is fluffy and the water absorbed. Fluff with a fork.

To Steam: Measure 2½ cups of water, 1 tablespoon of butter or margarine and 1 teaspoon of salt into the top of a double boiler; bring to boiling over direct heat, then stir in 1 cup of uncooked long-grain or processed (converted) white rice; cover. Place the top of the double boiler over the bottom (half-filled with boiling water); turn the heat to medium and cook for 45 minutes, or until the water is absorbed and the rice fluffy. Fluff with a fork.

To Bake Combine 1 cup of uncooked long-grain or processed (converted) white rice with 1 teaspoon of salt and 1 tablespoon of butter or margarine in a 4- or 6-cup baking dish. Pour in 2½ cups of *boiling* water; stir; cover. Bake in a moderate oven (350°) for 1 hour, or until the water is absorbed and the rice is tender. Fluff with a fork.

How Much Rice Should You Cook?

Rice swells 3 to 4 times as it cooks. Use this chart for reference.

Rice	Uncooked	Cooked	Servings
Long-Grain White Rice	1 cup	3 cups	3 to 4
Processed Converted White Rice	1 cup	4 cups	4 to 6
Precooked Instant White Rice	1 cup	2 cups	2 to 3
Brown Rice	1 cup	4 cups	4 to 6
Wild Rice	1 cup	4 cups	4 to 6

Zucchini Boats with Bulgur Pilaf

Bake at 350° for 20 minutes.
Makes 8 to 10 servings.

Nutrient Value Per Serving: 123 calories, 3 g protein, 3 g fat, 21 g carbohydrate, 294 mg sodium, 8 mg cholesterol.

¼ **cup chopped shallots OR: green onion**
2 **tablespoons butter or margarine**
1 **sweet red pepper, cored, seeded and finely chopped**
1 **cup bulgur**
2 **cups water OR: chicken broth**
½ **cup tomato juice**
¾ **teaspoon salt**
¼ **teaspoon ground pepper**
⅛ **teaspoon ground allspice**
8 **to 10 medium-size zucchini (5 or 6 inches long), halved lengthwise**

1. Sauté the shallots in the butter in a medium-size heavy saucepan for 5 minutes. Add the red pepper; sauté, stirring for 4 to 5 minutes. Stir in the bulgur, water, tomato juice, salt, pepper and allspice. Bring to boiling. Lower the heat; simmer, covered, for 15 minutes. Remove from the heat. Let stand, tightly covered, for 15 to 20 minutes.
2. Cook the zucchini in boiling salted water to cover in a large skillet, for 8 minutes, or until tender. Drain. Run under cold water. Scoop out the insides, leaving a ¼- to ½-inch shell. Spoon the bulgur pilaf into the zucchini shells. Serve hot or at room temperature. To serve hot, bake the zucchini in a shallow baking dish, loosely covered with foil, in a preheated moderate oven (350°) until heated through, for 20 minutes.

Vegetable Vinaigrette

Crisply cooked vegetables, such as carrots, green beans, lima beans, peas, corn or zucchini, can be coated with vinaigrette, stored in the refrigerator and be ready at a moment's notice to be added to salads.

Whisk the vinaigrette together, pour over the cooked or raw vegetables, and allow at least six hours before serving, so that the flavors marry. Marinated vegetables may be kept for at least a week in the refrigerator.

Grilled Vegetables with Goat Cheese Sauce

Broil for 10 minutes.
Makes 4 servings.

Nutrient Value Per Serving: 224 calories, 9 g protein, 14 g fat, 20 g carbohydrate, 412 mg sodium, 26 mg cholesterol.

1 **medium-size eggplant (about 1 pound), trimmed and cut into ½-inch-thick slices**
¼ **teaspoon salt**
½ **cup skim milk**
1 **teaspoon cornstarch**
   Pinch leaf thyme
   Pinch pepper
4 **ounces goat cheese, crumbled**
2 **medium-size zucchini, trimmed and halved lengthwise**
2 **medium-size onions, cut crosswise into ½-inch-thick slices**
2 **sweet red or green peppers, halved lengthwise and seeded**
½ **pound small mushrooms, trimmed (about 10)**
2 **tablespoons olive oil**

1. Sprinkle the eggplant with the ¼ teaspoon of salt. Drain in a colander for 30 minutes.
2. Combine the milk, cornstarch, thyme and pepper in a saucepan. Stir until the cornstarch dissolves. Bring to boiling over medium heat, stirring constantly. Cook for 1 minute. Remove from the heat. Add the cheese; stir until smooth. Keep warm in the top of a double boiler, over hot, not boiling, water.
3. Wipe the salt and moisture off the eggplant.
4. Brush the zucchini, onion, peppers and mushrooms with the oil. Arrange the vegetables on broiler pans. Broil 4 inches from the heat until brown, for 5 minutes. Turn over and cook until brown, for 5 minutes. Arrange on a serving platter. Serve with the warm cheese sauce.

Storing onions

All dry onions should be kept in as cool and dry an area as possible.

THE WINTER PRODUCE STALL

Besides the year-round favorites (such as bananas, cabbage, carrots, celery, onions, lettuce, red and green peppers and potatoes), winter features an abundance of apples, pears, avocados, grapes, citrus fruits, broccoli, cauliflower, Brussels sprouts, peas, spinach, winter squash and sweet potatoes.

The Roots Revisited

Don't ignore the earthy goodness of the following root vegetables.

Beets: Cook without trimming the stems or roots too closely, or they'll "bleed." Prepare vitamin A-rich tops as you would spinach. Serve hot sliced beets in an orange glaze, spiced with cloves.

Carrots: Add to soups and stews. Scrub very well; peeling is not necessary. Toss grated carrots with lemon juice, sherry, raisins and chopped nuts. Cut carrots into 2-inch chunks; boil until barely tender. Drain well and roll in orange-mint butter, then in dry bread crumbs; bake.

Parsnips: Parsnips are sweeter after prolonged exposure to cold temperatures; that's why they're best during the winter months. Steam them to bring out their rich nutty flavor. Toss diced cooked parsnips with a thin white sauce; sprinkle with crisp bacon bits and chopped parsley.

Radishes: Serve crisp radishes with butter, coarse salt, pumpernickle bread and icy cold beer.

Rutabagas and Turnips: Rutabagas, also called Swedes or Swedish turnips, are golden and larger than white turnips. Rutabaga tops, unlike turnip tops, are not eaten as a separate vegetable. Add a teaspoonful of sugar to cooking water to improve the mild flavor and sweetness. Mix mashed cooked rutabaga with applesauce. Toss diced cooked turnip with heavy cream and grated Parmesan cheese.

Salsify: Similar in appearance to parsnips, but with grass-like tops, salsify is also called Oyster plant. Serve gratinée, with minced chives or shallots. Mash until creamy; season with butter, salt and pepper.

Celeriac: Also known as celery root. Peel before cooking, adding vinegar to the water. Marinate raw celeriac in a vinaigrette dressing and serve over sliced tomatoes.

A FRUITFUL WINTER

Pears, bananas, oranges, grapefruit, apples, tangerines and cranberries are plentiful in winter.

- Fill apples with sugar, grated orange rind and coconut; place in a baking pan; squeeze orange juice over tops. Bake until tender, basting often.
- Top grapefruit halves with honey, rum and ground cinnamon; broil.
- Fill individual shortcakes with a cranberry relish; top with sweetened whipped cream.
- Sauté halved bananas in butter until golden; sprinkle with brown sugar and brandy; serve with ice cream.
- Add chopped orange to sweetened whipped cream cheese; use to top toasted pound cake.

- Combine diced pear with tangerine sections, whole almonds and ground ginger; toss with lemon juice and 10X sugar. Serve icy cold.

Other Accompaniments

Vegetable Rice Pilaf

Makes 8 servings.

Nutrient Value Per Serving: 205 calories, 4 g protein, 5 g fat, 36 g carbohydrate, 365 mg sodium, 12 mg cholesterol.

- **2 cups chopped leeks, both green and white parts (2 large)**
- **3 tablespoons butter or margarine**
- **1½ cups uncooked white rice**
- **1 can (13¾ ounces) chicken broth**
- **1 cup water**
- **1½ cups shredded carrots (about 2 large)**
- **½ teaspoon leaf thyme, crumbled**
- **½ teaspoon salt**
- **¼ cup chopped parsley**

1. Sauté the leeks in the butter in a large saucepan over low heat until wilted, for about 2 minutes. Add the rice, stirring until all the grains are coated with the butter.
2. Add the chicken broth, water, carrots, thyme and salt. Bring to boiling. Lower the heat and simmer, covered, for 20 minutes, or until all the water has been absorbed. Toss with the chopped parsley.

MICROWAVE DIRECTIONS FOR VEGETABLE RICE PILAF
650 Watt Variable Power Microwave Oven
Directions: Place the butter in a 3-quart microwave-safe casserole. Microwave, uncovered, at full power for 1 minute to melt. Add the leeks. Microwave, uncovered, at full power for 2 minutes. Stir in the rice; add the chicken broth, water, carrots, thyme and salt. Cover. Microwave at full power for 22 to 24 minutes until the rice is tender, stirring after 10 minutes. Let stand for 3 minutes. Toss with the chopped parsley.

Brandied Chestnut Stuffing

Use to stuff turkey, or bake at 350° for
45 minutes.
Makes 8 cups (enough for a 10 to 12 pound
turkey).

*Nutrient Value Per Serving: 312 calories, 10 g protein,
17 g fat, carbohydrate (not available), 797 mg sodium,
42 mg cholesterol.*

- **2 cups finely chopped mushrooms
  (about 5½ ounces)**
- **5 tablespoons butter**
- **1 large onion, finely chopped (1 cup)**
- **2 medium-size celery stalks, finely
  chopped (1 cup)**
- **1 pound sausage meat**
- **4 cups crumbled day-old white bread
  (8 slices)**
- **1 cup turkey or chicken broth**
- **1 can (15½ or 16 ounces) chestnuts,
  rinsed, drained and coarsely chopped,
  OR: 2 cups coarsely chopped, peeled,
  cooked fresh chestnuts**
- **¼ cup brandy**
- **¼ cup chopped parsley**
- **2 teaspoons leaf thyme, crumbled**
- **1 bay leaf, crumbled**
- **½ teaspoon salt**
- **¼ teaspoon pepper**

1. Sauté the mushrooms in 2 tablespoons of the
   butter in a large 12-inch skillet until golden,
   for about 5 minutes. Transfer with a slotted
   spoon to a small bowl.
2. Sauté the onion and celery in the remaining
   3 tablespoons of the butter for 3 minutes
   longer. Add the sausage, breaking up into
   small pieces with a wooden spoon; sauté
   until lightly browned and no longer pink, for
   about 5 minutes. Remove from the heat.
   Drain the excess fat.
3. Add the bread and the broth to the skillet;
   stir to moisten. Stir in the chestnuts, brandy,
   parsley, thyme, bay leaf, salt and pepper.
   Return to the heat; stir to mix thoroughly for
   2 minutes. Remove from the heat; stir in the
   reserved mushrooms.
4. Stuff the turkey and roast according to your
   favorite recipe. Or spoon the stuffing into a
   greased, shallow 2-quart baking dish. Bake,
   covered, in a preheated moderate oven (350°)
   for 45 minutes, or until heated through.
   Uncover for the last 10 minutes of baking for
   a crusty top.

Chestnuts

Buying and storing: Imported from Italy or Spain,
fresh chestnuts are found from October to March. Look
for plump, unblemished nuts that are heavy for their
size. Imported canned chestnuts packed in water and
puréed chestnuts are available in the gourmet section
of your supermarket, as are sweetened canned chestnuts or *marron,* imported from France.

Shelled, dried chestnuts are sold in Italian, Spanish
and Chinese markets. They can be used just like fresh
chestnuts after soaking overnight in water to cover,
then cooked until tender.

Store fresh chestnuts in a cool, dry place. They can be
refrigerated for several weeks. Canned chestnuts should
be refrigerated after opening. Dried chestnuts can be
kept in an air-tight comtainer on the shelf.

To Prepare Wash fresh chestnuts. Make a cut in the flat
side of each nut to keep the nut from exploding. To shell
and skin the nuts, place in a saucepan with water to
cover; bring to boiling. Boil for 3 minutes. Remove the
pan from the heat. With a spoon, remove several chestnuts and shell the nuts. Remove the inner skin from
each nut. (Keep the other chestnuts in hot water until
ready to shell and peel.)

To Cook: Fresh chestnuts can be boiled or roasted.

To serve as a vegetable, cook shelled and skinned
nuts in boiling water or chicken broth in a covered
saucepan over low heat until tender, for about 15
minutes. Drain and serve with cooked Brussels sprouts
or other green vegetable, or purée in a food processor.
If using chestnuts for dessert, cook in water or sugar
syrup.

To roast, place unshelled, slashed nuts in a shallow
baking pan; bake in a preheated very hot oven (475°) for
15 minutes, stirring occasionally. Serve piping hot.

To roast over an open fire, use a hole-punched metal
pan and roast over white coals until a nut can easily be
shelled and the kernel is soft.

Chestnut Math

1 pound of fresh chestnuts = 35 to 40 nuts =
2½ cups shelled.

Fruited Stuffing

Apples and raisins add the perfect touch to your holiday roast goose.

Bake at 325° for 1 hour.
Makes 8 servings.

Nutrient Value Per Serving: 320 calories, 5 g protein, 17 g fat, 40 g carbohydrate, 439 mg sodium, 17 mg cholesterol.

  1 **can (1 pound) sliced apples**
     Water
  ¼ **cup (½ stick) butter or margarine**
  1 **package (8 ounces) prepared bread stuffing mix**
  1 **cup chopped pecans**
  ½ **cup seedless raisins**

1. Drain the apple liquid into a 1-cup measure and add water to make 1 cup. Bring to boiling in a large saucepan. Stir in the butter or margarine until melted.
2. Add the prepared stuffing, apples, pecans and raisins; toss lightly to mix the fruits with the stuffing mix. Spoon into a 6-cup casserole; cover.
3. Bake in a slow oven (325°) for 1 hour, or until heated through.

Perfect Pan Gravy

Serve with Crisply Roasted Goose (page 126).

Makes 3 cups.

Nutrient Value Per ¼ Cup Serving: 64 calories, 1 g protein, 5 g fat, 3 g carbohydrate, 361 mg sodium, 4 mg cholesterol.

  ⅓ **cup all-purpose flour**
  ¼ **cup fat from roast**
  2¾ **cups chicken broth**
  1 **teaspoon salt**
  ¼ **teaspoon pepper**
  ¼ **cup Madeira wine**
  2 **teaspoons bottled gravy coloring (optional)**

1. Sprinkle the flour over the fat in a saucepan; cook, stirring constantly, until bubbly. Stir in the broth, salt and pepper.
2. Cook, stirring constantly, until the sauce thickens and bubbles, for 3 minutes. Stir in the Madeira and gravy coloring, if using. Strain into a medium-size saucepan; keep hot until ready to serve.

Bean Sprout Fritters

Makes 8 four-inch fritters.

Nutrient Value Per Serving: 160 calories, 6 g protein, 8 g fat, 18 g carbohydrate, 286 mg sodium, 34 mg cholesterol.

  1¼ **cups sifted all-purpose flour**
  1 **teaspoon salt**
  ¼ **teaspoon pepper**
  ½ **teaspoon ground ginger**
  1 **egg yolk**
  1 **cup ice water**
  ½ **pound fresh bean sprouts (2 cups)**
  1 **cup shredded carrots**
  ½ **cup chopped green onion**
  1 **package (10 ounces) tofu or bean curd, cut into ¼-inch cubes**
     Vegetable oil for frying
  ½ **cup bottled duck sauce**
  1 **tablespoon cider vinegar**

1. Combine the flour, salt, pepper and ginger in a large bowl. Beat the yolk with the ice water; beat into the flour mixture with the wire whip until the batter is smooth; let stand for 5 minutes.
2. Rinse the bean sprouts under cold running water; drain thoroughly. Add the bean sprouts, carrots, green onion and tofu to the flour batter; stir to coat the vegetables.
3. Pour oil to a depth of ½ inch in a 10-inch skillet. Heat to 375° on a deep-fat frying thermometer.
4. Place ½ cup of the vegetable mixture on a 5-inch flat saucer; spread to a 4-inch circle. Holding the plate slightly above the hot oil, *carefully* slide the mixture into the oil using a large spoon. (Fry one at a time.) Fry 1 minute on each side, or until lightly golden. Remove to paper toweling to drain.
5. Combine the duck sauce with the vinegar in a small bowl. Pass at the table.

Note: For a crisper fritter, place the cooked fritters in a single layer on a jelly-roll pan. Heat in a preheated very hot oven (475°) for 10 minutes.

Corn Tortilla Cups

Use a tortilla basket fryer (see Note*) to make these delicious, edible containers for chili and other suitable foods.

Makes 12 baskets.

Nutrient Value Per Serving: 80 calories, 1 g protein, 4 g fat, 11 g carbohydrate, 26 mg sodium, 0 mg cholesterol.

> **Vegetable oil for deep frying**
> **1 package 6-inch corn tortillas****
> **(10 ounces, 12 to a package)**

1. Pour enough oil for frying into a deep fat-fryer or heavy casserole. Heat the oil until a deep-fat frying thermometer registers 375°.
2. Place 1 corn tortilla in the large wire basket of the tortilla fryer. Gently place the smaller basket on top of the corn tortilla. Lower into the hot oil. Deep-fry until crisp and golden, for about 1 minute. Remove from the oil; carefully remove the smaller basket and turn the corn tortilla "basket" out onto paper toweling to drain. Repeat with the remaining corn tortillas.

*Note: Tortilla basket fryers can be found in the cookware section of department stores or specialty cookware shops, or can be mail-ordered from William-Sonoma, Mail-order Department, P.O. Box 7456, San Francisco, CA 94120-7456.

**Note: Use only the pliable tortillas found in the refrigerator case. If the tortillas are a little dry, refresh them before frying by steaming them for 20 to 25 seconds. Or place a tortilla on a sheet of microwave-safe paper toweling, then cover with another sheet of paper toweling. Microwave at full power for 20 seconds.

Charoseth

Some of the Charoseth, a paste of apples, nuts and wine, is placed on the Passover plate to symbolize the clay and bricks used by the Israelites to build cities for the Pharoahs. The rest of the Charoseth is placed in a bowl to be spread on matzo and eaten with the fish course or main course.

Makes 1½ cups.

Nutrient Value Per 2 Tablespoons: 53 calories, 1 g protein, 3 g fat, 1 mg sodium, 0 mg cholesterol.

> **1 cup finely chopped unpared apples**
> **½ cup finely chopped walnuts**
> **2 tablespoons honey**
> **¼ cup sweet red wine**
> **¼ teaspoon ground cinnamon**

Combine the apples and nuts in a bowl. Stir in the honey, wine and cinnamon. Mix thoroughly.

Corn Relish

Makes about 3½ cups.

Nutrient Value Per ¼-Cup Serving: 78 calories, .83 g protein, 5 g fat, 8 g carbohydrate, 43 mg sodium, .00 mg cholesterol.

> **1 package (10 ounces) frozen**
> **kernel corn, thawed**
> **1 cup finely chopped sweet red pepper**
> **(1 large)**
> **⅓ cup finely chopped onion**
> **¼ cup pickle relish**
> **¼ cup finely chopped celery**
> **⅓ cup distilled white vinegar**
> **⅓ cup vegetable oil**
> **1 tablespoon sugar**
> **2 teaspoons prepared mustard**
> **½ teaspoon mustard seed**
> **½ teaspoon celery seed**

1. Combine the corn, red pepper, onion, pickle relish and celery in a medium-size heatproof bowl.
2. Stir together the vinegar, oil, sugar, mustard seed and celery seed in a small saucepan. Bring to boiling; boil for 1 minute. Pour over the vegetables; stir well.
3. Refrigerate, covered, overnight, stirring occasionally.
4. Spoon the relish into a glass jar and tightly cover. Store in the refrigerator for up to 1 week.

*Pink-and-White Frosted Hearts, Cream-Filled Chocolate Cakes,
White-on-White Frosted Hearts (page 220)*

Treats and Sweets

A grand repertoire of dessert cakes and cookies awaits you! Serve any of these sumptuous treats, and they're sure to steal the show.

From an old favorite like Fresh Coconut Layer Cake (page 213) to unique and special Individual Birthday Cakes (page 226), homemade cakes are the ultimate in dessert dishes. Other culinary coups de grace you can make include cheesecakes, Valentine cakes-from-the-heart, plus five elegant and delectable cakes made from one Basic Cake Batter (page 204).

Who can forget the irrestistible smell of cookies that are fresh from the oven? We have something to tickle every cookie lover's tummy—from drop, sandwich and easy one-pan cookies, like Apricot-Coconut Cookie Squares (page 236), to elegantly decorated special-occasion cookies such as Lemon Slice Cookies (page 237).

Our extensive cake and cookie selection will give you all sorts of tasty ideas when you want to give a "special someone" a gift of love. After all, is there a better way to express that sentiment than with a delicious homemade cake or a fresh batch of scrumptious cookies?

 Quick

 Make Ahead

 Entertaining

 Low Cost

 Low Calorie

Cakes

Cake Baking Tips

- If you want your cake to have the best volume, shape and texture possible, use the ingredients, measurements and pan size called for in the recipe. Follow the directions carefully.
- For easier egg separation, separate yolks from whites when eggs are cold.
- Allow egg whites to come to room temperature for maximum volume when beating.
- Remember to preheat the oven to the proper temperature 10 minutes before baking.
- Cakes may turn out heavy and soggy if the oven temperature is too low.
- Cakes may fall if the oven door is opened too soon, if the oven is too hot or if there is not enough flour in the batter.
- Cakes are done when:
  The cake shrinks slightly from the sides of the pan.
  A fingertip is lightly pressed on the top of the cake and the top springs back to shape.
  A cake tester or wooden pick inserted near the center of the cake comes out clean, with no batter or moist particles clinging to it.
- Cool cakes thoroughly before splitting in half and assembling.
- To split cake evenly, measure its height and then mark cutting lines around outside of cake with wooden picks. Gently saw through cake with a long serrated knife.
- Brush off all loose crumbs from the cake before frosting.
- To prevent drips and frosting smears on the cake serving plate, cover the outer area of the plate with strips of wax paper that extend beyond the edge of the plate. Carefully remove strips once the cake is frosted.
- Frost the sides of the cake first, working from the bottom up. Then frost the top of the cake, spreading to edges and swirling.
- Heavy cream whips better if the cream is very cold and the mixing bowl and beaters have been chilled in the freezer for a few minutes.
- Cakes are best when served the same day they are frosted.

Basic Cake Batter

1 cup unsifted cake flour
1½ teaspoons baking powder
¼ teaspoon salt
5 eggs, separated
¼ cup water
1 cup granulated sugar
1½ teaspoons vanilla

1. Prepare the pan(s) and preheat the oven as directed in the individual cake recipe.
2. Sift together the flour, baking powder and salt onto a piece of wax paper.
3. Beat the egg whites in a large mixer bowl with an electric mixer at high speed until soft peaks form. Set aside.
4. Beat together the egg yolks and water in a second large bowl until foamy. Gradually beat in the sugar and vanilla; beat until thickened and light in color. Fold in the flour mixture just until all the flour is incorporated. Gently fold in the beaten egg whites with a whisk or rubber spatula just until no streaks remain.
5. Pour the batter into the prepared pan(s). Bake and cool as directed in the individual recipes.

Chocolate Cake: Reduce the sugar to ½ cup. Melt and cool 1 package (6 ounces) of semi-sweet chocolate pieces. Fold into the flour-egg-yolk mixture before adding the beaten egg whites.

Lemon Cake: Add 2 teaspoons of grated lemon rind when adding the vanilla.

Almond Cake: Reduce the flour to ½ cup and the baking powder to ¾ teaspoon. Fold 1 cup of the finely ground almonds into the flour-egg-yolk mixture.

Hazelnut Cake: Reduce the flour to ½ cup and the baking powder to ¾ teaspoon. Fold 1 cup of finely ground hazelnuts into the flour-egg-yolk mixture.

Cake Flour

Cake flour is milled from soft wheat. It is especially suitable for cakes, cookies and pastries. Soft wheat contains less gluten-forming protein. Gluten is the substance that gives structure and elasticity to batters and doughs.

Basic Butter Cream Filling

Makes about 1 cup.

Nutrient Value Per Cup: 1,155 calories, 10 g protein, 103 g fat, 51 g carbohydrate, 90 mg sodium, 795 mg cholesterol.

- **1 egg**
- **1 egg yolk**
- **¼ cup granulated sugar**
- **½ cup (1 stick) unsalted butter, softened**
- **½ teaspoon vanilla**

1. Whisk together the egg, egg yolk and sugar in the top of a double boiler. Place over simmering water and stir constantly until thick and velvety, for about 10 minutes. Remove from the top of the double boiler and set aside to cool to room temperature.

2. Beat the butter in a small bowl with an electric mixer until light and fluffy. On low speed, add the vanilla, then the egg mixture, a tablespoon at a time. Beat until smooth.

Almond Butter Cream Filling: Add ½ teaspoon of almond extract with the vanilla. Makes about 1 cup. Nutrient Value Per Cup: 1,162 calories, 10 g protein, 103 g fat, 51 g carbohydrate, 90 mg sodium, 795 mg cholesterol.

Chocolate Butter Cream Filling: Melt 3 squares (1 ounce each) of semisweet chocolate; cool to room temperature. Add to the butter before adding the egg mixture. Makes about 1 cup. Nutrient Value Per Cup: 1,586 calories, 13 g protein, 133 g fat, 51 g carbohydrate, 92 mg sodium, 795 mg cholesterol.

Basic Cream Pudding Filling

Makes 2 cups.

Nutrient Value Per 2 Cups: 682 calories, 14 g protein, 55 g fat, 35 g carbohydrate, 320 mg sodium, 210 mg cholesterol.

- **1 package (4 ounces) vanilla-flavor instant pudding and pie filling**
- **1 cup cold milk**
- **½ cup cold heavy cream**

1. Blend together the pudding mix and milk in a small mixer bowl with the mixer on low speed. Add the heavy cream; beat for about 1 minute at medium speed.

2. Chill for 10 minutes before folding in any additional ingredients.

Orange Cream Pudding Filling: Prepare as directed above. After chilling for 10 minutes, fold in 2 tablespoons of Triple Sec or other orange-flavored liqueur and ¼ cup of finely chopped mixed candied fruit. Makes 2 cups. Nutrient Value Per 2 Cups: 965 calories, 14 g protein, 56 g fat, 96 g carbohydrate, 506 mg sodium, 110 mg cholesterol.

Butterscotch-Pecan Cream Pudding Filling: Prepare as directed above, using 1 package (3½ ounces) of butterscotch-flavor instant pudding and pie filling. After chilling for 10 minutes, fold in ½ cup of chopped pecans. Makes 2 cups. Nutrient Value Per 2 Cups: 1,366 calories, 15 g protein, 93 g fat, 130 g carbohydrate, 1,946 mg sodium, 197 mg cholesterol.

Vanilla

A fragrant flavoring, vanilla extract is extracted or percolated from the vanilla bean with alcohol and water. The vanilla bean is the fruit of an exquisite, pale yellow orchid that is native to Mexico and grows in clusters of 12 or more blossoms on a vine. The orchid is now grown in Madagascar, Island of Reunion and Comores, Tahiti and Java although the best are still produced in Mexico.

When the fruit is harvested, it resembles a green bean. It is then dried and covered to induce fermentation. The process is repeated until the bean turns dark brown. The process of curing and drying takes 6 months, thus accounting for the high price of a single bean.

English Toffee Cake

7. Cut the cake horizontally into 3 equal layers. Place the top layer, cut-side up, on a serving platter. Spread with half of the glaze and half of the pudding filling. Place the middle layer on top of the filling, pressing down gently. Spread with the remaining glaze and pudding filling. Place the third layer, cut-side down, on top. Gently press down to seal the layers together.
8. Frost the sides and top with the Toffee Whipped Cream. Garnish with the pecan halves, if you wish. Refrigerate until ready to serve.

Toffee Whipped Cream: Beat 1½ cups of heavy cream, ½ teaspoon of instant coffee granules and 3 tablespoons of brown sugar in a chilled bowl until stiff.

English Toffee Cake

Bake at 325° for 40 to 45 minutes.
Makes 14 servings.

Nutrient Value Per Serving: 365 calories, 5 g protein, 23 g fat, 38 g carbohydrate, 284 mg sodium, 154 mg cholesterol.

**1 recipe Basic Cake Batter
   (see recipe, page 204)
1 recipe Butterscotch-Pecan Cream
   Pudding Filling (see recipe, page 205)
1 recipe Deep Chocolate Glaze
   (recipe follows)
   Toffee Whipped Cream (recipe follows)
   Pecan halves for garnish (optional)**

1. Preheat the oven to slow (325°). Grease the bottom of a 9-inch angelcake tube pan. Line the bottom with wax paper.
2. Prepare the Basic Cake Batter as directed. Pour into the prepared pan.
3. Bake in the preheated slow oven (325°) for 40 to 45 minutes, or until a wooden pick inserted in the center comes out clean. Invert the pan on a bottle or wire rack. Let the cake cool completely.
4. Loosen the cake with a knife around the edge and tube. Remove the cake from the pan; peel off the wax paper.
5. Prepare the Butterscotch-Pecan Cream Pudding filling.
6. Prepare the Deep Chocolate Glaze.

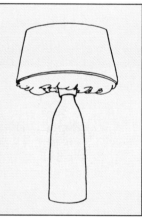

Hanging Foam Cakes

Remove angel food, chiffon or sponge cakes from the oven. Cool by placing over the top of a filled *glass* 1-quart or 1-liter bottle for 1 hour, or until cold. (The cake will not fall out and the air can circulate around whole cake which will cool faster.)

Deep Chocolate Glaze

Makes ⅓ cup.

Nutrient Value Per ⅓ Cup: 736 calories, 4 g protein, 65 g fat, 48 g carbohydrate, 353 mg sodium, 93 mg cholesterol.

**3 tablespoons butter
½ cup (3 ounces) semisweet
   chocolate pieces**

Combine the butter and chocolate in the top of a double boiler. Place over simmering water; stir constantly until smooth. Use while still warm. The glaze will harden as it sits.

CHOCOLATE HISTORY

There's no question that one of America's most beloved flavors is chocolate. Chocolate has a unique, satisfying and sensuous taste and is enjoyed in many forms.

Chocolate is a product of the New World. As early as the 16th century, Mexicans were already enjoying a frothy chocolate drink and the Spanish invaders under Cortez took the dark brown mystery product back to Europe. Hot chocolate in particular became an instant favorite. It wasn't long before there were chocolate shops galore where people went to enjoy a cup of the brew.

Chocolate is produced from cacao beans. Cacao beans are the seeds of a large, oval fruit. The fruit grows directly on the main branches of the cacao tree. Each fruit contains about 25 to 40 olive-size seeds or beans. The seeds are removed from the pulp and dried. Then they are roasted and ground until the fat in them liquefies. The rich, dark liquid is unsweetened chocolate. Cacao beans are also called cocoa beans.

In Colonial America, chocolate was imported from Europe until the first chocolate factory in Massachusetts started production in 1765.

TIPS ON CHOCOLATE

Melting Chocolate

● Chocolate scorches easily, so melt it over *hot*, not boiling water. A double boiler is best, but you can improvise by using a cup or bowl in a small saucepan. Either way, keep the water just below simmering. If steam gets into melting chocolate it will thicken the mixture and make it difficult to mix with the other ingredients. However, if this happens, simply soften the chocolate by adding 1 to 2 tablespoons vegetable shortening (not butter) and stir vigorously.

● If there is liquid in a chocolate recipe such as milk, water, or spirits, melt the chocolate in the liquid in a small saucepan over direct heat. There should be at least ¼ cup of liquid for every 6 ounces of chocolate. Stir constantly while melting to blend with the liquid.

You can also melt chocolate with the fat in the recipe directly over very low heat. Use a heavy saucepan and watch mixture carefully.

Storing Chocolate

When chocolate is stored in too warm a place, or during hot weather, it often develops a whitish film known as "bloom." This is caused by the cocoa butter rising to the surface. It will not affect the eating quality. Chocolate keeps best stored at a temperature of from 60°F to 70°F, with a low humidity factor.

Storing Cocoa

Store cocoa in a tightly covered container at moderate temperature and humidity to keep it from forming lumps or hardening.

DECORATING WITH CHOCOLATE

Cakes, pies, cookies, candies, puddings and ice-cream desserts take on a professional look with a garnish of grated chocolate curls.

To grate: Start with cold chocolate, a dry, cold grater and cold hands. Rub the square up and down over the grating surface, working quickly and handling the chocolate as little as possible.

To make curls: Warm a square of chocolate slightly at room temperature; then, for little curls, shave thin strips from the narrow side with a vegetable parer; for large ones, from the bottom. Pick up the curls with a wooden pick (otherwise they shatter) and chill until firm before arranging on food.

Sacher Torte

Bake at 350° for 30 to 35 minutes.
Makes 12 servings.

Nutrient Value Per Serving: 390 calories, 5 g protein, 20 g fat, 50 g carbohydrate, 168 mg sodium, 149 mg cholesterol.

**1 recipe Chocolate Cake Batter
 (see recipe, page 204)
1 jar (12 ounces) apricot preserves
2 tablespoons apricot brandy
1 recipe Deep Chocolate Glaze
 (see recipe, page 206)
 Apricot Whipped Cream (recipe follows)
 Apricot Rose for garnish (optional)**

1. Preheat the oven to moderate (350°). Grease the bottom of a 9-inch springform pan. Line the bottom with wax paper.

2. Prepare the Chocolate Cake Batter as directed. Pour into the prepared pan.

3. Bake in the preheated moderate oven (350°) for 30 to 35 minutes until a wooden pick inserted in the center comes out clean. Cool in the pan for 10 minutes. Loosen the cake around the edge with a knife. Turn out onto a wire rack; cool completely. Peel off the wax paper.

4. Heat the preserves in a saucepan until simmering. Press through a fine sieve; discard the solids. Stir in the brandy. Reserve and refrigerate ½ cup for the Apricot Whipped Cream; keep the remainder warm for the glaze.

5. Trim the cake to level the top. Cut in half horizontally. Place the top layer, cut-side up, on a serving platter. Brush the sides and top with the warm glaze. Place the bottom layer on top, cut-side down. Brush the sides and top with the remaining glaze. Refrigerate the cake for 15 minutes to allow the preserves to set.

6. Prepare the Deep Chocolate Glaze. Frost the cake sides and top. Refrigerate to set.

7. Prepare the Apricot Whipped Cream. ▶

Sacher Torte

8. Garnish the center of the torte with the Apricot Rose, if you wish. Top each serving with a generous dollop of the Apricot Whipped Cream.

Apricot Whipped Cream: Beat 1 cup of heavy cream, 2 teaspoons of 10X sugar and ½ teaspoon of vanilla in a small chilled mixer bowl until stiff. Fold in the reserved chilled ½ cup of apricot preserves.

Apricot Rose: Use 6 to 8 dried apricot halves for a rose. Flatten and slightly stretch each half with your thumbs and index fingers. To form the center bud, roll up an apricot half, sticky-side in. Wrap another apricot half around the bud, sticky-side in, so it adheres to the bud. Repeat with the other halves. Flare the top of each half outward to resemble rose petals. Pinch together at the bottom.

Splitting a Baked Cake Layer

Using a long, sharp serrated knife, draw a line around the side of the cake at the point where it needs to be cut. Continue cutting deeper into the cake, revolving the cake against the knife and keeping the knife parallel to the work surface.

Whipping Heavy Cream

Whipping cream is easy, unless the weather is very hot or the cream has been allowed to reach room temperature. For best results, place the bowl and beaters in the freezer ½ hour prior to whipping the cream. In very warm weather, also place the cream in the freezer until it is very cold—a few ice crystals are fine and won't impede the whipping process. Use medium speed for whipping, adding any sugar called for after the cream has been allowed to thicken slightly.

Orange Loaf (page 210)

⚡ 《 ⛏ 💲

Orange Loaf

Bake at 350° for 20 to 25 minutes.
Makes 10 servings.

Nutrient Value Per Serving: 426 calories, 6 g protein, 24 g fat, 49 g carbohydrate, 205 mg sodium, 183 mg cholesterol.

 **1 recipe Basic Cake Batter
  (see recipe, page 204)
 1 recipe Orange Cream Pudding Filling
  (see recipe, page 205)
 1 recipe Silky Chocolate Mocha Frosting
  (see recipe page 211)**

1. Preheat the oven to moderate (350°). Grease the bottoms of two 9¼ x 5¼ x 2¾-inch loaf pans. Line the bottoms with wax paper.
2. Prepare the Basic Cake Batter as directed. Pour into the prepared pans.
3. Bake in the preheated moderate oven (350°) for 20 to 25 minutes, or until a wooden pick

inserted in the centers comes out clean. Cool in the pans for 10 minutes.
4. Loosen the cakes around the edge with a knife. Turn out onto a wire rack. Cool completely. Peel off the wax paper.
5. Prepare the Orange Cream Pudding Filling.
6. Trim the crusts from the short ends of the cakes. Level the tops, if necessary. Cut each cake in half horizontally. Place one layer on a serving platter, cut-side up. Spread with a third of the pudding filling. Repeat with another cake layer, another third of the filling, a third cake layer and the remaining filling. Place the fourth layer on top, cut-side down. Gently press down. Refrigerate, covered, until firm, for about 2 hours.
7. During the last 30 minutes of chilling time, prepare the Silky Chocolate Mocha Frosting.
8. Frost the sides and top of the cake with the Silky Chocolate Mocha Frosting. Garnish with fresh orange slices, if you wish.

Orange Cream Loaf with Chocolate-Mocha Topping

Reduced Calorie

In the cake batter, we've reduced the number of eggs and the amount of sugar; in the filling, we've substituted a low-calorie, whipped topping mix made with skim milk; and we've made a topping with unsweetened cocoa powder.

Bake at 400° for 8 to 10 minutes.
Makes 14 servings.

Nutrient Value Per Serving: 125 calories, 3 g protein, 3 g fat, 22 g carbohydrate, 107 mg sodium, 78 mg cholesterol.

 **1 recipe Basic Sponge Cake (see
  Berry Cream Roll, page 216)**
Orange Cream Filling:
 1 envelope whipped topping mix
 ½ cup cold skim milk
 1 teaspoon grated orange rind
Chocolate-Mocha Topping:
**1¼ cups unsifted 10X (confectioners')
  sugar**
 **¼ cup unsifted unsweetened cocoa
  powder**
 1 teaspoon instant coffee granules
 2 to 3 tablespoons water

1. Prepare the Basic Sponge Cake, as directed in Steps 1 through 5 in the

Berry Cream Roll.
2. Prepare the Filling: Prepare the topping mix following package directions, using skim milk instead of whole milk. Fold in the rind. Refrigerate for 10 minutes.
3. Remove the cake with the foil underneath to a flat surface. Slice crosswise into 3 equal pieces.
4. Place one cake slice, top-side up, on a small cookie sheet. Spread with half the cream filling. Place the second cake layer, top-side up, on the filling. Spread with the remaining filling. Place the last cake layer, top-side down, on top. Gently press down to seal the layers together. Refrigerate.
5. Prepare the Topping: Stir together the 10X sugar, cocoa powder and coffee granules in a small bowl. Gradually stir in 2 tablespoons of the water. Gradually stir in enough of the remaining tablespoon to make a loose-spreading consistency. Spread the topping over the top of the cake, allowing it to drizzle down the sides.
6. Refrigerate the cake for 30 minutes until the filling is firm and the topping is set. Garnish with fresh mint and orange slices, if you wish.

⬛🔳 Silky Chocolate Mocha Frosting

Makes 1½ cups.

Nutrient Value Per 1½ Cups: 1,676 calories, 8 g protein, 153 g fat, 97 g carbohydrate, 16 mg sodium, 248 mg cholesterol.

1 package (6 ounces) semisweet chocolate pieces
¼ cup hot, strong black coffee
½ cup (1 stick) unsalted butter, cut into small pieces

1. Melt the chocolate, stirring constantly, in a small saucepan over low heat.
2. Pour the chocolate into a small mixer bowl. Beat in the hot coffee at low speed. When the mixture is smooth, beat in the butter, 1 piece at a time; beat until smooth.
3. Refrigerate the frosting until slightly thickened, for about 30 minutes.

The Best Way to Divide Cake Batter Evenly Between Pans

The easiest way is to use a spoon or ladle to divide the batter between the pans. Another way, if you have kitchen scales, is to weigh the batter and divide it between the pans.

🔳⬛💲 Orange-Mocha Cream Cake

Bake at 350° for 18 to 20 minutes.
Makes 24 servings.

Nutrient Value Per Serving: 748 calories, 7 g protein, 52 g fat, 71 g carbohydrate, 180 mg sodium, 187 mg cholesterol.

Orange Cake:
4 cups unsifted all-purpose flour
4 teaspoons baking powder
2 teaspoons baking soda
2 cups (4 sticks) unsalted butter, at room temperature
2½ cups sugar
6 eggs
2 tablespoons grated orange rind
1⅓ cups fresh orange juice
1 cup milk
Mocha Cream Filling (recipe follows)
Chocolate Ganache Icing (recipe, page 212)

1. Preheat the oven to moderate (350°). Grease two 15½ x 10½ x 1-inch jelly-roll pans. Line each with wax paper. Grease the paper.
2. Prepare the Orange Cake: Sift together the flour, baking powder and baking soda onto the wax paper. Set aside.
3. Beat together the butter and sugar in a large bowl until light and fluffy, for 3 to 4 minutes. Add the eggs one at a time, beating well after each addition. Add the orange rind. Gradually pour in the orange juice while beating. (Mixture may look as though it will separate, but it will become smooth.)
4. Beat in half the flour mixture. Gradually beat in the milk. Beat in the remaining flour mixture just until smooth. Divide the batter evenly between the prepared pans, spreading the batter to the corners with a spatula.
5. Bake one pan at a time, keeping the second pan at room temperature, in the preheated moderate oven (350°) for 18 to 20 minutes, or until golden brown and a wooden pick inserted in the center comes out clean. Carefully invert the cakes onto wire racks. Peel off the wax paper. Cool the cakes.
6. Prepare the Mocha Cream Filling.
7. Prepare the Chocolate Ganache Icing.
8. Assemble the cake: Place one cake layer on a large serving plate or tray. Spread the Mocha Cream Filling evenly over the cake. Place the second layer on top. Trim ¼ inch off all the edges to even the sides. Frost top and sides with about 2¼ cups of the ganache. Pipe the remainder decoratively around the base and top edge of the cake.

⬛🔳 Mocha Cream Filling

Makes about 2¾ cups.

Nutrient Value Per ¼-Cup Filling: 291 calories, .37 g protein, 26 g fat, 15 g carbohydrate, 5 mg sodium, 70 mg cholesterol.

1 to 2 tablepoons instant espresso powder
1 to 2 teaspoons hot water
1½ cups (3 sticks) unsalted butter
1¼ cups 10X (confectioners') sugar
2 tablespoons Chocolate Ganache Icing (recipe, page 212)

1. Mix the espresso and water in a small cup.
2. Beat together the butter and sugar in a large bowl until light and fluffy, for about 3 minutes. Beat in the espresso mixture and icing.

Chocolate Ganache Icing

Makes about 4½ cups.

Nutrient Value Per 1 Tablespoon Icing: 86 calories, .59 g protein, 8 g fat, 6 g carbohydrate, 4 mg sodium, 15 mg cholesterol.

   3 cups heavy cream
**1½ pounds semisweet chocolate,
        coarsely chopped**
   3 tablespoons unsalted butter

1. Heat the cream in a medium-size saucepan until bubbles form around the edge. Pour over the chocolate in a glass bowl. Whisk together gently until the chocolate is completely melted. Whisk in the butter.
2. Place the chocolate mixture over a large bowl half filled with ice. Stir the mixture constantly with a wooden spoon or rubber spatula until the chocolate is the consistency of a raw egg white, for about 15 minutes.
3. To make the icing firm enough to pipe, place the icing in a bowl over a bowl of ice. Stir constantly until the chocolate is the consistency of stiff whipped cream, for about 5 minutes. Spoon about ½ cup of stiffened icing into a pastry bag; refrigerate the remainder. Pipe as desired, working quickly so the icing won't soften. Refill the bag as necessary with the refrigerated icing.

Cream of Coconut Cake

A delicately flavored coconut cake with an old-fashioned cooked white icing.

Bake at 350° for 40 to 55 minutes.
Makes 12 servings.

Nutrient Value Per Serving: 413 calories, 5 g protein, 20 g fat, 56 g carbohydrate, 362 mg sodium, 111 mg cholesterol.

   3 eggs, separated
1¼ cups sugar
2½ cups sifted cake flour
   2 teaspoons baking powder
  ½ teaspoon salt
   1 cup butter or margarine
  ½ cup cream of coconut
   1 teaspoon vanilla
  ¼ cup milk
        Coconut Icing (recipe follows)
  ¼ cup shredded coconut

1. Preheat the oven to moderate (350°). Grease and flour a 10-inch Bundt or tube pan.
2. Beat the egg whites in a medium-size bowl until soft peaks form. Gradually beat in ¼ cup of the sugar, a tablespoon at a time, until stiff, shiny peaks form.
3. Sift together the flour, baking powder and salt onto a piece of wax paper.
4. Beat together the butter and remaining 1 cup of sugar in a large bowl until light and fluffy, for about 3 minutes. Add the 3 egg yolks, cream of coconut and vanilla; beat until smooth. Beat in the flour mixture alternately with the milk, beginning and ending with the flour. Gently fold in the beaten egg whites. Spoon the batter evenly into the prepared pan.
5. Bake in the preheated moderate oven (350°) for 40 to 55 minutes, or until a wooden pick inserted in the center comes out clean.* Cool the cake in the pan on a wire rack for 10 minutes. Unmold.
6. Prepare the Coconut Icing.
7. Frost the cake with the Coconut Icing. Sprinkle with the shredded coconut.

***Note:** If using a nonstick, black-coated baking pan, check the cake after 35 minutes.

Coconut Icing: Combine 1 cup of granulated sugar and ½ cup of water in a small saucepan. Cover the pan; bring to boiling. Uncover the pan; boil until the mixture registers 234° to 240° on a candy thermometer (soft-ball stage) or a small drop forms a flattened ball when dropped into cold water. Beat 3 egg whites in a small bowl with an electric mixer until soft peaks form. Pour the hot syrup into the egg whites in a thin stream while beating. Add ½ teaspoon of lemon juice and ½ teaspoon of coconut extract. Beat an additional 3 to 5 minutes, or until the frosting is cooled to room temperature.

When To Use Cake Flour in a Baking Recipe

Obviously, if a recipe calls for cake flour, it is best to use it. In general, cakes with a high proportion of sugar to flour, such as pound cakes, work well with cake flour. Pastries in which some strength is needed but too much would produce a tough dough, such as puff pastry, work well with a combination of all-purpose and cake flours. (*Note:* As a basic rule, if you want to substitute all-purpose flour for cake flour in a recipe, measure the flour needed, then remove 2 tablespoons of flour for each cup.)

Fresh Coconut Layer Cake

Bake at 350° for 20 to 25 minutes.
Makes 12 servings.

Nutrient Value Per Serving: 517 calories, 5 g protein, 21 g fat, 78 g carbohydrate, 409 mg sodium, 84 mg cholesterol.

Cake:
2½ cups **uns**ifted cake flour
2½ teaspoons baking powder
 1 teaspoon salt
 1 cup milk
 ¼ cup cold water
 1½ teaspoons vanilla
 4 egg whites, at room temperature
 1½ cups sugar
 ½ cup vegetable shortening
 ¼ cup (½ sitck) butter, softened
Lemon Filling:
 ⅔ cup sugar
 2 tablespoons cornstarch
 ⅛ teaspoon salt
 ¾ cup water
 ⅓ cup strained fresh lemon juice
 1 tablespoon butter
 3 egg yolks, slightly beaten
 1 tablespoon grated lemon rind
Fluffy White Frosting:
 1 cup sugar
 ⅛ teaspoon cream of tartar
 ⅛ teaspoon salt
 2 egg whites
 ¼ cup cold water
 1½ teaspoons vanilla
 2 to 3 cups grated fresh* or
    canned coconut

1. Preheat the oven to moderate (350°). Grease and flour three 9-inch-round layer-cake pans; set aside.
2. Prepare the Cake: Sift together the cake flour, baking powder and salt onto a sheet of wax paper; set aside. Combine the milk, water and vanilla in a 2-cup glass measure or small bowl; set aside.
3. Beat the egg whites in a medium-size bowl until frothy. Gradually beat in ¼ cup of the sugar until soft peaks form; set aside.
4. Combine the shortening, butter and remaining sugar in a large bowl. Beat on medium-high speed until light, for 2 to 3 minutes. Reduce the speed to low; beat in the dry ingredients alternately with the milk mixture, beginning and ending with the dry ingredients. Fold in the beaten whites, half at a time. Divide the batter among the prepared pans, spreading evenly to the edges.
5. Bake in the preheated moderate oven (350°) for 20 to 25 minutes, or until the edges start to pull away from the sides of the pan. Cool the cakes in the pans on wire racks for 10 minutes. Turn the cakes out onto wire racks to cool completely.
6. Prepare the Filling: Combine the sugar, cornstarch and salt in a small saucepan. Stir in the water, lemon juice and butter. Cook, stirring, over medium heat until the mixture comes to boiling, for 3 to 4 minutes. Lower the heat; cook 1 minute, stirring constantly. Stir ¼ cup of the hot mixture into the yolks in a small bowl. Quickly stir the yolk mixture into the saucepan. Cook, stirring for 1 minute. Do not boil.
7. Remove the saucepan from the heat. Add the lemon rind. Cool for 10 minutes, stirring once or twice. Cover; refrigerate until chilled.
8. Prepare the Frosting: Combine the sugar, cream of tartar, salt, egg whites and water in the top of a double boiler. Beat for 1 minute. Then beat over simmering water, for 5 to 7 minutes, or until the frosting is thick, shiny and holds firm peaks. Remove from the simmering water. Beat a little longer until cool. Beat in the vanilla; set aside.
9. Stir in the Lemon Filling to soften. Place the cake layer on a serving plate. Spread with half the filling. Top with the second layer. Spread with the remaining filling. Top with the remaining layer. Frost the top and sides with frosting. Sprinkle the top and sides with the coconut. ▶

Note: For grated fresh coconut, pierce the "eyes" of a coconut with a screwdriver; drain off the liquid. Heat the coconut on a baking sheet for 20 minutes in 400° oven. Tap all over to loosen the meat; crack open with a hammer. Pry the chunks of white meat from the shell; peel off the brown skin. Grate the meat on a hand grater or in a food processor.

How to Salvage a Baked Cake with an Uneven Top

Using a long, sharp serrated knife, trim the top of the cake so it is even and straight. Proceed with frosting and decorating.

◀◀◀ $

Banana Chiffon Cake

Bake at 325° for 1 hr., 10 min.
Makes 12 servings (one 10-inch tube cake).

Nutrient Value Per Serving: 333 calories, 5 g protein, 12 g fat, 53 g carbohydrate, 236 mg sodium, 114 mg cholesterol.

2¼ cups **sifted** *cake flour*
 1 cup sugar
 1 tablespoon baking powder
 1 teaspoon ground cinnamon
 ½ teaspoon salt
 ½ cup vegetable oil
 5 egg yolks
 2 tablespoons lemon juice
 2 to 3 bananas, mashed (about 1 cup)
 7 to 8 egg whites (1 cup)
 ½ teaspoon cream of tartar
    Vanilla Glaze (recipe follows)

1. Preheat the oven to slow (325°).
2. Sift together the *sifted* cake flour, ¾ cup of the sugar, baking powder, cinnamon and salt into a large bowl. Make a well in the center; add the following in order: oil, egg yolks, lemon juice and banana; stir with a spoon until well blended and smooth.
3. Beat together the egg whites and cream of tartar in a large bowl until foamy. Gradually beat in the remaining ¼ cup of sugar until soft peaks form.
4. Fold the batter gently into the beaten whites until no streaks of white remain. Turn the batter into an ungreased 10-inch tube pan.
5. Bake in the preheated slow oven (325°) for 1 hour and 10 minutes, or until the top springs back when lightly pressed with a fingertip.
6. Invert the pan, placing the tube of the pan over a funnel or large bottle. Cool completely. Loosen the cake around the tube and sides with a spatula. Remove the cake from the pan to a serving platter. Drizzle top and sides with the Vanilla Glaze.

Vanilla Glaze: Stir together 2 cups of *sifted* 10X (confectioners') sugar with 3 tablespoons of milk and 2 teaspoons of vanilla in a small bowl until very smooth. Thin with a little more milk, a teaspoon at a time, if necessary, to make good drizzling consistency.

Sifting

If a recipe calls for sifted flour, it should be sifted onto a piece of paper, spooned into a measuring cup and leveled off with a knife or spatula. Some recipes call for flour to be sifted directly into a measuring cup, then leveled off. The recipe should indicate what is preferred.

In using either of these methods, use dry measuring cups (as opposed to liquid ones), which will level off at the right measurement.

If a recipe doesn't call for sifted flour, it's best to stir the flour slightly to aerate it, spoon it into a dry measuring cup, then level it off.

Angel, Chiffon and Sponge Cakes

Should always be baked in ungreased pans so these light, airy cakes can cling to the sides of the pan and rise to their full height.

Rolling a Cake Roll

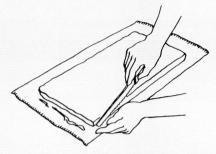

Step 1 Invert the cake onto a clean towel which has been sprinkled with confectioners' sugar; cut off the crisp edges with a long, thin serrated knife.

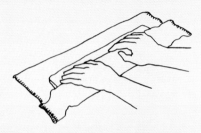

Step 2 Gently roll the warm cake and towel along the length of the cake. Place the cake and towel on a wire rack to cool.

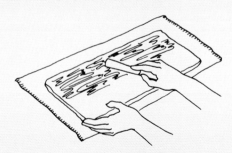

Step 3 Gently unroll the cake and spread with the filling.

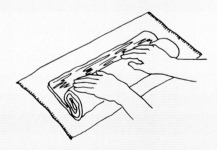

Step 4 Reroll the cake and filling without the towel.

Raspberry Cream Roll

Raspberry Cream Roll

Bake at 400° for 8 to 10 minutes.
Makes 10 servings.

Nutrient Value Per Serving: 431 calories, 6 protein, 22 g fat, 54 g carbohydrate, 173 mg sodium, 249 mg cholesterol.

> **1** recipe Basic Cake Batter
>   **(see recipe, page 204)**
> **¼** cup 10X (confectioners') sugar
> **1** recipe Basic Cream Pudding Filling
>   **(see recipe, page 205)**
> **⅓** cup seedless raspberry preserves
>   **Raspberry Whipped Cream**
>   **(recipe follows)**
> **½** recipe Deep Chocolate Glaze
>   **(optional; see recipe, page 206)**

1. Preheat the oven to hot (400°). Grease the bottom and sides of a 15½ x 10½ x 1-inch jelly-roll pan. Line with wax paper; grease the paper.

2. Prepare the Basic Cake Batter as directed. Pour into the pan.

3. Bake in the preheated oven (400°) for 8 to 10 minutes, or until a wooden pick inserted in the center comes out clean.

4. Sprinkle the top of the cake with the 10X sugar. Place a dish towel over the cake. Invert the cake and towel onto the counter. Peel off the wax paper. Trim ¼ inch from the edges. Starting at the short end, roll up the cake with the towel. Cool on a wire rack. ▶

5. Prepare the Basic Cream Pudding Filling.

6. Unroll the cake slowly and carefully on a flat surface. Spread the preserves over the cake. Spread the Basic Cream Pudding Filling over the cake, leaving a ½-inch border around the edges. Reroll the cake using the towel as an aid. Place on a serving platter, seam-side down.

7. Prepare the Raspberry Whipped Cream. Frost the sides and top with the cream.

8. Prepare the Deep Chocolate Glaze, if using. Drizzle the glaze with a spoon over the cake in a back-and-forth motion to create lines. Refrigerate until ready to serve.

Raspberry Whipped Cream: Beat 1 cup of heavy cream, 2 teaspoons of 10X sugar and ½ teaspoon of vanilla in a small chilled mixer bowl until stiff. Fold in ⅓ cup of seedless raspberry preserves.

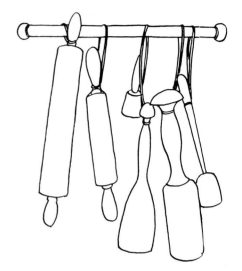

Berry Cream Roll

We've reduced the number of eggs and the amount of sugar in the cake batter. For the filling, we've substituted a whipped topping mix made with skim milk and a low-sugar strawberry spread.

Bake at 400° for 8 to 10 minutes.
Makes 14 servings.

Nutrient Value Per Serving: 89 calories, 3 g protein, 3 g fat, 13 g carbohydrate, 107 mg sodium, 78 mg cholesterol.

Basic Sponge Cake:
  4 eggs separated
  ½ teaspoon salt
  ¼ cup sugar
  2 teaspoons vanilla
  ⅔ cup sifted all-purpose flour
Berry Cream Filling:
  1 envelope whipped topping mix
  ½ cup cold milk
  ⅓ cup low-sugar strawberry spread
Topping:
  **1 tablespoon 10X (confectioners')
     sugar**

1. Preheat the oven to hot (400°). Grease a 15½ x 10½ x 1-inch jelly-roll pan. Line the bottom with aluminum foil, with a 2-inch overhang on the short ends. Lightly grease foil.

2. Prepare the Cake: Beat the egg whites and salt in a large bowl until fluffy.

Gradually beat in the sugar until the mixture forms peaks.

3. Beat together the yolks and vanilla in a large bowl. Fold in ½ cup of the beaten whites. Fold in the remaining whites along with the flour. Spread evenly into the prepared pan.

4. Bake in the preheated oven (400°) for 8 to 10 minutes, or until golden on top.

5. Place another sheet of aluminum foil on a wire rack. Spray with non-stick vegetable cooking spray. Loosen the cake around the edges of the pan with a knife. Invert the cake onto the prepared foil. Peel the foil from the bottom of the cake. Cool to room temperature.

6. Prepare the Filling: Prepare the whipped topping mix following the package directions, using skim milk instead of whole milk. Fold in the strawberry spread. Refrigerate for 10 minutes.

7. Transfer the cake with the foil underneath to a flat surface. Spread the chilled filling evenly over the cake. Using the foil as an aid and starting with a long side, roll up the cake. Place on a serving plate, seam-side down. Cover loosely with plastic wrap. Chill.

8. To serve, sift the 10X sugar down the center of the roll. Garnish with strawberries and fresh mint leaves, if you wish.

Reduced Calorie

Hazelnut Roll

🔖 🍴 🍸 💲
Hazelnut Roll

Bake at 400° for 8 to 10 minutes.
Makes 10 servings.

Nutrient Value Per Serving: 457 calories, 6 g protein, 32 g fat, 40 g carbohydrate, 132 mg sodium, 194 mg cholesterol.

1 **recipe Hazelnut Cake Batter
(see recipe, page 204)**
¼ **cup 10X (confectioners') sugar
Rum Whipped Cream (recipe follows)**
1 **recipe Silky Chocolate Mocha Frosting
(see recipe, page 211)**
Whole and ground hazelnuts

1. Preheat the oven to hot (400°). Grease the bottom and sides of a 15½ x 10½ x 1-inch jelly-roll pan. Line with wax paper; grease the paper.
2. Prepare the Hazelnut Cake Batter as directed. Pour into the prepared jelly-roll pan.
3. Bake in the preheated hot oven (400°) for 8 to 10 minutes, or until a wooden pick inserted in the center comes out clean.
4. Sprinkle the top of the cake with the 10X sugar. Place a dish towel over the cake. Invert the cake and towel. Peel off the wax paper. Trim ¼ inch from the edges. Starting at the short end, roll up the cake with the towel. Cool completely on a wire rack.
5. Prepare the Rum Whipped Cream.
6. Prepare the Silky Chocolate Mocha Frosting.
7. Unroll the cake slowly and carefully on a flat surface. Spread the Rum Whipped Cream over the cake, leaving a ½-inch border around the edges. Reroll the cake using the towel as an aid. Place on a platter, seam-side down.
8. Frost the sides and top with the Silky Chocolate Mocha Frosting. Garnish with whole and ground hazelnuts. Store in the refrigerator.

Rum Whipped Cream: Beat 1 cup of heavy cream, 1 tablespoon of 10X (confectioners') sugar and 1 tablespoon of rum in a small chilled mixer bowl until stiff.

Fresh Coconut Layer Cake (page 213), Pecan Candy Cake (page 225)

Cranberry-Nut Cheesecake (page 220), Christmas Stollen (page 38)

Sweetheart Cakes

Bake yellow cakes at 325° for 20 to 22 minutes; bake chocolate cakes at 325° for 22 to 25 minutes.
Makes 12 Frosted Yellow Cakes or 13 Cream-Filled Chocolate Cakes.

Frosted Yellow Cakes: Prepare 1 package (1 pound) of pound cake mix, following package directions. Preheat the oven to slow (325°). Grease and flour 4-ounce (½ cup) heart-shaped tart pans. Measure ⅓ cup of the batter into each pan. If making 4 cakes at a time, cover the remaining batter and refrigerate until ready to use. Bake in the preheated slow oven (325°) for 20 to 22 minutes, or until the tops are browned and the edges start to shrink from the sides of the pan. Let the cakes cool in the pans on a wire rack for 5 minutes. Remove the cakes from the pans and cool completely on the rack.
Pink-and-White Frosted Hearts: Frost the tops and sides of the cakes with half of a 1-pound tub of prepared vanilla frosting. Tint two-thirds of the remaining frosting pale pink and the remaining dark pink with red food coloring. Spoon into pastry bags fitted with a fancy tip and decorate as pictured on page 202.
White-on-White Frosted Hearts: Frost the tops and sides of the cakes with about half of a 1-pound tub of prepared vanilla frosting. Fill a pastry bag fitted with a fancy tip with the remaining frosting. Pipe a white ruffle around the top and bottom edges as pictured on page 202. Garnish with a chocolate heart, icing rose and silver dragees, if you wish.

Cream-Filled Chocolate Cakes: Melt ½ cup of semisweet chocolate pieces in a small saucepan over very low heat. Prepare 1 package (1 pound) of pound cake mix, following the package directions. Stir in the melted chocolate. Preheat the oven to slow (325°). Grease and flour 4-ounce (½ cup) heart-shaped tart pans. Measure ⅓ cup of the batter into each pan. If making 4 cakes at a time, cover the remaining batter and refrigerate until ready to use. Bake in the preheated slow oven (325°) for 22 to 25 minutes, or until the tops are browned and the edges start to shrink from the sides of the pan. Let the cakes cool in the pans on a wire rack for 5 minutes. Remove the cakes from the pans and cool completely on the rack. Beat 1 cup of heavy cream in a small bowl until stiff.

Carefully cut the cakes in half horizontally. Spread the bottom halves with the whipped cream. Frost the top halves with about one-third of a 1-pound tub of prepared chocolate frosting. Set on top of the cream. Place a heart-shaped cookie cutter on the frosting. Sprinkle red decorating sugar or colored sprinkles into the center. Carefully lift off the cutter. Outline the sugar heart with silver dragees, if you wish.

Preparing Pans for Baking

Spray baking pans with vegetable spray-on, following the label directions. Grease pans with vegetable shortening and sprinkle with flour; turn and pat pan to coat evenly, tap out excess. (*Note:* Use shortening—butter or margarine can make cake stick.)

Cranberry-Nut Cheesecake

Bake crust at 400° for 10 minutes. Bake cake at 475° for 10 minutes; then at 200° for 1 hour.
Makes 16 servings.

Nutrient Value Per Serving: 526 calories, 9 g protein, 36 g fat, 43 g carbohydrate, 329 mg sodium, 232 mg cholesterol.

Crust:
- 1 cup sifted *all-purpose flour*
- 1 teaspoon sugar
- ¼ teaspoon ground cinnamon
- ½ cup (1 stick) butter, at room temperature
- 1 egg yolk, slightly beaten
- ¼ teaspoon vanilla
- ½ cup finely ground walnuts (2 ounces)

Cheese Filling:
- 5 packages (8 ounces each) cream cheese, softened
- 1¾ cups sugar
- 3 tablespoons all-purpose flour
- ⅛ teaspoon salt
- 5 eggs, at room temperature
- 2 egg yolks, at room temperature
- ¼ cup dairy sour cream
- 1 teaspoon grated lime rind
- ½ teaspoon grated lemon rind
- 2 tablespoons fresh lime juice
- 1 teaspoon vanilla
  Cranberry Topping (recipe follows)

1. Preheat the oven to hot (400°). Butter the sides of a 9 x 3-inch springform pan; set aside.

2. Prepare the Crust: Combine the flour, sugar and cinnamon in a medium-size bowl; mix well. Cut in the butter with pastry blender until the mixture resembles coarse crumbs. Add the egg yolk and vanilla; mix just until dough holds together. Set aside two-thirds of the dough. Mix the walnuts into the remaining third.

3. Press the walnut dough evenly into the bottom of the prepared pan. Press the remaining dough evenly over the sides to a height of 2 inches. If the crust becomes soft, refrigerate for 10 minutes.

4. Bake in the preheated hot oven (400°) for 10 minutes, or until lightly golden. (Crust may shrink on the sides.) Cool on a wire rack. Increase the oven temperature to very hot (475°).

5. Prepare the Cheese Filling: Beat the cream cheese in a large bowl until smooth. Combine the sugar, flour and salt in a small bowl. Gradually beat into the cheese. Beat in the eggs and yolks, one at a time, beating well after each addition.

6. Combine the sour cream, lime and lemon rinds, lime juice and vanilla in a small bowl. Blend into the cheese mixture.

7. Place the prepared pan on the foil-lined jelly roll pan. Pour the cheese mixture into the pan.

8. Bake in the preheated very hot oven (475°) for 10 minutes. Lower the heat to slow (200°). Bake for 1 hour longer or until the cake is set. Turn the oven off. Let the cake sit in the oven with the door ajar for ½ hour. Transfer to a wire rack to cool completely. Cover and refrigerate until thoroughly chilled.

9. Remove the sides of the pan. Spread the top of the cheesecake with the Cranberry Topping. Chill for at least ½ before serving. Garnish with walnut halves and frosted cranberries, if you wish.

Cranberry Topping: Combine 2 cups of fresh or frozen cranberries (about 7½ ounces), ¾ cup of sugar, ¼ teaspoon of ground cinnamon, ⅛ teaspoon of salt and ⅔ cup of water in a medium-size saucepan. Cook over medium heat, stirring occasionally, until the berries begin to pop, for about 7 minutes. Reduce the heat to low; cook for 6 minutes longer. Force the mixture through a strainer. Stir in 1 tablespoon of fresh lime juice. Cool.

Valentine Cheesecake

Valentine Cheesecake

The best way to anyone's heart is with this love of a cheesecake! Topped with a luscious maraschino cherry glaze, it has an easy-to-prepare graham cracker crust and cream cheese filling—and will make any dinner special.

Bake crust at 350° for 5 minutes; bake cheese cake at 350° for 1 hour and 10 minutes. Makes 10 servings.

Nutrient Value Per Serving: 577 calories, 10 g protein, 37 g fat, 53 g carbohydrate, 388 mg sodium, 216 mg cholesterol.

Crumb Crust:
- 1 cup graham cracker crumbs
- 2 tablespoons sugar
- 2 tablespoons butter or margarine, softened

Filling:
- 2 pounds cream cheese, at room temperature
- 1 cup sugar
  Grated rind of 1 orange
- 4 eggs
  Cherry Glaze **(recipe follows)**

1. Preheat the oven to moderate (350°). Coat the inside of a heart-shaped cake pan (8½ x 1¾ inches) with nonstick vegetable cooking spray.

2. Prepare the Crumb Crust: Thoroughly blend together the graham cracker crumbs, the 2 tablespoons of sugar and butter in a small bowl. Press firmly in an even layer over the bottom of the prepared pan.

3. Bake in the preheated moderate oven (350°) for 5 minutes. Remove the pan to a wire rack. Leave the oven on.

4. Prepare the Filling: Combine the cream cheese, the 1 cup of sugar and orange rind in a large bowl. Beat just until the mixture is smooth. Add the eggs, one at a time, beating just until the eggs are incorporated. Pour over the crumb crust. Place the pan in a larger pan. Pour in enough water to come 1 inch up the sides of the heart pan.

5. Bake in the preheated moderate oven (350°) for 1 hour and 10 minutes, or until a small knife inserted in the center comes out clean. Remove the heart pan from the water bath to a wire rack to cool to room temperature.

6. Run a small sharp knife around the sides of the cake. Cover the top with wax paper. Place a wire rack over the top of the cake; carefully invert the pan and rack. Carefully remove the pan. Place the serving plate, upside down, over the crumb bottom of the cake; invert the plate, cake and rack. Remove the rack and wax paper. Cover the cake loosely and refrigerate until chilled.

7. Cover the top of the cheesecake with the Cherry Glaze. Refrigerate until serving time.

Cherry Glaze: Drain ⅔ cup of maraschino cherry syrup (from a 16-ounce jar of maraschino cherries) into a glass measure; pour into a small saucepan. Whisk in 2 teaspoons of cornstarch until smooth. Cook over low heat, stirring constantly, until the mixture thickens and bubbles; cook for 1 more minute. Set aside. Arrange 2¼ cups of the drained maraschino cherries (about one and a half 16-ounce jars) over the top of the cheesecake. Carefully spoon the thickened cherry syrup over the cherries.

Note: If you prefer, use a canned cherry pie filling to top the cheesecake.

Sparkling Cookie Cake

Bake cake at 375° for 40 minutes.
Bake cookies at 375° for 9 to 10 minutes.
Makes 8 cake servings and about 33 cookies.

Nutrient Value Per Serving of Cake: 557 calories, 6 g protein, 14 g fat, 96 g carbohydrate, 287 mg sodium, 4 mg cholesterol.

Nutrient Value Per Cookie: 98 calories, 1 g protein, 3 g fat, 17 g carbohydrate, 54 mg sodium, 16 mg cholesterol.

1 recipe Christmas Tree Cookies dough (see recipe, page 243)
1 unused, clean, clay flowerpot (7¼ inches across inside top, and 6¾ inches, or more, deep), or see Editor's Note (follows recipe)
Extra-wide, heavy-duty aluminum foil
1 box (14.5 ounces) angel food cake mix*
1 container (16 ounces) vanilla-flavored frosting
Yellow food color paste**
Green food color paste
Silver candy decorator balls
1 container (16 ounces) frozen non-dairy whipped topping, thawed, OR: 1 box (2.8 ounces) whipped topping mix
Sugar fruit candies*** (optional)

1. Prepare the Christmas Tree Cookies dough *(see recipe, page 243),* following the recipe directions through Step 2. Refrigerate and reserve.

2. Remove the top oven rack and place the bottom rack at the lowest postition. Center a 10-inch square of aluminum foil on the rack to catch any spills. Preheat the oven to moderate (375°).

3. Prepare the flowerpot: Turn the flowerpot, bottom-end up, on a counter. Center a 26 x 18-inch piece of extra-wide, heavy-duty aluminum foil over the bottom of the pot. Press the foil gently to the outside of the pot to shape the foil. Remove the foil. Invert the pot and place the shaped foil inside the pot, gently easing the foil into the pot. Be careful not to tear the foil. Gently press the foil against the sides of the pot to flatten all the creases. Fold the excess foil over the top and press firmly to the outside of the pot, anchoring under the flowerpot rim.

4. Prepare the angel food cake batter, following the package directions. Remove 1 generous cup of batter and discard. (The full amount of batter will overflow the pot ▶

Sparkling Cookie Cake

during baking; *see Editor's Note.*) Pour the remaining batter into the prepared flowerpot, being careful not to create any air pockets. Smooth the top gently with a spatula.

5. Place in the preheated moderate oven (375°) on the aluminum foil square. Bake for 40 minutes, or until a cake tester inserted in the center of the cake comes out clean. Check the cake after 25 minutes. If the top is becoming too brown, gently lay an 8-inch square of foil on top. Open and close the oven door carefully so as not to disturb the cake.

6. When the cake is done, remove from the oven and cool, inverted, resting the edges of the flowerpot on the edges of three 8- or 9-inch-round cake pans.

7. Make the patterns for the tree cookies. For the large tree: Use a ruler to draw a rectangle, 2½ x 4¼ inches. Label one 2½-inch side TOP. Make a mark to indicate the center 1¼ inches from either side on TOP. Draw a line connecting the mark at the center TOP with the bottom right corner. Draw a line connecting the mark at TOP with the bottom left corner. You should have a tree-shaped triangle. Cut out.

8. For the small tree cookies: Draw a rectangle 2½ x 3½ inches and proceed as in Step 7.

9. Divide the reserved cookie dough in half. Roll out, half at a time, on a floured surface to a ⅜-inch thickness. Cut out a star cookie, using a 3-inch star cookie cutter. Lightly flour the tree patterns and place on the dough. Cut out equal amounts of small and large trees with a small sharp knife. Place the trees 1 inch apart on greased cookie sheets. Repeat with the remaining dough. Reroll and use all the scraps. You should have about 16 large trees, 16 small trees and 1 star cookie.

10. Bake the cookies in the preheated moderate oven (375°) for 9 to 10 minutes or until lightly browned around the edges. Remove the cookies to wire racks to cool.

11. Remove 1 tablespoon of vanilla-flavored frosting from the container to a small bowl. Stir in the yellow food color paste and use to frost the star.

12. Stir a small amount of green food color paste into the container with the remaining frosting, to tint a pale green. Frost one-third of the cookies. Stir additional green food color paste into the pale green to tint medium green. Use to frost another third of the cookies. Add more green food color paste to the medium green frosting to make a dark green frosting. Frost the remaining cookies. Decorate the cookies with the silver candy decorator balls. Reserve the cookies.

13. When the cake is completely cooled, lift the foil with the cake from the pot. Place the cake, top-side down, on a serving plate. Trim if the cake does not sit evenly. Carefully peel off and discard the foil.

14. Frost the sides and top of the cake with the frozen non-dairy whipped topping. Or prepare the whipped topping mix, following the package directions and use to frost the cake. Top the cake with the star cookie. Arrange some of the trees around the base of the cake. Pass the remaining cookies when you serve the cake. Garnish the plate around the base of the cake with the sugar fruit candies, if you wish. Store in the refrigerator.

15. To serve, remove the cookies and pass. Cut the cake with a serrated knife.

*Do not use any other cake mix except the angel food cake mix specified in the recipe.
**Food color paste produces deeper shades than regular food coloring. They are available wherever cake decorating supplies are sold.
***We used 1 pound of assorted fruit-shaped hard candies.

Editor's Note: If you wish, use the whole angel food cake mix and bake in a 10-inch tube pan as directed on the package. You may then proceed with recipe as directed. The tube cake will yield a shorter, fuller centerpiece.

Pecan Candy Cake

Serve this rich, fruitcake-like confection sparingly. Make at least 2 weeks ahead so flavors can mellow.

Bake at 250° for 1½ hours.
Makes one 9-inch cake (32 thin slices).

Nutrient Value Per Slice: 218 calories, 2 g protein, 12 g fat, 28 g carbohydrate, 26 mg sodium, 4 mg cholesterol.

½ **pound candied red cherries, cut in quarters (1⅓ cups)**
½ **pound candied pineapple, coarsely chopped (1 cup)**
½ **pound pitted dates, coarsely snipped (1½ cups)**
1 **tablespoon all-purpose flour**
4⅓ **cups coarsely chopped pecans (1 pound, shelled)**
4 **ounces flaked coconut (about 1¼ cups)**
1 **can (14 ounces) sweetened condensed milk**

1. Preheat the oven to slow (250°). Grease and flour a 9 x 3-inch tube pan with a removable bottom; set the pan aside.
2. Combine the cherries, pineapple and dates in a very large bowl. Sprinkle with the flour; toss to coat well. Add the pecans and coconut; toss to mix. Add the sweetened condensed milk; stir to mix well. Spoon evenly into the prepared pan, smoothing the top.
3. Bake in the preheated slow oven (250°) for 1½ hours. Cool in the pan on a rack. Remove from the pan. Wrap tightly in foil. Refrigerate for at least 2 weeks. Cake cuts best when cold. Slice very thin with a serrated knife.

Storing Pecans

Store unshelled pecans in a cool, dry place and use within 6 months. Shelled pecans are best kept under refrigeration in an airtight container; use within 9 months or freeze up to 2 years.

Lemon Loaf Cake

Use as the base for Baked Alaska (page 265) or cut into slices, toast and top with a scoop of ice cream and sweetened strawberry slices.

Bake at 325° for 1 hour, 15 minutes.
Makes one 9 x 5 x 3-inch loaf (12 slices).

Nutrient Value Per Slice: 359 calories, 5 g protein, 18 g fat, 46 g carbohydrate, 345 mg sodium, 133 mg cholesterol.

2½ **cups all-purpose flour**
2 **teaspoons baking powder**
½ **teaspoon salt**
1 **cup (2 sticks) butter or margarine, softened**
1½ **cups sugar**
1 **tablespoon grated lemon rind**
4 **eggs**
¼ **cup milk**
2 **teaspoons vanilla**
Vegetable spray

1. Sift the flour, baking powder and salt onto wax paper.
2. Preheat the oven to slow (325°).
3. Beat the butter or margarine, sugar and lemon rind until light and fluffy in a large bowl with an electric mixer at high speed. Beat in the eggs, one at a time, until well blended.
4. Stir in the dry ingredients, alternately with the milk and vanilla, beginning and ending with the dry ingredients, to make a smooth batter.
5. Line a 9 x 5 x 3-inch loaf pan with two thicknesses of wax paper; spray generously with vegetable spray-on. Pour the batter into the prepared pan and smooth the batter into the corners.
6. Bake in the preheated slow oven (325°) for 1 hour, 15 minutes, or until a wooden pick inserted near the center comes out clean; cool in the pan on a wire rack for 15 minutes; loosen the cake around the edges with a sharp knife. Invert onto the wire rack; cool completely. Place in a large plastic bag and tie to seal.

🎀 💲 Family Circle's Carrot Cake

For a rich ending to a family dinner or for a wonderful have-on-hand winter snack, this super carrot cake fills the bill.

Bake at 325° for 1 hour and 20 minutes.
Makes 12 servings (one 10-inch tube cake).

Nutrient Value Per Serving: 621 calories, 7 g protein, 36 g fat, 70 g carbohydrate, 320 mg sodium, 92 mg cholesterol.

3⅓ cups **sifted** *all-purpose flour*
 2 cups sugar
 1 teaspoon baking powder
 1 teaspoon baking soda
 1 teaspoon salt
 1 teaspoon ground nutmeg
 2 teaspoons ground cinnamon
 4 eggs
1½ cups vegetable oil
 2 teaspoons vanilla
 2 cups coarsely shredded carrots
 1 cup chopped walnuts
    Confectioners' Frosting (recipe follows)

1. Preheat the oven to slow (325°). Grease a 10-inch Bundt or angel-cake tube pan.
2. Sift together the flour, sugar, baking powder, baking soda, salt, nutmeg and cinnamon into a large bowl. Make a well in the center. Add the eggs, oil and vanilla; beat with a wooden spoon until smooth. Stir in the carrots and walnuts. Turn the mixture into the prepared pan.
3. Bake in the preheated slow oven (325°) for 1 hour and 20 minutes, or until the top springs back when lightly pressed with a fingertip.
4. Cool the cake in the baking pan on a wire rack for 10 minutes. Remove the cake from the pan. Cool completely before frosting.
5. Drizzle with the Confectioners' Frosting.

Confectioners' Frosting: Place 1 cup of *sifted* 10X (confectioners') sugar in a small bowl. Gradually stir in 1 to 2 tablespoons of milk, whisking constantly, until the mixture is a good drizzling consistency.

Confectioners' Sugar

Granulated sugar that is crushed and screened. The degree of fineness is indicated by the number of X's. For example, 4X sugar is fine, 6X is very fine and 10X is ultra fine. 10X sugar is often mixed with cornstarch to prevent it from caking.

How to Chop Nuts

The most efficient way is with a heavy French chopping knife. Place a small mound of nuts on a chopping block or board, then chop back and forth in an arc until they're the desired degree of fineness. Blenders can be used for chopping, but they work so fast that they may overchop the nuts.

🗲 🎀 ⊤ 💲 Individual Birthday Cakes

The bonus with these minicakes is everyone gets their own.

Bake at 325° for 25 to 30 minutes.
Makes 14 minicakes.

Nutrient Value Per Serving: 473 calories, 5 g protein, 27 g fat, 56 g carbohydrate, 227 mg sodium, 124 mg cholesterol.

 3 cups **sifted** *cake flour*
 2 teaspoons baking powder
 ¼ teaspoon salt
 ⅔ cup butter or margarine, softened
1¾ cups sugar
 2 eggs
 2 teaspoons vanilla
1¼ cups milk
    Chocolate Cream Frosting
      (recipe follows)
    Sliced blanched almonds for garnish

1. Preheat the oven to slow (325°). Butter fourteen 4-ounce (½ cup) soufflé dishes.
2. Combine the flour, baking powder and salt in a medium-size bowl.
3. Beat together the butter, sugar, eggs and vanilla in a large bowl until light and fluffy. Mix in the flour mixture alternately with the milk, beginning and ending with the flour mixture. Spoon a scant ½ cup of the batter into the prepared dishes. Place on a cookie sheet.

At right: Individual Birthday Cake with Chocolate Cream Frosting (page 226). On server clockwise from top:
Carrot Cake with Cream Cheese Hard Sauce (page 233), Baby Brownie Cake (page 228),
Mini Cheesecake (page 229), Chocolate-Cream Cheese Cupcakes (page 229).
At center: Spice Cake with Banana Cream Filling (page 228).

4. Bake in preheated slow oven (325°) for 25 to 30 minutes, or until a wooden pick inserted in the center comes out clean. Cool the cakes in the soufflé dishes on wire racks for 10 minutes.

5. Run a knife around the edges of the cakes to loosen. Remove from the dishes. Turn the cakes upside down; trim the edges to form a neat cylinder. Slice into two layers. Frost the middle, sides and top of the cakes with the Chocolate Cream Frosting. Garnish with the almonds.

Note: These cakes can be baked in batches. Cover and refrigerate unused batter while baking the first batch.

Chocolate Cream Frosting: Combine 2½ cups of heavy cream, ¾ cups of sugar, ½ cup of *sifted* unsweetened cocoa powder and 2 teaspoons of vanilla in a large bowl. Beat until stiff.

Baby Brownie Cakes

They're as scrumptious as full-size cakes, but these mini versions are fun (and festive!) for special occasions.

Bake at 350° for 20 to 25 minutes.
Makes 18 cakes.

Nutrient Value Per Cake: 293 calories, 4 g protein, 20 g fat, 29 g carbohydrate, 123 mg sodium, 72 mg cholesterol.

- ¾ **cup butter or margarine**
- 4 **squares (1 ounce each) unsweetened chocolate**
- 3 **eggs**
- ¼ **teaspoon salt**
- 1½ **cups sugar**
- 2 **teaspoons vanilla**
- 1 **cup all-purpose flour**
- 1 **cup chopped walnuts or pecans**
  Chocolate Glaze (recipe follows)
  White chocolate, melted (optional)

1. Preheat the oven to moderate (350°). Line eighteen 2½-inch muffin-pan cups with paper or foil baking cups.
2. Melt together the butter and chocolate in the top of a double boiler over hot water. Let cool slightly.
3. Beat together the eggs and salt in a large bowl until foamy. Gradually add the sugar and beat until thick and pale yellow, for about 3 to 5 minutes. Beat in the vanilla. Blend in the melted chocolate mixture. Add the flour, stirring just until combined. Stir in the nuts. Spoon into the lined cups, dividing the batter equally.
4. Bake in the preheated moderate oven (350°) for 20 to 25 minutes or until a wooden pick inserted in the centers comes out slightly moist. Remove the cakes to a wire rack to cool.
5. Frost the tops with the Chocolate Glaze. Drizzle with the melted white chocolate, if you wish.

Chocolate Glaze: Melt together 1 package (4 ounces) of sweet cooking chocolate, coarsely chopped, and ⅓ cup of heavy cream in the top of a double boiler over hot water, stirring until smooth. Remove from the heat.

Spice Cakes with Banana Cream Filling

Bake at 325° for 20 to 25 minutes.
Makes 8 minicakes.

Nutrient Value Per Serving: 405 calories, 3 g protein, 24 g fat, 45 g carbohydrate, 284 mg sodium, 79 mg cholesterol.

- 1½ **cups sifted cake flour**
- ½ **teaspoon baking soda**
- ½ **teaspoon ground cinnamon**
- ¼ **teaspoon salt**
- ¼ **teaspoon ground allspice**
- ¼ **teaspoon ground cloves**
- ½ **cup (1 stick) butter or margarine, softened**
- ¾ **cup firmly packed light brown sugar**
- 2 **eggs**
- ½ **cup buttermilk**
  Maple Cream (recipe follows)
- 1 **or 2 small bananas, peeled and thinly sliced**
- ½ **cup flaked coconut, toasted**

1. Preheat the oven to slow (325°). Butter eight 4-ounce (½ cup) soufflé dishes.
2. Combine the flour, baking soda, cinnamon, salt, allspice and cloves in a small bowl; set aside.
3. Beat the butter and brown sugar in a large bowl until light and fluffy, for 3 to 5 minutes. Add the eggs, one at a time, beating well after each addition. Mix in the flour mixture alternately with the buttermilk, beginning and ending with the flour mixture. Spoon about ⅓ cup of batter into each prepared dish. Place on a cookie sheet.
4. Bake in a preheated slow oven (325°) for 20 to 25 minutes, or until a wooden pick inserted in the centers comes out clean. Cool the cakes in soufflé dishes on wire racks. Run a knife around the edges of the cakes to loosen. Remove from the dishes. Trim the rounded tops with a serrated knife. Turn the cakes cut-side down; slice horizontally into two layers.
5. Spread the bottom layers with the Maple Cream. Top with the banana slices. Cover with the top layers of the cakes. Spread with the Maple Cream, leaving the sides unfrosted. Sprinkle with the toasted coconut.

Note: These cakes can be baked in 2 batches. Cover and refrigerate unused batter while baking the first batch.

Maple Cream: Beat 1 cup heavy cream with 2 tablespoons of maple syrup in a small bowl until stiff.

⬛⬛⬛⬛⬛

Chocolate-Cream Cheese Cupcakes

Bake at 350° for 25 to 30 minutes.
Makes 18 minicakes.

Nutrient Value Per Serving: 227 calories, 3 g protein, 12 g fat, 28 g carbohydrate, 148 mg sodium, 29 mg cholesterol.

Cream Cheese Filling (recipe follows)
1½ cups unsifted all-purpose flour
1 cup sugar
¼ cup unsweetened cocoa powder
1 teaspoon baking soda
½ teaspoon salt
1 cup water
⅓ cup vegetable oil
1 tablespoon distilled white vinegar
1 teaspoon vanilla

1. Preheat the oven to moderate (350°). Line eighteen 2½-inch muffin-pan cups with foil or paper baking cups.
2. Prepare the Cream Cheese Filling. Set aside.
3. Sift together the flour, sugar, cocoa powder, baking soda and salt into a large bowl.
4. Combine the water, oil, vinegar and vanilla in a small bowl. Stir into the flour mixture until blended.
5. Half-fill each lined muffin-pan cup with batter. Place a spoonful of the Cream Cheese Filling into the center of the batter in each cup.
6. Bake in the preheated moderate oven (350°) for 25 to 30 minutes, or until a wooden pick inserted into the chocolate part comes out clean. Remove the pans from the oven and let the cakes cool in the pans for 5 to 10 minutes. Remove from the pans to wire racks to cool completely.

Cream Cheese Filling: Beat 1 package (8 ounces) cream cheese, softened, 1 egg and ¼ cup of sugar in a bowl until smooth. Stir in 1 cup (6-ounce package) of semisweet chocolate pieces.

⬛⬛⬛⬛⬛

Mini Cheesecakes

Individual creamy cheesecakes with a graham cracker crust and topped with a sour cream glaze.

Bake at 325° for 15 to 17 minutes; bake with glaze at 400° for 3 minutes.
Makes 18 minicakes.

Nutrient Value Per Serving: 196 calories, 3 g protein, 15 g fat, 14 g carbohydrate, 127 mg sodium, 49 mg cholesterol.

Sour Cream Lemon Glaze
  (recipe follows)
Crumb Crust:
1⅓ cups fine graham cracker crumbs OR:
    ⅔ cup fine gingersnap crumbs and
    ⅔ cup fine graham cracker crumbs
  2 tablespoons sugar
  ¼ teaspoon ground cinnamon
  4 tablespoons (½ stick) butter or
    margarine, melted
Cheese Filling:
  2 packages (3 ounces each) cream cheese,
    softened
  1 container (16 ounces) dairy sour cream
  1 egg
  ⅓ cup sugar
  2 teaspoons vanilla
    Raspberries and mint leaves for garnish
    (optional)

1. Prepare the Sour Cream Lemon Glaze. Set aside.
2. Line eighteen 2½-inch muffin-pan cups with foil or paper baking cups.
3. Prepare the Crumb Crust: Combine the crumbs, sugar and the cinnamon in a small bowl. Stir in the melted butter until well mixed. Spoon a rounded tablespoon of crumb mixture into each cup; press evenly and firmly in the bottom. Set aside.
4. Preheat the oven to slow (325°).
5. Prepare the Filling: Beat the cream cheese in a medium-size bowl until creamy. Beat in the sour cream, egg, sugar and vanilla until well blended. Spoon a scant ¼ cup of filling into each muffin-pan cup.
6. Bake in the preheated slow oven (325°) for 15 to 17 minutes, or until the tops are set but the centers are still creamy; do not overbake. (The cheesecakes will firm up as they chill.) Remove cups from the oven. Increase the oven temperature to hot (400°).
7. Gently spread the top of each cake with 1 tablespoon of Sour Cream Lemon Glaze. Bake in the hot oven (400°) for 3 minutes. ▶

8. Remove the pans with the cheesecakes to a wire rack to cool to room temperature. Remove the cakes from the pans; refrigerate until cold. Garnish with the raspberries and mint leaves, if you wish.

Sour Cream Lemon Glaze: Mix together 1 cup of dairy sour cream, 2 tablespoons of sugar, ½ teaspoon of grated lemon rind and ¼ teaspoon of vanilla in a small bowl.

MICROWAVE DIRECTIONS FOR MINI CHEESECAKES
650 Watt Variable Power Microwave Oven
Directions: Place the butter in a 1-cup microwave-safe measure. Microwave, uncovered, at full powder for 30 to 45 seconds to melt. Combine the crumb crust as in Step 3 on the previous page. Place the paper baking cups in microwave-safe muffin-pan cups. Spoon a rounded tablespoon of the crumb mixture into each; press into an even layer on the bottom. Place the cold cream cheese mixture in a medium-size microwave-safe bowl. Microwave, uncovered, at full power for 30 seconds to soften. Prepare the cheese filling as in Step 5 on the previous page. Spoon a scant ¼ cup of filling into each crumb-lined cup. Microwave 6 cheesecakes at a time, uncovered, at half power for 2 minutes, turning once. Remove from the microwave; spread a scant 1 tablespoon of Glaze over each. Microwave, uncovered, at full power for 30 seconds. Let stand in the cups for 5 minutes. Carefully transfer to other regular muffin cups to cool completely so the cakes hold their shape. Cover and refrigerate to chill. Repeat twice more to make 18 cakes.

Slim Mini Cheesecakes

Reduced Calorie

Substituting low-fat cottage cheese for cream cheese makes the calorie difference in this recipe.

Makes 18 mini cakes.

Nutrient Value Per Cheesecake: 76 calories, 6 g protein, 1 g fat, 9 g carbohydrate, 169 mg sodium, 33 mg cholesterol.

18 vanilla wafers
2 envelopes unflavored gelatin
½ cup water
3 containers (8 ounces each) low-fat cottage cheese (1% milk fat)
½ cup sugar
2 eggs
1 teaspoon lemon juice
¼ teaspoon grated lemon rind
2 teaspoons vanilla
18 raspberries (optional)

1. Line eighteen 2½-inch muffin-pan cups with paper or foil baking cups. Place 1 cookie in the bottom of each liner.
2. Sprinkle the gelatin over the water in a small cup. Let stand for 5 minutes to soften. Set the cup in a pan of simmering water, stirring to the dissolve the gelatin. Remove from the heat.
3. Place the cottage cheese in the container of a food processor. Cover; whirl until very smooth. Add the sugar, eggs, lemon juice, lemon rind and vanilla; whirl until well blended. With the motor running, pour in the dissolved gelatin, whirling until incorporated.
4. Spoon the mixture into the lined cups, using about ¼ cup for each. Refrigerate for 3 hours, or until set.
5. Remove the cheesecakes from the liners and garnish with the raspberries, if you wish.

⬛⬛⬛⬛
Chocolate Cheesecakes

Bake at 325° for 15 to 17 minutes.
Makes 16 minicakes.

Nutrient Value Per Cake: 254 calories, 4 g protein, 20 g fat, 18 g carbohydrate, 199 mg sodium, 97 mg cholesterol.

Crust:
1¼ cups fine chocolate wafer crumbs
     (about 26 wafers)
 ¼ cup (½ stick) butter or margarine,
     melted
Filling:
 1 package (8 ounces) cream cheese,
     softened
 ¼ cup sugar
 ½ cup heavy cream
 ½ teaspoon vanilla
 ¼ teaspoon salt
 3 eggs
 1 package (6 ounces) semisweet chocolate
     pieces, melted over low heat
     Whipped Cream Topping (recipe follows)
     Chocolate Hearts
     (optional; recipe follows)

1. Preheat the oven to slow (325°). Line sixteen 2½-inch muffin-pan cups with foil or paper baking cups.
2. Prepare the Crust: Combine the crumbs and butter in a small bowl. Press into the bottoms of the lined muffin-pan cups.
3. Prepare the Filling: Beat the cream cheese in a small bowl until smooth. Beat in the sugar, cream, vanilla and salt. Add the eggs, one at a time, beating well after each. Blend in the melted chocolate. Spoon into the muffin-pan cups, dividing equally.

4. Bake in the preheated slow oven (325°) for 15 to 17 minutes, or until the tops are just set. Remove the cheesecakes from the oven to the wire rack; cool in the pans to room temperature. Remove from the pans and refrigerate until cold.
5. Spoon or pipe the Whipped Cream Topping onto the cheesecakes. Garnish with the Chocolate Hearts, if you wish.

Whipped Cream Topping: Beat ½ cup of heavy cream and 2 teaspoons of sugar in a small bowl until stiff.

Chocolate Hearts: Melt ½ cup of the semisweet chocolate pieces in the top of a double boiler set over hot water. Let cool slightly. Spoon into a pastry bag fitted with a small writing tip. Pipe the heart shapes onto wax paper-lined cookie sheets. Chill until firm.

MICROWAVE DIRECTIONS FOR
CHOCOLATE CHEESECAKES
650 Watt Variable Power Microwave Oven
Directions: Line microwave-safe muffin-pan cups with paper baking cups. Place the butter in a 1-cup microwave-safe measure. Microwave, uncovered, at full power for 30 to 45 seconds to melt. Combine the melted butter with the wafer crumbs. Press a rounded tablespoonful into the bottom of each prepared muffin cup. Place the chocolate pieces in a 2 cup microwave-safe measure. Microwave, uncovered, at half power for 4 minutes to melt; set aside. Place the cream cheese in a large microwave-safe bowl. Microwave, uncovered, at full power for 30 seconds to soften. Prepare the cheese filling as in Step 3 at left. Spoon about 3 tablespoons of the cheese mixture into each prepared muffin cup. Microwave 6 cakes at a time, uncovered, at half power for 2½ minutes until set around the edges, rotating the muffin pan one-quarter turn twice. Or microwave 4 cakes at a time for 1 minute and 45 seconds, turning once. Let the cakes cool in the pan on the wire rack for 5 minutes. Remove the cakes from the pans; place in other regular muffin cups to cool so the cakes hold their shape. Cover and refrigerate to chill. Serve with the Whipped Cream Topping, and Chocolate Hearts, if you wish.

⚡ 🎂 Master Cupcake Recipe

It's easy to bake cupcakes for a crowd when you use our master recipe, which utilizes your favorite cake mix plus a package of instant pudding. Add some nuts, or chocolate or other extras; top with ready-to-spread frosting and decorate as you like.

Bake at 350° for 20 minutes.
Makes 36 cupcakes.

Nutrient Value Per Cupcake: 101 calories, 1 g protein, 4 g fat, 15 g carbohydrate, 129 mg sodium, 30 mg cholesterol.

- **1 package (about 18½ ounces) cake mix, without pudding**
- **1 package (3½ ounces) instant pudding mix**
- **1 cup water**
- **⅓ cup vegetable oil**
- **4 eggs**
  Optional addition (see chart)
  Ready-to-spread frosting

1. Preheat the oven to moderate (350°).
2. Combine the cake mix, pudding mix, water, oil and eggs. Beat with an electric mixer at low speed until blended. Beat at medium speed, 2 minutes, scraping down the side of the bowl often. Stir in the optional addition, if using.
3. Place paper liners in twelve 2½-inch muffin-pan cups. Divide about 1¾ cups of batter evenly among the 12 cups. Refrigerate the unused batter, covered, while the cupcakes are baking.
4. Bake in the preheated moderate oven (350°) for 20 minutes or until the tops spring back when lightly pressed with a fingertip. Remove from the pans; cool on wire racks. Repeat twice using the remaining batter.
5. Frost the cooled cupcakes with your choice of ready-to-spread frosting and decorate as you wish.

Note: To save cupcakes for another time, wrap the cooled cakes in freezer paper or heavy-duty aluminum foil, or place in a freezer-proof container with a tight-fitting lid. When ready to use, remove the desired number from freezer, thaw, frost, decorate and serve. Leftover decorated cakes can be frozen also.

SUPER COMBINATIONS CHART

Cupcake	Cake Mix	Instant Pudding	Optional Addition	Ready-to-Spread Frosting Plus
Snowball	Devil's food	Chocolate	½ cup chopped walnuts	Vanilla and flaked coconut
South Seas	Pineapple	Banana	½ cup chopped macadamia nuts	Vanilla with ½ teaspoon rum extract
Citrus Glow	Orange	Lemon	⅔ cup flaked coconut	Orange with 1 teaspoon coconut extract
Pecan Spice	Spice	Butter pecan	½ cup milk chocolate pieces	Milk chocolate
Chocolate Fleck	Yellow	French vanilla	1½ squares unsweetened chocolate, grated	Chocolate fudge
Vanilla Lover's	Yellow	Vanilla	½ cup raisins	Vanilla
Choco-Ana	Deep chocolate	Banana	1 teaspoon ground cinnamon	Chocolate fudge with 1 teaspoon banana extract
Double Lemon	Lemon	Lemon	½ cup pitted chopped prunes	Lemon
Mocha	Sour cream chocolate	Coffee	½ cup chopped pecans	Milk chocolate with 1 teaspoon instant coffee powder
Pistachio	Devil's food	Pistachio	¼ cup chopped pistachios	Vanilla
Banana Scotch	Banana	Butterscotch	½ cup butterscotch pieces	Milk chocolate with 1½ teaspoons brandy extract

Carrot Cakes with Cream Cheese Hard Sauce

Bake at 350° for 20 to 25 minutes.
Makes 24 minicakes.

Nutrient Value Per Cake: 251 calories, 2 g protein, 16 g fat, 26 g carbohydrate, 135 mg sodium, 32 mg cholesterol.

1½ cups unsifted all-purpose flour
2¼ teaspoons ground cinnamon
1 teaspoon baking soda
¾ teaspoon baking powder
¾ teaspoon ground nutmeg
½ teaspoon salt
1⅓ cups sugar
1 cup vegetable oil
2 eggs
3 cups grated carrots (about 1 pound)
1 cup coarsely chopped walnuts
  Cream Cheese Hard Sauce
    (recipe follows)
  Shredded carrot for garnish (optional)

1. Preheat the oven to moderate (350°). Line twenty-four 2½-inch muffin-pan cups with foil or paper baking cups.
2. Combine the flour, cinnamon, baking soda, baking powder, nutmeg and salt in a small bowl; stir to mix. Set aside.
3. Beat together the sugar, oil and eggs in a large bowl. Stir in the grated carrot. Add the dry ingredients, stirring until just combined. Stir in the nuts. Spoon the batter into lined muffin-pan cups, dividing equally.
4. Bake in the preheated moderate oven (350°) for 20 to 25 minutes, or until a wooden pick inserted in the centers comes out clean. Remove the cakes from the pans to wire racks to cool.
5. Prepare the Cream Cheese Hard Sauce.
6. Frost the cakes with the Hard Sauce. Garnish with the shredded carrot, if you wish.

Cream Cheese Hard Sauce: Beat ¼ cup (½ stick) of softened butter or margarine, 1 package (3 ounces) of softened cream cheese and 1 teaspoon of a vanilla in a bowl until well blended. Gradually beat in 1½ cups of *sifted* 10X sugar until smooth and creamy.

Cake Storage

Cover the cut surface of the cake with plastic wrap and place it in a cake keeper, or invert a large bowl over the cake plate. The cake will keep for 2 or 3 days this way. Cakes with a cream frosting or filling should be refrigerated, with plastic wrap over the cut part.
● Unfrosted cakes freeze best—up to 4 months. Wrap in aluminum foil, plastic wrap or large plastic bags; thaw at room temperature for 1 hour.
● Frosted cakes should be frozen on a piece of cardboard or a cookie sheet until firm, then wrapped in aluminum foil, plastic wrap or very large plastic bags; freeze cakes for up to 3 months and thaw at room temperature for 2 hours.

Raspberry-Nut Pinwheels (page 235), Butternut Bars (page 237), Mocha Bar Cookies (page 235), Apricot–Coconut Cookie Squares (page 236), Rainbow Venetians (page 236), Lemon Slice Cookie (page 237)

Cookies

⬛⬛⬛⬛
Mocha Bar Cookies

Bake at 350° for 20 minutes.
Makes 30 diamonds.

Nutrient Value Per Cookie: 127 calories, 2 g protein, 6 g fat, 17 g carbohydrate, 63 mg sodium, 14 mg cholesterol.

1½ **cups** sifted *all-purpose flour*
 1 **teaspoon baking powder**
 ¼ **teaspoon baking soda**
 ¼ **teaspoon salt**
 ½ **teaspoon ground cinnamon**
 ¼ **cup (½ stick) butter, softened**
 1 **cup firmly packed light brown sugar**
 1 **egg**
 ½ **cup strongly brewed coffee**
 ½ **cup raisins**
 1 **cup chopped walnuts**
 ½ **cup semisweet chocolate pieces**
 1 **white chocolate candy bar (3 ounces)**

1. Preheat the oven to moderate (350°). Grease a 13 x 9 x 2-inch baking pan.
2. Sift the flour, baking powder and soda, salt and cinnamon onto wax paper.
3. Beat together the butter, brown sugar and egg in a medium-size bowl until light and fluffy, for about 2 minutes. Stir in the coffee alternately with the flour mixture until the batter is smooth. Add the raisins and ½ cup of the nuts.
4. Spread the batter evenly into the prepared baking pan. Sprinkle the remaining nuts and chocolate pieces over the batter.
5. Bake in the preheated moderate oven (350°) for 20 minutes, or until the tip springs back when lightly touched with a fingertip. Cool in the pan on a wire rack. Cut into 30 diamonds.
6. Melt the white chocolate in the top of a double boiler over hot, not boiling water. Drizzle over each diamond, using a spoon or pastry bag fitted with a small writing tip.

⬛⬛⬛
Raspberry-Nut Pinwheels

Bake at 375° for 9 minutes.
Makes 3 dozen cookies.

Nutrient Value Per Serving: 99 calories, 1 g protein, 5 g fat, 13 g carbohydrate, 41 mg sodium, 15 mg cholesterol.

2 **cups** unsifted *all-purpose flour*
1 **teaspoon baking powder**
½ **cup (1 stick) butter or margarine, softened**
1 **cup sugar**
1 **egg**
1 **teaspoon vanilla**
¼ **cup seedless raspberry jam**
1 **cup finely chopped walnuts**

1. Sift together the flour and baking powder onto wax paper.
2. Beat together the butter, sugar and egg in a large bowl with an electric mixer until fluffy. Stir in the vanilla. Gradually add the flour mixture, stirring until well combined.
3. Roll out the dough between two pieces of wax paper to a 12 x 10-inch rectangle. Remove the top piece of wax paper. Spread the jam evenly over the entire surface of the dough. Sprinkle evenly with the nuts.
4. Firmly roll up the dough from a long side, jelly-roll style, removing the wax paper as you roll. Wrap the roll in wax paper and refrigerate for several hours or overnight.
5. When ready to make the cookies, preheat the oven to moderate (375°).
6. Cut the roll into generous ¼-inch-thick slices with a thin, sharp knife. Transfer the slices to an ungreased cookie sheet, spacing 2 inches apart.
7. Bake in the preheated moderate oven (375°) for 9 minutes, or until golden around the edges. Cool on wire racks.

> ### To Prevent Cookies from Burning on the Bottom
>
> Bake cookies in the middle level of the oven. Also, double up the cookie sheets, or use the new insulated sheets.

Apricot-Coconut Cookie Squares

Bake bottom cookie layer at 350° for 25 minutes; bake whole cookie at 350° for 35 minutes.
Makes 36 squares.

Nutrient Value Per Square: 144 calories, 2 g protein, 6 g fat, 21 g carbohydrate, 86 mg sodium, 28 mg cholesterol.

¼ **cup sugar**
1⅓ **cups sifted all-purpose flour**
½ **cup (1 stick) butter or margarine,** softened
1 **package (6 ounces) dried apricots**
½ **teaspoon baking powder**
¼ **teaspoon salt**
2 **eggs, well beaten**
1 **can (15 ounces) sweetened** condensed milk
1 **package (7 ounces) flaked coconut**
⅓ **cup apricot preserves**

1. Preheat the oven to moderate (350°). Butter a 9 x 9 x 2-inch-square baking pan.
2. Combine the sugar and 1 cup of the flour in a medium-size bowl. Cut in the butter with a pastry blender until coarse crumbs form.
3. Press the crumbs firmly over the bottom of the pan to form the bottom crust.
4. Bake in the preheated moderate oven (350°) for 25 minutes, or until pale golden. Remove the pan to a wire rack. Leave the oven on.
5. Reserve 4 apricots for garnish. Finely chop the remaining apricots. Combine with the remaining ⅓ cup of flour, baking powder, salt, eggs, condensed milk and half the coconut in a bowl. Spread evenly over the baked cookie layer.
6. Bake in the preheated moderate oven (350°) for 35 minutes, or until the top is firm to the touch. Cool in the pan on a wire rack.
7. Spread the preserves over the top and sprinkle with the remaining coconut. Cut into 36 squares. Cut the reserved apricots into small pieces. Decorate the top of each square with an apricot piece.

Is It Ever Necessary to Sift Sugar

It's only necessary to sift granulated sugar if it is lumpy. Confectioners' powdered sugar (10X) is best sifted before using. It can cake, especially if the package has already been open for a while.

Rainbow Venetians

Bake at 350° for 15 minutes.
Makes about 6 dozen.

Nutrient Value Per Serving: 98 calories, 1 g protein, 6 g fat, 11 g carbohydrate, 51 mg sodium, 26 mg cholesterol.

1 **can (8 ounces) almond paste** (not marzipan)
1½ **cups (3 sticks) butter or margarine,** softened
1 **cup sugar**
4 **eggs, separated**
1 **teaspoon almond extract**
2 **cups sifted all-purpose flour**
¼ **teaspoon salt**
10 **drops green food coloring**
8 **drops red food coloring**
1 **jar (12 ounces) apricot preserves**
5 **squares (1 ounce each) semisweet** chocolate

1. Preheat the oven to moderate (350°). Grease three 13 x 9 x 2-inch baking pans; line with wax paper; grease the paper.
2. Beak up the almond paste in a large bowl with a fork. Add the butter, sugar, egg yolks and almond extract. Beat with an electric mixer until light and fluffy, for about 5 minutes. Beat in the flour and salt.
3. Beat the egg whites in a medium-size bowl with an electric mixer until stiff peaks form. Stir into the almond mixture with a wooden spoon, using a turning motion similar to folding.
4. Remove 1½ cups of batter; spread evenly into one of the prepared pans. Remove another 1½ cups of batter to a small bowl; tint with the green food coloring. Spread evenly into the second prepared pan. Add the red food coloring to the remaining 1½ cups of the batter and spread into the third prepared pan.
5. Bake in the preheated moderate oven (350°) for 15 minutes, or until the edges are lightly golden. *(Note: Cake layers will each be ¼ inch thick.)* Immediately remove the cakes from the pans onto large wire racks. Cool thoroughly.
6. Place the green layer on an upturned jelly-roll pan. Heat the apricot preserves in a small saucepan; strain. Spread half the warm preserves over the green layer to the edges. Place the yellow layer on top. Spread with the remaining preserves. Place the pink layer, top-side up, on the yellow layer.

7. Cover with plastic wrap. Weight down with a large wooden cutting board or heavy flat tray. Refrigerate overnight.
8. Melt the chocolate in the top of a double boiler over hot water. Trim the cake edges even. Cut the cake crosswise into 1-inch-wide strips. Frost the top (pink layer) with the chocolate. Turn the strip on the side. Frost the bottom (green layer). Let the chocolate dry. Cut into 1-inch pices. Repeat with the remaining strips.

Butternut Bars

Bake at 350° for 15 minutes.
Makes about 4 dozen.

Nutrient Value Per Cookie: 57 calories, 1 g protein, 4 g fat, 5 g carbohydrate, 31 mg sodium, 8 mg cholesterol.

  ½ **cup chopped blanched almonds**
 1½ **tablespoons granulated sugar**
  ¾ **cup (1½ sticks) butter or margarine, softened**
  ⅓ **cup granulated sugar**
  1 **teaspoon almond extract**
 1¾ **cups sifted all-purpose flour**
  1 **egg white, slightly beaten**
     10X (confectioners') sugar (optional)

1. Preheat the oven to moderate (350°).
2. Combine the almonds with the 1½ tablespoons of sugar in a small bowl. Reserve.
3. Beat together the butter, ⅓ cup of sugar and the almond extract in a medium-size bowl until smooth. Stir in the flour. Gather the dough into a ball and flatten slightly. Divide in half.
4. Roll out each half on a floured surface to a rectangle, ¼ inch thick and about 3 inches wide and 12 inches long. Even the edges with a ruler to measure 2½ inches wide. Cut crosswise into bars, ¾ inch wide. Brush the tops with the egg white. Sprinkle evenly with the almond-sugar mixture. Lift the bars with a spatula to an ungreased cookie sheet, spacing 1 inch apart.
5. Bake in the preheated moderate oven (350°) for 15 minutes, or until golden brown. Transfer to racks to cool. Store in a tightly covered container for up to 2 weeks. Dust with the 10X sugar, if you wish.

Lemon Slice Cookies

Bake at 400° for 6 minutes.
Makes about 7 dozen.

Nutrient Value Per Cookie: 60 calories, 1 g protein, 2 g fat, 11 g carbohydrate, 38 mg sodium, 11 mg cholesterol.

 2½ **cups** sifted **all-purpose flour**
  1 **teaspoon baking powder**
  ½ **teaspoon salt**
  ¾ **cup (1½ sticks) butter or margarine, softened**
  1 **cup sugar**
  2 **eggs**
  2 **teaspoons grated lemon rind**
  1 **teaspoon lemon juice**
     Decorator Frosting (recipe follows)
     Yellow food coloring
     Small white mint candies (½-ounce package)

1. Sift together the flour, baking powder and salt onto wax paper.
2. Beat together the butter, sugar and eggs in a large bowl until well blended. Stir in the lemon rind and juice, then the flour mixture, until the dough is smooth.
3. Wrap the dough in plastic wrap and refrigerate for several hours or overnight.
4. When ready to make the cookies, preheat the oven to hot (400°).
5. Roll out the dough to a ⅛-inch thickness on a lightly floured surface. Cut out the cookies, using a 3-inch-round cutter. Cut each cookie in half and place 1 inch apart on an ungreased cookie sheet.
6. Bake in the preheated hot oven (400°) for 6 minutes, or until lightly golden. Remove the cookies to wire racks to cool.
7. Tint the Decorater Frosting pale yellow with several drops of the yellow food coloring. Divide the frosting in half. Set half aside, covered with damp paper toweling. Use the other half to frost the tops of the cookies. Tint the reserved frosting dark yellow. Spoon into a pastry bag fitted with a plain writing tip. Pipe a lemon rind and sections on each cookie as pictured on page 234. Add 1 or 2 small white mint candies for the lemon seeds. ▶

Decorator Frosting: Combine 3 egg whites, at room temperature, 1 box (1 pound) of 10X (confectioners') sugar and ½ teaspoon of cream of tartar in a medium-size bowl. Beat with an electric mixer until the frosting reaches a good spreading consistency.

Krumcake

This Scandinavian favorite is made in a special mold available in the cookware section of large department stores.

Makes 3 dozen.

Nutrient Value Per Cookie: 78 calories, 1 g protein, 5 g fat, 8 g carbohydrate, 8 mg sodium, 31 mg cholesterol.

1¼ **cups** sifted *all-purpose flour*
½ **teaspoon** *ground cardamom*
2 **eggs**
¾ **cup** *sugar*
¾ **cup** *heavy cream*
  Whipped Cream Filling (recipe follows)
  10X (confectioners') sugar (optional)

1. Sift together the flour and cardamom onto wax paper.
2. Beat together the eggs and sugar in a bowl with an electric mixer until very thick and lemon colored, for about 5 minutes; do not underbeat. Beat in the flour mixture alternately with the cream until blended.
3. Heat the krumcake iron in its holder, to moderately hot, on top of the stove; a few drops of water sprinkled on the iron will dance about. Do not let the iron become too hot.
4. Drop about a tablespoon of batter on the hot iron. Bring the cover down; do not press hard. Cook over medium heat for 30 seconds on each side of the iron. Carefully peel the cookie from the iron with a spatula. Quickly roll around the handle of a wooden spoon or form that may come with the krumcake iron. Cookie will stiffen at once. Remove from the handle. Continue with the remaining batter. Store the cookies in an airtight container.
5. To serve, spoon the Whipped Cream Filling into a pastry bag with a medium-size plain or star tip. Pipe into the ends of the cookies. Sprinkle with the 10X sugar, if you wish.

Whipped Cream Filling: Combine 1 cup of heavy cream, 2 tablespoons of 10X sugar, 1 tablespoon of cherry-flavored liqueur and 2 drops of red food coloring, if you wish, in a bowl. Refrigerate for 30 minutes to chill. Beat with an electric mixer until stiff.

Butter Cookies

Refrigerate this soft dough several hours or overnight before rolling. If the dough becomes too soft to handle when rerolling, refrigerate until firm.

Bake at 375° for 6 minutes.
Makes forty 3-inch cookies (10 sandwich cookies and 20 frosted cookies).

Nutrient Value Per Sandwich Cookie: 154 calories, 1 g protein, 5 g fat, 26 g carbohydrate, 96 mg sodium, 26 mg cholesterol.

Nutrient Value Per Frosted Cookie: 119 calories, 1 g protein, 6 g fat, 17 g carbohydrate, 70 mg sodium, 19 mg cholesterol.

1½ **cups** unsifted *all-purpose flour*
1 **teaspoon** *baking powder*
½ **teaspoon** *baking soda*
½ **cup (1 stick)** *butter or margarine, softened*
1 **egg**
½ **cup** *sugar*
1½ **tablespoons** *milk*
1 **teaspoon** *vanilla*
⅔ **cup** *currant or other flavor jelly*
  Butter-Cream Frosting (recipe follows)
¼ **cup** *chopped pistachio nuts*

1. Sift together the flour, baking powder and baking soda onto wax paper.
2. Beat together the butter, egg and sugar in a large bowl with an electric mixer until fluffy, for about 3 minutes. Stir in the milk and vanilla. Stir in the flour mixture until blended and smooth. Wrap the dough and chill for several hours or overnight.
3. Preheat the oven to moderate (375°).
4. Divide the dough into fourths. Roll out one-fourth of the dough, keeping the remainder of the dough refrigerated, on a lightly floured surface to a ⅛-inch thickness. Cut out the cookies from the dough with a 3-inch-round cookie cutter. Reroll the scraps of dough and cut out as many rounds as you can (you should have a total of about 10). Arrange on an ungreased cookie sheet, 1 inch apart.
5. Repeat with the remaining dough, cutting the centers out of the last fourth of dough with a 1½-inch star-shape or round cookie cutter.

Carefully remove the cut-out stars and place on a separate cookie sheet, 1 inch apart.

6. Bake the rounds in the preheated moderate oven (375°) for 6 minutes, or until the cookies are set and lightly browned. Bake the stars for 4 minutes, or until set and lightly browned. Transfer the cookies and stars to wire racks to cool.

7. For sandwich cookies, spread about 1 tablespoon of the jelly on the bottom side of 10 of the cookies. Place a cookie with a cut-out center on each, to make 10 sandwich cookies. Spread the remaining cookies with the Butter-Cream Frosting and top half of them with a cookie star. Sprinkle the remaining cookies with the chopped pistachios.

Butter-Cream Frosting: Beat together ¼ cup of softened butter, 1 tablespoon of milk, ½ teaspoon of vanilla and 1 cup *sifted* 10X (confectioners') sugar in a medium-size bowl until smooth. Slowly beat in 1 additional cup of *sifted* 10X sugar until the frosting is good spreading consistency. Beat in several drops of food coloring to tint, if you wish. Makes about ¾ cup.

Pistachio

The pistachio is the stone or seed of the fruit of the pistachio tree. The fruit is red, about ½ inch long, and grows in bunches. A pistachio nut has a double shell. The red outer shell is removed; the inside shell is grayish-white, thin, smooth, and brittle. Pistachio nuts are often dyed red to make the shell a uniform color.

Butter Cookies

Macaroon Tartlets

Macaroon Tartlets

Bake at 350° for 25 to 30 minutes.
Makes 22 tartlets.

Nutrient Value Per Tartlet: 158 calories, 3 g protein, 8 g fat, 20 g carbohydrate, 57 mg sodium, 50 mg cholesterol.

Dough:
- 9 tablespoons (1 stick plus 1 tablespoon) butter, at room temperature
- 4½ tablespoons sugar
- 3 egg yolks
- 1½ cups sifted all-purpose flour

Filling:
- ¾ cup 10X (confectioners') sugar
- ⅔ cup blanched whole almonds, finely ground
- 2 egg whites
- ⅛ teaspoon almond extract
- ¼ teaspoon grated lemon rind (optional)
  White Icing (recipe follows)
  Glacé Cherries

1. Prepare the Dough: Beat together the butter and sugar in a small bowl until light and fluffy. Beat in the yolks and flour until well blended. Chill in the freezer for 5 minutes.

2. Prepare the Filling: Combine the 10X sugar, almonds, egg whites, almond extract and lemon rind, if using, in a small bowl.

3. Spray twenty-two 2-to 3½-inch tartlet pans with nonstick vegetable cooking spray. Press about 2 teaspoons of dough into each pan, forming an even layer over the bottom and up the sides. (If you have less than 22 pans, work in batches.) If the tart shells become too soft, refrigerate before filling. ▶

4. Spoon about 2 teaspoons of the filling into each shell, so each is about three-quarters full. Arrange on cookie sheets.

5. Bake in a preheated moderate oven (350°) for 25 to 30 minutes, or until the fillings puff and are golden.

6. Remove the cookie sheets to wire racks. When cool enough to handle, carefully remove the tartlets from the pans. Drizzle each with the White Icing. Decorate each tartlet with a tiny piece of the glacé cherry.

White Icing: Stir together 1 egg white, ¼ teaspoon of cream of tartar and 1½ cups of sifted 10X sugar in a small bowl until good drizzling consistency.

Gobblin' Good Cookies

Gobblin' Good Cookies

Your little gremlins will love these treats.
(Use Halloween cookie cutters for extra fun!)

Bake at 375° for 5 minutes.
Makes about 5½ dozen 3-inch cookies.

Nutrient Value Per Cookie: 58 calories, .75 g protein, 2 g fat, 9 g carbohydrate, 31 mg sodium, 4 mg cholesterol.

 3 cups unsifted all-purpose flour
 2 teaspoons baking soda
1½ teaspoons ground ginger
 ½ teaspoon ground cinnamon
 ½ teaspoon ground cloves
 ¼ teaspoon salt
 ½ cup vegetable shortening
 ½ cup sugar
 1 egg
 ½ cup molasses
1½ teaspoon cider vinegar
  Orange Decorator Frosting
  (recipe follows)

1. Sift together the flour, baking soda, ginger, cinnamon, cloves and salt onto wax paper.

2. Beat together the shortening, sugar and egg in a large bowl with an electric mixer until fluffy, for about 3 minutes. Beat in the molasses and cider vinegar. Stir in the flour mixture until blended and smooth. Gather the dough into a ball, wrap and chill for several hours.

3. Preheat the oven to moderate (375°).

4. Divide the dough in half. Roll out one-half of the dough on a lightly floured surface to a ⅛-inch thickness. (Keep the remainder of the dough refrigerated.) Cut out cookies from the dough with cookie cutters (use Halloween shapes, if you wish). Reroll the scraps of dough and cut out as many as you can. Arrange on ungreased cookie sheets 2 inches apart.

5. Bake in the preheated moderate oven (375°) for 5 minutes, or until firm. Transfer the cookies to wire racks to cool.

6. Repeat with the remaining dough.

7. Decorate and/or frost with melted semisweet chocolate and the Orange Decorator Frosting.

Orange Decorator Frosting: Beat together 1 egg white, ⅛ teaspoon of cream of tartar and 1¼ cup of *sifted* 10X (confectioners') sugar in a small bowl until thick and creamy. Tint with orange food coloring.

Molasses

A thick, dark to light brown syrup made either by boiling down sugar cane juice or separating the liquid from raw sugar in the process of making granulated sugar. Molasses is used as a sweetener and a flavoring ingredient.

Cookie Tiers (page 244), Italian Star (page 243), Grand Marnier Christmas Wreaths (page 244), Christmas Trees Cookies (page 243), Spritz Cookie Sandwich (page 242), Chocolate Pistachio Meringues (page 245), Almond–Raspberry Sandwich Cookies (page 242), Cottage Cheese Thumb Print (page 245)

◣ ◀◀ ▼

Finska Kakor (Almond-Raspberry Sandwich Cookies)

Bake at 350° for 8 to 10 minutes.
Makes about 2 dozen sandwich cookies.

Nutrient Value Per Sandwich Cookie: 116 calories,
1 g protein, 6 g fat, 14 g carbohydrate, 4 mg sodium,
16 mg cholesterol.

¾ cup (1½ sticks) unsalted butter or
 margarine, softened
¼ cup sugar
1 teaspoon almond extract
2 cups sifted *all-purpose flour*
1 egg white, slightly beaten
1 tablespoon finely chopped almonds
1½ teaspoons sugar
½ cup seedless red raspberry preserves

1. Beat together the butter, the ¼ cup of sugar and almond extract in a large bowl until well mixed. Stir in the flour until well blended. Shape the dough into a ball. Cover and refrigerate until chilled, for about 1 hour.
2. To roll out cookies, slightly dampen a cookie sheet. Cover with wax paper; flour the paper. Divide the dough into thirds. Roll out, one-third at a time, on the prepared sheet to a ⅛-inch thickness. Make cutouts in the dough with a 2-inch hexagonal or round cookie cutter, leaving the dough intact on the sheet. In the center of half the cookies, make a cutout for a small opening with a small cookie cutter (about ¾ inch). Place the cookie sheet with the dough in the freezer for 5 minutes to stiffen.
3. Remove the cookie sheet from the freezer. Remove the cookie cutouts from the dough with spatula. Place on ungreased cookie sheet, leaving about 1½ inches between cookies. Remove the small cutouts from the centers of half the cookies to make cookie rings.
4. Preheat the oven to moderate (350°).
5. Repeat rolling and cutting with the remaining thirds of dough. Press all the scraps together and roll and cut as above.
6. Brush the rings with egg white. Combine the almonds and the 1½ teaspoons of sugar; sprinkle over the egg white.
7. Bake in the preheated moderate oven (350°) for 8 to 10 minutes, or until the cookies are a light golden brown. Remove the cookies to a wire rack to cool. Spread bottom of whole cookies with the raspberry perserves. Top each with a cookie ring.

◀◀ ▼

Spritz Cookie Sandwiches

Bake at 350° for 10 to 12 minutes.
Makes about 3½ dozen sandwiches.

Nutrient Value Per Sandwich Cookie: 159 calories,
1 g protein, 8 g fat, 20 g carbohydrate, 80 mg sodium,
29 mg cholesterol.

4 cups sifted *all-purpose flour*
1 teaspoon baking powder
1 teaspoon salt
1½ cups (3 sticks) unsalted butter or
 margarine, softened
1 cup sugar
1 egg
1 teaspoon vanilla
1 tablespoon grated orange rind
2 tablespoons unsweetened cocoa powder
 Orange Butter Cream (recipe follows)

1. Preheat the oven to moderate (350°).
2. Sift together the flour, baking powder and salt onto wax paper.
3. Beat together the butter and sugar in a large bowl until light and fluffy. Beat in the egg and vanilla. Stir in the flour mixture until well mixed. Remove half of the cookie dough to another bowl. Stir the orange rind into half; stir the cocoa powder into the other half of the dough.
4. Fill the cookie press with the orange dough. Press out onto an ungreased cookie sheet into a desired design, leaving about 2 inches between cookies.
5. Bake in the preheated moderate oven (350°) for 10 to 12 minutes, or until lightly browned around the edges. Transfer the cookies to wire racks to cool. Wash the cookie press; fill with the remaining chocolate dough. Press out as above, using the same design. Bake and cool as above.
6. Sandwich an orange cookie together with a chocolate cookie with the Orange Butter Cream or Chocolate-Orange Butter Cream. Decorate with a piping of Orange Butter Cream, if you wish.

Orange Butter Cream: Beat together ¼ cup (½ stick) of butter and ½ teaspoon of grated orange rind in a medium-size bowl until light and fluffy. Stir in 2 cups of *unsifted* 10X (confectioners') sugar and 1 to 2 tablespoons of orange juice until the frosting is a good spreading consistency. *To make the Chocolate-Orange Butter Cream,* remove half of the frosting to a small bowl; stir in 2 teaspoons of unsweetened cocoa powder until well mixed. Makes enough to fill 3½ dozen sandwich cookies.

Christmas Tree Cookies

Bake at 375° for 9 to 10 minutes.
Makes about 2½ dozen 4-inch cookies.

Nutrient Value Per Cookie: 108 calories, 1 g protein, 3 g fat, 18 g carbohydrate, 59 mg sodium, 17 mg cholesterol.

2½ cups sifted *all-purpose flour*
1 teaspoon baking powder
⅛ teaspoon salt
½ cup (1 stick) butter or margarine, softened
1 cup sugar
1 egg
1 teaspoon vanilla
½ teaspoon almond extract
   Decorator Icing (recipe follows)
   Silver candy decorator balls

1. Sift the flour, baking powder and salt onto wax paper. Grease 2 cookie sheets.
2. Beat together the butter and sugar in a large bowl until light and fluffy. Beat in the egg, vanilla and almond extract. Gradually stir in the flour mixture to make a stiff dough. (If the mixture is too dry, mix in 1 to 2 tablespoons of milk.) Shape into a ball; wrap in wax paper and refrigerate until chilled, for about 30 minutes.
3. Preheat the oven to moderate (375°).
4. Divide the dough into thirds. Roll out, one-third at a time, on a floured surface to a ⅜-inch thickness. Cut with a floured tree-shaped cookie cutter. Place the cookies on the prepared cookie sheets, leaving about 2 inches between each.
5. Bake in the preheated moderate oven (375°) for 9 to 10 minutes, or until lightly browned around the edges. Remove the cookies from the sheets to wire racks to cool.
6. Pipe the Decorator Icing through a plain or fancy tip onto the cookies. Decorate with the silver candy decorator balls.

Decorator Icing: Combine 1 egg white, 1¼ cups of *sifted* 10X sugar and ⅛ teaspoon of cream of tartar in a small bowl. Beat at high speed until the mixture forms stiff peaks. Tint light green with food coloring, if you wish.

Italian Stars

Bake at 350° for 15 to 17 minutes for large stars, 10 to 12 minutes for small stars.
Makes 16 large stars and 30 small stars.

Nutrient Value Per Large Star: 134 calories, 2 g protein, 7 g fat, 16 g carbohydrate, 63 mg sodium, 63 mg cholesterol.

Nutrient Value Per Small Star: 89 calories, 1 g protein, 4 g fat, 11 g carbohydrate, 42 mg sodium, 42 mg cholesterol.

½ cup (1 stick) butter, softened
½ cup (1 stick) margarine, softened
1 cup sugar
6 egg yolks
1 teaspoon vanilla
4 cups sifted *all-purpose flour*
1 egg, slightly beaten
   Colored nonpareils

1. Beat together the butter, margarine and sugar in a large bowl until light and fluffy. Beat in the egg yolks and vanilla until thoroughly mixed. Stir in the flour until well mixed. Shape the mixture into a ball. Wrap in wax paper; refrigerate for 15 minutes.
2. Preheat the oven to moderate (350°). Lightly grease 2 cookie sheets.
3. Divide the dough into thirds. Roll out the dough, one-third at a time, on a lightly floured surface to a ¼-inch thickness. Cut out with 3- or 2½-inch star cookie cutters. Transfer the cookies to the prepared sheets, leaving 2 inches between each. Brush the tops with the egg. Sprinkle with the nonpareils.
4. Bake in the preheated moderate oven (350°) for 15 to 17 minutes for the large stars, and 10 to 12 minutes for the small stars. Remove the cookies to wire racks to cool.

Cookie Tiers

Bake at 350° for 10 to 12 minutes for large cookies, and 8 to 10 minutes for small cookies. Makes 2½ dozen cookie tiers.

Nutrient Value Per Cookie Tier: 112 calories, 1 g protein, 5 g fat, 14 g carbohydrate, 21 mg sodium, 49 mg cholesterol.

- ¾ **cup (1½ sticks) unsalted butter**
- ¾ **cup sugar**
- 4 **hard-cooked egg yolks**
- 2 **tablespoons white rum**
- 2 **cups sifted all-purpose flour**
- ¼ **teaspoon salt**
- ⅓ **cup currant jelly**
  10X (confectioners') sugar

1. Beat the butter and sugar in a large bowl until light and fluffy. Press the yolks through a strainer into the butter mixture. Add the rum; mix well. Mix in the flour and salt until well blended. Shape the dough into a ball; wrap in plastic wrap. Refrigerate overnight.
2. When ready to bake the cookies, preheat the oven to moderate (350°).
3. Divide the dough into thirds. Roll out the chilled dough, one-third at a time, between sheets of wax paper to a ⅛-inch thickness. Carefully peel off the top paper. Cut cookie rounds with plain or scalloped cutters in three sizes (2-, 1½- and 1-inch). Place on ungreased cookie sheets, keeping the large cookies on one sheet and the two smaller sizes on another sheet.
4. Bake in the preheated moderate oven (350°) for 10 to 12 minutes for the large cookies, and 8 to 10 minutes for the smaller cookies; the edges of the cookies should be lightly browned. Cool the cookies on wire racks.
5. To assemble, spread the bottoms of the middle-size cookies thinly with the jelly. Press onto the center of the large cookies. Repeat with the small cookies to make the three-tiered cookies. Dust with the *sifted* 10X sugar. Garnish with a glacé cherry wedge, if you wish.

Grand Marnier Christmas Wreaths

Bake at 350° for 10 to 12 minutes. Makes about 3 dozen cookies.

Nutrient Value Per Cookie: 93 calories, 1 g protein, 4 g fat, 14 g carbohydrate, 18 mg sodium, 17 mg cholesterol.

- 2¼ **cups unsifted all-purpose flour**
- 1 **teaspoon ground nutmeg**
- ¼ **teaspoon salt**
- ⅔ **cup unsalted butter or margarine, softened**
- ⅓ **cup sugar**
- 2 **tablespoons grated orange rind**
- 1 **egg**
- 2 **tablespoons Grand Marnier liqueur**
- ½ **cup glacé red cherries, chopped**
  Glaze (recipe follows)
  Red and green glacé cherries

1. Preheat the oven to moderate (350°). Grease cookie sheets.
2. Sift the flour, nutmeg and salt onto wax paper.
3. Beat together the butter, sugar and orange rind in a large bowl until light and fluffy. Beat in the egg and liqueur until smooth. Stir in the flour mixture until well blended. Gently stir in the cherries. Using 1 tablespoon of dough for each cookie, roll the dough into 5-inch-long ropes. Shape into wreaths; pinch the edges together to seal. Place on the prepared cookie sheets, leaving about 2 inches between each.
4. Bake in the preheated moderate oven (350°) for 10 to 12 minutes, or until lightly browned around the edges. Transfer the cookies to wire racks to cool. Spread the Glaze lightly over each cookie. Decorate with red and green glacé cherries.

Glaze: Combine 1¼ cups of *sifted* (confectioners') sugar, 1 tablespoon of Grand Marnier liqueur, ⅛ teaspoon of ground nutmeg and 1 tablespoon of milk in a small bowl; mix until smooth and good spreading consistency. Add additional milk as needed.

Chocolate Pistachio Meringues

Bake at 250° for 30 minutes.
Makes about 3 dozen cookies.

Nutrient Value Per Cookie: 28 calories, 0 g protein, 1 g fat, 5 g carbohydrate, 0 mg sodium, 3 mg cholesterol.

⅓ **cup pistachio nuts**
¼ **cup semisweet chocolate pieces**
2 **egg whites**
⅛ **teaspoon cream of tartar**
⅔ **cup superfine sugar**
½ **teaspoon vanilla**

1. Preheat the oven to slow (250°). Grease and flour 2 cookie sheets.
2. Combine the pistachios and chocolate in a blender or food processor. Cover; whirl until very finely chopped. Reserve.
3. Beat together the egg whites and cream of tartar in a small bowl until soft peaks form. Gradually beat in the sugar, 1 tablespoon at a time, until the mixture forms very stiff peaks. Fold in the chocolate mixture and vanilla. Using a teaspoon, drop small mounds of meringue on the prepared sheets, leaving 1 inch between.
4. Bake in the preheated slow oven (250°) for 30 minutes, or until firm but not browned. Let stand for several minutes on the cookie sheets. Loosen the meringues carefully with a small knife; transfer to a wire rack to cool completely. Store in a tightly covered container in a dry place.

Leftover Yolks

Store leftover uncooked egg yolks, covered with water, in an airtight container for 2 or 3 days in the refrigerator. Drain the water from the yolks before using them in custards or sauces.

Cottage Cheese Thumb Prints

Bake at 400° for 12 to 14 minutes.
Makes about 8 dozen cookies.

Nutrient Value Per Cookie: 69 calories, 1 g protein, 4 g fat, 7 g carbohydrate, 32 mg sodium, 11 mg cholesterol.

1 **container (16 ounces) cottage cheese**
1 **pound (4 sticks) unsalted butter or margarine, softened**
1 **teaspoon vanilla**
4 **cups unsifted all-purpose flour**
½ **teaspoon salt**
  Granulated sugar
1 **cup seedless raspberry preserves**

1. Press the cottage cheese through a wire sieve into a large bowl, or purée in a food processor. Add the butter and vanilla; beat until light and fluffy. Stir in the flour and salt until well blended. Shape into a ball; refrigerate for 30 minutes to firm.
2. Preheat the oven to hot (400°). Spray cookie sheets with nonstick vegetable cooking spray.
3. Break off pieces of the chilled dough; roll into balls the size of a small walnut. Roll in the sugar. Place on the prepared sheets, leaving about 2 inches between. Make an indentation in the middle of each cookie with your thumb. Fill each center with ½ teaspoon of preserves.
4. Bake in the preheated hot oven (400°) for 12 to 14 minutes, or until the cookies are lightly browned and crispy. Remove from the sheets to wire racks to cool.

Freezing Cookies

• Both dough and baked cookies can be frozen and stored for 9 to 12 months.
• Baked cookies should be frozen in a strong box lined with plastic wrap or foil; separate each layer with more wrap or foil; thaw cookies at room temperature for 10 minutes.
• Cookie dough may be frozen in foil or plastic.
• Drop-cookie dough should be thawed until just soft enough to use.
• Rolled cookies can be frozen already shaped; place, still frozen, onto cookie sheets.
• Freeze bar-cookie dough in the pan in which it is to be baked; cover with plastic wrap, then foil.
• Refrigerator-cookie rolls should be thawed just enough to slice.

Choco-Berry Pie (page 269)

Just Desserts

Cakes and cookies aren't the only decadent desserts—in this chapter, you'll find more "sweet treats" to tempt your palate. You can choose from scrumptious pies, velvety ice creams, refreshing fruit combinations, no-bake specialties and many others that are sure to please.

Family and friends always appreciate the extra effort you put into planning a special ending. In general, follow a heavy meal with a light, refreshing dessert that complements the other foods you've served. Likewise, a light meal will welcome a richer dessert. Warm weather will seem much cooler with a cool and creamy Lemon-Lime Soufflé Pie (page 252), or take the chill off a brisk wintery day with a warm and spicy Apple Crisp (page 257).

Why not take advantage of the fresh fruits that are available? For the tastiest results, use them in desserts during their peak season. Or try our ice-cream desserts, which rate high all year long but reach record highs during the summer months. Plan an ice-cream party and be sure to incude a few exotic flavors for everyone to try. There are also the seasonless, no-bake favorites like No-Bake Pineapple Upside-Down Cake (page 271). You can make these delicacies several hours in advance or even a day or two ahead of time so that last-minute garnishing is all that's necessary before serving.

Not only do these delectable morsels satisfy "sweet attacks," but they also meet some daily nutritional requirements—surprise!—when they include dairy products, fruits or eggs. So the next time you feel guilty about turning to the dessert chapters first—don't!

Quick

Make Ahead

Entertaining

Low Cost

Low Calorie

Dessert Pies

MAKING PASTRY

Cut cold vegetable short-ening into all-purpose flour and salt in large bowl with a pastry blender or two knives.

Keep cutting in the vege-table shortening until the mixture is crumbly and the shortening is evenly distributed. (*Note:* This is the step that assures a light and flaky pastry after baking.)

Stir in ice-cold water, 1 tablespoon at a time, with a fork, adding just enough cold water to moisten the mixture.

Keep mixing the dough with a fork, just until the pastry forms a ball that leaves the side of the mixing bowl clean. Divide the ball in half.

Fit a stocking onto the rolling pin and sprinkle flour over pastry cloth. (*Note:* A stocking and pastry cloth are two of the most important tools for the pastry chef. The set of stocking and pastry cloth are not expensive and can be found in most houseware departments of stores.)

Flour the pastry cloth lightly by sprinkling flour on the cloth and rolling pin over the cloth to coat both evenly.

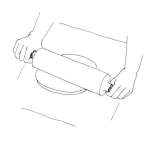

Shape pastry for bottom crust into a 1-inch-thick round and place on the pastry cloth. Start from the center and roll the pastry evenly with a circular motion, so the pastry will retain its circular shape, to desired diameter. As you roll out the dough, turn it gently to prevent sticking. Use pie plate for a good size guide. Turn it upside down on rolled dough. Check for additional rolling needed.

Use the pastry cloth to lift and fold the rolled out pastry over the rolling pin to the center of the pastry and transfer to the pie plate.

Unroll the pastry into the pie plate gently. Be sure to fit dough loosely in pie plate. If dough is stretched taut, it will shrink during baking and break.

Trim the edge to ½ inch and roll with fingers to make a smooth edge. Choose any of the edges on the next page as the finishing touch to your pastry.

GIVE YOUR PIES A PERFECT EDGING

Scalloped Edge: Place left thumb and forefinger on the outside of the rim. With a teaspoon, press the inside of rim between fingers, forming a large, rounded scallop. Repeat about every inch around pastry rim.

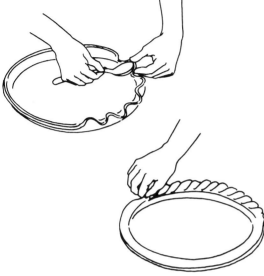

Rope Edge: Press pie rim firmly between thumb and forefinger of right hand, pressing down, toward the right, with thumb. Continue pressing, turning pie clockwise as you do, until entire rim is finished.
Note: Lefthanded people should reverse hands.

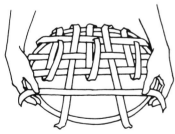

Lattice Top: Roll remaining half of Flaky Pastry dough or other dough being used, to a 12 x 8-inch rectangle. Cut lengthwise into ½-inch strips. Weave into a lattice over pie filling. Trim overhang even with bottom crust. Pinch to seal edge. Turn sealed edge *under.* Pinch again to make stand-up edge; flute.
Note: You may find it easier to weave the lattice on a piece of wax paper or heavy-duty aluminum foil, then flop it over filling. Also, a pastry wheel will make pretty, unusually shaped lattice strips.

Baking Pie Pastry Blind

Baking pastry blind means baking the empty crust for a pie or tart, partially or completely, before filling.

To bake blind, line the pan with dough; dock well (prick with a fork all over), then line the pastry with parchment paper or wax paper. Fill with dried beans to weight down dough (these beans should be kept specifically for this purpose and may be reused). Bake the dough until it sets and no longer has a raw, shiny appearance. Remove the paper and beans, then return the pastry shell to the oven to dry further. For a shell that's partially baked, filled and returned to the oven (as in quiches), the dough should bake only until it is partially cooked. For a shell that's completely baked before being cooled and filled, bake longer, until it turns golden.

Prevent Overbrowning

If the pastry edge is browning too quickly, cover it with strips of aluminum foil.

Strawberry-Rhubarb Cream Pie

🔽 《《 🍴 💲

Strawberry-Rhubarb Cream Pie

The perfect finale to a delightful meal.

Bake crust at 375° for 8 to 10 minutes.
Makes 8 servings (one 9-inch pie).

*Nutrient Value Per Serving: 316 calories, 5 g protein, 14 g fat,
45 g carbohydrate, 203 mg sodium, 46 mg cholesterol.*

Gingersnap Crust:
1½ **cups ground gingersnap cookie crumbs**
    (about 26 gingersnaps)
 2 **tablespoons sugar**
¼ **cup melted butter or margarine**
Filling:
 1 **package (16 ounces) frozen rhubarb**
    (about 3 cups) OR: 1 pound fresh
    rhubarb, trimmed and cut into
    1-inch pieces
 1 **cup strawberries, washed, hulled**
¾ **cup plus 2 tablespoons sugar**
 3 **slices (⅛ inch thick) gingerroot**
 2 **envelopes unflavored gelatin**
⅓ **cup cold water**
 3 **egg whites**
½ **cup heavy cream**
½ **teaspoon vanilla**
Garnish (optional)
½ **cup heavy cream, whipped**
    Fresh strawberries
    Fresh mint leaves

1. Preheat the oven to moderate (375°).
2. Gingersnap Crust: Combine the gingersnap crumbs and sugar in a small bowl. Stir in the melted butter until well blended. Press the crumbs evenly over the bottom and sides of a 9-inch pie plate.
3. Bake in the preheated moderate oven (375°) for 8 to 10 minutes. Cool on a wire rack. Refrigerate until ready to fill.
4. Filling: Combine the rhubarb, strawberries, ½ cup of the sugar and gingerroot in a medium-size saucepan. Cook over medium heat, stirring occasionally, until the fruit is well cooked, for about 15 minutes. Remove from the heat. Remove the gingerroot.
5. Meanwhile, sprinkle the gelatin over cold water in a measuring cup; let stand to soften, for about 5 minutes.
6. Add the softened gelatin to the hot rhubarb mixture, stirring until the gelatin is completely dissolved, for about 1 minute. Blend the mixture in a blender or food processor just until smooth. Pour into a bowl. Place the bowl in a large bowl of ice water. Chill, stirring occasionally, until the mixture is partially set; mixture will mound when dropped from a spoon. Remove from the ice water and set aside.
7. Beat the egg whites in a small bowl until soft peaks form. Gradually add ¼ cup of the sugar, beating until stiff, shiny peaks form.

8. Beat the cream, the 2 tablespoons of sugar and vanilla in a small bowl until stiff.

9. Gently fold the egg whites and whipped cream into the fruit mixture. Mound into the piecrust. Refrigerate for 1 to 2 hours, or until set. Garnish with the whipped cream, strawberries and mint leaves, if you wish.

MICROWAVE DIRECTIONS
650 Watt Variable Power Microwave Oven
Directions: Crust: Place the butter in a small microwave-safe bowl. Microwave, uncovered, at full power for 1 minute to melt. Mix and shape the crust in a 9-inch microwave-safe pie plate as directed in Step 2. Microwave, uncovered, at full power for 2 minutes. Cool. Filling: Combine the frozen rhubarb, strawberries, gingerroot and ½ cup of sugar in a 2-quart microwave-safe casserole. Cover. Microwave at full power for 8 to 10 minutes until very tender, stirring once. Remove the ginger. Meanwhile, continue with Step 4 and complete the recipe.

Flaky Pastry

Makes enough pastry for 9-inch double crust.

2 cups unsifted all-purpose flour
1 teaspoon salt (¾ teaspoon if using salted butter)
6 tablespoons vegetable shortening
6 tablespoons unsalted butter or margarine, cut into ½-inch slices
¼ cup cold water

Combine the flour and salt in a large bowl. Cut in half of the shortening and half of the butter with a pastry blender or 2 knives until the mixture resembles fine meal. Cut in the remaining shortening and remaining butter until the largest pieces are the size of peas. Gradually add the water, stirring with the fork, until the dough leaves the sides of the bowl clean and can be gathered into a ball. Wrap the ball of dough in plastic wrap. Refrigerate for at least 30 minutes before rolling.

Strawberry-Rhubarb Parfait

Reduced Calorie

The filling from the pie, without the high-calorie crust, makes a delicious parfait. We've made it even more low-calorie by eliminating the heavy cream, reducing the amount of sugar and increasing the number of servings.

Makes 10 servings.

Nutrient Value Per Serving: 75 calories, 3 g protein, 0 g fat, 16 g carbohydrate, 28 mg sodium, 0 mg cholesterol.

1 package (16 ounces) frozen rhubarb (3 cups)
1 cup strawberries, washed and hulled
½ cup plus 2 tablespoons sugar
2 envelopes unflavored gelatin
⅓ cup cold water
5 egg whites
Fresh mint leaves (optional)

1. Cook the rhubarb, strawberries and ½ cup of the sugar in a medium-size saucepan, stirring occasionally, until the fruit is well-cooked, for about 15 minutes. Remove from the heat.

2. Meanwhile, sprinkle the gelatin over the cold water in a measuring cup; let stand to soften, for about 5 minutes.

3. Add the softened gelatin to the hot rhubarb mixture, stirring until the gelatin is completely dissolved, for about 1 minute.

4. Place the fruit mixture in the container of an electric blender or food processor, working in batches if necessary. Cover; whirl just until smooth. Pour into a medium-size bowl. Place the bowl in a larger bowl of ice and water. Chill, stirring occasionally, until the mixture is partially set; the mixture will mound when dropped from a spoon. Remove from the ice water and set aside.

5. Beat the egg whites in a medium-size bowl until soft peaks form. Gradually add the 2 tablespoons of sugar, beating until stiff, shiny peaks form.

6. Gently fold the egg whites into the fruit mixture. Spoon into 10 dessert glasses or bowls. Serve immediately or refrigerate for up to 1 hour. Garnish with the mint, if you wish.

Chewy Pecan Pie

An easy version of an old Southern favorite.

Bake at 375° for 15 minutes.
Makes 8 servings.

Nutrient Value Per Serving: 547 calories, 5 g protein, 38 g fat, 52 g carbohydrate, 255 mg sodium, 44 mg cholesterol.

> **1   cup firmly packed light brown sugar**
> **1/3 cup margarine**
> **1/3 cup light corn syrup**
> **1/4 cup heavy cream**
> **1   egg, slightly beaten**
> **2   cups pecan pieces, toasted (8 ounces)**
> **1/2 teaspoon vanilla**
> **1   baked 9-inch pie shell**

1. Preheat the oven to moderate (375°).

2. Combine the brown sugar, margarine, corn syrup and heavy cream in a heavy 10-inch skillet. Bring to boiling over medium heat, stirring constantly. Once the mixture has come to a boil, stop stirring. Boil for 4 minutes; the mixture should be thick with large bubbles on the surface. Remove from the heat. Quickly stir some of the hot mixture into the egg in a small cup. Stir back into the skillet. Stir in the pecans and vanilla until well combined. Do not let boil. Pour into the prebaked pie shell.

3. Bake in the preheated moderate oven (375°) for 15 minutes, or until bubbly and the center is almost set. Cool on a wire rack.

Tips for Making Perfect Meringues

● Choose a cool, dry day—humid air tends to soften meringues. Be sure your tools—non-plastic bowl and beater—are clean and dry. The tiniest speck of fat will spoil meringues.
● Egg whites will beat higher if allowed to stand at room temperature to warm slightly.
● Depend on your electric mixer, since long beating is a must to dissolve sugar completely and prevent meringue from "weeping." To test if sugar is completely dissolved: Rub a bit of meringue between your fingers. Meringue should feel smooth.

Lemon-Lime Soufflé Pie

Lemon-lime filling topped with a golden meringue lattice. Make sure you grate the lemon rind before you squeeze the juice.

Bake at 400° for 7 to 8 minutes.
Makes 8 servings (one 9-inch pie).

Nutrient Value Per Serving: 376 calories, 5 g protein, 15 g fat, 56 g carbohydrate, 355 mg sodium, 182 mg cholesterol.

> **One 9-inch baked pie shell**
> **1 1/3 cups sugar**
> **1/3 cup cornstarch**
> **1/2 teaspoon salt**
> **1 3/4 cups cold water**
> **1/3 cup lemon juice (about 2 medium-size lemons)**
> **3   tablespoons lime juice (2 limes)**
> **5   egg yolks**
> **1   tablespoon grated lemon rind**
> **3   tablespoons butter or margarine**
> **3   egg whites**
> **Meringue:**
> **2   egg whites**
> **1/8 teaspoon cream of tartar**
> **1/4 cup sugar**

1. Prepare the baked pie shell, using your favorite recipe or store-bought crust.

2. Combine 1 cup of the sugar, the cornstarch and salt in a medium-size saucepan. Gradually stir in the water, lemon juice and lime juice. Cook over medium-high heat, stirring constantly, until the mixture thickens and bubbles and turns clear, for about 5 minutes. Cook for 1 more minute.

3. Beat the egg yolks lightly in a small bowl. Slowly stir in about 1/2 cup of the hot cornstarch mixture; stir back into the saucepan. Cook over low heat, stirring constantly, for 2 minutes. Remove from the heat. Stir in the lemon rind and butter.

4. Beat the 3 egg whites in a medium-size bowl until foamy. Gradually beat in the remaining 1/3 cup of the sugar until stiff peaks form. Fold the egg whites into the hot lemon mixture until no streaks of white remain. Pour into the baked pastry shell. Refreigerate for 3 to 4 hours, or until firm.

5. Prepare the Meringue: Preheat the oven to hot (400°). Beat the 2 egg whites with the cream of tartar in a medium-size bowl until foamy white and doubled in volume. Beat in 1/4 cup of sugar, 1 tablespoon at a time, until the meringue forms stiff peaks.

6. Spoon the meringue into a pastry bag fitted with a small star tip. Pipe out stars over the lemon filling in a lattice pattern and in the border around the edges.

7. Bake in the preheated hot oven (400°) for 7 to 8 minutes, or until the meringue is golden brown.

Optimum Temperature for Separating Eggs

Cold eggs separate more easily than those at room temperature, because the whites hold together better. After separating, however, egg whites should be brought to room temperature for maximum volume with beating. Avoid getting yolks into the egg whites; the fat in them will prevent the whites from beating up.

Correct Procedure for Beating Egg Whites

If egg whites are refrigerator-cold, they should be warmed slightly, just to get the chill off. Place them in a bowl; place the bowl over another bowl of warm water; stir briefly, just until they are no longer ice-cold.

Add a pinch of salt to help egg whites liquefy to a point where they will begin absorbing air. Then start beating the egg whites slowly. If using a machine, set it on medium speed. Continue whipping on medium speed until the egg whites are very white and opaque. *Then,* increase the speed to high and beat until whites are the desired consistency, soft peaks or firm. If sugar is added, it should be added in a very slow, thin stream when the speed is increased.

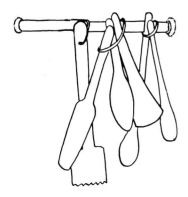

Banana Cream Pie

Creamy-smooth, and oh, so delicious!

Makes 8 servings (one 9-inch pie).

Nutrient Value Per Serving: 437 calories, 8 g protein, 25 g fat, 47 g carbohydrate, 294 mg sodium, 160 mg cholesterol.

One 9-inch baked pie shell
⅔ cup sugar
3 tablespoons unsifted all-purpose flour
2 tablespoons cornstarch
¼ teaspoon salt
3 cups milk
3 eggs
2 teaspoons vanilla
3 medium-size ripe bananas
1 cup heavy cream

1. Prepare the baked pie shell, using your favorite recipe or store-bought crust.

2. Combine the sugar, flour, cornstarch and salt in a large saucepan. Gradually stir in the milk.

3. Cook, stirring constantly, over moderate heat, until the mixture thickens and bubbles. Continue cooking and stirring until the mixture is very thick, for about 6 minutes longer.

4. Beat the eggs in a medium-size bowl until frothy. Slowly stir in half of the cooked mixture until blended. Return to the saucepan, blending in the mixture. Cook over low heat, stirring constantly for 2 minutes more.

5. Remove from the heat; stir in the vanilla. Place a piece of plastic wrap directly on the surface; cool.

6. Peel and slice the bananas into the pie shell. Pour the cooled cream filling over the bananas; chill for several hours. Whip the cream in a medium-size bowl until stiff. Spoon over the top of the pie.

Banana Math

1 pound = 3 medium-size bananas
1 medium-size banana = ⅔ cup sliced or ½ cup diced or ⅓ cup mashed.

Down-Home Deep-Dish Rhubarb Pie

Down-Home Deep-Dish Rhubarb Pie

The fruits of summer, such as rhubarb, taste especially delicious on winter nights.

Bake at 400° for 40 minutes.
Makes one 8-cup deep-dish pie.

Nutrient Value Per Serving: 326 calories, 3 g protein, 14 g fat, 47 g carbohydrate, 222 mg sodium, 0 mg cholesterol.

6 cups dry-frozen diced rhubarb
1 cup sugar
¼ cup unsifted all-purpose flour
½ teaspoon ground nutmeg
2 cups unsifted all-purpose flour
1 teaspoon salt
⅔ cup vegetable shortening
4 to 5 tablespoons ice water
2 tablespoons sugar
1 teaspoon grated lemon rind

1. Toss the frozen rhubarb with 1 cup of sugar, ¼ cup of flour and nutmeg in a medium-size bowl until well blended. Pour into an 8-cup shallow baking dish.
2. Preheat the oven to hot (400°).
3. Combine the 2 cups of flour and salt in a medium-size bowl; cut in the shortening with a pastry blender until the mixture is crumbly. Toss in the ice water, 1 tablespoon at a time, until the mixture forms a ball and leaves the side of the bowl clean; wrap in wax paper.

4. Roll out the pastry to the length and width of the pastry dish on a lightly floured pastry cloth or board. Cut the pastry, lengthwise, into 1-inch strips. Lay the strips in a diagonal pattern on top of the fruit. Trim the edge of the baking dish. (Bake the pastry trims as extra nibbles.)
5. Combine the 2 tablespoons of sugar and the lemon rind in a cup. Sprinkle over the pastry to coat well. Place the baking dish on a cookie sheet. (This catches drips and keeps the oven clean.)
6. Bake in the hot oven (400°) for 40 minutes, or until the rhubarb bubbles and the pastry is golden. Serve warm with ice cream, if you wish.

Cook's Tip: You can buy dry-frozen rhubarb in 1-pound bags (this recipe will use 1½ bags) or other sizes in the rhubarb season. Wipe the rhubarb with a damp paper towel; trim and cut into 1-inch pieces. Arrange in a single layer in a jelly-roll pan. Freeze until firm. Pack in 6-cup quantities in plastic freezer containers or heavy plastic bags. Label, date and freeze.

Freezing Pie Shells

Make 2 pie shells, use 1 and freeze the other for future use.
● Wrap unbaked pie shells in aluminum foil and freeze. To use, thaw the unbaked shell at room temperature for about 30 minutes and use in the recipe as directed.
● Cool a baked pie shell before wrapping and freezing. Warm the frozen shell in a preheated moderate (375°) oven for 10 minutes, if you wish.

Fruit Desserts

Pink Grapefruit Snow with Warm Orange Sauce

⚡ ⟪⟫ ⊥ $ ▦
Pink Grapefruit Snow with Warm Orange Sauce

Makes 6 servings.

Nutrient Value Per Serving: 114 calories, 3 g protein, 0 g fat, 26 g carbohydrate, 27 mg sodium, 0 mg cholesterol.

1 envelope unflavored gelatin
¼ cup cold water
⅔ cup sugar
½ teaspoon grated lemon rind
1 cup pink grapefruit juice
3 egg whites
   Orange Sauce (recipe follows)
   Pink grapefruit sections (optional)

1. Sprinkle the gelatin over the cold water in a small bowl; let soften, for 5 minutes. Set the bowl in hot water; stir the gelatin to dissolve.
2. Combine the dissolved gelatin, ⅓ cup of the sugar, the lemon rind and grapefruit juice in a large bowl. Set the bowl in a pan of ice and water; stir often just until the mixture begins to set, for 15 to 20 minutes.
3. Beat the egg whites in a medium-size bowl with an electric mixer until soft peaks form. Gradually beat in the remaining sugar; continue beating until stiff peaks form.
4. Beat the gelatin mixture on high speed until light and frothy. Fold in the egg whites until well-blended. Turn into a 1-quart mold. Refrigerate until firm, for at least 3 hours.
5. To serve, run a small, thin spatula around the edge of the mold. Dip the mold quickly in the pan of hot water. Cover the mold with a plate; invert the plate and mold together. Shake gently to release snow. Carefully lift off the mold.
6. Prepare the Orange Sauce.
7. Spoon the warm Orange Sauce around the base of the snow. Garnish with the pink grapefruit sections, if you wish. Pass additional warm Orange Sauce.

⚡ ⟪⟫ ⊥ $
Orange Sauce

Grate the rinds before squeezing the juice.

Makes about 1¾ cups.

Nutrient Value Per ¼ Cup: 160 calories, 3 g protein, 9 g fat, 18 g carbohydrate, 97 mg sodium, 135 mg cholesterol.

3 eggs
½ cup sugar
¾ cup orange juice (2 oranges)
1 tablespoon lemon juice (1 lemon)
¼ cup butter or margarine, cut into small pieces
1 tablespoon grated orange rind
¼ teaspoon grated lemon rind

1. Beat together lightly the eggs and sugar in the top of a double boiler. Stir in the orange juice, lemon juice and butter.
2. Place over barely simmering water. Cook, stirring constantly, until the sauce thickens slightly and coats the back of a spoon, for 10 to 15 minutes. Stir in the grated rinds.
3. Remove from the heat. Serve warm or cold.

Orange Math

2 to 4 medium-size oranges = 1 cup of juice
1 medium-size orange = 4 teaspoons of grated rind

Yogurt-Lime Parfaits

⚡🗡🍸💲
Yogurt-Lime Parfaits

Mixed fruits and strawberries are spooned into individual dessert glasses, and then topped with a frothy yogurt-lime gelatin. Make several hours ahead.

Makes 6 servings.

Nutrient Value Per Serving: 287 calories, 4 g protein, 17 g fat, 33 g carbohydrate, 48 mg sodium, 62 mg cholesterol.

- **1 envelope unflavored gelatin**
- **¼ cup cold water**
- **1½ cups unflavored yogurt**
- **⅔ cup sugar**
- **2 teaspoons grated lime rind**
- **¼ cup lime juice (about 2 limes)**
- **1 cup heavy cream, whipped**
- **1 package (10 ounces) quick-thaw frozen mixed fruits, partly thawed**
- **9 fresh or frozen strawberries**
- **6 thin lime slices, halved and seeded**

1. Sprinkle the gelatin over the cold water in a small bowl; let stand to soften, for 5 minutes. Set the bowl in simmering water; stir the gelatin until completely dissolved.
2. Combine the dissolved gelatin, yogurt, sugar, lime rind and juice in a bowl. Place a bowl in a pan of ice water; stir often until slightly thickened. Fold in the whipped cream.
3. Divide the mixed fruits with their juice among six 8-ounce dessert glasses.

4. Reserve 3 strawberries for garnish; refrigerate. Slice the remaining strawberries and divide among the glasses. Spoon the lime mixture over the fruits. Refrigerate for several hours, or until ready to serve.
5. Halve the reserved strawberries. Garnish each parfait with a strawberry half and 2 lime slices.

Lime Math

1 medium-size lime = 2 tablespoons of juice
1 medium-size lime = 2 teaspoons of grated rind

💲
Rhubarb-Strawberry Cobbler

Bake at 400° for 25 minutes.
Makes 8 servings.

Nutrient Value Per Serving: 336 calories, 4 g protein, 5 g fat, 71 g carbohydrate, 427 mg sodium, 2 mg cholesterol.

- **1 pound fresh rhubarb, washed and cut into 1-inch pieces, OR: 1 package (1 pound) frozen unsweetened cut rhubarb, thawed (about 4 cups)**
- **1¼ cups sugar**
- **½ cup water**
- **2½ tablespoons cornstarch**
- **2 pints fresh strawberries, washed, dried and hulled, OR: 1 package (1 pound) frozen unsweetened strawberries, thawed (about 4 cups)**
- **½ cup milk**
- **2 cups buttermilk baking mix**
- **1 tablespoon grated orange rind**
- **⅓ cup sugar**

1. Combine the rhubarb, ¾ cup of the sugar and ¼ cup of the water in a large saucepan. Cook over low heat, stirring occasionally, just until the rhubarb is tender. Do not overcook.
2. Combine the remaining ¼ cup of water, the cornstarch and the remaining ½ cup of sugar in a bowl; stir until smooth. Stir into the rhubarb. Cook, stirring constantly, until the mixture thickens and bubbles. Remove from the heat. Stir in the strawberries. Pour into a 2-quart shallow baking dish (11¾ x 7½ x 1¾ inches).

3. Place the baking dish in the oven. Turn on the oven to hot (400°). Place a cookie sheet on an oven rack below the dish to catch drips.

4. Stir the milk into the baking mix in a medium-size bowl until soft dough forms. Turn out onto a lightly floured surface. Knead 8 to 10 times. Roll out to 13 x 12-inch rectangle.

5. Combine the orange rind with the sugar. Sprinkle over the surface of the dough. Roll up jelly-roll style, starting with a long side. Cut crosswise into 18 slices, about ¾ inch thick.

6. Remove the dish from the oven. Arrange the pinwheels over top. Bake for 25 minutes, or until the biscuits are golden brown.

Strawberry Math

1 pint strawberries = 3¼ cups whole berries or 2¼ cups sliced
1 bag (20 ounces) frozen strawberries = 4 cups whole berries or 2½ cups sliced
1 package (10 ounces) frozen sliced strawberries = 1¼ cups berries in syrup

---

Rhubarb

A hardy vegetable that is used like a fruit, rhubarb is native to Mongolia. Only the stems or stalks of the rhubarb are cut up and made into pie, sauces, desserts and jams. The large green leaves are poisonous.

A 3½-ounce serving of cooked rhubarb with sugar added is 141 calories with a fair amount of vitamin A and vitamin C.

Buying and Storing: Fresh rhubarb is marketed from February to June. Buy fresh, firm, crisp stalks either pink or cherry red in color. Refrigerate and use them as soon as possible. One pound will yield about 2 cups when cooked.

Frozen, dry-packed, cut-up rhubarb is also available.

Apple Crisp

Roast at 375° for 30 to 40 minutes.
Makes 6 servings.

Nutrient Value Per Serving: 354 calories, 2 g protein, 12 g fat, 63 g carbohydrate, 126 mg sodium, 31 mg cholesterol.

2½ pounds tart apples, pared, cored and sliced (about 8 cups sliced)
¾ cup firmly packed light brown sugar
½ teaspoon ground cinnamon
¼ teaspoon ground nutmeg
2 teaspoons lemon juice
¾ cup unsifted all-purpose flour
6 tablespoons butter or margarine

1. Preheat the oven to moderate (375°). Spray the inside of a 2-quart baking dish with nonstick vegetable cooking spray.

2. Combine the apple slices, 6 tablespoons of the sugar, cinnamon, nutmeg and lemon juice in the prepared baking dish; stir gently to mix well.

3. Combine the flour and the remaining 6 tablespoons of sugar in a small bowl. Cut in the butter with a pastry blender or 2 knives until the mixture is crumbly. Sprinkle evenly over the apples.

4. Bake in the preheated moderate oven (375°) for 30 to 40 minutes, or until the apples are tender and the top is browned. Serve warm or cold.

Grape and Sour Cream "High Hats"

Grape and Sour Cream "High Hats"

Refrigerated ready-to-make biscuits are the secret shortcut for these crowd-pleasing shortcakes.

Makes 10 small servings.

Nutrient Value Per Shortcake: 171 calories, 3 g protein, 7 g fat, 25 g carbohydrate, 261 mg sodium, 10 mg cholesterol.

> 1   tube (10 ounces) refrigerated
>   ready-to-bake flaky biscuits
> 1   cup dairy sour cream
> 4   tablespoons dark brown sugar
> 2   cups seedless green grapes

1. Bake the biscuits, following the package directions.
2. Split the biscuits in half. Lightly toast the cut sides.
3. To serve, place the bottom halves of the biscuits on small dessert plates. Spoon about ⅔ cup of the sour cream onto the biscuit bottoms. Sprinkle with a total of 3 tablespoons of the brown sugar, dividing equally.
4. Reserve 10 grapes for garnish. Divide the remaining grapes over the sour cream-topped biscuits. Cover with the tops. Garnish each with the remaining sour cream, brown sugar and grapes. Serve immediately.

Sliced Nectarines on Pound Cake with Cream Cheese Topping

A delicious, easy treat to prepare when you're expecting company.

Makes 6 servings.

Nutrient Value Per Serving: 407 calories, 5 g protein, 26 g fat, 42 g carbohydrate, 108 mg sodium, 104 mg cholesterol.

> 4   cups sliced ripe nectarines
>   (8 nectarines)
> 1   tablespoon lemon juice
> 3   tablespoons sugar
> Cream Cheese Topping:
> 4   ounces (half 8-ounce package)
>   cream cheese
> 2   tablespoons honey
> 1   tablespoon milk
> ½   teaspoon grated lemon rind
> ½   cup heavy cream
> 12   thin slices store-bought pound cake,
>   fresh or frozen (about three-quarters
>   of a frozen 10¾-ounce cake)

1. Toss the sliced nectarines with the lemon juice in a medium-size bowl. Sprinkle with the sugar; stir to mix. Let stand for 30 minutes at room temperature, stirring occasionally.
2. Prepare the Cream Cheese Topping: Beat together the cream cheese, honey, milk and grated lemon rind in small bowl until smooth.
3. In another bowl, beat the heavy cream until stiff. Fold into the Cream Cheese Topping mixture.
4. To serve, overlap 2 slices of the pound cake on each of 6 individual dessert plates. Top with the undrained nectarines. Spoon the Cream Cheese Topping over each.

Peach Blueberry Cream Tart

Bake crust at 350° for 8 to 10 minutes.
Makes 8 servings.

Nutrient Value Per Serving: 539 calories, 4 g protein, 28 g fat, N/A g carbohydrate, 224 mg sodium, 80 mg cholesterol.

Graham-Cracker Crust (recipe follows)
1 can (21 ounces) blueberry pie filling
2 packages (3 ounces each) cream cheese, at room temperature
⅓ cup sugar
1 tablespoon milk
½ teaspoon ground nutmeg
1 cup heavy cream
1 can (16 ounces) sliced peaches, drained
½ cup apricot preserves, melted and strained

1. Preheat the oven to moderate (350°).
2. Prepare the Graham-Cracker Crust.
3. Bake the crust for 8 to 10 minutes, or until lightly colored. Cool on a wire rack.
4. Pour the blueberry filling into the cooled crust.
5. Beat together the cream cheese, sugar, milk and nutmeg in a medium-size bowl until well

blended. Beat the cream in a small bowl until stiff. Fold into the cream cheese mixture. Spread evenly over the blueberry layer. Or spoon the cream cheese mixture into a pastry bag fitted with a large star tip; pipe decoratively over the blueberry layer. Arrange the drained peach slices over the cream cheese layer. Spoon the preserves over the peaches. Chill for several hours or overnight.

Graham-Cracker Crust: Combine 1 cup of graham-cracker crumbs, ¼ cup (1 ounce) of ground pecans or walnuts, 2 tablespoons of sugar and ¼ cup (½ stick) of melted butter in a bowl until well blended. Press evenly over the bottom and sides of a 9-inch pie plate.

Banana Kabobs

Banana Kabobs

Peanut butter, jelly and bananas—a yummy combination.

Makes 6 servings.

Nutrient Value Per Serving: 108 calories, 3 g protein, 6 g fat, 13 g carbohydrate, 27 mg sodium, 0 mg cholesterol.

2 firm medium-size or 3 small bananas
2 tablespoons creamy peanut butter
1 tablespoon fruit preserves
¼ cup finely chopped nuts, such as walnuts or pecans
6 lollipop sticks

▶

1. Peel the bananas and cut off the ends. Cut the bananas crosswise into 1-inch chunks; you should have about 12 chunks. Spread one end of each piece with the peanut butter, top with the preserves and dip in the ground nuts.

2. To assemble the kabobs: Skewer 2 pieces of banana on each lollipop stick, pushing the stick through the plain sides first. Press the pieces together to achieve the layered effect. Serve immediately, or wrap the kabobs in plastic wrap, freeze and serve frozen.

Note: Try substituting coconut, wheat germ or Homemade Granola Crunch *(see recipe, page 274)* for the chopped nuts. For variety, try 2 or 3 different combinations on one kabob.

Going Bananas

Batter's up For a change of pace, add sliced ripe bananas to your pancake batter instead of blueberries. Go a step further and add chopped walnuts, too.

For chocoholics Bananas and chocolate make great mates. Top your next chocolate pie with sliced bananas. Or add a little mashed banana to chocolate-chip cookie batter.

On the side Sauté peeled, sliced, firm bananas in butter until golden brown, sprinkle with a dash of nutmeg and serve with ham or chicken.

Wrap-around Try wrapping bacon slices around a whole, peeled banana and broiling it for breakfast or brunch.

Hold the bread Peanut butter and bananas make great "sandwiches." Slice a banana lengthwise and spread peanut butter on each side; then reassemble. Make sure you squeeze lemon juice on the banana to keep it from darkening.

For your sweet tooth Blend half a ripe banana (cut into pieces), a cup of skim milk and a dash of nutmeg.

Pineapple-Strawberry Fruit Pops

Makes 6 pops.

Nutrient Value Per Serving: 48 calories, 0 g protein, 0 g fat, 12 g carbohydrate, 1 mg sodium, 0 mg cholesterol.

- **6 paper bathroom drinking cups (about 3 ounces each)**
- **1 can (8 ounces) pineapple chunks packed in juice, drained and juice reserved**
- **½ cup fresh or frozen dry-pack strawberries**
- **1 cup pineapple juice**
- **6 popsicle sticks**

1. Place the cups on a cookie sheet.

2. Combine the pineapple chunks and strawberries in the bowl of a food processor. Cover; whirl just until chunky. Stir in the reserved pineapple juice and the 1 cup of pineapple juice.

3. Pour or ladle the fruit-juice mixture into the cups. Place a sheet of aluminum foil over the cups; press down lightly on the foil so the cup rims show. Make ¼-inch slits in the foil over the center of each cup; insert a popsicle stick in each.

4. Place the pops on a cookie sheet in the freezer. Freeze until firm, for 5 hours or overnight.

5. To serve, remove the foil and carefully peel off the paper cups.

Orange Banana Fruit Pops

Makes 6 pops.

Nutrient Value Per Serving: 47 calories, 1 g protein, 0 g fat, 12 g carbohydrate, 1 mg sodium, 0 mg cholesterol.

- **6 paper bathroom drinking cups (about 3 ounces each)**
- **1 cup orange sections, white pith and seeds removed (about 2 medium-size oranges)**
- **½ cup sliced ripe banana (about 1 small)**
- **1 cup orange juice**
- **6 popsicle sticks**

1. Place the paper cups on cookie sheets.

2. Combine the orange sections and banana slices in a bowl of a food processor. Cover; whirl just until chunky. Stir in the orange juice.

3. Pour or ladle the fruit-juice mixture into the cups. Place a sheet of aluminum foil over the cups; press down lightly on the foil so the cup rims show. Make ¼-inch slits in the foil over the center of each cup; insert a popsicle stick in each.
4. Place the pops on a cookie sheet in the freezer. Freeze until firm, for 5 hours or overnight.
5. To serve, remove the foil and carefully peel off the paper cups.

◤◤◤◤ ◤ *California Oranges Jubilee*

Makes 8 ice-cream "snowballs".

Nutrient Value Per Serving: 336 calories, 4 g protein, 12 g fat, 61 g carbohydrate, 92 mg sodium, 30 mg cholesterol.

1 quart vanilla ice cream
1 can (3½ ounces) flaked coconut
6 seedless oranges
   Orange juice
¾ cup sugar
3 whole cloves
1 cup water
1½ tablespoons cornstarch
3 tablespoons brandy

1. Using a 2-ounce ice-cream scoop, scoop the ice cream into 8 balls. Roll in the coconut and freeze until ready to serve.
2. Cut the peel from the oranges, removing all the white membrane. Separate the oranges into segments, over a bowl, reserving the juice. Place the segments in a second bowl. Add enough orange juice to the reserved juice, if necessary, to make 1 cup.
3. Combine the sugar, cloves, orange juice and ¾ cup of the water in a 10-inch skillet. Bring to boiling. Lower the heat to medium-low; simmer for 15 minutes. Discard the cloves. Blend the cornstarch with the remaining ¼ cup of water in a small cup until smooth. Stir into the hot orange juice mixture. Cook, stirring, until the mixture comes to boiling, for about 10 minutes. Lower the heat; boil gently for 30 seconds. Add the orange segments; heat through. Carefully add the brandy; heat for 30 seconds.
4. Remove the ice-cream "snowballs" from the freezer. Place in heatproof dessert bowls. Spoon the hot sauce over.

◤◤ ◤ *Cranberry Linzer Torte*

Bake at 350° for 40 minutes.
Makes 8 servings.

Nutrient Value Per Serving: 668 calories, 7 g protein, 28 g fat, 101 g carbohydrate, 183 mg sodium, 115 mg cholesterol.

2¾ cups granulated sugar
½ cup orange juice
1 package (12 ounces) fresh or frozen cranberries (3 cups)
1 small to medium-size apple, pared, cored and chopped
1¾ cups sifted all-purpose flour
½ teaspoon ground cinnamon
¼ teaspoon ground cloves
1 cup finely ground almonds
¾ cup (1½ sticks) butter or margarine
1 tablespoon grated orange rind
2 egg yolks
1 teaspoon vanilla
   10X (confectioners') sugar

1. Heat 2 cups of the sugar and the orange juice in a large saucepan until the sugar dissolves. Add the cranberries and apple. Bring to boiling. Lower the heat; simmer, uncovered, for 20 minutes or until slightly thickened. Cool completely.
2. Sift together the flour, cinnamon and cloves into a large bowl. Add the remaining ¾ cup of sugar and the almonds. Cut in the butter with a pastry blender until crumbly. Blend in the orange rind, egg yolks and vanilla. Knead the dough a few times until smooth. Chill for 1 hour.
3. Roll half of the dough between 2 sheets of wax paper to a 10-inch round, using a tart pan with removable bottom as a guide. Remove the top sheet of paper; turn the dough out onto a cookie sheet; remove the paper. Trim the edges evenly. Trace and cut 2 stars in the dough, one 10 inches with points touching the outer rim of the dough, and one 4-to-5-inches in the center, lined up with the larger star. Remove the dough between two cuts, leaving the center star and outer pieces on the cookie sheet. Place the cookie sheet in the freezer for a few minutes, until the dough is firm.
4. Preheat the oven to moderate (350°). ▶

5. Combine the trimmings with remaining dough. Press evenly over the bottom and up the sides of a 10-inch tart pan with a removable bottom. Spread 1 cup of the cranberry mixture over the dough. Place a star on the cranberry mixture in the center. Arrange the corresponding outer pieces along the edge of the pan, so the cutout lines up with the star in the center. Press the edge down together with the side all around to form an even rim.

6. Bake in the preheated moderate oven (350°) for 40 minutes, or until lightly browned. Cool in the pan for 15 minutes. Remove the outer rim of the pan. Cool the torte completely.

7. Fill in the open space with ⅓ to ½ cup cranberry filling.* Sprinkle the center star with 10X sugar. Garnish with fresh cranberries and strips of orange peel, if you wish.

Note: Extra cranberry filling can be served as a condiment with roast turkey or chicken.

Pear-Ginger Pudding with Two Sauces

Steam for 2 hours and 15 minutes.
Makes 8 to 10 servings (without sauce).

Nutrient Value Per Serving: 529 calories, 7 g protein, 29 g fat, 64 g carbohydrate, 391 mg sodium, 123 mg cholesterol.

 2 *slightly underripe pears*
 1 *tablespoon lemon juice*
 1 *tablespoon granulated sugar*
 2 *cups* sifted *all-purpose flour*
 2 *teaspoons ground ginger*
 1 *teaspoon ground cinnamon*
 1 *teaspoon baking powder*
 1 *teaspoon baking soda*
 3 *tablespoons chopped crystallized ginger*
14 *tablespoons (1¾ sticks) butter or margarine*
 ¾ *cup light brown sugar*
 2 *eggs*
 1 *cup applesauce*
 ¾ *cup chopped walnuts or pecans*
    Nesselrode Sauce **(see recipe, page 263)**
    Lemon Sauce **(see recipe, page 264)**

1. Butter an 8-cup steamed-pudding mold or a heatproof bowl.

2. Pare, quarter and core the pears. Cut each quarter crosswise into ⅛-to-¼-inch-thick slices. Toss with the lemon juice and sugar in a heavy medium-size skillet. Cook, stirring often, over medium-high heat until tender, for 10 to 15 minutes. Cool completely.

3. Sift together the flour, ginger, cinnamon, baking powder and baking soda onto wax paper; mix in the crystallized ginger.

4. Beat the butter in a large bowl until soft. Add the sugar and eggs. Beat until light and fluffy, for 3 to 5 minutes. Stir in the applesauce, then the flour mixture, a third at a time, adding the nuts with the last addition. Fold in the pear mixture. Spoon into the prepared mold or bowl; cover with the lid of the mold or foil. Fasten tightly with string.

5. Place the mold on the rack in a deep kettle. Pour in boiling water to come halfway up the side of the mold. Cover the ketttle. Keep the water gently boiling, adding more boiling water if necessary. Steam for 2¼ hours, or until a wooden skewer tests clean.

6. Cool the pudding in the mold for 10 minutes on a rack. Turn out onto a plate. Serve warm with the Lemon Sauce and Nesselrode Sauce.

Note: Pudding can be steamed 2 to 3 days ahead. Cool and unmold as in Step 6. Wrap tightly in foil; refrigerate. Reheat wrapped pudding on a cookie sheet in a slow oven (300°) for 30 minutes.

MICROWAVE DIRECTIONS FOR PUDDING
650 Watt Variable Power Microwave Oven
Ingredient Changes: Add dry bread crumbs for coating the pan.
Directions: Toss together the pear pieces, lemon juice and 1 tablespoon of butter in a microwave-safe 9-inch pie plate. Cover. Microwave at full power for 5 minutes, stirring after 3 minutes. Cool. Grease a 2-quart microwave-safe tube pan; sprinkle the sides with the dry bread crumbs. Assemble the pudding as in the above recipe. Spoon the batter into the prepared pan. Cover tightly with plastic wrap. Place the pan on an inverted saucer in the microwave oven. Microwave at half power for 16 to 17 minutes, rotating the pan a quarter turn after 8 minutes. Pudding will pull away slightly from the sides and a wooden pick inserted in the center will come out clean. Let stand for 10 minutes. Loosen the pudding sides with a small knife. Invert onto the plate. (Small pieces of the pudding may remain in the mold; patch on top of the pudding. Microwaving saves about 1 hour and 50 minutes.)
To Reheat: Place the unmolded pudding on a microwave-safe plate. Cover loosely with paper toweling. Microwave at half power for 7 minutes. Let stand for 5 minutes.

Choosing Pears

Pears are harvested green because they develop a better flavor as the sugar content increases due to the conversion of starch to sugar. Pears used for cooking or baking should be firm and slightly underripe. Pears to be used fresh, eaten out of hand, in salads and desserts should be fully ripe. If pears are hard, let them ripen at room temperature until the fruit feels soft. Some green pears, such as the Bartlett, will turn yellow when ripe, but others do not change color upon ripening.

Nesselrode Sauce

Makes about 1¼ cups.

Nutrient Value Per ¼ Cup: 182 calories, 2 g protein, 12 g fat, 13 g carbohydrate, 42 mg sodium, 196 mg cholesterol.

- **3 egg yolks**
- **3 tablespoons 10X (confectioners') sugar**
- **2 tablespoons brandy**
- **½ cup heavy cream, whipped**
- **3 tablespoons chopped mixed candied fruits**

Beat the egg yolks and sugar in a small bowl until thick and fluffy, for 3 to 5 minutes. Beat in the brandy. Fold in the whipped cream and candied fruits.

Nesselrode

Count Karl Robert Nesselrode was a Russian count who lived from 1780 to 1862 and loved good eating. The most famous dish created and named in his honor was a dessert using chestnut pieces, candied peel, cherries, raisins and currants flavored with maraschino liqueur and mixed with cream, then frozen in a mold. Today, Nesselrode sauces are commercially bottled containing candied fruits and peel in a heavy syrup. Use them for desserts.

Major Pear Varieties

Bartlett: Known as the summer pear, this variety is named for Enoch Bartlett, the owner of the property that this variety was grown on in 1817. Over two-thirds of the pears harvested in this country are Bartlett. They are available from mid-July to October. The fruit is bell-shaped; the skin is fairly thin and clear yellow when ripe. The flesh is white, smooth and juicy. Bartlett is the only variety of pears commercially canned. Canned pears are available in halves or slices, packed in syrup, water or juice.

Anjou: A green, round, heart-shaped pear available from October to May. It is medium to large in size with a short neck. The flesh is yellowish-white, fine-textured, juicy and sweet. The color is not an indication of ripeness because this variety does not change color. When ripe, it yields to gentle pressure at the stem end.

Bosc: This variety has a long, tapering neck, a russet-brown skin and crunchy, sweet, white flesh. The fruit is medium or large in size. This pear is ideal for eating and baking. Available from September to March.

Comice: A medium to large fruit in size, almost round in shape, comice pears are famous as a holiday-gift fruit. The skin is yellow-green, often with a red blush. The flesh is very fine, extremely juicy and not gritty. It is marketed from October to March.

Seckel: A late-summer pear, small, sweet and ideal for fresh eating, canning and pickling. It has a yellow-brown skin; available from September to December.

Winter Nelis: A medium- to small-size pear with a yellow-green skin. The flesh is sweet and firm, good for cooking and canning. Available from February to May.

Red Bartlett: Similar to Bartlett, differing only in skin color. The skin is bright crimson.

Forelle: A golden yellow pear with a bright red blush and red freckles. Available from December to February.

Apple-pear: A small fruit shaped like a pear with a brownish-yellow skin; the flesh is crisp and white like an apple. It looks somewhat like a small Anjou or Comice. This variety was introduced by Chinese gold miners in the California Gold Rush days. The Chinese call them Sha-li. They are also known as Japanese pears, Chalea or pear-apples. Apple-pears are available in gourmet or specialty markets from October to February.

Lemon Sauce

Makes 1½ cups.

Nutrient Value Per Serving: 131 calories, 1 g protein, 4 g fat, 24 g carbohydrate, 25 mg sodium, 96 mg cholesterol.

- **⅔ cup sugar**
- **1 tablespoon cornstarch**
- **⅔ cup water**
- **2 egg yolks, slightly beaten**
- **1 tablespoon butter**
- **1 tablespoon grated lemon rind**
- **¼ cup fresh lemon juice, strained**

1. Combine the sugar and cornstarch in a small saucepan; stir in the water until smooth. Cook, stirring constantly, until the mixture thickens and bubbles, for 1 minute. Remove from the heat.
2. Beat half of the cornstarch mixture into the beaten yolks in a small bowl; stir back into the saucepan. Cook, stirring, for 1 minute longer. Remove from the heat. Stir in the butter, lemon rind and juice.
3. Pour into a serving bowl. Place a piece of plastic wrap directly on the surface to prevent a skin from forming. Serve warm or cold.

MICROWAVE DIRECTIONS FOR LEMON SAUCE
650 Watt Variable Power Microwave Oven
Directions: Combine the sugar, cornstarch, water and egg yolks in a 4-cup microwave-safe measure; stir to mix. Microwave, uncovered, at full power for 2 to 3 minutes, stirring well every minute, until thickened and bubbly. Stir in the butter, lemon rind and juice.

Orange Bread Pudding

Orange Bread Pudding

Just-squeezed orange juice is the secret to this dessert.

Bake at 350° for 45 minutes.
Makes 6 servings.

Nutrient Value Per Serving: 436 calories, 12 g protein, 17 g fat, 60 g carbohydrate, 452 mg sodium, 220 mg cholesterol.

- **10 to 12 slices French bread, about ¾ inch thick and with crust**
- **¼ cup (½ stick) butter or margarine, softened**
- **4 eggs**
- **½ cup sugar**
- **2 teaspoons grated orange rind**
- **⅔ cup orange juice (2 oranges)**
- **2¾ cups milk**
- **¼ cup orange marmalade, melted**

1. Spread the bread slices generously on one side with the butter. Arrange the slices, buttered-side up, overlapping in a lightly buttered 2-quart shallow baking dish.
2. Beat the eggs, sugar and orange rind in a bowl just until blended. Gradually stir in the orange juice and milk. Pour evenly over the bread. Let stand for 15 minutes.
3. Preheat the oven to moderate (350°).
4. Set the dish in a large baking pan. Place on the oven rack. Pour boiling water into the pan so it comes halfway up the sides of the bread pudding dish.
5. Bake in the preheated moderate oven (350°) for 45 minutes, or until a knife inserted in the center comes out clean. The center will be almost set but still soft.
6. Remove the pudding from the water bath. Cool for at least 30 minutes.
7. Brush the melted marmalade over the top. Serve the pudding warm or chilled with light cream to pour over, or with whipped cream on the side, if you wish.

⬛⬛⬛⬛
Orange Soufflé

Makes 8 servings.

Nutrient Value Per Serving: 421 calories, 7 g protein, 26 g fat, 44 g carbohydrate, 68 mg sodium, 253 mg cholesterol.

2 envelopes unflavored gelatin
½ cup water
5 eggs, at room temperature
1 cup sugar
2 cups heavy cream
1 tablespoon grated orange rind
½ cup orange juice

1. Sprinkle the gelatin over the water in a small saucepan. Let stand for 10 minutes to soften. Place over very low heat; stir to dissolve. Cool.
2. Prepare a collar for a 5-cup clear-glass soufflé dish: Measure off a length of foil long enough to encircle the dish. Fold in half lengthwise. Fasten securely around the dish with tape or string, so the collar is 3 inches higher than the rim of the dish.
3. Beat the eggs and sugar in a large bowl until very thick and light, for 7 to 8 minutes.
4. Beat 1½ cups of the cream in a small bowl until stiff peaks form. Refrigerate.
5. Combine the grated rind and juice with the cooled gelatin. Pour into the egg mixture. Beat until well blended. Chill briefly, stirring frequently, just until thick enough to mound when spooned, for about 5 minutes. Fold in the whipped cream. Pour the soufflé mixture into the dish. Refrigerate for 4 hours, or until set.
6. Remove the collar gently, freeing the soufflé from the foil, if necessary, with a small paring knife.
7. Beat the remaining ½ cup of cream in a small bowl until stiff. Garnish the soufflé with whipped cream.

Glazed Orange Decoration: Combine ½ cup of water and ½ cup of sugar in a large skillet. Simmer until the sugar is dissolved. Slice one juice orange into ⅛-inch-thick slices. Remove the seeds. Add the slices to the skillet. Simmer over medium-high heat for 5 minutes, turning the slices halfway through. Transfer to a wire rack to cool. Use to garnish the soufflé.

Ice Cream Desserts

⬛⬛⬛
Baked Alaska

President Thomas Jefferson served a version at a White House Dinner in 1802. Now, see how simple it is to serve this show-stopper.

Bake at 425° for 3 minutes.
Makes 8 servings.

Nutrient Value Per Serving: 1,421 calories, 18 g protein, 78 g fat, 167 g carbohydrate, 678 mg sodium, 518 mg cholesterol.

3 cups mint-chocolate chip ice cream, slightly softened
3 cups strawberry ice cream slightly softened
Lemon Loaf Cake (see recipe, page 225)
4 egg whites
¾ cup sifted sugar
Cherries Jubilee Amandine (recipe follows)

1. Line a 9 x 5 x 3-inch loaf pan with a sheet of heavy-duty aluminum foil long enough to seal the pan.
2. With the back of a spoon, firmly pack the mint-chocolate chip ice cream onto the bottom of a foil-lined pan, spreading evenly. Repeat, making a second layer, with the strawberry ice cream. Cover and seal with the overlapping edges of the foil; freeze for 2 hours, or until firm.
3. Slice the Lemon Loaf Cake in half horizontally. Place on a foil-wrapped wooden board. (Use the second half to make another Baked Alaska or save for snacking.)
4. Unmold the ice cream layers onto the cake. Remove the aluminum foil from the ice cream. Freeze the layers while making the meringue topping.
5. Beat the egg whites until foamy white in a large bowl with an electric mixer at high speed. Beat in the sifted sugar, 1 tablespoon at a time, until the meringue forms firm peaks.
6. Spread the meringue over the ice cream and cake to coat completely, making deep swirls on top with a spatula. Freeze until the meringue is firm, then cover with plastic wrap. (Meringue-covered cake can be wrapped and frozen for up to one week.) ▶

Baked Alaska (page 265), Cherries Jubilee Amandine

7. Just before serving, bake in a preheated hot oven (425°) for 3 minutes, or just until the meringue peaks turn golden. Slide onto a serving platter and serve immediatly with the Cherries Jubilee Amandine. Return any remaining dessert to the freezer.

Cherries Jubilee Amandine: Makes 4 cups. Drain the syrup from 1 can (1 pound, 13 ounces) of pitted sweet dark cherries into a 2-cup measure. Add water to make 2 cups. Combine ¼ cup of the sugar and 2 tablespoons of cornstarch in a large, heavy saucepan; stir in the cherry liquid. Cook, stirring constantly, until the sauce thickens and bubbles for 1 minute; stir in the cherries and ¼ cup of almond-flavored liqueur or brandy. Simmer for 5 minutes. Sprinkle with sliced almonds.

Note: Sauce may be made ahead; cool to room temperature; refrigerate. Reheat before serving.

Pineapple-Yogurt Sherbet

This easy-to-make and refreshing dessert can be served alone or with fresh berries.

Makes about 8 servings (1 quart).

Nutrient Value Per Serving: 136 calories, 3 g protein, .92 g fat, 31 g carbohydrate, 75 mg sodium, 3 mg cholesterol.

2 cans (8 ounces each) crushed pineapple in pineapple juice
½ cup honey
1 container (16 ounces) plain yogurt
1 teaspoon vanilla
⅛ teaspoon salt

1. Drain the juice from the pineapple (about ½ cup) into a small saucepan; add the honey. Bring to boiling, stirring until the honey is dissolved. Boil, uncovered, over low heat for 5 minutes. Pour into a large bowl; cool. Stir in the pineapple, yogurt, vanilla and salt.

2. Spoon the mixture into a 9 x 9 x 2-inch pan. Freeze, stirring several times, until mushy, about 3 hours.

3. Turn partially frozen mixture into a chilled bowl; beat with an electric mixer until smooth. Return to the pan and freeze until firm, for at least 6 hours. Leave at room temperature for 15 to 30 minutes before serving. Scoop into sherbet glasses; garnish with fresh mint or fresh berries, if you wish.

Chestnut Ice Cream Log

Honeyed chestnut-vanilla ice cream curled around green-cherry-dotted strawberry ice cream.

Makes 10 servings.

Nutrient Value Per Serving: 456 calories, 7 g protein, 13 g fat, 80 g carbohydrate, 110 mg sodium, 48 mg cholesterol.

1 can (15½ ounces) chestnut purée
½ cup honey
1 quart vanilla ice cream, softened
1 quart strawberry ice cream, softened
½ cup candied green cherries, halved

1. Line a 15½ x 10½ x 1-inch jelly-roll pan with plastic wrap.
2. Beat the chestnut and honey in a large bowl with an electric mixer at medium speed until smooth. Gradually beat in the vanilla ice cream until no streaks of white remain. Spoon evenly into the prepared pan. Freeze until firm to the touch, for several hours or overnight.
3. Soften the strawberry ice cream in a large bowl; spoon dollops over the surface of the chestnut layer; spread in an even layer; sprinkle with the cherries. Roll up, beginning with a short side, by lifting up the plastic wrap. (If the chestnut layer cracks on rolling, wait until it softens.) Cover with the plastic wrap; refreeze until very firm.
4. Transfer the log to a serving plate. Smooth the outer surface with a metal spatula. Use a serrated knife or the tip of a fork to score the surface to give a rough-textured look. Garnish with whipped cream, candied chestnuts, candied cherries and citron, if you wish.

Peach Melba Ripple Ice Cream

Swirls of raspberry juice ripple through this fresh peach ice cream.

Makes 16 servings (2 quarts).

Nutrient Value Per Serving: 295 calories, 3 g protein, 18 g fat, 31 g carbohydrate, 52 mg sodium, 116 mg cholesterol.

1 cup sugar
3 tablespoons unsifted all-purpose flour
**   Dash of salt**
1½ cups milk
3 eggs, slightly beaten
3 cups heavy cream
½ teaspoon almond extract
2 packages (10 ounces each) frozen peaches, thawed and drained
1 package (10 ounces) frozen raspberries, thawed
2 tablespoons sugar (for raspberries)
1 teaspoon cornstarch

1. Combine the 1 cup of sugar, the flour and salt in a medium saucepan; add the milk gradually. Cook over medium heat, stirring constantly, until the mixture thickens and bubbles. Remove the saucepan from the heat.
2. Stir half the mixture slowly into the beaten eggs in a medium-size bowl; stir back into the remaining mixture in the saucepan. Cook, stirring constantly, for 1 minute. Remove from the heat; pour into a large bowl; cool. Stir in the cream and almond extract; chill.
3. Crush the peaches with a potato masher in a medium bowl; reserve.
4. Press the raspberries through a fine sieve into a small saucepan; add the 2 tablespoons of sugar. Mix the cornstarch and the 1 tablespoon of water in a cup; add to the raspberries. Cook over medium heat, just until thickened and bubbly, for about 1 minute. Cool completely; reserve.
5. Pour the ice cream mixture into a 4-to-6-quart freezer can; add the peaches; freeze, following the ice-cream freezer manufacturer's directions.
6. When the ice cream is frozen, working very fast, spoon about one-fifth of the ice cream into a large plastic container or bowl; drizzle the raspberry sauce over. Continue to layer the ice cream and sauce this way. Freeze until firm.

Frozen Semi-Freddo

3. Beat the egg whites in a medium-size bowl until soft peaks form. Gradually add half the sugar and ¼ teaspoon of the vanilla, beating until stiff, but not dry, peaks form.
4. Beat the egg yolks in a small bowl until foamy. Gradually add the remaining sugar and ¼ teaspoon of the vanilla, beating until almost white, for about 3 minutes. Set aside.
5. Beat the cream and the remaining ½ teaspoon of the vanilla in a clean medium-size bowl until stiff peaks form. Gently fold in the beaten yolks and beaten whites just until mixed. Layer one-third of the mixture in the bottom of the prepared pan. Sprinkle on half of the cookie mixture. Spoon on another third of the cream mixture. Sprinkle on the remaining cookie mixture. Spoon the remaining cream mixture on top. Tap the pan lightly on the counter to settle.
6. Cover the pan with aluminum foil or plastic wrap. Freeze for at least 8 hours or overnight.
7. To serve, remove the top wrapping. Invert onto a serving platter. Remove the pan. Peel off the foil or plastic wrap. Garnish the top with stripes of chopped almonds, crushed cookies and chopped chocolate, if you wish.

Frozen Semi-Freddo

This rich dessert, inspired by the original from Italy, is similar to a frozen mousse.

Makes 8 servings.

Nutrient Value Per Serving: 244 calories, 5 g protein, 19 g fat, 15 g carbohydrate, 45 mg sodium, 145 mg cholesterol.

2 ounces milk chocolate, finely chopped
⅓ cup crushed amaretti cookies
¼ cup chopped almonds
1 tablespoon brandy
3 eggs, separated
⅓ cup superfine sugar
1 teaspoon vanilla
1 cup heavy cream
Garnish (optional):
2 tablespoons chopped almonds
2 tablespoons crushed amaretti cookies
1 ounce milk chocolate, finely chopped

1. Line a 8½ x 4½ x 2⅝-inch loaf pan with aluminum foil or plastic wrap. Set aside in the freezer while preparing the filling.
2. Toss the chocolate, cookie crumbs, almonds and brandy in a bowl. Reserve.

Pineapple-Orange Ice

Makes about 2½ pints.

Nutrient Value Per Serving: 75 calories, 0 g protein, 0 g fat, 16 g carbohydrate, 1 mg sodium, 0 mg cholesterol.

1 ripe pineapple, peeled, quartered, cored and cut into 1-inch chunks (about 4 cups)
½ cup 10X (confectioners') sugar
1 cup orange juice
2 to 4 tablespoons white rum

1. Working in batches if necessary, combine the pineapple, sugar and juice in a food processor; purée. Add the rum.
2. Pour the mixture into an 8-inch-square metal pan. Freeze until almost frozen, 2 to 4 hours; stir several times so the ice freezes evenly.
3. Transfer the mixture to a food processor or large chilled bowl. Quickly process or beat until smooth and fluffy. Return to the pan. Freeze for 30 minutes. Process or beat again.
4. Freeze, tightly covered, until almost firm, for 1 to 2 hours. If the ice freezes solid, soften in the refrigerator for 30 minutes.

No-Bake Desserts

▚ ⧉ ⊤ ⑊

Choco-Berry Pie

Makes 8 servings (one 9-inch pie).

Nutrient Value Per Serving: 313 calories, 4 g protein, 17 g fat, 36 g carbohydrate, 237 mg sodium, 55 mg cholesterol.

1 package (10 ounces) quick-thaw frozen strawberries, thawed and drained
35 chocolate wafer cookies
3 egg whites
¼ cup sugar
1¼ cups heavy cream
Fresh strawberries for garnish

1. Purée the berries in an electric blender.
2. Line the bottom of a 9-inch pie plate with 7 chocolate cookies. Line the edge of the plate with 12 cookies.
3. Beat the egg whites in a small bowl with an electric mixer until soft peaks form. Gradually add the sugar, beating until stiff, but not dry, peaks form. Reserve.
4. Beat 1 cup of the heavy cream in a medium-size bowl until stiff. Fold in the strawberry purée and egg whites. Spoon half the mixture evenly over the cookies in the pie plate. Place a double layer of cookies (12 cookies) over the top. Mound the remaining mixture on top. Break the remaining 4 cookies in half. Arrange 8 halves vertically in a spoke pattern on top. Cover lightly with plastic wrap. Freeze for at least 8 hours or overnight.
5. Just before serving, beat the remaining ¼ cup of cream in a small bowl until stiff. Garnish the pie with the whipped cream and fresh strawberries.

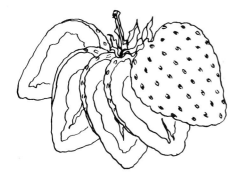

Choco-Berry Pie

Still a luscious dessert, but lower in calories since we use fewer cookies, dry-pack frozen or fresh strawberries instead of frozen packed in syrup and imitation sour cream dressing instead of heavy cream. And we've shrunk the serving size.

Makes 10 servings.

Nutrient Value Per Serving: 138 calories, 3 g protein, 6 g fat, 19 g carbohydrate, 96 mg sodium, 1 mg cholesterol.

12 chocolate wafer cookies
2 cups (1 pint) fresh or dry-pack frozen strawberries
3 egg whites
½ cup sugar
2 envelopes unflavored gelatin
⅓ cup water
1 cup imitation sour cream dressing*

1. Line a 9-inch pie plate with 7 chocolate cookies. Break the remaining 5 cookies in half; reserve.
2. Purée the strawberries in a blender or food processor. Set aside.
3. Beat the egg whites in a small bowl until foamy-white. Slowly beat in the sugar until soft peaks form. Set aside.
4. Sprinkle the gelatin over the water in a small cup. Let stand to soften, for 3 minutes. Set the cup in a pan of simmering water, stirring the gelatin until dissolved.
5. Transfer the dissolved gelatin to a large bowl. Beat in the strawberry purée until well blended. Beat in the sour cream dressing. Place the bowl in a pan of ice and water to speed setting; chill, stirring often, until the mixture just begins to thicken, for about 3 minutes. Remove the bowl and fold in the egg whites.
6. Return the bowl to the pan of ice and water; stir occasionally until the mixture mounds when spooned.
7. Spoon into the pie plate, mounding the mixture. Insert the reserved cookie halves around the edge of the pie. Refrigerate until set, for about 4 hours.

*Note: You can find imitation sour cream dressing in the dairy section of your supermarket.

Blueberry Lemon Tarts

These individual tarts are filled with lemon curd, a tart custardy pudding, which can be purchased in jars from the gourmet section of your supermarket or specialty food shops.

Makes 6 servings.

Nutrient Value Per Serving: 224 calories, 2 g protein, 13 g fat, 26 g carbohydrate, 201 mg sodium, 45 mg cholesterol.

2 cups pressurized whipped cream
½ cup lemon curd
1½ cups fresh blueberries
1 package (4 ounces) 6 graham cracker tart-size ready-to-use crusts

1. Spray the cream into a glass measure to measure 2 cups. Beat the lemon curd with a spoon in a medium-size bowl until smooth; gently fold in the whipped cream.
2. Arrange a layer of blueberries in the bottom of each tart shell. Mound the lemon cream into each shell. Garnish with the remaining blueberries.

Note: To remove the tart crusts from aluminum foil pans, remove any plastic covers from the shells and add to the ones you may have collected previously. Freeze the crusts in their foil pans for several hours. Carefully turn back the edges of the foil pans. Carefully lift out the crusts and transfer to the plastic covers. Fill as directed in the above recipe.

Regal Peach Crown

A frozen charlotte-like dessert with a peach-flavored ricotta cheese filling.

Makes 8 servings.

Nutrient Value Per Serving: 282 calories, 8 g protein, 8 g fat, 46 g carbohydrate, 87 mg sodium, 67 mg cholesterol.

10 plain ladyfingers*, split
1 bag (20 ounces) frozen peach slices OR: 3 cups fresh peach slices
4 tablespoons sugar
¾ cup peach preserves
⅛ teaspoon ground cinnamon
1 container (15 ounces) part-skim ricotta cheese
½ cup dairy sour cream
2 teaspoons lemon juice
Whipped cream for garnish

1. Line the bottom of a 5½-cup brioche mold or 1½-quart bowl with aluminum foil. Arrange 3 or 4 ladyfinger halves on the bottom, cutting to fit exactly in a single layer. Line the sides with the ladyfinger halves slightly overlapping. (The brioche mold needs 17 halves; the bowl may require more.)
2. Combine 1 cup of the peach slices, 2 tablespoons of the sugar, the preserves and cinnamon in the container of an electric blender or food processor. Cover; whirl until smooth. Transfer to a clean bowl. Stir in the ricotta cheese and sour cream. Pour into the prepared mold. Cover with plastic wrap. Freeze for at least 8 hours or overnight.
3. Prepare the peach sauce up to 1 hour before serving: Set aside 6 or 7 peach slices for garnish. Combine the remaining peaches, the remaining 2 tablespoons of the sugar and the lemon juice in the container of the blender or food processor. Cover; whirl until puréed. Set aside in the refrigerator.
4. Turn the mold out onto a serving platter. Let stand at room temperature for 20 minutes before serving. Garnish the top with the reserved peach slices and whipped cream. Serve with the peach sauce on side.

Note: Make sure the ladyfingers are very fresh, or they will "float."

Peanut Brittle and Rice Pudding with Nectarines

Makes 4 servings.

Nutrient Value Per Serving: 556 calories, 12 g protein, 11 g fat, 107 g carbohydrate, 195 mg sodium, 29 mg cholesterol.

1 cup peanut brittle pieces OR: 2 bars (1.6 ounces each) peanut candy
4 large nectarines, halved, pitted and cut into ½-inch-thick slices
4 cups canned or deli rice pudding
½ teaspon grated lemon rind

1. Reserve 4 small pieces of the peanut brittle for garnish. Coarsely crush the remaining candy.
2. Reserve 4 nectarine slices for garnish. Decoratively overlap half the remaining nectarine slices in the bottoms of 4 large dessert glasses.

3. Stir together the rice pudding and lemon rind in a large bowl. Layer each glass of fruit with ½ cup of rice pudding, the crushed brittle, remaining nectarines, ½ cup of rice pudding and the remaining crushed brittle.

4. Garnish each glass with one of the reserved nectarine slices and a small piece of brittle.

Sunshine Sundae

Sunshine Sundae

Makes 2 servings.

Nutrient Value Per Serving: 150 calories, 7 g protein, 4 g fat, 21 g carbohydrate, 90 mg sodium, 7 mg cholesterol.

1 **container (8 ounces) plain yogurt**
1 **tablespoon orange marmalade**
3 **tablespoons granola**
  Fresh fruit

1. Combine the yogurt and marmalade in a small mixing bowl. Place 1 tablespoon of the granola in each of two sundae glasses. Spoon half of the yogurt mixture into each dish. Sprinkle the remaining 1 tablespoon of granola over the yogurt, dividing evenly.

2. Garnish with fresh fruit.

Chocolate-Glazed Strawberry Pound Cake

A frozen pound cake never had it so good!

Makes 8 servings.

Nutrient Value Per Serving: 353 calories, 4 g protein, 22 g fat, 37 g carbohydrate, 159 mg sodium, 41 mg cholesterol.

1 **frozen pound cake (10¾ ounces)**
1 **pint strawberries**
1 **cup heavy cream, whipped**
3 **tablespoons strawberry preserves**
½ **cup bottled chocolate fudge topping**

1. Slice the frozen pound cake horizontally into 3 equal layers, using a long, thin knife. Place the layers on a cookie sheet to defrost.

2. Reserve ½ cup of the strawberries for garnish. Slice the remaining berries; stir into the whipped cream.

3. Brush the bottom cake layer with half the preserves; spread with half the sliced strawberries and cream mixture. Place the second cake layer on top. Brush with the remaining preserves; spread with the remaining sliced strawberries and cream mixture. Gently place the third layer on top. Refrigerate.

4. To serve, spread the fudge topping over the top layer with metal spatula, allowing some to drip down the sides. Garnish each slice with the reserved strawberries.

No-Bake Pineapple Upside-Down Cake

Our fruit-topped sponge cake is a naturally sweet concoction that's heavy on flavor and light on calories.

Makes 10 servings.

Nutrient Value Per Serving: 235 calories, 3 g protein, 7 g fat, 40 g carbohydrate, 157 mg sodium, 0 mg cholesterol.

1 **can (20 ounces) sliced pineapple in juice**
1 **envelope unflavored gelatin**
¼ **cup cold water**
7 **fresh ripe or canned dark red cherries, halved and pitted**
1 **small banana, thinly sliced 8- or 9-inch round purchased sponge cake layer**

1. Drain the sliced pineapple, reserving the juice; reserve 7 pineapple rings for the cake. Add enough water to the juice to make 1 cup. ▶

2. Sprinkle the gelatin over the cold water in a small saucepan. Let stand to soften, for 5 minutes. Place over very low heat; stir to dissolve. Stir into the pineapple juice mixture. Refrigerate until slightly syrupy.

3. Arrange the reserved pineapple rings in a single layer in the bottom of a 9-inch-round layer-cake pan. Place a cherry half, cut-side up, in the center of each pineapple ring and between the rings. Arrange a thin slice of banana between the rings. Spoon the syrupy gelatin mixture evenly over the fruit.

4. If using a 9-inch sponge cake layer, slice horizontally in half with a long, thin serrated knife. Wrap, label and freeze one layer for another use. Gently place the remaining layer on the gelatin mixture. If using an 8-inch sponge cake layer, slice horizontally into 2 thin layers. Gently place one layer on the gelatin mixture. Cut the remaining layer in pieces to fill the spaces around the edge of the pan. Refrigerate until set, for about 3 hours.

5. To serve, run the knife around the edge of the pan. Invert onto a serving platter. If the cake does not easily release from the pan, gently pry the knife under the gelatin layer to release the cake.

Other Desserts

Meringue Rice Pudding

Meringue Rice Pudding

Get a head start on dessert by making the pudding the day before.

Bake meringue at 425° for 5 minutes.
Makes 10 servings.

Nutrient Value Per Serving: 228 calories, 6 g protein, 5 g fat, 40 g carbohydrate, 102 mg sodium, 97 mg cholesterol.

- ½ **cup long-grain white rice**
- 1 **cup water**
- 4¼ **cups milk**
- ¼ **cup raisins**
- 3 **eggs, separated**
- ½ **cup plus 2 tablespoons sugar**
- 2 **teaspoons vanilla**
- ⅛ **teaspoon salt**
- ½ **cup raspberry preserves**

1. Combine the rice and water in a 2-quart saucepan. Bring to boiling; boil for 8 to 10 minutes, or until the water is absorbed. Stir in the milk. Return to boiling. Lower the heat and simmer, stirring often, for 25 minutes. Add the raisins; cook for 5 to 10 minutes longer, or until the rice is very tender.

2. Beat the egg yolks in a small bowl until frothy. (Reserve the whites in a small bowl.) Beat in ¼ cup of the sugar, vanilla and salt. Stir in ⅓ cup of the hot rice mixture into the yolks; return the mixture to the saucepan. Cook over very low heat for 2 minutes, or until the mixture thickens slightly; the mixture should be very loose and creamy.

3. Pour into a 1½-quart casserole dish. Cover the surface of the pudding and egg whites with plastic wrap. Refrigerate overnight.

4. Bring the egg whites to room temperature. Preheat the oven to hot (425°).

5. Beat the egg whites until frothy. Gradually beat in at high speed the remaining 6 tablespoons of sugar, a tablespoon at a time, until the meringue forms firm peaks.

6. Blot any accumulated moisture on top of the pudding with paper toweling. Spread a layer of preserves over the rice pudding. Mound the meringue over the top. Spread with the back of the spoon so the meringue touches all sides of the casserole; swirl to form peaks.

7. Bake in the preheated hot oven (425°) for 5 minutes, or until the peaks of the meringue are golden brown. Serve immediately.

Red, White and Blue Waffle Shortcake

Belgian Waffles

Electric Belgian waffle makers or irons are available in a variety of shapes and sizes—square and round, with 1, 2 or 4 waffles to a griddle. Here's our basic recipe for crisp and puffy Belgian waffles, and 7 ideas for quickly transforming them into festive desserts.

Makes enough batter for 6 servings.

Nutrient Value Per Serving (without toppings): 392 calories, 9 g protein, 25 g fat, 34 g carbohydrate, 361 mg sodium, 213 mg cholesterol.

1¾ **cups** sifted *all-purpose flour*
 2 **teaspoons baking powder**
 ¼ **teaspoon salt**
 2 **tablespoons sugar**
 3 **eggs, separated**
 1 **cup milk**
 1 **cup heavy cream**
 1 **tablespoon plus 1 teaspoon grated lemon rind**
 3 **tablespoons melted butter**

1. Sift together the flour, baking powder, salt and sugar in a large bowl.
2. Beat the egg yolks slightly in a small bowl. Stir in the milk and cream. Blend in the flour mixture until smooth. Stir in the lemon rind and melted butter.
3. Beat the egg whites, in a medium-size bowl until stiff, but not dry peaks form. Fold gently into the batter.
4. Bake in the waffle iron, following the manufacturer's instructions. Serve hot, sprinkle with 10X (confectioners') sugar and garnished with sliced fresh fruit. Or serve with one of the following toppings.

Red, White and Blue Waffle Shortcake For each serving, cut large square or round waffles into triangles or wedges. Layer with whipped cream or thawed frozen whipped topping, strawberries and fresh or frozen blueberries. Garnish with whipped cream and fresh mint leaves.

Maple Blueberry Topping Combine ¼ cup of brown sugar and 1 tablespoon of cornstarch in a saucepan. Gradually blend in ½ cup of maple syrup and ½ cup of water. Cook, stirring until thick and bubbly, for 1 minute. Stir in 2 cups of fresh or frozen blueberries, 1 tablespoon of lemon juice and ⅛ teaspoon of nutmeg. Cool slightly. Serve over the waffles with a dollop of sour cream.

Baked Alaska Meringue: Beat 3 egg whites and ⅛ teaspoon of cream of tartar in a bowl until foamy. Gradually beat in 9 tablespoons of granulated sugar, 1 tablespoon at a time, until stiff peaks form. Raspberry Sauce: Purée a thawed package (10 ounces) of frozen raspberries in juice in a blender. Strain. Place 1 tablespoon of cornstarch in a small saucpan. Blend in the purée. Bring to boiling, stirring; cook for 1 minute. Cool. Place 1 scoop or slice of vanilla or strawberry ice cream for each serving on waffle(s), leaving a ½-inch border. Spread evenly with the meringue, sealing the edges to the waffle. Sprinkle with sliced almonds. Hold in the freezer, for up to 2 or 3 hours. To serve, bake in a preheated very hot oven (450°) until golden, for 3 to 5 minutes. Serve with Raspberry Sauce. Makes 6 servings.

Banana Split Waffles For each serving, cut square waffles in half into triangles and place in a dish. Slice or split a small banana lengthwise; arrange over the waffles. Add small scoops of vanilla, strawberry and chocolate ice creams. Spoon prepared strawberry, pineapple and chocolate toppings over the top. Garnish with whipped cream and chopped nuts.

Black Forest Waffles Cherry Sauce: Drain a 8¾-ounce can of dark sweet pitted cherries, reserving the syrup. Place 2 teaspoons of cornstarch in a small saucepan. Blend in the reserved syrup and 2 tablespoons of port wine. Bring to boiling, stirring; cook for 1 minute. Stir in the cherries. Cool slightly. Spoon 3 to 4 tablespoons of sauce over each serving of waffles. Top with whipped cream, shaved semi-sweet chocolate and maraschino cherry.

Peach & Chocolate Shortcake For each serving, stack 2 small waffles on a serving plate with drained, canned, sliced peaches and whipped cream or thawed frozen whipped topping. Top with a dollop of whipped cream and peach slices. Serve with warm chocolate fudge sauce.

Cherry-Cheese Waffles Ricotta-Cheese Topping: Beat 1 cup of ricotta cheese with 4 tablespoons of sugar, 2 teaspoons of amaretto liqueur and ½ teaspoon of grated lemon rind. For each serving, spoon ¼ cup of cherry pie filling over 2 overlapped small waffles. Garnish with 2 to 3 tablespoons of ricotta topping and grated lemon rind.

Homemade Granola Crunch

Homemade Granola Crunch

Serve with low-fat milk for breakfast or a snack and use in some of our other recipes.

Bake at 300° for 1 hour.
Makes 9 cups.

Nutrient Value Per ½ Cup: 288 calories, 6 g protein, 15 g fat, 37 g carbohydrate, 134 mg sodium, 0 mg cholesterol.

4   cups old-fashioned oats (11 ounces)
1   cup flaked coconut (about 2 ounces)
1   cup coarsely chopped pecans (4 ounces)
½   cup unsalted sunflower seeds (2½ ounces)
½   cup wheat germ (about 2 ounces)
½   cup firmly packed light brown sugar
1   teaspoon ground cinnamon
1   teaspoon salt
½   cup vegetable oil
½   cup water
2   tablespoons honey
1   teaspoon vanilla
1   cup raisins
1   cup coarsely chopped dates (about 5 ounces)

1. Preheat the oven to slow (300°). Lightly grease a 15½ x 10½ x 1-inch jelly-roll pan.
2. Combine the oats, coconut, pecans, sunflower seeds, wheat germ, sugar, cinnamon and salt in a large bowl.
3. Stir together the oil, water, honey and vanilla in a small bowl. Pour over the oat mixture; mix well. Spread the mixture evenly in the prepared jelly-roll pan.
4. Bake in the preheated slow oven (300°) for 1 hour, stirring every 15 minutes, until the mixture is golden brown and slightly crunchy. Cool in the pan on a wire rack. Stir in the raisins and dates. Store in an airtight container.

◪◪▣▣

Mint Bavarian with Chocolate Sauce

Makes 8 servings.

Nutrient Value Per Serving: 284 calories, 4 g protein, 16 g fat, 28 g carbohydrate, 98 mg sodium, 113 mg cholesterol.

1 envelope unflavored gelatin
½ cup sugar
1 cup milk
2 eggs, separated
¼ cup green créme de menthe
¾ cup heavy cream
     Whipped cream for garnish
     Fresh mint leaves (optional)
     Chocolate Sauce (recipe follows)

1. Generously grease or spray with nonstick vegetable cooking spray a 5-cup decorative mold. Set aside.
2. Combine the gelatin and ¼ cup of the sugar in a small saucepan; mix well. Stir in the milk and egg yolks; blend well. Let stand for 1 minute. Cook over low heat, stirring constantly, until hot and the gelatin is dissolved, for about 4 minutes. Do not let boil.
3. Remove the saucepan from the heat. Stir in the créme de menthe. Pour into a medium-size bowl. Place in a large bowl of ice and water to speed setting. Stir often until the mixture begins to thicken, for about 15 minutes.
4. Meanwhile, beat the cream in a small bowl until soft peaks form. Refrigerate.
5. Beat the egg whites in the small bowl until frothy. Gradually beat in the remaining ¼ cup of sugar until soft peaks form.
6. Fold the beaten whites into the gelatin mixture. Then fold in the whipped cream. Pour into the prepared mold. Chill until firm, for at least 5 hours or overnight.
7. To serve, unmold onto a serving dish. Garnish with additional whipped cream, and the fresh mint, if you wish. Serve with the Chocolate Sauce.

Chocolate Sauce: Melt 2 squares (1 ounce each) of semisweet chocolate and 1 tablespoon of butter in the top of a double boiler over simmering water. Blend in 3 tablespoons of sugar, ⅛ teaspoon of salt and 1 tablespoon of light corn syrup. Stir in ¼ cup of milk and 2 tablespoons of heavy cream. Cook, stirring occasionally, for 10 minutes, or until slightly thickened. Remove the top from the double boiler. Add ½ teaspoon of vanilla. Cool to room temperature before serving. Makes about ¾ cup.

◪◪▣▣

Strawberry Port Wine Sauce

Spoon over vanilla or chocolate ice cream.

Makes about 3 cups.

Nutrient Value Per ¼ Cup: 53 calories, 0 g protein, 0 g fat, 13 g carbohydrate, 1 mg sodium, 0 mg cholesterol.

2 pints fresh strawberries
½ cup sugar
1 tablespoon cornstarch
½ cup port wine

1. Wash, hull and halve the strawberries. Purée through a food mill or in a food processor.
2. Combine the purée and sugar in a medium-size saucepan; stir to blend.
3. Dissolve the cornstarch in the wine in a small bowl. Stir into the berry mixture.
4. Cook over medium heat, stirring frequently, until the sauce thickens and bubbles, for about 5 minutes. Do not overcook.
5. Cool to room temperature. Store in a tightly covered container in the refrigerator.

Fresh Lemonade (page 285)

Best Beverages

Beverages can do so much to enhance a meal. Certain foods are just naturals with certain drinks, like wine and cheese, beer and pizza or milk and cookies. Whether you prefer to casually sip a beverage all through your meal, or to save it for shortly afterward, you now have several flavorful drinks to choose from and to enjoy.

Frothy cold drinks can cool the heat wave on a sweltering summer day. How about a tall frosty glass of ice-cold Fresh Lemonade (page 285)? It's garnished with a bright yellow lemon wedge and clean, crisp mint leaves. Or on a bone-chilling winter's evening, gently swirl a cinnamon stick in a mug of steaming Brandied Cider (page 287) beside a blazing fire.

Like all foods, beverages are more inviting when served in complementary containers. The beauty of a Hawaiian Sunrise (page 282), for instance, can only be fully appreciated in a crystal-clear, stemmed round goblet. Children will love a yogurt-based Banana-Berry Shake (page 284) if you serve it in an old-fashioned soda fountain glass with a strawberry nestled on top.

Even if you're not planning a meal, why not fix a favorite beverage just for yourself? After all, it's always beverage time: morning, noon or night, summer or winter, with family, friends—or just to spoil yourself.

 Quick

 Make Ahead

Entertaining

Low Cost

Low Calorie

Punches

Punch

An alcoholic beverage introduced to England from India, made with five ingredients—a spirit, lime, sugar, spices and water. The word is derived from the Hindi word *panch,* meaning five. Nowadays a punch may be made of any number of ingredients, served hot or cold and contain no alcohol or spirit.

◥ ◰ ⛉

Fruit-Tea Punch

A nonalcoholic punch that's perfect for any and all summer gatherings.

Makes 20 servings.

Nutrient Value Per Serving: 57 calories, .61 g protein, .13 g fat, 14 g carbohydrate, 10 mg sodium, 0 mg cholesterol.

¾ **cup natural lemon-flavored iced tea mix**
    with sugar
4 **cups water**
1 **can (6 ounces) frozen orange juice**
    concentrate
1 **can (6 ounces) frozen pineapple**
    juice concentrate
2 **cups sliced strawberries**
2 **cups melon balls**
1 **cup blueberries**
1 **bottle (28 ounces) club soda, chilled**
    Ice Ring (recipe follows)

1. Stir together the lemon-flavored iced tea mix with the sugar, water and orange and pineapple juice concentrates in a large punch bowl or pitcher until blended. Chill until ready to serve.
2. Just before serving, stir in the strawberries, melon, blueberries and club soda. Slide in the Ice Ring.

Ice Ring: Pour water, club soda or mineral water into a decorative mold or container that will fit inside the punch bowl. Freeze for 8 hours, or overnight. To release, dip the mold or container quickly in and out of a pan of hot water, or allow to stand at room temperature for 5 minutes, then invert onto a cookie sheet. Slide the mold into a punch bowl.

◥ ◰ ⛉

Della Robbia Fruit Punch

Luca della Robbia, a 15th-centruy Florentine sculptor and painter, sculpted beautiful wall wreaths decorated with birds and fruit. Our holiday punch is cooled by a lovely wreathlike ice ring.

Makes about 14 servings.

Nutrient Value Per Cup: 187 calories, 1 g protein, 0 g fat, 49 g carbohydrate, 7 mg sodium, 0 mg cholesterol.

Ice Ring:
1 **bunch green grapes**
1 **can (8 ounces) apricot halves,**
    well drained
1 **lime, thinly sliced**
1 **navel orange, thinly sliced**
½ **pint fresh strawberries**
    Fresh sprigs of mint
2½ **cups ginger ale**
½ **cup fresh lemon juice, strained**
Punch:
2 **packages (10 ounces each) frozen**
    strawberries in syrup, thawed
3 **cups apricot nectar, chilled**
3 **cups club soda, chilled**
1 **cup fresh lemon juice, chilled**
1 **can (6 ounces) orange juice concentrate,**
    thawed
1 **cup sugar**
1 **bottle (28 ounces) ginger ale, chilled**

1. Prepare the Ice Ring: Arrange small bunches of the green grapes, apricot halves, lime slices, orange slices, strawberries and mint decoratively in a 1¼-quart, 8-inch-diameter ring mold. Combine the ginger ale and lemon juice in a measuring cup. Carefully pour over the fruit. Freeze until firm.
2. When ready to serve, prepare the Punch: Combine the thawed frozen strawberries, apricot nectar, club soda, lemon juice, orange juice concentrate and sugar in a large punch bowl. Stir until the sugar is dissolved. Pour in the ginger ale.
3. Remove the ice ring from the freezer. Let stand for 3 or 4 minutes, or until it is slightly melted and can be removed easily from the mold. Place the ice ring in the punch bowl. Garnish the ice with mint leaves, if you wish.

Holiday Punch

Our versatile holiday punch, with or without Champagne.

Makes 20 servings (10 cups).

Nutrient Value Per Serving: 112 calories, 0 g protein, 0 g fat, 16 g carbohydrate, 4 mg sodium, 0 mg cholesterol.

- **1 cup Crème de Cassis (black currant liqueur)**
- **2 tablespoons lime juice**
- **3 to 4 tablespoons honey**
- **1 quart cranberry juice, chilled**
- **1 bottle (750 ml.) Champagne, chilled***
- **1 bottle or can (12 ounces) carbonated water (seltzer or soda water), chilled Ice cubes (optional)**

1. Stir together the Cassis, lime juice and honey in a punch bowl or large pitcher until blended. Add the cranberry juice. Chill until ready to serve.

2. Just before serving, add the Champagne and carbonated water. Add the ice, if you wish.

*Note: One quart of carbonated water may be substituted for the Champagne.

Autumn Harvest Punch

Makes 20 servings (10 cups).

Nutrient Value Per Serving: 109 calories, .33 g protein, .51 g fat, 26 g carbohydrate, 13 mg sodium, 1 mg cholesterol.

- **2 quarts apple cider**
- **1 container (6 ounces) frozen grape juice concentrate, thawed**
- **1 pint orange sherbet**
- **1 bottle (750 ml.) ginger ale, chilled**

1. Combine the cider and grape juice in a 5- to 6-quart punch bowl. Chill until ready to serve.

2. Just before serving, scoop out the sherbet and float on top of the punch. Add the ginger ale. Stir gently to combine the ingredients and make the top look frothy.

Cocktails

Strawberry Kir

This is a twist on the summertime Continental cooler. Strawberry liqueur replaces crème de cassis.

Makes 1 serving.

Nutrient Value Per Serving: 181 calories, .11 g protein, 0 g fat, 14 g carbohydrate, 6 mg sodium, 0 mg cholesterol.

- **1 ounce strawberry liqueur**
- **4 ounces dry white wine**

Pour the strawberry liqueur into the bottom of a chilled stemmed glass. Carefully pour the chilled white wine down the side of the glass. Serve with a stirrer to blend both of the layers before drinking.

Minted Lemon and Lime

A new drink for the warm weather. Crème de menthe combines with lemon-lime soda.

Makes 1 serving.

Nutrient Value Per Serving: 207 calories, 0 g protein, 0 g fat, 28 g carbohydrate, 0 mg sodium, 0 mg cholesterol.

- **1½ ounces crème de menthe**
- **6 ounces lemon-lime soda**
- **2 lemon wedges**
- **1 maraschino cherry**

Fill a glass with ice cubes. Pour the crème de menthe down the side and add the lemon-lime soda. Garnish with a kabob of lemon wedges and a maraschino cherry, if you wish.

Strawberry Kir (page 279), Minted Lemon and Lime (page

ngria Spritzer (page 282) Mexican Margarita (page 282), Rosé Spritzer (page 282)

Mexican Margaritas

This version is mixed in the blender.

Makes 2 servings.

Nutritional analysis not available.

> **Coarse salt**
> **Lime wedge**
> **1½ cups ice cubes**
> **1½ ounces Tequila**
> **4 ounces Margarita mixer**

1. Pour the salt into a shallow saucer; moisten the rim of two 4-ounce stem glasses with the lime wedges; dip the glasses into salt to coat evenly. Allow to dry.
2. Place the ice cubes in the container of an electric blender; add the Tequila and Margarita mixer. Cover the blender; process on high speed for 10 seconds, or until the mixture is smooth; strain into the prepared glasses, dividing evenly.

Rosé Spritzer

Mineral water, rather than club soda, adds a new touch.

Makes 1 servings.

Nutrient Value Per Serving: 99 calories, .11 g protein, 0 g fat, 5 g carbohydrate, 6 mg sodium, 0 mg cholesterol.

> **4 ounces rosé wine**
> **4 ounces mineral water, chilled**
> **Lemon slice**

Fill a glass with ice and add the rosé wine, then the mineral water; garnish the glass with a lemon slice.

Sangria Spritzer

Red wine and orange juice plus club soda and fruits make such a refreshing combo.

Makes 1 serving.

Nutrient Value Per Serving: 63 calories, .26 g protein, .01 g fat, 6 g carbohydrate, 35 mg sodium, 0 mg cholesterol.

> **2 ounces red wine**
> **1 ounce orange juice**
> **Club soda, chilled**
> **Fruit kabob of orange and lime wedges**

Fill a tall glass with ice; stir in the red wine and orange juice until blended. Fill with the club soda and stir in the kabob.

Scorpion

Very exotic and a great favorite in Polynesian restaurants.

Makes 1 servings.

Nutrient Value Per Serving: 295 calories, .60 g protein, .12 g fat, 15 g carbohydrate, 1 mg sodium, 0 mg cholesterol.

> **¼ cup dark rum**
> **2 tablespoons brandy**
> **¼ cup fresh orange juice**
> **3 tablespoons fresh lemon juice**
> **1 tablespoon orgeat syrup or amaretto liqueur**
> **1 cup crushed ice**
> **Gardenia**

Combine the rum, brandy, orange and lemon juices, orgeat and ice in the container of an electric blender. Cover; whirl until well blended. Serve over ice cubes in a large footed champagne-type glass. Garnish with a gardenia.

Hawaiian Sunrise

Makes 1 serving.

Nutrient Value Per Serving: 277 calories, .85 g protein, .16 g fat, 28 g carbohydrate, 2 mg sodium, 0 mg cholesterol.

> **2 teaspoons grenadine syrup**
> **Ice cubes**
> **¼ cup light rum**
> **1 tablespoon orange-flavored liqueur**
> **¼ cup unsweetened pineapple juice**
> **¼ cup fresh orange juice**
> **2 tablespoons fresh lime juice**
> **1 tablespoon fresh lemon juice**
> **Lemon slice and strawberry**

1. Pour the grenadine syrup in the bottom of a large, round, footed (about a 16-ounce) glass. Fill the glass with ice.
2. Combine the rum, orange liqueur and pineapple, orange, lime and lemon juices in a small pitcher; mix well. Carefully pour over the ice. Stir slightly, if necessary, to give the sunrise effect. Garnish with the lemon and strawberry.

Pineapple-Mint Cooler

Sparkling pineapple juice with the cool zip of mint.

Makes about 12 servings.

Nutrient Value Per Serving: 84 calories, .37 g protein, .04 g fat, 18 g carbohydrate, 3 mg sodium, 0 mg cholesterol.

- **4 cups unsweetened pineapple juice, chilled**
- **½ cup lemon juice**
- **¼ cup green crème de menthe**
- **1 bottle (28 ounces) lemon-lime carbonated beverage**
  Canned or fresh pineapple slices

1. Combine the pineapple and lemon juices and crème de menthe in a 2½-quart container; mix well. (Can be prepared ahead up to this point.)
2. Add the carbonated beverage just before serving. Serve over ice cubes in 8-ounce highball glasses; or pour over an ice ring in a punch bowl. Garnish each serving with the pineapple.

Cold Drinks

Very Berry Milk Punch

Makes 3 servings.

Nutrient Value Per Serving: 127 calories, 6 g protein, 4 g fat, 18 g carbohydrate, 90 mg sodium, 15 mg cholesterol.

- **1 cup milk**
- **1 container (8 ounces) vanilla yogurt**
- **6 medium-size strawberries**
- **2 teaspoons honey**
  Ice cubes

1. Combine the milk, yogurt, strawberries, honey and ice cubes in the container of an electric blender. Cover; whirl at high speed until all of the ice pieces are gone, for about 1 minute.
2. Pour into three 12-ounce glasses. Garnish each with a strawberry and serve with a straw.

Double Orange Fizz

Makes 1 serving.

Nutrient Value Per Serving: 229 calories, 2 g protein, 2 g fat, 53 g carbohydrate, 46 mg sodium, 7 mg cholesterol.

- **½ cup chilled orange juice**
  Lemon or pineapple sherbet
- **½ cup chilled orange soda**
  Orange slices

Pour the juice into a 12-ounce glass. Add 1 scoop of the sherbet. Add the orange soda. Serve with a straw and a long-handled spoon.

Pink Lemon-Lime Cooler

Makes 1 serving.

Nutrient Value Per Serving: 101 calories, .05 g protein, .04 g fat, 26 g carbohydrate, 3 mg sodium, 0 mg cholesterol.

- **⅓ cup chilled cranberry juice**
- **⅔ cup chilled lemon-lime soda**
  Ice cubes
  Lime wedge

Pour the cranberry juice and the lemon-lime soda over the ice cubes in a 12-ounce glass. Squeeze the juice from the lime wedge into the drink and add the wedge for garnish. Stir lightly and serve with a straw.

Tips for Making Perfect Tea

- Rinse teapot with boiling water, then drain.
- Bring fresh cold tap water to a full rolling boil.
- Use 1 teaspoon of loose tea or 1 tea bag for each cup of water.
- When making iced tea, use 50 percent more tea to allow for melting ice.
- Allow tea to steep 3 to 5 minutes; then serve with sugar and lemon or milk.
- Tea for iced tea should be kept at room temperature until ready to serve. If refrigerated, it may turn murky or cloudy. Although the flavor is not affected, the clear appearance can be restored by adding a little boiling water.

Apple Iced Tea

Makes 4 servings.

Nutrient Value Per Serving: 34 calories, .18 g protein, .10 g fat, 9 g carbohydrate, 5 mg sodium, 0 mg cholesterol.

2 cups boiling water
3 tea bags
1 cup apple juice
¼ cup lemon juice

Pour the boiling water over the tea bags; steep for 3 minutes; remove the tea bags; let stand at room temperature until ready to serve. Combine the tea, apple juice and lemon juice in a pitcher. Pour into ice-filled glasses. Sweeten to taste; garnish with mint leaves, if you wish.

Sunrise Milk Shake

Makes 1 serving.

Nutrient Value Per Serving: 213 calories, 9 g protein, 8 g fat, 27 g carbohydrate, 121 mg sodium, 35 mg cholesterol.

1 cup chilled milk
1½ tablespoons thawed orange juice
    concentrate
1 teaspoon honey
    Ice cubes

Combine the milk, orange juice concentrate and honey in a 12-ounce glass. Stir until well blended and smooth. Add the ice cubes.

Banana-Berry Shake

Banana-Berry Shake

Makes 1 serving.

Nutrient Value Per Serving: 187 calories, 9 g protein, 3 g fat, 33 g carbohydrate, 82 mg sodium, 7 mg cholesterol.

½ cup low-fat plain yogurt
⅛ cup water
1 cup fresh or frozen unsweetened
    strawberries
½ small banana
1 tablespoon wheat germ
⅛ teaspoon ground cinnamon
¼ teaspoon lemon juice
    Artificial sweetener (optional)

Combine the yogurt, water, strawberries, banana, wheat germ, cinnamon, lemon juice and artificial sweetener (if using) in the container of an electric blender. Cover; whirl at high speed until smooth, for about 30 seconds. Serve immediately.

Fruit Smoothie

Fruit Smoothie

Makes 5 servings (8 ounces each).

Nutrient Value Per Serving: 135 calories, 3 g protein, 0 g fat, 32 g carbohydrate, 27 mg sodium, 1 mg cholesterol.

**1   can (6 ounces) frozen orange juice
      concentrate
1   large ripe banana, sliced (1 cup), OR:
      1½ cups fresh or frozen dry-pack
      strawberries OR: 1½ cups fresh, frozen
      dry-pack or drained canned peaches
1   cup skim milk
1   cup water
2   tablespoons honey
5   ice cubes**

1. Combine the orange juice concentrate, banana or other fruit, skim milk, water and honey in the container of an electric blender. Cover; whirl at high speed until thick and smooth, for about 1 minute.

2. Add the ice cubes, one at a time, and blend until smooth and frothy. Garnish with a whole strawberry, if you wish. Serve.

Fresh Lemonade

Make the lemonade syrup ahead and refrigerate. When ready for a glass of lemonade, simply combine water and ice with a little syrup; make it as lemony as you wish.

Makes 6 servings.

Nutrient Value Per Serving: 127 calories, 0 g protein, 0 g fat, 35 g carbohydrate, 1 mg sodium, 0 mg cholesterol.

**1   teaspoon grated lemon rind
1   cup lemon juice (4 to 5 lemons)
¾   to 1 cup sugar
4½ cups water
1   lemon, sliced
      Ice cubes
      Fresh mint leaves or lemon slices for
      garnish (optional)**

1. Prepare the lemon syrup: Combine the lemon rind, lemon juice and sugar in a 4-cup glass measure; stir to dissolve the sugar. Chill, covered, until ready to use.

2. Lemonade by the pitcher: Combine the lemon syrup, the 4½ cups of water and the lemon slices in a large pitcher. Stir to mix. Add the ice cubes just before serving. Garnish with the mint leaves or lemon slices, if you wish.

3. Lemonade by the glass: Measure 3 tablespoons of the lemon syrup (or more or less according to taste) into a tall 10- or 12-ounce glass. Add the ice cubes and water; stir to mix. Garnish with the mint or lemon slices, if you wish.

Lemon Spritzer: Measure 2 to 3 tablespoons of the lemon syrup into a 10-ounce stemmed glass. Add chilled club soda and garnish with a lemon wedge.

Hot Drinks

Café Brûlot

A New Orleans classic flamed just before serving.

Makes 8 servings.

Nutrient Value Per Serving: 45 calories, 0 g protein, 0 g fat, 2 g carbohydrate, 1 mg sodium, 0 mg cholesterol.

- **5 lumps sugar**
- **1 cup brandy**
- **4 cups very strong hot coffee**
- **1 3-inch piece stick cinnamon**
- **6 whole cloves**
- **1 piece vanilla bean**
- **1 3-inch strip orange rind**

1. Soak a sugar lump in the brandy, remove and set aside. Add the remaining 4 sugar lumps to the brandy.
2. Pour the coffee into a chafing dish or metal bowl with a flame underneath it. Add the cinnamon stick, cloves, vanilla bean and orange rind. Stir together. Add the brandy.
3. Place the brandy-soaked lump of sugar on a serving ladle and ignite. Add, flaming, to the Café Brûlot and serve immediately.

Cappucino

A sophisticated Italian after-dinner coffee. The name comes from the color of the coffee—that of the robe of a Capuchin monk.

Makes 8 servings.

Nutrient Value Per Serving: 58 calories, 3 g protein, 3 g fat, 4 g carbohydrate, 46 mg sodium, 13 mg cholesterol.

- **3 cups hot espresso coffee**
- **3 cups scalded milk**
  Ground cinnamon
  Ground nutmeg

Combine the coffee and milk. Pour into heated demitasse cups; sprinkle with cinamon and nutmeg. Add some sugar to taste, if you wish.

Spiced Coffee Vienna

Makes 6 servings.

Nutrient Value Per Serving: 2 calories, .01 g protein, 0 g fat, .24 g carbohydrate, 1 mg sodium, 0 mg cholesterol.

- **3 cups extra-strong hot coffee**
- **2 3-inch pieces stick cinnamon**
- **4 whole cloves**
- **4 whole allspice**
  Softly whipped cream
  Ground nutmeg

1. Pour the coffee into a chafing dish with a flame underneath. Add the cinnamon, cloves and allspice. Steep the mixture over very low heat for 10 to 15 minutes. Strain.
2. Pour into heatproof wine glasses or cups; top with the cream and nutmeg. Serve with sugar.

Blazing Spiced Wine Punch

Makes about 24 four-ounce servings.

Nutrient Value Per Serving: 155 calories, 2 g protein, 3 g fat, 15 g carbohydrate, 6 mg sodium, 0 mg cholesterol.

- **¼ cup sugar**
- **2 4-inch pieces stick cinnamon, broken**
- **8 whole cardamom seed pods, crushed**
- **8 whole cloves**
- **4 whole allspice**
  Thin rind from 1 orange (no white)
- **½ cup water**
- **½ gallon (8 cups) dry red wine**
- **2 cups ruby port wine**
- **1 cup raisins**
- **1 cup whole blanched almonds**
- **1 orange, sliced**
- **20 tiny sugar cubes (½-inch size)**
- **1 2-inch piece lemon rind stuck with 2 whole cloves**
- **1 cup brandy, warmed**

1. Combine the sugar, cinnamon, cardamom, cloves, allspice, orange rind and water in a small saucepan; bring to boiling. Cover; simmer over low heat for 5 minutes. Let stand for several hours, or until ready to make the punch. Strain, discarding the spices and orange rind.
2. Just before serving, combine the wine, port, raisins and almonds in a large saucepan; add the strained spice mixture. Bring just to boiling. Pour into a warm, heatproof punch bowl; float the orange slices on top.

3. Place the sugar cubes and lemon rind in a large ladle; add about ¼ cup of the warm brandy; carefully pour the remaining brandy over the surface of the punch. Hold the ladle over the punch bowl. Ignite the mixture in the ladle; rotate and shake the ladle until the sugar is almost dissolved.

4. Lower the ladle into the punch to ignite the brandy floating on top; stir slowly a few times. When the flames have died, serve in small mugs or punch cups with a few raisins and almonds in each serving. Give each guest a spoon to eat the raisins and almonds.

Wassail Bowl

A traditional punch from medieval England whose name means "good health."

Bake apples at 350° for 10 minutes.
Makes 12 half-cup servings.

Nutrient Value Per Serving: 141 calories, 2 g protein, 2 g fat, 25 g carbohydrate, 19 mg sodium, 69 mg cholesterol.

  2 **Red Delicious apples**
  2 **whole cloves**
  2 **whole allspice**
  2 **whole cardamom pods, crushed**
  1 **3-inch piece stick cinnamon**
  1 **quart ale**
  ½ **teaspoon ground ginger**
  ½ **teaspoon ground nutmeg**
  1 **cup sugar**
1½ **cups dry sherry**
  3 **eggs, separated**

1. Core the apples; cut crosswise into ¼-inch-thick slices. Place the slices in a shallow baking pan.

2. Bake in a moderate oven (350°) for 10 minutes, or until the apples are tender, but still firm enough to hold their shape; reserve.

3. Tie the cloves, allspice, cardamom and cinnamon in a small piece of cheesecloth. Place in a kettle or Dutch oven with 1 cup of the ale, the ginger and nutmeg. Heat very slowly for 20 minutes over low heat (do not allow to boil). Remove the spice bag. Stir in the remaining ale, ½ cup of the sugar and the sherry. Heat slowly for 20 minutes.

4. Beat the egg whites in a large bowl until foamy-white. Slowly beat in the remaining ½ cup of sugar until soft peaks form.

5. Beat the egg yolks in a small bowl until light; fold into the beaten whites. Slowly beat the hot ale mixture into the eggs until the mixture is smooth.

6. Carefully pour the wassail into a heatproof punch bowl; float the baked apple slices on top. Serve in heatproof mugs with a cinnamon stick in each, if you wish.

Brandied Cider

Makes 8 servings.

Nutrient Value Per Serving: 211 calories, .18 g protein, .37 g fat, 30 g carbohydrate, 9 mg sodium, 0 mg cholesterol.

  2 **quarts apple cider**
1½ **teaspoons whole cloves**
  ¾ **teaspoon whole allspice**
  2 **three-inch pieces stick cinnamon**
1¼ **cups California brandy**
     Orange or lemon slices (optional)

1. Combine the cider, cloves, allspice and cinnamon in a large saucepan. Bring slowly to boiling; lower the heat. Simmer for 15 minutes. Remove the spices. Add the brandy.

2. Pour into a 2½- to 3-quart punch bowl or individual cups. Add the orange or lemon slices to each cup of cider, if you wish.

Overstuffed Italian Bread Pizza (page 291)

Meals in Minutes

Time is something that most of us never seem to have enough of. So we've put together 10 complete meals that can be ready to serve in 30 minutes or less, complete with a main course, accompaniments, bread, dessert and even beverage selections. We've given extra attention to recipes and foods that are quick and easy to prepare, but we haven't sacrificed nutrition.

Our menus are an assorted and taste-tempting bunch. Some, such as the Chicken Swiss Menu (page 292), are elegant enough to entertain guests with, while children will be elated with the 28-Minute Pizza Parlor (page 290).

Along with each menu is a complete shopping list—with check-off boxes—plus a step-by-step work plan to make sure you spend as little time in the kitchen as possible. We've even included the staple items needed, though you probably already have them on hand. If not, just add them to the list.

After trying just one of these menus, you'll be amazed at how much you can do in just half an hour! Then see how many other Meals in Minutes you can create using other recipes from our book. A hint: Look for recipes with the symbol.

Quick

Make Ahead

Entertaining

Low Cost

Low Calorie

28-MINUTE PIZZA PARLOR

Overstuffed Italian Bread Pizza*
Green Salad
Creamy Italian Dressing*
Raspberry-Almond Dream*

*Recipe Included

SHOPPING LIST

- [ ] 1 package (3½ ounces) sliced pepperoni
- [ ] 1 package (8 ounces) shredded mozzarella
- [ ] Grated Parmesan cheese
- [ ] 1 small container dairy sour cream
- [ ] Salad greens
- [ ] 1 bunch curly parsley
- [ ] 1 lemon
- [ ] 8 oil-cured black olives
- [ ] 1 small jar roasted red peppers
- [ ] 1 small jar marinara spaghetti sauce
- [ ] 1 large loaf Italian bread
- [ ] 1 package (12 ounces) individually frozen raspberries
- [ ] 1 container (8 ounces) frozen non-dairy whipped topping

TO HAVE ON HAND
- garlic • leaf oregano • pepper • olive oil
- mayonnaise • Dijon-style mustard • 10X (confectioners') sugar • almond extract

WORK PLAN

1
28 minutes before serving time: Prepare dessert, an easy put-together of frozen raspberries and whipped topping.

2
Spoon the mixture into four dessert dishes; refrigerate, or freeze.

3
18 minutes before serving time: Clean and assemble ingredients for green salad. Make Creamy Italian Dressing; refrigerate.

4
10 minutes before serving time: Toast split Italian loaf slices. Layer "pizza" ingredients on top. Broil pizzas in toaster oven for about 2 minutes until cheese is melted and bubbly!

Overstuffed Italian Bread Pizza

Makes 4 pizzas.

Nutrient Value Per Pizza: 509 calories, 23 g protein, 29 g fat, 40 g carbohydrate, 1,351 mg sodium, 64 mg cholesterol.

- **1 large loaf Italian bread (about ½ pound), cut in half horizontally and crosswise**
- **½ cup prepared marinara spaghetti sauce**
- **1 package (8 ounces) shredded mozzarella cheese**
- **16 slices pepperoni (part of 3½-ounce package)**
- **¼ cup drained roasted red peppers (part of 7-ounce jar), cut into strips**
- **8 oil-cured black olives, halved and pitted**
- **2 tablespoons grated Parmesan cheese**
- **1 teaspoon olive oil**
- **½ teaspoon leaf oregano, crumbled**

1. Place the bread on the broiler rack. Broil 4 inches from the heat, for 2 minutes on each side, or until crisp.

2. Spread the cut sides of the bread with the marinara sauce. Sprinkle with the mozzarella cheese and top with the pepperoni, peppers, olives, Parmesan, oil and oregano, dividing the ingredients equally.

3. Broil the pizzas for 2 minutes until the cheese is melted and bubbly.

Creamy Italian Dressing

Makes about 1 cup.

Nutrient Value Per 2 Tablespoons: 132 calories, 1 g protein, 14 g fat, 1 g carbohydrate, 115 mg sodium, 14 mg cholesterol.

- **½ cup dairy sour cream**
- **½ cup mayonnaise**
- **¼ cup chopped parsley**
- **1½ teaspoons lemon juice**
- **1½ teaspoons Dijon-style mustard**
- **1 or 2 cloves garlic, finely chopped**
- **¼ teaspoon leaf oregano, crumbled**
- **⅛ teaspoon pepper**

Combine the sour cream, mayonnaise, parsley, lemon juice, mustard, garlic, oregano and pepper in a bowl. Mix until well combined. Store in an airtight container in the refrigerator for up to 1 week.

Creamy Garlic Dressing

Reduced Calorie

Makes about 1 cup.

Nutrient Value Per 1 Tablespoon: 42 calories, 0 g protein, 4 g fat, 2 g carbohydrate, 127 mg sodium, 5 mg cholesterol.

- **1 cup mayonnaise-type salad dressing OR: reduced calorie mayonnaise**
- **¼ cup chopped fresh parsley**
- **1½ teaspoons lemon juice**
- **1½ teaspoons Dijon-style mustard**
- **1 or 2 cloves garlic, finely chopped**
- **¼ teaspoon leaf oregano, crumbled**
- **⅛ teaspoon pepper**

Beat together the dressing, parsley, lemon juice, mustard, garlic, oregano and pepper with a whisk or wooden spoon in a bowl. Mix until well blended. Store in an airtight container in the refrigerator for up to 1 week.

Raspberry-Almond Dream

Makes 8 servings.

Nutrient Value Per Serving: 131 calories, 1 g protein, 7 g fat, 16 g carbohydrate, 7 mg sodium, 0 mg cholesterol.

- **1 package (12 ounces) individually frozen raspberries**
- **1 container (8 ounces) frozen nondairy whipped topping, thawed**
- **⅓ cup 10X (confectioners') sugar**
- **½ teaspoon almond extract**
  Frozen nondairy whipped topping for garnish (optional)

Place the raspberries in the container of an electric blender or food processor. Cover; whirl until puréed. Place the whipped topping in a large bowl. Gradually fold in the raspberry purée, 10X sugar and almond extract. Spoon into dessert dishes and refrigerate or freeze until ready to serve. Garnish with a dollop of the whipped topping, if you wish.

FAMILY OR COMPANY DINNER IN 30 MINUTES

*Chicken Swiss**
Long-Grain and Wild Rice
Buttered Broccoli
Rolls
Strawberry Cream   Chablis

Recipe Included

SHOPPING LIST

- ☐ 4 boneless skinned chicken breast halves (1½ pounds)
- ☐ 1¼ pounds broccoli
- ☐ 1 pint fresh strawberries
- ☐ 1 package (6 ounces) long-grain and wild rice mixture
- ☐ Plain dried bread crumbs
- ☐ 4 ounces Gruyère or Swiss cheese
- ☐ ½ pint heavy cream
- ☐ Small dinner rolls
- ☐ Raspberry-flavored brandy
- ☐ Chablis
- **TO HAVE ON HAND**
  - • butter • eggs • flour • milk • salt • pepper
  - • leaf thyme • 10X (confectioners') sugar
  - • Dijon-style mustard

WORK PLAN

1 Heat water for the rice.
2 Prepare the Chicken Swiss through Step 3.
3 Cook the rice, following the label directions.
4 Cut the broccoli into flowerets. Cook in 1 cup of water, covered, until tender. Drain.
5 Preheat the broiler.
6 Prepare dessert: Hull the strawberries; reserve 4. Purée the remaining berries with 2 teaspoons of brandy in the blender. Whip 1 cup of cream with 2 tablespoons 10X sugar. Fold in the purée; pour into 4 goblets. Garnish with the berries. Refrigerate.
7 Complete the chicken.

Chicken Swiss

Makes 4 servings.

Nutrient Value Per Serving: 545 calories, 54 g protein, 28 g fat, 17 g carbohydrate, 827 mg sodium, 241 mg cholesterol.

- **4 boneless skinned chicken breast halves (1½ pounds)**
- **1 egg**
- **1 tablespoon water**
- **2 tablespoons Dijon-style mustard**
- **½ cup plain dried bread crumbs**
- **½ teaspoon leaf thyme, crumbled**
- **¼ teaspoon salt**
- **Dash pepper**
- **All-purpose flour**
- **¼ cup (½ stick) butter**
- **1¼ cups milk**
- **1 cup shredded Gruyère or Swiss cheese (4 ounces)**

1. Gently flatten the chicken breasts between pieces of wax paper with a rolling pin or the flat side of a meat mallet.

2. Combine the egg, water and 1 tablespoon of the mustard in a bowl. Combine the bread crumbs, thyme, salt and pepper on a piece of wax paper. Coat the chicken evenly with the flour. Dip the chicken in the egg mixture; roll in the bread crumbs.

3. Sauté the chicken in 2 tablespoons of the butter in a skillet until golden and cooked through, for about 15 minutes.

4. Meanwhile, melt the remaining butter in a saucepan. Stir in 2 tablespoons of flour. Stir in the milk; cook, stirring, until thickened. Remove from the heat; stir in the cheese and remaining mustard.

5. Arrange the chicken in a broiler-proof serving dish. Pour the sauce over. Broil 3 inches from the heat until the sauce is bubbly and browned, for 3 minutes.

20–MINUTE PORK AND APPLE DINNER

*Herb-Sautéed Pork Cutlets**
Sautéed Apple Rings
*Whipped Potatoes with Bacon and Chives**
*Banana-Chocolate Chip Mousse**

*Recipe Included

SHOPPING LIST

- [ ] 4 boneless pork cutlets (1 pound)
- [ ] 1 envelope (3½ ounces) instant mashed potatoes
- [ ] 2 medium-size ripe bananas
- [ ] 2 apples
- [ ] Frozen chives
- [ ] Real bacon bits
- [ ] 1 small bag mini-chocolate pieces
- [ ] Brandy or apple juice
- [ ] ½ pint heavy cream

TO HAVE ON HAND
- milk • butter or margarine • vegetable oil
- garlic • leaf thyme • salt and pepper
- sugar • vanilla

WORK PLAN

1 Prepare the Banana-Chocolate Chip Mousse.
2 Prepare the Herb-Sautéed Pork Cutlets through Step 2.
3 Prepare the Whipped Potatoes with Bacon and Chives, following the package directions, but using 2 cups of milk, ¾ cup of water and 4 tablespoons of butter. After whipping the potatoes, beat in 1 tablespoon of real bacon bits, 2 tablespoons of frozen chopped chives and salt and pepper to taste.
4 Sauté the apple rings in a second skillet.
5 Complete the pork cutlets.

Herb Sautéed Pork Cutlets

Makes 4 servings.

Nutrient Value Per Serving: 299 calories, 25 g protein, 17 g fat, 0 g carbohydrate, 407 mg sodium, 87 mg cholesterol.

- **4 boneless pork loin cutlets (about 1 pound), trimmed of excess fat**
- **½ teaspoon salt**
- **¼ teaspoon leaf thyme, crumbled**
- **⅛ teaspoon pepper**
- **2 tablespoons butter or margarine**
- **1 tablespoon vegetable oil**
- **1 clove garlic, finely chopped**
- **¼ cup brandy or apple juice**

1. Pound the cutlets to a ¼-inch thickness between sheets of wax paper. Season with the salt, thyme and pepper.
2. Meanwhile, heat a large heavy skillet over medium-high heat. Add 1 tablespoon of the butter and the oil to the skillet. Sauté the cutlets for 3 minutes on each side, or until cooked through. Remove to a platter; cover. Discard the fat from the skillet.
3. Lower the heat to medium. Add the remaining 1 tablespoon of butter and garlic to the skillet. Sauté for 30 seconds. Add the brandy; cook for 30 seconds, or until the liquid is syrupy. Add any accumulated meat juices from the platter to the skillet; stir. Pour the sauce over the cutlets.

Banana-Chocolate Chip Mousse

Makes 4 servings.

Nutrient Value Per Serving: 249 calories, 2 g protein, 19 g fat, 21 g carbohydrate, 18 mg sodium, 61 mg cholesterol.

- **¾ cup heavy cream**
- **1 tablespoon sugar**
- **1 teaspoon vanilla**
- **2 medium-size ripe bananas, peeled and broken into chunks**
- **2 tablespoons mini-chocolate pieces**

1. Beat together the cream, sugar and vanilla in a small bowl until stiff.
2. Purée the bananas in a blender or food processor. Fold into the whipped cream along with the chocolate pieces. Spoon into 4 dessert dishes. Refrigerate for up to 1 hour.

14-MINUTE HOT DELI PLATTER

*Mile-High Hot Turkey Sandwich
with Chutney Mayonnaise**
*Deli Coleslaw
Low-Salt Potato Chips
Vanilla Ice Cream with
Butterscotch Sauce and
Chopped Walnuts*

*Recipe Included

SHOPPING LIST

- ☐ 1 pound sliced cooked turkey
- ☐ 1 head leaf lettuce
- ☐ 1 medium-size purple onion
- ☐ 1 medium-size sweet red pepper
- ☐ Vanilla ice cream
- ☐ 4 club rolls
- ☐ Deli coleslaw
- ☐ Chutney
- ☐ Low-salt potato chips
- ☐ Butterscotch sauce
- ☐ Chopped walnuts
  TO HAVE ON HAND
  - butter or margarine • mayonnaise
  - ground cumin • cayenne pepper

WORK PLAN

1 Prepare the Mile-High Hot Turkey Sandwich through Step 1.
2 Prepare the Chutney Mayonnaise.
3 Complete the Turkey Sandwich.
4 Place the coleslaw and chips in serving bowls.
5 Scoop the ice cream and top with sauce and walnuts when ready to serve.

Mile-High Hot Turkey Sandwich with Chutney Mayonnaise

Makes 4 open-faced sandwiches
(2 halves per serving).

Nutrient Value Per Sandwich: 537 calories, 40 g protein, 22 g fat, 44 g carbohydrate, 564 mg sodium, 103 mg cholesterol.

- **2 tablespoons butter or margarine**
- **1 pound thinly sliced cooked turkey breast**
- **4 club (rectangular) rolls, split and toasted**
  Leaf Lettuce
  Chutney Mayonnaise (recipe follows)
- **1 medium-size purple onion, cut into rings**
- **1 medium-size sweet red pepper, cut into rings**

1. Melt the butter in a large skillet over medium-high heat. Heat the sliced turkey, turning slices often, for about 3 minutes.
2. Place the rolls, cut-side up, on a work surface. Cover both halves of each roll with the leaf lettuce. Arrange the hot turkey over the lettuce and spread with the Chutney Mayonnaise. Top with the onion and red pepper.

Chutney Mayonnaise: Combine ¼ cup of mayonnaise, ¼ cup of chutney, ½ teaspoon of ground cumin and a pinch of cayenne pepper in the container of an electric blender or food processor. Cover; whirl until fairly smooth.

Open-Faced Turkey Sandwich with "Chutney Mayonnaise"

Makes 4 open-faced sandwich halves.

Nutrient Value Per Sandwich: 314 calories, 29 g protein, 10 g fat, 25 g carbohydrate, 304 mg sodium, 66 mg cholesterol.

- ¼ **cup mayonnaise-type salad dressing OR: reduced-calorie mayonnaise**
- 3 **tablespoons golden raisins**
- ½ **teaspoon ground cumin**
- ¼ **teaspoon ground ginger**
  Dash red pepper flakes
  Leaf Lettuce
- 2 **unseeded club (rectangular) hard rolls, split lengthwise and toasted**
- 12 **ounces thinly sliced cooked turkey breast, warmed or at room temperature**
- 1 **medium-size purple onion, sliced and separated into rings**
- 1 **medium-size sweet red pepper, seeded and cut into rings**

1. Combine the salad dressing, raisins, cumin, ginger and red pepper flakes in a blender or food processor. Cover; whirl until well blended and the raisins are finely chopped.
2. Arrange the lettuce on each roll half. Top with the turkey, then the dressing, and onion and red pepper.

Reduced Calorie

17-MINUTE MEXI-BURGER SUPPER

Mexi-Burgers with Cheddar Cheese*
Spiced-Up Iceberg Lettuce Relish*
Confetti Ice Cream with Shredded Coconut and Almonds

*Recipe Included

SHOPPING LIST

- ☐ 1 pound lean ground beef
- ☐ 1 sweet green pepper
- ☐ 1 head iceberg lettuce
- ☐ 1 ripe tomato
- ☐ 1 egg
- ☐ 1 package (6 ounces) sliced Cheddar cheese
- ☐ Ice cream
- ☐ 4 sesame seed buns
- ☐ Plain bread crumbs
- ☐ 1 small jar mild taco sauce
- ☐ Shredded coconut
- ☐ Sliced almonds
  TO HAVE ON HAVE:
  - ● vegetable oil ● liquid red-pepper seasoning
  - ● leaf oregano ● chili powder
  - ● ground cumin ● salt and pepper

WORK PLAN

1 Prepare the Mexi-Burgers.
2 While the burgers are cooking, prepare the Spiced-Up Iceberg Lettuce Relish.
3 Scoop the ice cream and sprinkle with coconut and almonds when ready to serve dessert.

Mexi-Burgers with Cheddar Cheese

Makes 4 burgers.

Nutrient Value Per Burger: 535 calories, 31 g protein, 31 g fat, 32 g carbohydrate, 783 mg sodium, 170 mg cholesterol.

1 **pound lean ground beef**
¼ **cup mild taco sauce**
1 **egg**
2 **tablespoons plain bread crumbs**
1 **teaspoon leaf organo, crumbled**
½ **teaspoon chili powder**
½ **teaspoon ground cumin**
½ **teaspoon salt**
⅛ **teaspoon pepper**
6 **drops liquid red-pepper seasoning**
1 **tablespoon vegetable oil**
4 **sesame seed buns**
4 **square slices Cheddar cheese**
 (part of 6-ounce package)
4 **large slices ripe tomato**
8 **thin sweet green pepper rings**

1. Mix the beef, taco sauce, egg, crumbs, oregano, chili powder, cumin, salt, pepper and red-pepper seasoning in a bowl until combined. Shape into four 4-inch burgers.

2. Cook the hamburgers in the oil in a large skillet, for 3 minutes on each side, or until desired doneness.

3. Split the buns in half. Place the burger on the bottom of each bun. Top with the cheese, tomato, green pepper and bun.

Spiced-Up Iceberg Lettuce Relish

Makes about 4 servings (2 cups).

Nutrient Value Per Serving: 74 calories, 1 g protein, 4 g fat, 10 g carbohydrate, 249 mg sodium, 0 mg cholesterol.

1 **tablespoon vegetable oil**
6 **cups shredded iceberg lettuce**
⅓ **cup mild taco sauce**
¼ **teaspoon salt**
 Pinch pepper
 Liquid red-pepper seasoning

Heat the oil over high heat in a large skillet. Stir-fry the lettuce for 1 minute, until wilted. Transfer to a serving dish; lightly toss with the taco sauce, salt, pepper and red-pepper seasoning.

Skinny Mexi-Burgers

Reduced Calorie

Makes 4 servings.

Nutrient Value Per Serving: 277 calories, 26 g protein 13 g fat, 13 g carbohydrate, 669 mg sodium, 141 mg cholesterol.

1 **pound prepared ground turkey,**
 thawed if frozen
¼ **cup mild taco sauce**
1 **egg**
4 **tablespoons plain bread crumbs**
1 **teaspoon leaf organo, crumbled**
½ **teaspoon chili powder**
½ **teaspoon ground cumin**
½ **teaspoon salt**
⅛ **teaspoon pepper**
6 **drops liquid red-pepper seasoning**
 Shredded lettuce
2 **slices (¾ ounce each) individually**
 wrapped reduced calorie
 American-flavored cheese product,
 halved
4 **large ½-inch-thick tomato slices**
8 **thin sweet green pepper rings**

1. Mix the turkey, taco sauce, egg, crumbs, oregano, chili powder, cumin, salt, pepper and red-pepper seasoning in a medium-size bowl until blended. Shape into four 4-inch burgers. The burgers should be moist; add additional bread crumbs only if necessary.

2. Broil the burgers for about 4 minutes on each side, or until the centers are fully cooked. Arrange each burger on a bed of shredded lettuce on a plate. Top with a band of cheese, tomato slices and green pepper rings.

18-MINUTE HAM STEAK DINNER

Citrus-Glazed Ham Steak*
Winter Applesauce*
Corn Muffins
Frosted Devil's Food Cake

*Recipe Included

SHOPPING LIST

- ☐ 11 ounces fully cooked ham steaks (about ¼ inch thick)
- ☐ 2 all-purpose apples (about ¾ pound)
- ☐ 2 small parsnips
- ☐ 2 lemons
- ☐ 1 can (11 ounces) mandarin oranges
- ☐ 1 can (8 ounces) jellied cranberry sauce
- ☐ Frozen grapefruit concentrate
- ☐ Corn muffins
- ☐ Frozen Devil's food cake
  - **TO HAVE ON HAND**
    - ● butter or margarine ● cornstarch
    - ● Dijon-style mustard ● leaf rosemary
    - ● pepper ● ground cinnamon ● sugar

WORK PLAN

1 Prepare the Winter Applesauce through Step 2.
2 Prepare the Citrus-Glazed Ham Steak.
3 Complete the applesauce.

Citrus-Glazed Ham Steak

Makes 4 servings.

Nutrient Value Per Serving: 232 calories, 18 g protein, 13 g fat, 11 g carbohydrate, 1,210 mg sodium, 62 mg cholesterol.

**2 tablespoons unsalted butter
    or margarine**
**11 ounces fully cooked ham steaks
    (about ¼ inch thick)**

**⅓ cup mandarin orange juice
    (from 11-ounce can)**
**2 tablespoons frozen grapefruit juice
    concentrate**
1 teaspoon cornstarch
1 teaspoon Dijon-style mustard
⅛ teaspoon pepper
⅛ teaspoon leaf rosemary, crumbled
**⅓ cup canned mandarin orange segments
    (from 11-ounce can)**

1. Melt the butter in a large skillet over high heat. Sauté the ham for 2 minutes on each side, or until heated through. Transfer to a platter; cover and keep warm.
2. Stir together the orange juice, grapefruit juice concentrate, cornstarch, mustard, pepper and rosemary in a small bowl until smooth. Pour into the skillet. Cook over high heat, whisking constantly, until bubbly and thick. Remove from the heat and stir in the orange segments. Pour over the ham steak.

Winter Applesauce

Makes 4 servings.

Nutrient Value Per Serving: 195 calories, 1 g protein, 0 g fat, 50 g carbohydrate, 21 mg sodium, 0 mg cholesterol.

½ cup cold water
¼ cup sugar
2 tablespoons lemon juice
**2 all-purpose apples (about ¾ pound),
    pared, cored and cut into chunks**
**2 small parsnips (about ¼ pound), pared
    and cut into chunks**
1 can (8 ounces) jellied cranberry sauce
⅛ teaspoon ground cinnamon

1. Combine the water, sugar and lemon juice in a saucepan. Bring to boiling, stirring, until the sugar is dissolved.
2. Working in batches, place the apples and parsnips in a blender or food processor. Pulse on and off to chop fine. Stir into the boiling sugar syrup. Cover and cook over medium heat, until the apples and parsnips are soft, for about 5 minutes.
3. Combine the apple mixture, cranberry sauce and cinnamon in the container of an electric blender or processor. Cover; whirl until puréed. Serve warm.

297

FAST FRITTATA FEAST

Ratatouille Frittata

Ratatouille Frittata*
Garlic Toast
Garden Salad*
Strawberries in Lemon Yogurt

*Recipe Included

SHOPPING LIST

- ☐ 8 eggs
- ☐ 1 package (10 ounces) frozen ratatouille
- ☐ 2 ounces grated Cheddar cheese
- ☐ 1 loaf of crusty bread
- ☐ 1 medium-size head romaine
- ☐ 1 small red onion, or slices from salad bar
- ☐ 2 carrots, or shredded or sliced carrots from salad bar
- ☐ Italian salad dressing
- ☐ 1 pint strawberries
- ☐ 1 container (8 ounces) lemon yogurt

TO HAVE ON HAND
- • butter or margarine • salt • garlic powder

WORK PLAN

1
In the morning, place the frozen ratatouille in the refrigerator to thaw. Rinse and trim the romaine. Wrap in paper towels and refrigerate.

2
25 minutes before dinner, rinse, hull and halve the strawberries. Divide among 4 dessert bowls. Spoon yogurt over; refrigerate.

3
Prepare the Garden Salad, cover; refrigerate until serving time. Toss with the dressing at the last moment.

4
Prepare the Ratatouille Frittata, a tasty combination of eggs, butter, cheese and vegetables. Serve directly from the skillet.

5
Butter thick slices of crusty bread and sprinkle with garlic powder; broil just before serving.

298

Ratatouille Frittata

Makes 4 servings.

Nutrient Value Per Serving: 265 calories, 16 g protein, 19 g fat, 6 g carbohydrate, 471 mg sodium, 571 mg cholesterol.

8 eggs
¼ teaspoon salt
1 tablespoon butter or margarine
1 package (10 ounces) frozen ratatouille, thawed
½ cup grated Cheddar cheese

1. Beat the eggs with the salt in a large bowl until foamy. Set aside.
2. Melt the butter in a heavy, ovenproof 10-inch skillet. Add the ratatouille, cook until bubbly.
4. Add the beaten eggs to the ratatouille. Cook, stirring, until the eggs are almost set on top. Sprinkle with the cheese.
5. Place under the broiler until the cheese melts, for about 30 seconds. Cut into wedges.

Garden Salad

Makes 4 servings.

Nutrient Value Per Serving: 107 calories, 3 g protein, 7 g fat, 8 g carbohydrate, 137 mg sodium, 0 mg cholesterol.

1 medium-size head romaine, rinsed and trimmed
1 small red oinion, sliced
1 cup shredded or sliced carrots
¼ cup bottled Italian salad dressing

1. Break the romaine into bite-size pieces into a salad bowl.
2. Scatter the onion rings and carrots over the lettuce. Drizzle with the salad dressing; toss.

CHICKEN IN A JIFFY

Sautéed Chicken Breasts with Mustard*
Long-Grained and Wild Rice
Creamed Spinach
Salad Bar Toss
Ricotta Cups with Mandarin Oranges*

*Recipe Included

SHOPPING LIST

- ☐ 1½ pounds boneless, skinned, split chicken breast halves
- ☐ Chicken broth
- ☐ Dijon-style mustard
- ☐ 1 box (6¼ ounces) fast-cooking long-grain and wild rice
- ☐ 1 package (16 ounces) frozen creamed spinach in boil pouch
- ☐ 1 pound mixed sliced mushrooms, red pepper strips and chopped green onion, and salad dressing from salad bar
- ☐ 1 container (15 ounces) part-skim ricotta cheese
- ☐ ¼ cup powdered chocolate milk flavoring
- ☐ 1 can (16 or 11 ounces) mandarin oranges
- **TO HAVE ON HAND**
  - butter or margarine • salt • lemon juice
  - cornstarch

WORK PLAN

1 In the morning, if the chicken is frozen, place in the refrigerator to thaw. Place the can of mandarin oranges in the refrigerator to chill.
2 Heat water for the spinach.
3 Prepare the Ricotta Cups.
4 Toss the deli salad with the deli dressing and chill.
5 Start the spinach.
6 Start the rice.
7 Prepare the Sautéed Chicken Breasts with Mustard.

Sautéed Chicken Breasts with Mustard

Makes 4 servings.

Nutrient Value Per Serving: 257 calories, 41 g protein, 8 g fat, 2 g carbohydrate, 457 mg sodium, 114 mg cholesterol.

1½ pounds boneless, skinned chicken breast halves, thawed if frozen
2 tablespoons butter or margarine
1 tablespoon lemon juice
2 teaspoons cornstarch
1 cup chicken broth
2 to 3 teaspoons Dijon-style mustard

1. Pat the chicken dry with paper toweling. Sauté the chicken in the butter in a large skillet over medium heat until lightly browned and cooked through, for about 5 minutes each side.
2. Sprinkle with the lemon juice and transfer to a serving platter; keep warm.
3. Dissolve the cornstarch in the chicken broth in a small cup. Pour into the skillet. Bring to boiling, scraping up any browned bits from the bottom; cook for 1 minute. Remove the pan from the heat. Whisk in the mustard. Spoon the sauce over the chicken.

Ricotta Cups with Mandarin Oranges

Makes 4 servings.

Nutrient Value Per Serving: 281 calories, 14 g protein, 9 g fat, 38 g carbohydrate, 175 mg sodium, 33 mg cholesterol.

¼ cup powdered chocolate milk flavoring
1 container (15 ounces) part-skim ricotta
1 can (16 or 11 ounces) mandarin oranges, drained

1. Stir the chocolate flavoring into the ricotta in a medium-size bowl until well blended.
2. Fold in all but ¼ cup of the orange segments. Spoon into 4 individual ramekins or other dessert dishes. Chill until serving time. Garnish with the remaining orange segments.

PASTA PRONTO

Tortellini with Cream Sauce*
Marinated Artichoke Salad
Italian Bread
Raspberry Sherbet with
Shredded Coconut

*Recipe Included

SHOPPING LIST

☐ 1 pound frozen cheese tortellini
☐ 1 bunch broccoli, or ½ pound flowerets from salad bar
☐ ½ cup heavy cream
☐ ½ cup grated Parmesan cheese
☐ 1 can (10½ ounces) chick-peas
☐ 1 jar (6 oz.) marinated artichoke hearts
☐ 1 pint cherry tomatoes
☐ Italian Bread
☐ 1 pint raspberry sherbet
TO HAVE ON HAND
  ● butter ● pepper ● shredded coconut

WORK PLAN

1 In the morning, refrigerate the jar of marinated artichoke hearts and the can of chick-peas.
2 Heat water for the tortellini.
3 Trim the broccoli; save the stems for another use.
4 Prepare the Marinated Artichoke Salad.
5 Slice the bread.
6 Prepare the Tortellini with Cream Sauce.
7 Sprinkle the coconut over the sherbet just before serving.

Tortellini with Cream Sauce

Makes 4 servings.

Nutrient Value Per Serving: 410 calories, 21 g protein, 22 g fat, 33 g carbohydrate, 752 mg sodium, 90 mg cholesterol.

1 pound frozen cheese tortellini
   Flowerets from 1 bunch of broccoli
   (about 2 cups)
½ cup heavy cream
½ cup grated Parmesan cheese
   Pepper

1. Cook the tortellini in 3 quarts of boiling salted water in a large pot for 5 minutes. Add the broccoli flowerets and continue cooking for 1 to 2 minutes, or until the tortellini are tender. Drain in a colander; set aside.
2. In the same pot, heat the heavy cream to boiling; cook for 1 minute.
3. Add the tortellini and broccoli to the cream. Sprinkle with the Parmesan. Gently toss to coat. Add the pepper to taste. Serve immediately.

Marinated Artichoke Salad

Makes 4 servings.

Nutrient Value Per Serving: 150 calories, 5 g protein, 8 g fat, 16 g carbohydrate, 129 mg sodium, 0 mg cholesterol.

1 jar (6 ounces) marinated artichoke
   hearts, halved and undrained
1 can (10½ ounces) chick-peas, drained
1 pint cherry tomatoes, rinsed and halved
   if large
   Pepper to taste

Combine all the ingredients in a bowl. Let stand to blend the flavors.

SHRIMP IN A DASH

Greek-Style Shrimp with Pasta*
Green Beans in Butter Sauce*
Cucumber Salad
Fresh Pears and Cookies

*Recipe Included

SHOPPING LIST

☐ 1 pound fresh or frozen medium-size shrimp, shelled and deveined
☐ 4 ounces feta cheese
☐ 1 can (16 ounces) stewed tomatoes
☐ 8 ounces rotelle or fusilli pasta
☐ 1 pound frozen, cut green beans
☐ Cucumber salad from a deli
☐ 4 pears
☐ Packaged cookies
   TO HAVE ON HAND
   ● Olive oil ● garlic ● leaf oregano
   ● butter or margarine ● Worcestershire sauce
   ● lemon juice ● pepper

WORK PLAN

1 Heat the water for the rotelle or fusilli pasta and green beans.
2 Rinse the pears. Cube the feta.
3 Start cooking the pasta.
4 Prepare the Green Beans in Butter Sauce.
5 Prepare the Greek-Style Shrimp with Pasta.

Greek-Style Shrimp with Pasta

Makes 4 servings.

Nutrient Value Per Serving: 339 calories, 29 g protein, 13 g fat, 28 g carbohydrate, 897 mg sodium, 195 mg cholesterol.

- **1 clove garlic, finely chopped**
- **1 tablespoon olive oil**
- **1 can (16 ounces) stewed tomatoes**
- **½ teaspoon leaf oregano, crumbled**
- **1 pound fresh or frozen medium-size shrimp, shelled and deveined**
- **4 ounces feta cheese, cut into ½-inch cubes**
- **8 ounces hot cooked rotelle or fusilli pasta**

1. Sauté the garlic in the oil in a large skillet over low heat for 1 minute. Stir in the tomatoes and oregano; cook for 3 minutes.
2. Stir in the shrimp and feta. Cook for 2 to 3 minutes, or just until the shrimp is pink and cooked through.
3. Toss with the cooked pasta in a large serving bowl.

MICROWAVE OVEN DIRECTIONS FOR GREEK-STYLE SHRIMP WITH PASTA
650 Watt Variable Power Microwave Oven
Ingredient Changes: Drain off ¼ cup of liquid from the 16-ounce can of stewed tomatoes.
Directions: Combine the garlic and olive oil in a microwave-safe 2-quart casserole. Microwave, uncovered, at full power for 1 minute. Add the tomatoes and oregano. Cover. Microwave at full power for 4 minutes until boiling. Add the shrimp. Cover. Microwave at full power for 3 minutes, stirring once. Stir in the feta cheese and hot cooked pasta.

Green Beans in Butter Sauce

Makes 4 servings.

Nutrient Value Per Serving: 64 calories, 2 g protein, 3 g fat, 9 g carbohydrate, 47 mg sodium, 8 mg cholesterol.

- **1 pound frozen, cut green beans**
- **1 tablespoon butter or margarine**
- **1 teaspoon Worcestershire sauce**
- **1 teaspoon lemon juice**
- **Freshly ground pepper**

1. Cook the green beans, following the package directions.
2. Drain well. Return to the pot. Add the butter, Worcestershire sauce, lemon juice and pepper. Stir over low heat just until the beans are coated. Keep warm.

SO GOOD— YET—SO QUICK

Mixed English Grill*
Potatoes O'Brien
Orange and Roquefort Salad
Lemon-Coconut Cake with
Peach Purée
Coffee

*Recipe Included

SHOPPING LIST

- ☐ 4 shoulder lamb chops
- ☐ 2 large tomatoes
- ☐ 1 bunch fresh mint, or dried
- ☐ 1 small head green leafy lettuce
- ☐ 2 oranges
- ☐ 1 medium-size red onion
- ☐ 4 ounces Roquefort cheese
- ☐ 1 package (8 ounces) frozen brown-and-serve sausages
- ☐ 1 package (16 ounces) frozen Potatoes O'Brien
- ☐ 1 package (10 ounces) dry-pack frozen peaches
- ☐ Orange-flavored liqueur
- ☐ Lemon-coconut cake
  - **TO HAVE ON HAND:**
    - ● butter ● salt ● leaf mint ● leaf oregano
    - ● leaf thyme ● bottled salad dressing

WORK PLAN

1. Thaw the frozen peaches, according to the label directions.
2. Preheat the broiler.
3. Tear the lettuce into bite-size pieces. Peel and section 2 oranges. Peel and thinly slice the red onion. Arrange the lettuce, orange and onion in a salad bowl. Sprinkle with 4 ounces of crumbled Roquefort cheese. Serve with the bottled salad dressing.
4. Cook the Potatoes O'Brien.
5. Prepare the English Grill.
6. Purée the peach slices with 2 tablespoons liqueur. Serve as a sauce with the cake.

Mixed English Grill

Makes 4 servings.

Nutrient Value Per Serving: 653 calories, 34 g protein, 55 g fat, 4 g carbohydrate, 447 mg sodium, 173 mg cholesterol.

4 shoulder lamb chops, 1 inch thick (2 pounds)
1 package (8 ounces) frozen brown-and-serve sausages*
2 large tomatoes, halved
3 tablespoons butter, softened
1 teaspoon leaf thyme, crumbled
1 teaspoon leaf oregano, crumbled
2 tablespoons finely chopped mint, or 1 teaspoon dried
⅛ teaspoon salt

1. Wipe the lamb chops with damp paper toweling. Cut the fat around the edges in several places to prevent curling. Arrange with the sausages on the rack of a large broiler pan.
2. Place the tomato halves, cut-side up, on the broiler rack.
3. Combine the butter, thyme, oregano, mint and salt in a small bowl. Brush half over the meat and tomatoes.
4. Broil 3 inches from the heat for 5 minutes. Turn the chops and sausages over; brush with the remaining butter mixture. Broil until the chops and sausages are no longer pink in the center, about 4 minutes.

***Note:** For 1 sausage per serving instead of 2, only remove 4 from the package. Freezer-wrap the remainder; return to the freezer.

Super-Speedy Menu Ideas

- Coarsely chop cooked "sea legs" or crab legs and stir into store-bought potato salad; add chopped parsley, chives and/or green onion; add a dash of mustard.
- Heat store-bought, ready-to-use taco shells and a can of chili; spoon the chili into the taco shells. Serve with grated cheese, shredded lettuce and chopped onions.
- Buy canned lentil soup, grated Swiss cheese and garlic bread. Heat the soup and pour over a tablespoon of cheese in a soup bowl. Top with more cheese and serve with garlic bread.
- Heat fully cooked chicken pieces with bottled barbecue sauce; serve over sesame rolls.
- Cook a package of frozen fish sticks, according to label directions. Serve in hot-dog rolls and top with Russian dressing. Store-bought coleslaw makes a zesty topping or side dish.
- Treat your family to pizza—it's delicious and nutritious. If you're eating pizza at home, serve with a salad and fixings from your supermarket salad bar.
- Combine canned chicken gravy, precooked chicken pieces or canned chicken pieces and canned mushrooms (drained); heat and serve on toast points or prepared biscuits.

Ways to Save Time & Money

Grocery Know-How

- Plan a once-a-week shopping trip for perishables (meat, dairy, etc.). Shop in bulk once a month for nonperishables and buy the most economical sizes—as much as you can afford and can store.
- Delegate shopping to your husband or children. Make a list stating brand names and sizes; group items according to aisles (frozen foods, canned goods, etc.).
- Exchange shopping trips with a friend: Let her go to the butcher, while you go to the fruit market.
- Patronize stores that deliver.
- Seek out stores with extended shopping hours. Stop at off-peak times to avoid crowds.

Cooking Glossary

A

À la In the manner of, as in *à la maison:* in the style of the house—"the house specialty."

Al dente An Italian phrase meaning "to the tooth," used to describe spaghetti or other pasta at the perfect stage of doneness— tender, but with enough firmness to be felt between the teeth.

Antipasto Another Italian word, this one meaning "before the meal." Antipasto is a selection of hors d'oeuvres, such as salami, marinated mushrooms, tuna or anchovies.

Aspic A jelly made from the cooking liquids of beef or poultry, principally. It will jell by itself, but is often strengthened with additional gelatin and used for coating and garnishing cold foods.

Au gratin Usually a creamed mixture topped with bread crumbs and/or cheese and browned in the oven or broiler.

Au naturel A French phrase referring to foods that are cooked simply or served in their natural state.

B

Bake To cook cakes, pies, cookies, breads, other pastries and doughs, as well as casseroles, fish, ham, etc., in the oven by dry heat.

Barbecue To roast meat, poultry or fish over hot coals or other heat, basting with a highly seasoned sauce. Also, the food so cooked and the social gathering.

Baste To ladle pan fat, marinade or other liquid over food as it roasts in order to add flavor and prevent dryness.

Batter A flour-liquid mixture of fairly thin consistency, as for pancakes.

Beat To stir vigorously with a spoon, eggbeater or electric mixer.

Blanch To plunge foods, such as tomatoes and peaches, quickly into boiling water, then into cold water, to loosen skins for easy removal. Also, a preliminary step to freezing vegetables.

Blend To mix two or more ingredients until smooth.

Boil To cook in boiling liquid.

Bone To remove the bones from meat, fish or poultry. This is usually done to make eating, carving or stuffing easier.

Bouillon A clear stock made of poultry, beef or veal, vegetables and seasonings.

Bouquet garni A small herb bouquet, most often sprigs of fresh parsley and thyme plus a bay leaf, tied in cheesecloth. Dried herbs can be used in place of the fresh. The *bouquet garni* is dropped into stocks, stews, sauces and soups as a seasoner and is removed before serving—usually as soon as it has flavored the dish.

Braise To brown in fat, then to cook, covered, in a small amount of liquid.

Bread To coat with bread crumbs, usually after dipping in beaten egg or milk.

Broil To cook under a broiler or on a grill by direct dry heat.

Broth A clear meat, fish, poultry or vegetable stock made of a combination of them.

Brush To spread with melted butter or margarine, beaten egg, water or other liquid, using a small brush.

C

Calorie The measure of body heat energy produced by the burning (oxidation) of the food we eat.

Candy To cook fruit, fruit peel or ginger in a heavy syrup until transparent, which is later drained and dried. Also to cook vegetables, such as carrots or sweet potatoes, in sugar or syrup.

Caramelize To melt sugar in a skillet, over low heat, until it becomes golden brown.

Chantilly Heavy cream whipped until soft, not stiff; it may or may not be sweetened.

Chop To cut into small pieces.

Coat To cover with flour, crumbs or other dry mixture before frying.

Coat the spoon A term used to describe egg-thickened sauces when cooked to a perfect degree of doneness; when a custard coats a metal spoon, it leaves a thin, somewhat jelly-like film.

Combine To mix together two or more ingredients.

Crimp To press the edges of a piecrust together with the tines of a fork or your fingertips.

Croutons Small, fried bread cubes.

Crumb To coat food with bread or cracker crumbs. So that the crumbs will stick, the food should first be dipped in milk or beaten egg.

Crumble To break between the fingers into small, irregular pieces.

Crush To pulverize food with a rolling pin or whirl in a blender until it is granular or powdered.

Cube To cut into cubes.

Cut in To work shortening or other solid fat into a flour mixture with a pastry blender or two knives until the texture resembles coarse meal.

Cutlet A small, thin, boneless piece of meat—usually cut from the leg of veal or chicken or turkey breast.

D

Dash A very small amount—less than $1/16$ teaspoon.

Deep-fry To cook in hot, deep, temperature-controlled fat.

Deglaze To loosen the browned bits in a skillet or roasting pan by adding liquid while stirring and heating. A glaze is used as a flavor base for sauces and gravies.

Demitasse French for "half cup," it refers to the small cups used for after-dinner coffee and also to the strong, black coffee served in them.

Devil To season with mustard, pepper and other spicy condiments.

Dice To cut into small, uniform pieces.

Dissolve To stir a powder or solid ingredient into a liquid to make a solution.

Dot To scatter bits of butter or margarine or other seasoning over the surface of a food to be cooked.

Dough A mixture of flour, liquid and other ingredients stiff enough to knead.

Drain To pour off liquid. Also, to place fried foods on paper toweling to soak up the excess fat.

Drawn butter Melted, clarified butter or margarine; often served with boiled shellfish.

Dredge To coat with flour prior to frying.

Drizzle To pour melted butter or margarine, marinade or other liquid over food in a thin stream.

Duchesse Mashed potatoes mixed with egg, butter or margarine and cream, piped around meat, poultry or fish dishes as a decorative border, then browned in the oven or broiler just before serving.

Dust To cover lightly with flour, 10X (confectioners') sugar or other dry ingredient.

Dutch oven A large, heavy, metal cooking pot with a tight-fitting cover; used for cooking pot roasts and stews and for braising large cuts of meat and poultry.

E

Entrée A French term applying to the third course in a full French dinner. We use the term to designate the main dish of a meal.

Escalope A thin slice of meat or fish, slightly flattened and most often sautéed quickly in oil or butter.

Espresso Robust, dark Italian coffee brewed under steam pressure. It is traditionally served in small cups and, in this country (though usually not in Italy), accompanied by twists of lemon rind.

Evaporated milk Canned unsweetened milk slightly thickened by the removal of some of its water.

F

Fillet A thin, boneless piece of meat or fish.

Fillo See "Phyllo."

Fines herbes A mixture of minced fresh or dried parsley, chervil, tarragon and, sometimes, chives, used to season salads, omelets and other dishes.

Flake To break up food (salmon or tuna, for example) into smaller pieces with a fork.

Flambé, flambéed French words meaning "flaming." In the culinary sense, the verb *flamber* means to pour warm brandy over a food and to set it afire with a match.

Florentine In the style of Florence, Italy, which usually means served on a bed of spinach, topped with a delicate cheese sauce and browned in the oven. Fish and eggs are often served Florentine style.

Flour To coat with flour.

Flute To form a fluted edge with the fingers, on a piecrust edging.

Fold in To mix a light, fluffy ingredient, such as beaten egg white, into a thicker mixture, using a gentle under-and-over motion.

Fondue Switzerland's gift to good eating: a silky concoction of melted cheese, white wine and kirsch served in an earthenware crock set over a burner. To eat the fondue, chunks of bread are speared with special, long-handled fondue forks and then twirled in the semiliquid cheese mixture. *Fondue Bourguignonne* is a convivial Swiss version of a French dish: Cubes of raw steak are speared with the fondue forks, fried at the table in a pot of piping hot oil, then dipped into assorted sauces.

Frappé A mushy, frozen dessert.

Fricassee To simmer a chicken covered in water with vegetables and often wine. The chicken may be browned in butter first. A gravy is made from the broth and served with the chicken.

Fritter A crisp, golden, deep-fried batter bread, often containing corn or minced fruits or vegetables. Also, pieces of fruit or vegetable, batter-dipped and deep-fried.

G

Garnish To decorate with colorful and/or fancily cut pieces of food.

Glaze To coat food with honey, syrup or other liquid so it glistens.

Gluten The protein of wheat flour that forms the framework of cakes, breads, cookies and pastries.

Goulash A beef or pork stew, flavored with paprika.

Grate To shred into small pieces with a grater.

Grease To rub food or a container with butter, margarine or other fat.

Grill To cook on a grill, usually over charcoal.

Grind To put through a food grinder.

H

Hors d'oeuvres Bite-size appetizers served with cocktails.

Hull To remove caps and stems from berries.

I

Ice To cover with icing. Also, a frozen, water-based, fruit-flavored dessert.

Italienne, à la Served Italian style with a garnish of pasta.

J

Julienne To cut food into uniformly long, thin slivers (1½ x ¼ inches).

K

Kabobs Cubes of meat, fish or poultry and/or vegetables threaded on long skewers and grilled over coals or under the broiler.

Kasha Buckwheat groats, braised or cooked in liquid and usually served in place of rice, potatoes or another starch.

Knead To work dough with the hands until it is smooth and springy. Yeast breads must be kneaded to develop the gluten necessary to give them framework and volume.

Kosher salt A very coarse salt.

L

Lard Creamy, white, rendered pork fat.

Line To cover the bottom, and sometimes sides, of a pan with paper or thin slices of food.

Lyonnaise Seasoned in the style of Lyons, France, meaning with parsley and onions.

M

Macerate To let food, principally fruits, steep in wine or spirits (usually kirsch or rum).

Maître d'hôtel Simply cooked dishes seasoned with minced parsley, butter and lemon. *Maître d'hôtel* butter is a mixture of butter (or margarine), parsley, lemon juice and salt. It is most often used to season broiled fish, grilled steaks or chops or boiled carrots.

Marinade The liquid in which food is marinated.

Marinate To let food, principally meats, steep in a piquant sauce prior to cooking. The marinade serves to tenderize and add flavor.

Marzipan A confection made from almond paste, sugar and egg whites—often colored and shaped into tiny fruit and vegetable forms.

Mash To reduce to a pulp.

Mask To coat with sauce or aspic.

Melt To heat a solid, such as chocolate or butter, until liquid.

Meringue A stiffly beaten mixture of sugar and egg white.

Mince To cut into fine pieces.

Mix To stir together.

Mocha A flavoring for desserts, usually made from coffee or a mixture of coffee and chocolate.

Mold To shape in a mold.

Mole A sauce of Mexican origin, usually containing chilies, onion, garlic and other ingredients, especially bitter chocolate. It is usually served over poultry.

Mousse A rich, creamy, frozen dessert. Also, a velvety hot or cold savory dish, rich with cream, bound with eggs or—if cold—with gelatin.

Mull To heat a liquid, such as wine or cider, with whole spices.

N

Niçoise Prepared in the manner of Nice, France—with tomatoes, garlic, olive oil and ripe olives.

Nouvelle Cuisine A French cuisine established by classically trained younger chefs with a new and lighter twist on classic French dishes and preparation techniques. It has been adapted by many other cuisines.

O

Oil To rub a pan or mold with cooking oil.

P

Panbroil To cook in a skillet in a small amount of fat; drippings are poured off as they accumulate.

Parboil To cook in water until about half done; vegetables to be cooked *en casserole* are usually parboiled.

Pare To remove the skin of a fruit or vegetable with a swivel-blade vegetable peeler.

Pasta The all-inclusive Italian word for all kinds of macaroni, spaghetti and noodles.

Pastry A stiff dough, made from flour, water and shortening, used for piecrusts, turnovers and other dishes; it is also a rich cookie-type dough used for desserts.

Pastry bag A cone-shaped fabric, parchment or plastic bag with a hole at the tip for the insertion of various decorating tubes. Used to decorate cakes, pastries, etc.

Pâté A well-seasoned mixture of finely minced or ground meats and/or liver. *Pâté de foie gras* is made of goose livers and truffles.

Pectin Any of several, natural gelatinous substances found in the cellular structure of different fruits and vegetables. It is also manufactured in syrup form to use in helping jellies to jell.

Petits fours Tiny, fancily frosted cakes.

Phyllo Greek term for a flaky, tissue paper-thin pastry used in many Greek dishes. (Also spelled fillo.)

Pilaf Rice cooked in a savory broth, often with small bits of meat or vegetables, herbs and spices.

Pinch The amount of a dry ingredient that can be taken up between the thumb and index finger—less than ¼ teaspoon.

Pipe To press frosting, whipped cream, mashed potatoes or other soft mixtures through a pastry bag fitted with a decorative tube to make a fancy garnish or edging.

Plank A well-seasoned (oiled) hardwood plank used to serve a broiled steak or chop, usually edged with Duchesse potatoes.

Plump To soak raisins or other dried fruits in liquid until they are softened and almost returned to their natural state.

Poach To cook in barely simmering liquid, as fish fillets, for example.

Polenta A cornmeal porridge popular in Italy. Usually cooled, sliced or cubed, then baked or fried with butter and Parmesan cheese.

Pot cheese A soft uncured cheese from strained milk curds, almost identical to cottage cheese but perhaps a bit drier.

Pound To flatten by pounding.

Preheat To bring an oven or broiler to the correct temperature before cooking food.

Purée To reduce food to a smooth, velvety texture by whirling in an electric blender or pressing through a sieve or food grinder. Also, the food so reduced.

R

Ragôut A stew.

Ramekin A small, individual-size baking dish.

Reduce To boil a liquid, uncovered, until the quantity is concentrated.

Render To melt solid fat.

Rice To press food through a container with small holes. The food then resembles rice.

Risotto An Italian dish made with short-grain rice browned in fat and cooked with chicken broth until tender but firm. Mixture is creamy, not dry or runny.

Roast To cook meat or poultry in the oven by dry heat.

Roe The eggs of fish, such as sturgeon, salmon (caviar) or shad; considered delicacies.

Roll To press and shape dough or pastry with a rolling pin.

Roulade A slice of meat, most often veal or beef, rolled around any number of fillings. Also, a jelly-roll cake.

Roux A cooked, fat-flour mixture used to thicken sauces and gravies.

S

Sauté To cook food quickly in a small amount of hot fat in a skillet.

Scald To heat a liquid just until small bubbles

form around the pan, but the liquid does not boil.

Scallop To bake small pieces of food *en casserole,* usually in a cream sauce. Also a thin, boneless slice of meat, such as veal.

Score To make shallow, crisscross cuts over the surface of a food with a knife.

Scramble To stir eggs or an egg mixture while cooking until the mixture sets.

Scrape To remove fruit or vegetable skin by scraping with a knife.

Shirr To bake whole eggs in ramekins with cream and crumbs.

Short An adjective used to describe a bread, cake or pastry that has a high proportion of fat and is ultra-tender or crisp.

Shortening A solid fat, usually of vegetable origin, used to add tenderness to pastry, bread or cookies.

Shred To cut in small, thin slivers by rubbing food, such as Cheddar cheese, over the holes in a shredder-grater.

Sift To put flour or another dry ingredient through a sifter. (*Note:* In this book, recipes that call for *sifted* flour require that you sift the flour and then measure it, even if you use a flour that says "sifted" on the bag.)

Simmer To cook in liquid just below the boiling point.

Skewer To thread food on a long wooden or metal pin before cooking. Also, the pin itself.

Skim To remove fat or film from the surface of a liquid or sauce.

Sliver To cut in long, thin strips.

Soak To let stand in liquid.

Soufflé A light, fluffy, baked combination of egg yolk, sauce, purée and flavoring, with stiffly beaten egg whites folded in.

Spit To thread food on a long rod and roast over glowing coals or under a broiler. Also, the rod itself.

Steam To cook, covered, on a trivet over a small amount of boiling water.

Steep To soak food liquid until the liquid absorbs its flavor, as in steeping tea in hot water.

Stew To cook, covered, in simmering liquid.

Stir To mix with a spoon using a circular motion.

Stir-fry To cook in a small amount of oil, in a wok or skillet, over high heat, stirring or tossing constantly, for a short period of time.

Stock A liquid flavor base for soups and sauces made by long, slow cooking of meat, poultry or fish with their bones. Stock may be brown or white, depending on whether the meat and bones are browned first.

Stud To press whole cloves, slivers of garlic or other seasoning into the surface of a food.

T

Terrine A type of container used for baking dishes such as pâtés. The prepared dish may also be referred to as a terrine.

Thicken To make a liquid thicker, usually by adding flour, cornstarch or beaten egg.

Thin To make a liquid thinner by adding liquid.

Timbale A savory meat, fish, poultry or vegetable custard, baked in a small mold. Also, pastry shells made on special iron molds—Swedish Rosettes, for example.

Torte A very rich, multilayered cake made with eggs, and, often, grated nuts. Usually it is filled, but frequently it is not frosted.

Toss To mix, as a salad, by gently turning ingredients over and over in a bowl, either with hands or with a large fork and spoon.

Truffles A type of underground fungi considered a real delicacy. Black, dark brown or white in color and quite expensive because of their rarity and the method of obtaining them. Also, a term for a rich chocolate candy.

Truss To tie into a compact shape before roasting.

Turnover A folded pastry usually made by cutting a circle or square, adding a dollop of sweet or savory filling, folding into a semicircle or triangle, then crimping the edges with the tines of a fork. Most turnovers are baked, but some are deep-fat fried.

Tutti-Frutti A mixture of minced fruits used as a dessert topping.

V

Variety meats Organ and muscular meat, such as liver, heart, kidneys and tripe.

Véronique A dish garnished with seedless green grapes.

Vinaigrette A sauce, French in origin, made from oil, vinegar, salt, pepper and herbs; usually served on cold meat, fish or vegetables.

W

Whip To beat until frothy or stiff with an eggbeater or an electric mixer.

Wok A round-bottomed, bowl-shaped Chinese cooking utensil used for stir-frying.

Z

Zest The oily, aromatic, colored part of the rind of citrus fruits.

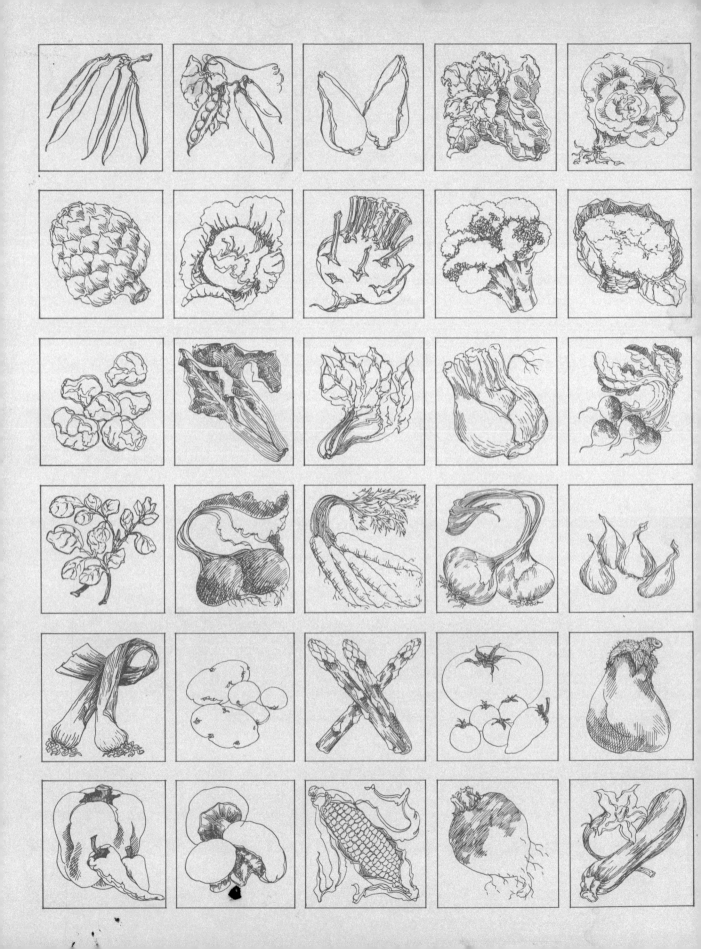